D1265162

Emotional Growth

Psychoanalytic Studies of the Gifted and a Great Variety of Other Individuals

Volume 2

PHYLLIS GREENACRE

Emotional Growth

Psychoanalytic Studies of the Gifted and a
Great Variety of Other Individuals

Volume 2

PHYLLIS GREENACRE

INTERNATIONAL UNIVERSITIES PRESS, INC.
New York

Manufactured in the United States of America

Contents

VOLUME 2

Part II
Studies in Creativity

Part III
Psychoanalytic Therapy and Training

Part II
STUDIES IN CREATIVITY

The Mutual Adventures of Jonathan Swift and Lemuel Gulliver: A Study in Pathography (1955)

This study has emerged from an interest in distortions in the body image involving sensations of change in size, either of the entire body or some part of the body, sensations which I believe to be of particular significance in fetishism (ch. 2). It is extracted from a book about Dean Swift and Lewis Carroll, with special reference to their lives in connection with their famous literary master-pieces, *Gulliver's Travels* and *Alice's Adventures in Wonderland*, in both of which such distortions of the body play a noteworthy role.[1]

I. SWIFT'S LIFE

Swift was a remarkable man of picturesque contradictions. He was secretive, enigmatic, touchy, inordinately power-driven and

---

[1] At the time this paper was written, this book, *Swift and Carroll*, was in preparation. It was published in 1955.

In order not to hamper the reading of this paper with documentation I here list the sources on which I have drawn: the complete works of Jonathan Swift (1735), the editions edited by Eddy (1951), Samuel Johnson (1778), Temple Scott (1913), and Williams (1937). With regard to Swift's life, see Acworth (1947), Ball (1914), Bullitt (1953), Craik (1882), Davis (1942, 1947), Forster (1876), Freeman (1921), Hardy (1949), Heilman (1950), Lane-Poole (1885), Orrery (1752), Quintana (1953), Scott (1841), Sheridan (1785), Smith (1935), Stephen (1889), Deane Swift (1755), Van Doren (1930), Wilde (1849), Williams (1948), Wilson (1804). Additional source material is contained in the References and Notes and the Bibliography of my book (1955).

active; always in the public eye, he was conspicuously afraid of gossip, and had many hiding places. He was a political power in his day in both England and Ireland, and in his activities swung like a pendulum between the two countries during much of his adult life. He rarely wrote or talked directly of his own experiences; yet he celebrated himself flagrantly in poetry and was never modest. He became known for his satirical prose and his obscene verses; yet in speech he was generally charming, immaculate, and witty. He wrote often under pseudonyms, a not uncommon practice of the time; he would wait until he could see the success of his anonymous pamphlet and when it was attributed to someone else, would come forth and angrily claim it, seemingly after having sat back and laughed at the commotion it had caused. He was known as a great practical joker too. His political writings especially revealed his unparalleled courage and his great timidity, together with his fierce resentment at what he had himself provoked. Of himself he wrote: "A person of great honor in Ireland . . . used to say that my mind was like a conjured spirit that would do mischief if I would not give it employment." The "person of great honor" seems to have been Swift himself.

He came of a Yorkshire family. In his one autobiographical account—which petered out after a few pages—he was inclined to stress the aristocracy of his English forebears, and showed especial admiration for his English clergyman grandfather, in whose honor he erected a tombstone. He had not known this grandfather, nor his father either. The father, also named Jonathan Swift, had come to Ireland with several brothers, and had proved the least successful of them all. This Jonathan died in the spring of 1667, seven and a half months before the birth of his only son on November 13 of that year. Swift always spoke of having been "dropped," not born, on Irish soil, and rather exhibitionistically mentioned that he was wont to read the third chapter of the Book of Job on his birthday—the chapter in which Job curses the day he was conceived. Yet Swift always celebrated his birthday with poetry and festivity as well as curses.

His mother, Abigail, was an Englishwoman of simple background, some eight to ten years older than her husband. They had married three years before Jonathan's birth, and he had a sister Jane, less than two years older. Some considered that Jonathan was illegitimate, others that he was really the posthumous child of the elder Jonathan. Whatever the facts, these two accounts of his birth must have been the gossip of the time and have contributed to the fantasies of the growing boy. The father died leaving many debts, and the records of the time indicate that the mother made great efforts to collect certain money due her husband in order to pay these debts. One is surprised to learn that in spite of this impoverishment the family had an English nurse for the two children, possibly furnished by the paternal uncle Godwin, a successful barrister and prolific husband and father. He married successively four wealthy wives and had in all eighteen children.

The events of Swift's infancy were more than dramatic and seem to have set an indelible pattern for his restless, driven, divided life. Swift wrote of himself that he had been a frail baby, and that when a year old he had been kidnapped by his nurse "without the knowledge or consent" of his mother or his uncle, and had been taken by the nurse to the town of Whitehaven in England; further, that his mother, on discovering his abduction and after some delay in learning his whereabouts, sent word that he was not to be returned until he was sufficiently sturdy to bear easily the trip across the Irish Sea. This was accomplished three years later, when young Jonathan was between four and five. The nurse, he says, had been so devoted and careful that she had taught him to read and write so well that he could read any chapter of the Bible. The immediate cause and circumstances of his return are nowhere described. It is rather striking, too, that a few months after his return his mother left him in Ireland with his uncle Godwin and herself returned to her home in England, where she continued to live unmarried the rest of her life, depending on a small annuity of which the source is unclear.

The mysteries of this early career are the more baffling in that, while Swift in the autobiographical fragment records the nurse's devotion to him and attributes to her his early literacy, he mentions her nowhere else, and seems generally to have consigned her to anonymity, which was his way in later life with those who displeased him. (We shall rediscover the nurse in Gulliver's account of *his* life.) The mother, who had apparently deserted Swift twice before he was five years old, was on the other hand described by

Swift's second cousin, grandson of uncle Godwin, as "a woman greatly beloved and esteemed by all the family of Swifts. Her conversation was so exactly polite, cheerful, and agreeable, even to the young and sprightly." He further remarked on her generosity, her decorum, her industrious reading and needlework. Whether this was sincere or a "face" for the world is difficult to say.

When Swift came to know his mother later in life, he was fond of her and visited her whenever he went to England. According to some accounts, the mother maintained a playful relationship with him, so that when she visited him unexpectedly once in Ireland and found him absent, she succeeded in persuading his landlady that he was her lover. She died when Swift was forty-three. He then wrote that with her passing he had lost the barrier between himself and death, and he put this memorandum away between the pages of an account book.

Swift's relationship to his sister Jane is obscure. She presumably stayed with her mother. The same second cousin who wrote amiably of Abigail Swift noted that she was equally fond of both her children, between whom disagreements often existed. This must have been in their young adulthood, for they did not know each other after the earliest months until then. After his mother's return with Jane to England, Jonathan was placed under the care of his uncle Godwin, who presently sent him to school at Kilkenny, which was considered the Eton of Ireland. At school he was with two of his cousins, while vacations may have been spent among the eighteen children in Godwin Swift's household. Certainly from age five or six until twenty-two the young Jonathan lived an institutional existence which he hated. He later referred to these school years as comprising "the education of a dog," and described himself as "discouraged and sunk in spirit." He was a poor student both at Kilkenny and at Trinity College in Dublin, where finally he got his degree only by a special dispensation at eighteen. He seems to have been compliant and inhibited in his work.

Swift later wrote to Lord Bolingbroke of an incident in his early days at Kilkenny—undoubtedly a screen memory of considerable significance:

> I remember when I was a little boy, I felt a fish at the end of my
> line which I drew up almost to the ground, but it dropped in and

the disappointment vexes me to this day and I believe it the type of all my future disappointments.

This incident is told in other terms in the first voyage of Gulliver, in which he loses his hat in the water because the cord has been broken. The hat is later retrieved and, attached by hooks on cords, is dragged in by five horses. This screen memory and its later literary elaboration, which we should regard as a corrective or restitutive version of the original screen memory, seems extremely significant, the two forming a picture not unlike the famous screen memory described by Freud (1899).

Swift described another incident from his student days, which he repeated to impecunious young people seeking to marry without adequate savings. He so much wanted a horse that he invested his entire capital in a worn-out nag which was the only horse he could afford, only to find that he had no money with which to buy feed for it. The horse finally solved the problem by lying down and dying. That Swift connected this story with marriage is significant, the tired horse quite possibly representing his own improvident father who also lay down and died. The horse was an important figure to both Swift and Gulliver, as we shall observe later.

Only after the attainment of his degree, disgraceful as it was, did the young man rebel, and as a graduate student at Trinity he became known as the writer of a scurrilous harangue which is described by one biographer as showing "the will and capacity to wound and above all a directness in insolence, a mercilessness in savage laughter." Thenceforward he seemed more or less freed from his intellectual serfdom and from his depressions, which now rather appeared in the form of savage laughter turned to a high moral purpose whenever possible. He left Trinity without a higher degree, ostensibly because of the illness and increasing dementia of his uncle Godwin, whom he hated and whose illness consequently made a deep impression on him. Swift then, at the age of twenty-two, turned to England and his mother, and embarked on his first flirtation with a rather undistinguished young woman named Betty Jones, who subsequently married a tavern keeper. Whatever this affair amounted to, it provoked some self-examination, for he wrote afterward to a friend that "his own cold temper and unconfined humor were the greatest hindrance to any kind of folly." He seems also to have turned to power and pride, for at the same time he wrote: "I hope my carriage will be so as my friends need not be ashamed of the name."

After a short time he obtained, through his mother and uncle, a position as a kind of secretary or literary steward in the home of Sir William Temple, who had previously been ambassador to Holland and active in affairs of state but was now retired and wanted the younger man to help him in the editing and sorting of his papers. Swift spent ten years in this household, the decade punctuated by several interruptions and some discontent. During his first year he developed symptoms of dizziness, deafness, and headache, probably Ménière's disease, which was to stalk him the rest of his life. He attributed it to eating too much "stone fruit" in the Temple garden and sought to cure it by returning to his native Ireland.

The onset of this illness seems to have precipitated a wealth of hypochondriacal fears to counteract which he intensified compulsive walking and exercising, keeping track of the amount of his daily walking and interrupting his work at regular intervals to keep up his pedal score. This continued throughout his life. His return to Ireland lasted only three months, after which he was back in the Temple household, this time not only editing and doing routine secretarial work but also attempting to write poetry. In this he was discouraged by his distant cousin Dryden, but he succeeded at this time in writing some of his famous satires, *The Battle of the Books* and *The Tale of the Tub,* which were not to be published until some years later.

Swift's second interruption of his sojourn in the Temple household occurred at twenty-seven, when he decided to enter the church. He had certainly been restless and resentful, and obviously felt unappreciated. He had obtained his Master's degree at Oxford at twenty-five without difficulty, much to his surprise, and had been busy with his own literary enterprises, but had not yet really tasted the heady wine of publication. The significance of his step in the direction of the church is not clear. He had already attacked religion like an atheist. But he was without a real home or family, and his position with the Temples was not well defined. His sister Jane was also a member of the Temple ménage, but he seemed not to care much for her, and she remains throughout Swift's life a shadowy, drab, and disappointing figure at best. It is possible he looked to the church to take the place of a family. (It will be remembered that the ancestor he most admired was a clergyman grandfather.) This position in the church also offered him an excellent rationalization for his neurotic fear of gossip and exposure. But he was again to be disappointed: the prebend of Kilroot which was granted him was a dreary country place near Belfast.

During his stay with the Temples, Swift had become acquainted with a Mrs. Johnson, widow of Sir William's steward. As a lady-in-waiting she was also part of the establishment, together with her little daughter Hester, who was eight years old when Jonathan first came there. The lonely young man took an interest in the child and taught her so effectively to read and write that her evenly formed letters were almost a replica of his own. This little girl was to play an important part in his life and in a most enigmatic relationship which has been puzzling and provocative of fantasy to students of literature throughout the more than two hundred and fifty years since then.

At Kilroot, however, he fell in love with a young lady, Jane Waring, the sister of a college classmate. He wanted to marry her, but he likened to distemper his infatuation for her, and he hoped the marriage would cure him. He renamed her Varina—a Latinized version of her last name—and she became the first of the three important women of his adult life: little Hester Johnson, the second, was to become the Stella who was most in his confidence and his companion until her death; and the third was another Hester whom he nicknamed Vanessa, again condensing her first name Hester with her last one, van Homrigh. The two Hesters were the daughters of widows; whether this was true of Jane Waring is not known.

The courtship of Varina was an odd affair, in which the tortured man was by turns suspicious and peremptory, obviously frightened, yet driven toward marriage, while the girl wavered irresolutely. Swift's letters to her, of which he seems to have kept careful copies, were strange mixtures of philosophizing and violence. Finally, at twenty-nine, he left and again returned to the Temples. Three years later, when at thirty-two he again visited Ireland, Varina got in touch with him. Hinting then that he felt she valued him for his better worldly standing, he wrote her an angry offer of marriage, in which he adjured her to be cleanly and obedient. This seems to have been the end of his relationship with Varina, and he did not mention her again.

His demand for cleanliness, and especially his fear of dirtiness in a woman, spoke loudly of the core of his neurosis. Characteristically he used the word slut as a term of endearment, while he called his cook "sweetheart" when she displeased him with over-done roasts. He was himself more than scrupulously clean at a time when to be so was a luxury and an achievement, and there are stories of his refusing to give alms to old women with unclean hands. In his repeated attacks on whatever seemed corrupt or evil, whether in a woman's body or in a matter of state, his language was itself so violent and foul that presently the stench seemed to come from him rather than from the object of his attack.

Just before his rupture with Varina, he wrote a series of pathetic "Resolutions when I come to be old"—seventeen resolutions for self-protection and self-strengthening. One was not to marry a young woman; another, not to harken to flatterers or conceive "that I can be loved by a young woman"; and another, "not to be fond of children or let them come near me hardly." Yet he remained the devoted tutor of little Hester Johnson (Stella).

Swift's thirty-second year (1699) was momentous: Sir William Temple died; Jane Swift married; Jonathan Swift made a final break with Jane Waring (Varina). This seems to have been the closing of an emotional epoch for him. Subsequently he became more cautious, negativistic, and aggressively touchy. He may have realized that he could not love, but was rather one who can feel that he is a person only if he opposes; the more so because he could thus save himself from the counterdemand of his nature which was to lose himself completely in another, in the unconditional love of infancy.

His relationship with the Temple family and with his sister Jane fell apart completely. He sought preferment in the church, and being disappointed wrote two of his bitterest and foulest poems, *The Discovery* and *The Problem,* which caused one of his biographers to remark that he had behaved like an animal that relieves itself on the despised carcass of an adversary. At this time too some of his writings, for example, *Meditations Upon a Broom-*

stick and *Digression on Madness,* showed an unmistakable pre-occupation with sexual inversion. He soon obtained a small country church at Laracor, a few miles from Dublin.

Swift had a theory that girls should be trained to be as much like boys as possible, and that only thus could they hope for a secure marriage. His education of Hester Johnson was continued in this way. He demanded great accuracy in spelling, reading, and writing, and he warned continuously against the frivolities of interest in dress, social chatter, or flirtations. He was training the first Hester to be a second version of himself. Two years after the death of Sir William, he persuaded Stella, who was living with a nurse-chaperon, Rebecca Dingley, to join him in Ireland. The great rationalization was that they would have more money because living was cheaper there. It is interesting that this move, referred to as the abduction of Stella, occurred at almost exactly the same interval after Sir William's death as Swift's own abduction by his nurse, traveling in the opposite direction, had occurred after the death of his father.

The life of Stella and Dingley in Ireland was unusual. They lived in a tiny cottage a discreet half mile or so from the rectory at Laracor, and when Swift was Dean of St. Patrick's in Dublin they lived near him there. He schooled them relentlessly to be discreet, meaning secretive. When he went to England they stayed behind in Ireland, but moved into his quarters, and Stella carried on his routine business for him, like a Junior Dean. It is said that he never saw her except in Dingley's presence. For twenty-seven years this strange triangle continued, with Swift complaining openly of Dingley's stupidity, but keeping her always as a guardian.

Stella's inner relationship to Swift, like so much else, is unclear. Her father had been a steward in Sir William Temple's household. (His father had been steward of the King's Inns.) We do not know the time of her father's death, nor her feeling for him. By some it was said that she was not his child. She was sickly till the age of fifteen, and later developed tuberculosis. Until her death in middle age, she lived in this synthetic family with the brilliant Jonathan Swift as her "father" (her platonic lover in fact), and Dingley as a nurse-mother. Her own mother remained in England until her death. Swift quarreled with his sister Jane about her marriage, but when she was widowed a few years later he dutifully helped to support her although he did not wish to see or hear much of her, and sent her to live with Stella's mother. It seems amply clear that the Swift-Stella-Dingley ménage was a condensed version of Swift's own early life, with Mrs. Johnson playing the part of Abigail Swift with her daughter Jane in keeping. The real Abigail continued to live in Leicester until her death.

There was nothing to indicate a sexual relationship between Swift and Stella, and much to suggest that for Swift the idea was loathsome and perhaps impossible. He addressed Stella as "Young Sir"; wrote to her, "Why are you not a young fellow and then I might prefer you?" and again declared that Stella and Dingley were not women. Swift pictured her as a stern and exacting idealist like himself; she was as prudent and frugal with money as he. When another clergyman sought Stella in marriage, Swift was pushed to a declaration "in conscience and in honour," in which he told "the naked truth," but proceeded to an appraisal of Stella's fortune and intellect such that the poor man retreated—for Swift seemingly supported the suit of his rival but ended with the pretense that the gentleman would presently be obliged to marry Stella in order to satisfy gossip. Swift's letter on the occasion is extraordinarily cold.

At the time of Swift's mother's death when he was forty-three (1710), he was at the height of his political power in England. He knew himself to be a genius, and savored his influence with arrogance and sometimes with revenge. Just then he began his famous *Journal to Stella*, a series of letters always frequent and sometimes daily, which continued for three years (1710-1713). This *Journal* is fascinating, for side by side with his account of his political and literary achievements are long chronicles of his complaints and illnesses, together with barely decipherable personal communications written in a kind of baby talk pig Latin, with many abbreviations known between Swift and Stella as the "little language."

It was in 1710 too that the third goddess, the second Hester, appeared on the scene—the girl who was to be Vanessa. Her father had been Lord Mayor of Dublin, and Swift met the widow and her children on the boat from Ireland to England. The new Hester was about seven years younger than the first. Swift frequently and seemingly carelessly misstated the ages of the two Hesters, often making them two or three years younger than they were. It is interesting to note that this is the difference in age between himself and his sister Jane. Hester van Homrigh was older when Swift met her, more worldly, but as direct and intolerant of deception as he had trained Stella to be. Swift once wrote to Vanessa's cousin about her in such terms that it provoked the young woman to protest that he sounded as though he were describing a hermaphrodite. This Hester was said actually to resemble Swift. She was, however, not as docile as Stella, and she was developed as a woman. While she reverenced his genius, she fell in love with him—a state which became distressing to all three and caused Swift finally to turn on her in coldness and destroy her.

For a time Swift kept up visits and correspondence with the two Hesters, often with amazingly similar expressions. One was in England, the other in Ireland, and for a long time they did not know each other. In these letters he addressed Vanessa as "agreeable bitch," Stella as "brat." His disappointing cook he addressed as "sweetheart." There is no doubt that his affection for Stella was more consistent than that for Vanessa. It was Vanessa, however, who elicited from him an attempt at a passionate response, which he "half revealed and all concealed" in his famous poem *Cadenus and Vanessa*. What remains of her letters to him is filled with the urgency of her desire to see him and her disappointment at his constantly broken promises. On his side, however, every expression of warm feeling for her is followed by one of coldness and desire to flee.

In 1711 Swift's satirical pamphlets were so successful that his *Conduct of the Allies* was credited with ending the war between France and England. In 1713 he became Dean of St. Patrick's Cathedral in Dublin. But by this time he was caught in the decline of the Tory power, was personally unpopular, and began to complain of being old and to write his epitaphs. Now too Vanessa unfortunately returned to Ireland to live on her family's estate at Celbridge, also a few miles from Dublin. The two young women heard rumors of each other. Swift's relationship to Vanessa progressively declined, and had throughout a desperate, tantalizing quality. Swift, often placating, sometimes sentimentally tender, treated her with what Scott described as "cruelty under the mask of mercy," and Vanessa complained that he kept her in "a languishing death." He even twitted her with behaving as though she were in love. Stella, however, remained generally steadfast but possibly more demanding.

In the years 1713-1718 Swift seems to have written only once to Vanessa, and his correspondence with Stella was not kept. The famous *Journal* stopped in 1713. Swift was personally uncourageous and seemed always afraid of being caught in scandal. In 1716 some event occurred which gave rise to stories that Swift had married or almost married Stella, but with the proviso that they should continue to live apart. There were evidently rumors that the marriage had not been finally accomplished, but the official version for nearly seventy-five years was that it was. Later investigations revealed no documentary evidence of any kind that it had occurred, and some indications that it had not. And so the secretive man who was always so afraid of the nasty tattle of the town succeeded in setting up a mystery that has stimulated the scoptophilia of students of English literary history ever since.

The marriage is said to have occurred in the garden of the Deanery in Dublin. Stella was ill and jealous. The reports come mostly from two clergymen friends, one of whom was said to be the officiating churchman. Just as the marriage ceremony was to have been performed someone, whose identity is not stated, revealed that it could not continue, as Swift and Stella were actually brother and sister, the natural children of Sir William Temple. The occurrence of any marriage was later denied by Dingley and by Stella's executor. That the rumors represent some sort of fantasy—with what grain of truth?—is obvious; but like the stories concerning Swift's birth, it is not clear whose fantasies predominated. One may well ask whether it is conceivable that these fantasies sprang primarily from Swift himself, representing some older longing of his own, and were advanced and "confessed" by him in a way to block the marriage and let the situation remain as it had been. The facts already presented rather clearly suggest Swift's fixation on and identification with the fantasied sister of his childhood, Jane, the child who was absent with the mother and who was actually so disappointing to him in the materialization. Swift's first love affair was with Jane Waring, sister of his school friend. It is my further suggestion that one of the many determinants in the choice of the two Hesters was the name itself, so alliteratively close to the word "sister." Both were the children of widowed mothers; one the daughter of a steward, and the other of a more distinguished sire, the Mayor of Dublin.

Eleven years after the supposed marriage, Swift was again writing to a young woman to prepare her for marriage and stressing the need for rational love and intellectual companionship. Always he emphasized cleanliness and avoidance of gossip, and warned the girl not to be sentimental or rapturous, or to taunt a man about his physical deformity or his lack of a family fortune. Of love itself, or of spirituality, he said nothing.

A few of Vanessa's letters remain, betraying a pathetic, growing disillusionment and hatred for the man who besought her to be sincere and was himself so indirect. Her idolatry turned to bitterness. When she wrote to him of the approaching death of her sister, of whom he had seemed to be fond, he advised her to get her friends around her but himself stayed away, writing, "I want comfort and can give little." One feels that he could not tolerate being called upon for personal help or being confronted with suffering. Then he felt worse himself, whether out of identification or guilt it is hard to say; but he stayed away, plagued and hypochondriacal, and considered the suffering of others as due to "unhappy imagination!"

Vanessa died in 1723 at the age of thirty-six. On hearing of her death, he hastened a southern trip which he had planned for some time and, leaving that very night, he stayed away for some months, traveling more than 500 miles on horseback seeking "companionship among those of least consequence and most compliance." He gave no indication of conscious grief or guilt, but spent his energy in riding, even as earlier he had required his compulsive walking. He could not go to England because of his unpopularity. True to the pattern of his earlier life, he climbed out of this period by becoming again politically active, and that in the interest of a noble cause. The next year he was writing the famous Drapiers letters, satire which was so successful that it forced the rescinding of a law permitting special coinage for Ireland in a way that would have ruined Irish trade. His popularity in Ireland now rose to new heights. It seems then that what he could do for Vanessa, who had been emotionally closer to him than anyone else in his life, he did on a grand scale for the suffering people of Ireland. Presently, however, he was playing a practical joke which showed his contempt for these same Irish he had just rescued.

It seems probable that Swift thought much about *Gulliver's Travels,* but especially of the fourth (and last) voyage, while he was on this journey of concealed mourning. It is known that he had long had the main ideas for the *Travels,* and had already written much, but the fourth voyage is but scantily mentioned in the earlier drafts. In 1726 *Gulliver's Travels* was published.

On the whole Swift seems to have been esteemed and feared by his contemporaries. His wit and his intellect won him social recognition and his periodic forays into politics brought great admiration. He could seldom sustain friendships of close intimacy with men, perhaps because of his possessiveness but also because of the interplay between his great charm and his implacably fierce principles. To be sure, Addison wrote of him as "the most agreeable companion, the truest friend, and the greatest genius of his age"—remarks on the flyleaf of a presentation copy of one of Addison's own books (1705), indicative of considerable enthusiastic respect. Charles Ford was the one man, however, with whom Swift maintained a close and confidential relationship over many years. The full extent of this relationship was probably not recognized by early biographers, as many of the letters between the two men did not come to light until 1896.

Charles Ford was Dublin born and of almost exactly the same age as Stella. Swift probably came to know him about 1707, when Ford was taking his Master's degree and was about to marry. The marriage never took place, however, and as the friendship between the two men grew, Ford became a real confidant, who knew about Vanessa and Stella and offered solace and help rather generally. He is described as gay, joyous, and bright, but never profound. He had Stella and Dingley visit him for months after Vanessa's death, while Swift was galloping along the South coast of Ireland. Sometime later, however, Ford seems gradually to have removed himself from Ireland and Swift, and he spent his last years in London.

The publication of *Gulliver's Travels* reinstated and increased

Swift's fame, and somewhat counteracted the ill feeling aroused by the poem, *Cadenus and Vanessa,* publication of which had been vengefully ordered in Vanessa's will but might well have been stopped by Swift. Characteristically he preferred to pretend that it meant nothing to him and was only a bit of a frolic among women, ignoring how much suffering its publication must have caused the faithful Stella.

Stella began to fail in health. Swift absented himself often and began to speak as though she were already dead. He was aware of his profound distaste for seeing her ill and found great difficulty in overcoming this enough to go to see her and comfort her during the last months of her life. He narrowly missed being present as her death in January, 1727; she died while he was entertaining friends at dinner. He had been overwhelmingly afraid that she would die in the Deanery. He could not bear to go to her funeral, and sat in an adjacent room writing a long eulogy of her during the service.

By 1730 both Stella and Vanessa were dead and Charles Ford had settled in London. Swift became increasingly lonely and resentful. He spent much time with the erratic and rather dirty but charming Sheridan, grandfather of the playwright, and began to write many things for which he had had ideas for years. He incessantly reviled the body, especially the body of woman; he expressed his resentment of children as dirty nuisances who cluttered the world. Under the strange guise of a savage attack upon conditions of poverty in Ireland, he wrote one of his most dreadful and fierce satirical essays, entitled *A Modest Proposal for Preventing the Children of Poor People Being a Burden to Their Parents,* in which he suggested that infants one year old be roasted and served at the tables of the rich. He wrote both fair and filthy verse, became pugnacious in espousing the causes of the distressed, and took on the minor problems of people who had little or no claim upon him.

During the next decade, he suffered increasingly from attacks of rage and from progressive failure of his memory. In 1742, it was necessary to have him declared to be mentally incompetent and to appoint a guardian. He was silent for almost one year. It is reported that before his capacity to think had become quite clouded, he would look at himself in a pierglass and mutter, "Poor old man.

Poor old man," and again, as though childishly philosophizing to himself, "I am what I am. I am what I am." He died in Dublin at seventy-eight, on October 19, 1745. He left his fortune to found a hospital for fools and madmen.

II. GULLIVER'S TRAVELS

This book is manifestly an adventure story burlesquing the reports of world explorations at a time when new areas of the strange world were being discovered and the explorer was a romantic storyteller, a conqueror, and a kind of amateur reporter of anthropological mysteries. Sometimes, as by Defoe, the book of travel was used as an allegorical medium. *Gulliver's Travels* contains bold satirical attacks upon the political policies of the day, but its enduring popularity as a fairy tale classic for children is obviously not based on its political significance but upon its closeness to profound and unconscious problems of mankind.

Gulliver's Travels was written between 1721 and 1725 and published in 1726. The outline of the voyages had long been cast, having been written but not fully published by Swift as early as 1711-1714, under the title of the *Memoirs of Scriblerus*. But the fourth and last voyage seems to have been largely a product of a later time, and its elaboration may have been influenced by the prolonged emotional strain which Swift suffered, culminating with Vanessa's death in 1723. The first voyage was to Lilliput, the land of tiny folk; the second to Brobdingnag, the land of the giants; the third to five places: Laputa, Balnibarbi, Glubdubdrib, Luggnagg, and Japan; the fourth was to the country of the strangest creatures of all, the Houyhnhnms.

Lemuel Gulliver, the traveler, is a young man of Nottinghamshire, England, the third among five sons, recently apprenticed to a surgeon, Mr. James Bates. He has always had an interest in travel, having prepared himself for it by studying navigation, mathematics, and two years of physics at Leyden. Bates, his master, recommends him as surgeon on a ship, the Swallow,[2] where he serves for three years on voyages to the Levant. Later, again under the influence of Bates, he settles down to the practice of his profession in London and marries a woman who brings him a modest dowry. But his good master Bates dying in two years, Gulliver

2 Swift liked to pun on the names Swift, Martin, and Swallow, all being birds.

finds himself failing in his profession and has so strong a conscience that he cannot imitate the corrupt practices of his colleagues. He returns to the sea, where his maritime career continues more than fifteen years (1699-1715).[3]

It is interesting to compare the lives of Lemuel Gulliver and
Jonathan Swift, his creator, both as to sequence of events and the
occurrences at specific dates in the two lives. There are no very
full or reliable accounts of either. Gulliver was born a few years
before Swift. Both men were travelers. Though Swift never traveled far, he was a constant voyager between Ireland and England,
sometimes dividing the year between the two countries, and many
times made plans for foreign travel. Swift was a clergyman, preoccupied with the ills of his own body and with the political ills
of the state, but could hardly bear to consider the bodies of
others. Gulliver was a surgeon's apprentice who went on to explore the topography of foreign lands and peoples. Gulliver went
to Cambridge at fourteen; Swift at the same age had gone to
Trinity. While Gulliver was being apprenticed to Mr. Bates,
Swift at a corresponding time was doing graduate work for his
Master's degree. Both left their native soil at the age of twenty-
one, Gulliver going to Leyden to prepare for travel, Swift to
England to find his mother. At twenty-seven, Gulliver married and
attempted to settle down in London. At the same age, Swift was
wishing to marry Jane Waring and settle into the life of a clergyman. Both men lost their benefactors, Mr. Bates and Sir William
Temple respectively, at the age of thirty-two. Gulliver then returned to the sea, and Swift to the church. The actual year 1699,
in which Gulliver set out on the first recorded voyage, was a landmark in the life of Swift, being the time of Sir William Temple's
death, of Swift's rupture with Jane Waring, and of the unap-
proved marriage of Jane Swift. The date, December, 1715, of
Gulliver's return from his last voyage, in a state of abhorrence
toward his wife, was only a few months before Swift's supposed
marriage to Stella.

If one may summarize the qualities of the voyages in a phrase

[3] After the publication of *Gulliver's Travels* Pope wrote humorously to Swift
that one Jonathan Gulliver had turned up in Boston as a member of the local
parliament; Swift replied in kind, that a Lemuel Gulliver had actually appeared in
England, had the reputation of being a liar, but that he, Swift, considered this a
coincidence.

or two apiece, it may be said that the first two are concerned with size of the body; while in the third, changes of size, and especially the movement of inanimate objects in a land of abstract geometric fantasies not subject to reality testing, are the striking factors. The land of the fourth voyage is inhabited by ideal creatures and foul creatures, and the interrelation of these, and their relation to the traveler, compose the climax of the travels.

The first and best known voyage to Lilliput took three years. The ship, headed for the East Indies, was wrecked and Gulliver was the only survivor. He found himself in a land of very tiny people who, having caught him napping, pinned him to the ground with lacings of rope, attempting so to hold him down. Later they conveyed him to a temple which had been profaned by the murder of a man. There he was placed on view, tethered by a chain. Unable to escape, he defecated once within the temple, but later went into the open air for this purpose. Gulliver tells all this in meticulous detail, much as a child who is striving to be good in a new and strange place. He resembles Swift in his preoccupation with involuntary moral guilt and unavoidable physical dirtiness.

> I would not have dwelt so long upon a circumstance which . . . may appear not very momentous, if I had not thought it necessary to justify my character in point of cleanliness to the world, which I am told some of my maligners have been pleased . . . to call into question.

The most pervasive motif of the first voyage is the disparity in size between Gulliver and the Lilliputians who are afraid that Gulliver's need for food and clothing will impoverish them. This seems to reproduce something of Swift's first year of life to which he returns in his horrible satire, *A Modest Proposal* . . . , in which he proposes that the child be roasted at the age of one, the age at which he was kidnapped and taken to England. In Lilliput, Gulliver pretends to eat up the little folk. Most conspicuous of all is the awesomeness and offensiveness to the Lilliputians of Gulliver's mountainous body: his sneeze produces a tornado, his urination creates a torrent of "noise and violence," his defecation causes a national problem of health. He brandishes his sword and the sunlight on the blade causes them to kneel down in blinded awe.

When he shoots his pistol into the air a hundred men fall from shock. One cannot but think that these experiences correspond in reverse to Swift's own infantile experiences when, still in an era of primary identification, he was transported on *his* first voyage to England, where his stay also lasted three years.

Threads, ropes, and cords play an important part, in many variations, in the game of Gulliver and the Lilliputians, reminding one strongly of the importance of ropes and thongs among fetishists. The interest, awe, and revulsion aroused by the human body is represented actively and passively by both Gulliver and the Lilliputians, with reciprocal exhibitionism and scoptophilia, with great attention to the excretory functions. Gulliver plays with the King's cavalry[4] like a child playing with toy soldiers, and in turn is directed by the Emperor to stand, like a colossus, with his legs apart while the soldiers parade under the arch thus formed, stealing covert glances at the torn crotch of the giant's pants.

The problem of size reappears in the Lilliputian religious and political problems, for the country is split into factions: the High-Heelers against the Low-Heelers, and the Big-Endians against the Little-Endians (who dispute the question, which end of a boiled egg is preferred). The Emperor's son wears heels of uneven height, so that he hobbles in compromise, and the country is in danger of being conquered by a neighboring country. But the giant Gulliver rescues Lilliput by dragging the enemy fleet out of the channel, like a child manipulating toys.

His visit to the Lilliputians culminates in his famous exploit of putting out a fire in the Queen's chamber by urinating upon it; but the Queen reacts in revenge rather than gratitude.

The system of education among the Lilliputians was certainly founded by the infant Swift. It is based on the principle that parents beget children from purely biological drives and therefore should not be permitted to educate them, nor to visit them for more than two hours in a year. Boys and girls are educated separately, but girls are educated to be as much like boys as possible, on the principle that a wife "should always be a reasonable and agreeable companion, since she cannot always be young." Through-

---

4 When King William encountered the young Swift in the Temple household, he taught him to eat asparagus and offered him a post in the cavalry.

out the story morals are valued higher than abilities. Consequently Gulliver finds himself impeached because his abilities are recognized and feared, and he finds it ultimately necessary to escape and return home. Thus ends the first voyage of Lemuel Gulliver and Jonathan Swift.

The second voyage is soon undertaken. Again the ship loses its course and after a year of wandering lands upon a new continent. Gulliver becomes separated from his companions and finds himself among giants in the land of Brobdingnag. This voyage seems but a continuation and reversed version of the first. Gulliver is now afraid of being trampled or eaten. The appearance of the nurse as an important figure is significant. She appears in two forms. In one she is the revolting adult nurse who bares her dry nipple to quiet the baby by suckling it, and in so doing reminds Gulliver that the Lilliputians had found his skin revolting, with its oversized pores and stumps of hairs. In the other she is the little girl nurse who teaches him the language and calls him her manikin. The impression of the disgusting adult woman is later reinforced by the sight of a woman with cancerous holes in her breast, so large that Gulliver might have crawled into one. The traveler himself suffers passive exhibition, being carried in a kind of doll cage dangling from a cord around the waist of the little girl nurse when she shows him at county fairs.

Ultimately he is protected by the Queen, who prepares a little closet in which he can go riding on horseback strapped to the belt of the rider. It is of interest that he is unimpressed by the tallest tower in the land, computing its height to be less than that of Salisbury Cathedral. He suffers exposure and mutual exhibitionism at the hands of the Maids of Honor, who use him for their erotic amusement, balance him astride their nipples, and disgust him by their copious urination and the odor of their bodies. This indeed is the first voyage in reverse. Finally he suffers the typical lesson of being brought to witness the beheading, with a dramatic spurt of blood, of a murderer. The Queen now makes a little boat for him, which is propelled down a water-filled trough by the breeze from the ladies' fans.

The common symbolism of the man-in-the-boat as the clitoris suggests the identification with the female phallus thought to be characteristic of the male transvestite. A further incident confirming this occurs when one of the ladies lifts him up between her thumb and forefinger to put him into his little boat, but he slides through and plunging downward is caught by a corking pin in the lady's stomacher. The head of the pin passing between his skin and his waistband, he is suspended in this way more or less attached to the lady's stomacher until rescued by his little nurse.

The theme of the kidnapping appears also, for Gulliver is carried away three times: by a dog, by a kite, and by a monkey. The monkey holds him "as a nurse does a child she is about to suckle." The further description of this event specifies that the monkey is a male, who crams food into Gulliver's mouth, squeezing it out from his chaps. This whole experience sickens Gulliver terribly, and the food has to be picked out again by the child nurse. Surely this is a fantasy of fellatio—of being at the mercy of a bisexual adult. Gulliver is forced to recognize his insignificance when the King chaffs him about this disgusting experience. Finally, when the King wishes to find him a mate, it is time for the traveler, who has been away two years, to return home. He cannot bear to propagate a race so diminutive as to be laughable. He escapes by being kidnapped again, this time by an eagle which carries him off in his box, then drops the box with its occupant into the sea. It is noteworthy that, after he is picked up by sailors, his return voyage takes exactly nine months, during which he suffers severe sensory feelings of unreality in trying to reconcile himself to the normal size of those around him. He has difficulty in focusing his vision.

After this homecoming, his wife begs Gulliver never to leave again, but he has an insatiable thirst for seeing the world and soon is off again. Many critics have thought the third voyage out of place; they feel it does not belong in this sequence. To me it seems an essential link. On this trip, his ship is attacked by pirates and he is cast adrift in a canoe. This leads to his discovery of a peculiar, exactly circular island suspended in the air over the body of a continent, and resting so delicately on a lodestone that a little child's hand can manipulate it; and its inhabitants can thus move it at will "to raise or sink, or put it in progressive motion." This is the Island of Laputa, and might be described as the Island of Abstract Fantasy without Reality Testing. The movement of the island, directed by the King, depends much upon mathematics and music. Ideas are expressed in geometrical figures, although there is great contempt for practical geometry. The Laputans are chronically anxious and fearful of total destruction of the earth, the planets, everything. Peculiar marital relations prevail, and the women are mostly restless and unsatisfied, a condition which reminds Gulliver of his home in England. Through the intervention of the stupidest man on the island, Gulliver succeeds in getting away to the adjacent Island of Balnibarbi, a place once rich and substantial, but recently ruined by the infiltration of smatterings of mathematics from the Laputans, which has produced too great a volatility of spirit. The Balnibarbians have attempted to put the ideas of the Laputans to practical tests, and consequently have impoverished their people. Their Institute of Scientific Exhibits, however, would be well worth a visit in our own day. It must have resembled a display of patents. In one place, words are mixed in a kind of grinding machine and then used for poetry, politics, law, and theology. In another, words are abolished, as each word uttered diminishes the lungs by corrosion. Following this, words are supplanted by things, in a kind of symbolic realization, and only the women rebel and insist upon using their tongues; moreover, a kind of lobotomy is performed, but with the advantage of an exchange of amputated lobes between individuals. In this progressive country, Gulliver recommends the establishment of a governmental department of spies, informers, discoverers, accusers, and witnesses, so that it can first be agreed who shall be accused; the papers of the accused can then be seized, and the anagrammatic method used for evaluating the evidence. This country makes Gulliver homesick for England and he feels, prophetically, that it may perhaps extend to America and the land of California. (Swift only missed using the name McCarthy.)

There is still another island, Glubdubdrib, inhabited by sorcerers and magicians, where the servants are ghosts, changing each twenty-four hours and being made to evaporate into thin air by a flick of the Governor's finger. Another stop is at Luggnagg, where he is met by a male interpreter, a contrast to his previous experiences of having been nursed and taught by girls, women, princesses, and queens. Here Gulliver has to lick the dust before the royal footstool and utter words which mean "my tongue is in the mouth of my friend!" He makes a final stop in the vicinity of the eerie Struldbrugs, variant creatures, human but undying, and finds them a dejected, opinionated, covetous group of immortals.

After a short stop at home, during which his wife enters her third pregnancy, Gulliver again leaves on the ship Adventure, not as a ship's surgeon this time, but as a sailing captain. There is a mutiny, and he is left on a strange, desolate island inhabited by strangely evil and by noble creatures. The evil ones are dirty, hairy, nightmarish animals that scamper about and climb trees, persecuting and tormenting the traveler by letting excrement drop on his head. In contrast to these are reasonable, gentle horses, the natural aristocrats of the land. Soon a pair of the gentle horses take him in hand, teach him the language, and give him a home. From them he learns that they are Houyhnhnms, and that the foul creatures are called Yahoos. From the way the Houyhnhnms look at his face and hands he realizes that they regard him as a special Yahoo, unexpectedly clean and teachable. When they see him at night, partly undressed and with the lower part of his body uncovered, they are sure that he is a Yahoo, and a complete examination of his body brings them to the opinion that he is a perfect specimen of Yahoo—a characterization which greatly displeases him. When he tries to explain to them the laws and customs of his native England, they feel even more strongly confirmed in their diagnosis, but feel also that Gulliver is not quite so hardy as their local members of the species. After a time he decides never to return home, but to stay permanently with the Houyhnhnms. They explain to him that the Yahoos hate each other more than they do any creatures of other species, the reason for this being the odiousness of their shapes which all can see in each other but none in himself. The Yahoos are greedy, lacking in discrimination, and foul in their sexuality, and their system of medicine is founded upon coprophagic practices. Gulliver himself, studying the Yahoos, confirms their unteachability but interestingly attributes it to a perverse, restive disposition rather than to inherent defect.

After three years in this country, Gulliver becomes convinced of his own indubitable Yahoo origin when a Yahoo maiden falls in love with him as she sees him bathing, and is so energetic in her advances that he has to be rescued by his devoted sorrel nag. In contrast to the Yahoos, the Houyhnhnms are reasonable, just, and friendly. In their education of children they depend upon reason rather than love; the marital relationship is one of mutual benevolence and friendship of a standardized communal variety. They train their youth after a Swiftian rule by having them run up and down hills in competitive races.

In this country, the Houyhnhnms embody equable reason and impersonal goodwill, while the Yahoos are creatures of primordial hate and passion. The former are minute and exact in their descriptions and "just" in their similes. When they die, by a process of gradual fading, there is no emotion, no mourning. The dead person is said "to have returned to his first mother," and before taking this final step he pays a last ceremonial call upon his friends, being sure to repay all past visits.

After Gulliver's discovery of his true Yahooness he settles down to stay in this strange country, hating himself in a way unique among them, and trying hard to emulate the behavior of the Houyhnhnms. After five years residence, he finds himself banished by the General Council of Houyhnhnms, who consider him dangerous, perhaps because he is mixing customs so much. He builds a boat and gets away. Ultimately picked up by a Portuguese ship, he is at first judged deranged because of his accounts of his experiences. He wants to isolate himself for the rest of his life on an island. He returns home, however, and finds that he cannot bear his wife for he is still under the influence of Houyhnhnm ideals and cannot endure the thought of having cohabited with a Yahoo and produced Yahoo children. It is more than a year before he can bear to be in the same room with his wife, and never afterward can he bring himself to drink from the same cup as his family or to be touched by one of them. In memory of the good Houyhnhnms he buys a pair of horses with whom he lives in amiable friendship, the smell of their stable being sufficient to revive his sagging spirits.

No account of Gulliver and Swift can be tolerably complete unless it links with these two names that of Martin Scriblerus, later known as Tim. The Scriblerus Club, originally the Tory Club, consisted of Swift, Pope, Gay, Oxford, Parnell, and Arbuthnot, and Swift proposed that all write in collaboration a comprehensive satire on the abuses of learning. They produced the *Memoirs of Scriblerus,* the major part of which was supposed to have been written by Swift. It was openly admitted, furthermore, that Swift himself was identified with Scriblerus, and Swift was temporarily nicknamed "Dr. Martin" for, as he explained in his *Journal to Stella*, surely a Martin was a kind of Swift, and both were swallows. (Swallow was the name of one of the ships on which Gulliver traveled.) In the early Scriblerus writings, Swift revealed certain fantasies regarding his birth, his grandiose dreams, and his attitudes toward his own genius. He projected the *Travels* (not to be published for another fifteen years) as consisting of four voyages: first to the pygmies; second to the giants; third to the mathematicians and philosophers; and fourth, one in which a "vein of melancholy proceeds almost to a disgust of his species." At this time he was preoccupied with his conservative plan of using cannibalism for the relief of the conditions of the poor. It was certainly a longstanding preoccupation, for the *Modest Proposal* was not published until 1729.

III. CLINICAL DISCUSSION

Swift's problems of identity and identification, inherent in the strange circumstances of his birth, were again evident at the end of his life, when he addressed the old man in the mirror as "poor old man," and philosophized "I am what I am. I am what I am." The complications of his kidnapping and the return to his mother, followed by her apparent desertion at the very height of the oedipal period, furnished in reality a fateful family romance that might otherwise have been a powerful fantasy. His living almost entirely in institutions from this time until his majority really completed the punishment of fate. Even his vacations were presumably spent among the eighteen children of uncle Godwin, and it is of interest that he mentions no girl among them.

His one attempt to write an autobiography petered out after a few pages, and about the kidnapping nurse we have only the barest statement that she prematurely taught him to read the Bible. Gulliver tells us more, as I have indicated, and splits the image of the nurse into two, the evil, repulsive, gaping old nurse, and the gentle, prepubertal little girl nurse, who protected him and kept him dangling in his cage attached to her belt. I have already indicated, in relating the histories of Dean Swift and Dr. Gulliver, that it is my belief that the infant Swift must have been in close bodily contact with the kidnapping nurse, and almost surely some-how built up a complementary fantasy of the sister from whom he had been separated at the age of one; and that he made a deep identification of himself with both by a direct primary bodily identification with the actual nurse, and with a sustaining ideal image of the sister, which seems to have been a phallic image whereby he became predominantly identified with the sister's phallus. (Recall the child nurse who has him dangling from her waist, the Maids of Honor who blow him in his little boat down a trough of water, and the incident of his getting impaled on the stomacher of the lady-in-waiting.) That the young adult Swift first sought a girl of his sister's name, Jane, and then formed at-tachments to two girls named Hester (sister), and that he broke with Jane Waring in bitter disillusionment at the same time that he practically banished sister Jane because he disapproved of her marriage, are not pure accidents. Furthermore, his mutual identi-fication between himself, his sister, and the nurse is consistently re-enacted in his arrangement of his own life as tutor to the two Hesters, whom he would also turn into boys by his education of them. All this seems to me so clinically clear as to need little fur-ther elucidation in this presentation.

Swift's physical health and symptoms are worthy of notice. He was said to have been a frail, premature infant, and certainly his mother was under stress during the pregnancy and throughout his first year. One cannot avoid the conclusion that her attitude to-ward this baby, whose birth caused so many complications in her life, must have been disturbed; but in just what direction is un-clear. Swift had two mothers, in fact; and that he had two fathers is indicated by the reports of illegitimacy and remarks that his father never even knew of his conception. This question of pater-nity was to reappear in the never-solved mystery story of how Swift's marriage to Stella was stopped by the rumor that they actu-ally were brother and sister. It seems to me important that Swift, whether or not he furthered the rumor, must have known of it, and certainly made no move to correct or deny it. It either sprang from his fantasy or closely corresponded to a latent fantasy and served this purpose for him.

In the *Memoirs of Scriblerus* Swift shows again his enormous anality—so evident in his character—and gives a clear picture of the anal birth of genius. Martin Scriblerus's mother, having difficulty in conceiving, was advised to take seven sheets of paper and write upon each with seven alphabets of seven languages in such a way that no letter would stand twice in the same posture (surely a fantasy of a polymorphously perverse conception); then to clip all letters apart and put them into a pillow which she was to use to support her in a certain position favorable to fecundity. This proved helpful and Scriblerus was conceived. But on the eve of his birth his mother dreamed that she had given birth to a monster in the shape of an inkpot spurting black liquid in rivulets throughout the room. These were interpreted by a sorceress as being symbols of the infant's genius, signifying the variety of the productions of human learning; the spout of the inkpot signified that the child would be a son. When he was born, the infant enjoyed the rattling of paper and dabbling in ink. When the child was thought to say "Papa" it was determined by the nurse that he had really said "paper." Thus was launched the Genius of the Age.

Swift does not seem to have been a sickly child after his infancy. Yet by adolescence he had instituted walking rituals as a way of preserving his health and of showing his strength. In adulthood he was a man of unusually fine physique, but from the age of twenty-two he frequently complained of ill health, weakness, pains, stomachaches, nausea, and rather diffuse bodily pains. He developed Ménière's disease, which caused him many attacks of dizziness and deafness, and his account of its origin from eating stone fruit in the Temple garden suggests a strong homosexual conflict, which was to appear also in his *Meditations Upon a Broomstick*. He was extremely fearful of insanity from an early age ("dying at the top" he said, likening himself to a fir tree), and his constant reiteration of his defiance of death seems an overprotestation. In the third voyage of Gulliver, his meeting with the Struldbrugs condenses these fears.

Swift suffered from severe chronic anxiety and diffuse hypochondriasis of the type that so often accompanies an inordinately severe castration complex, to which his early life inevitably predisposed him. This hypochondriasis always increased when he saw the suffering of another. While some of these situations suggested guilt, so that he turned away in seeming callousness, there is the further question whether the sight of suffering did not cause him to take it unto himself through a primary identification. In his *Life and Character of Dr. Swift* (1731), Swift states:

> I could give instances enough that Human Friendship
> is but stuff. . . .
>
>   . . .
>
> True friendship in two breasts requires the same
> aversions and desires;
> My friend should have when I complain, a Fellow
> feeling for my pain.

What was writ large, vividly, and constantly in Swift's letters was his preoccupation with the lower bowel. He suffered from hemorrhoids, and complained of them in letters to Charles Ford, but in general he was personally reticent about this part of his body. Gulliver's concern with the excretions is noteworthy, and Swift's character contained juxtaposed gratification and reaction formation against gratification from this primitive source. That all sexuality was dirty and confused with excretory functions is amply evident. The fourth voyage of Gulliver portrays the conflicts and attempt at resolution vividly. It is quite clear that the Yahoos represent the dirty, unrestrained sexual parents, while the Houyhnhnms are the idealized, gentle, reasonable ones, the superego ones, possessing all the reaction formations against the primitive animal instincts. In the second voyage, it is the older nurse who is described as the most loathsome of creatures, with foul and gaping bodily apertures. It should be noted that the sweet, charming, protective little girl nurse was at prepuberty, a period when actually the little girl's body more closely resembles that of the boy than at any other time. Swift made the resemblance closer by endowing her with a phallus, through the diminutive Gulliver. Swift's actual hatred of the adult nurse is large and is nowhere more clear than in the paragraph devoted to nurses in his essay on *Directions to Servants in General*. This, together with certain passages in *Gulliver*, suggests strongly that his own nurse had a baby during the time of his stay with her (ages one to four), of whom he was inordinately jealous. The constant intermingling of literary learning and toilet functioning seems to indicate the severe and simultaneous training in these lines that was to leave a permanent mark upon his character and abilities. In the *Memoirs of Scriblerus* are invectives against the "accursed nurse" who, among other things, made the infant's ears "lie forever flat and immovable"—surely a reference to the impotence, both genital and auditory, of the writer.

Another theme, so often found in Swift's writing and life, is the confusion, determinedly rationalized, between the sexes. It occurs in his frank attempts to make boys of Stella and Vanessa, in his treatises on education, in his descriptions of the bodies of men and women. This naturally was associated with the opposite, a polarization of characteristics between the sexes, so that women became the completely emotional, dirty, unreliable ones, and men were reasonable, just, temperate, and cleanly. In the land of the fourth voyage, the Houyhnhnm horses are both male and female, and so are the Yahoos, yet in spirit the horses are good male, and the Yahoos dirty, seducing female. In a letter Swift even referred to Stella as a Yahoo.

The alternating scoptophilia and exhibitionism, so much described in the first two voyages (they are inevitably great in a posthumous child), seem to have formed the basis of many of Swift's most charming and penetrating capacities. Physically he was well built and rather handsome, with clear, blue eyes, of which he was so proud that he would never permit himself to wear spectacles, much to the disgust of Samuel Johnson, who wrote one of the biographies of Swift.

Perhaps the most fascinating problem of Swift's development was the configuration of his oedipus complex. He had no real father on whom to play out his oedipal development. Indeed his oedipal crime was accomplished seemingly by his very conception, after which the father died, while the son lived, and possessed his mother, at least in fantasy. Whether he found a substitute father during those years with the nurse in Whitehaven is not clear, but he was again confronted with his actual fatherlessness exactly at the oedipal period. It is apparent that there was an attempt to find a father through his interest in his English clergyman grandfather, and later in his decade of wavering allegiance to Sir William Temple. The feeling of his oedipal crime may well be expressed in the second voyage of Gulliver, in which he is given as a place to stay a deserted temple which has long ago been defiled

by the murder of a man. Gulliver's recalling of the heroic ances-
tors of history on the Island of Glubdubdrib also belongs here.

Just at the height of the oedipal period Swift's mother left him
and he was from then until young manhood almost entirely in a
homosexual environment. This may well have heightened and
directed his postoedipal idealism by increasing his feelings of
guilt and his hostilities in a mutually reinforcing way. Much of
his conflict was played out in his relation to the church, which he
seems to have adopted and then to have fought with personal dis-
illusion and bitterness; yet he fell back on it time and again, and
finally made it the substance of his career. It is no wonder that
having "killed" his father by being conceived, and lost mothers
three times before the age of six, he should have accepted the protection of school with a chronic suppressed rage, low-spirited
compliance, and some difficulty in formal learning. This difficulty
of learning was further aggravated by the fact that his learning
inevitably acquired its pattern from his toilet functions, as is
shown by the life stories of Gulliver and Scriblerus. The early
death of the father, a prehistoric event for the child, inescapably
increased the fear of death for himself—a fear which he met by
the repeated denial that life was worth having.

That the lonely and disappointed child should have suffered
from worries over masturbation was also inevitable. Swift, the
man, wrote seldom of genital sexuality, though through Scriblerus
and Gulliver he made extensive expositions of his masturbatory
concern and fantasies. Dr. Martin Scriblerus treated a young
nobleman for distempers of the mind evident in his affectations of
speech and his tendency to talk in verse, to show a whimsicality of
behavior, and to choose odd companions. Scriblerus diagnosed his
condition as that of being in love, and since no woman was involved he must be in love with himself. "There are people," says
Swift through Scriblerus, "who discover from their youth a most
amorous inclination to themselves . . . [they] are so far gone in this
passion, they keep a secret intrigue with themselves and hide it
from all the world. . . . This patient has not the least care of the
Reputation of his Beloved, he is downright scandalous in his be-
haviour with himself." Scriblerus then prescribes the remedies
which Swift applied to himself and offered to others: to give up
extravagance, travel in hardship, look at "the naked truth and

purge himself" weekly. If these did not avail, nothing was left but for the sufferer to marry himself, and when he tired of himself he might drown himself in a pond. What a complete version of Narcissus!

The other traveling surgeon, Lemuel Gulliver, had had his training under a master named Bates. To repeat a quotation from Gulliver:

> My good Master Bates, dying in two years after, and I having few friends, my business began to fail, for my conscience would not suffer me to imitate the bad practice of too many among my brethren. . . .

Swift's peculiar relation to words and to punning lends support to the notion that this might be a sly and even conscious trick of self-revelation. The greatest exposition of the masturbation fantasies appears, however, in the third voyage. After a glorious start, Gulliver was much reduced by pirates, set adrift in a canoe, and he fell into a great despondency. He then came to a small, perfectly round island, already described as floating in the air, rising and falling above the body of the continent from which it sometimes shut out the sun. Many of the people here were so absorbed in speculation that they forgot to speak or pay attention to those around them. Consequently they kept "flappers" who tapped them on the mouth, eyes, or ears, with blown bladders attached like flails to short sticks. These bladders held small quantities of dried peas or pebbles. This island was balanced so delicately on a lodestone that the tenderest hand could move it up and down to a height of four miles. In also somewhat controlled the fate of the continent, Balnibarbi, beneath it; and since it was a place of intense speculation without reality, it had a deleterious effect on the Balnibarbians, who engaged in feats of scientific magic and concocted marvelous inventions of great intricacy and incompleteness, while the country itself was impoverished and wasted, and the senators suffered from "redundant, ebullient, and peccant humours, with many diseases, of head and heart."

Swift's early life certainly predisposed him to a stunting bisexuality which is apparent in the man's later life. That his genitality was impaired and degraded by its amalgamation with anal drives is also indicated in his character and his writings. He moreover tended to absorb friends into his service in a demanding and possessive way—the infantile oral quality of these relationships being partly obscured by his real genius, which could fascinate and command others so that they wanted to be absorbed by him, only to find themselves intolerably burdened. Two additional developments are of special interest: first, the influence of his special anal character on the texture of the family romance, which was determined in reality and stimulated in fantasy; second, the special nature of his relationship to his sister, which left a strong mark on his relations with other women.

There can be little doubt that the young child was aware that he was not the son of the nurse during his early stay in England, and must have had some fantasies about his own family. On returning to his mother and sister in Ireland, he had memories and thoughts about the family in England. Within a few months he had neither of these families, and only memories of both, when he became the peripheral and special child in the enormous family of his uncle Godwin. Later he repeated this in the decade spent with Sir William Temple.

The anal stamp on his character, which must have come from the period with the nurse in Whitehaven, appeared compellingly throughout his life. It is quite clear, too, that to Swift the spoken word and the written word were miles apart. The spoken word was airy, pure, and of the spirit. The vowels, especially, were "airy little creatures, all of different voice and features." The written word was discharged in secret and disclaimed until it had proved itself, and was in danger of appearing "fathered by another" as he once wrote. The spoken word was oral-respiratory; the written word was genito-anal. The consonants too seemed anal in contrast to the airy vowels, and the proper names in *Gulliver's Travels* are heavy with repeated consonants and duplicated syllables: Glubdubdrib, Luggnagg, Traldragdribh, Glumdalclitch, Clumeging, to name a few. These words suggest an onomatopoeic derivation from the sounds of drippings and droppings, possibly owing to the overly intense toilet preoccupation, which seemed to engulf and then to color the important infantile philosophies of the little child Jonathan.

Swift always played with words, with clang and pun, which concealed and revealed simultaneously. The original *Journal to Stella*

(1710-1713), which has suffered too much later editing, reveals Swift's language in its most infantile oral qualities, in terms of endearment in which "you" is "oo" "dearest" is "dealest"; r's and l's get strangely mixed up, and the effect is of a lisping child saying good night. For example, he writes to Stella: "Nite dealest richar M.D. Sawey dealest M.D. M.D. M.D. F.W. F.W. F.W. M E, Poo Pdfr. Lele, lele, lele." Swift himself said, "When I am writing in our language, I make up my mouth just as if I were speaking it." *"Our richar Gangridge"* is our little language. *M.D.* is "my dears"; *F.W.* is "farewell foolish wench"; *M E* is (myself and) Madame Elderly—i.e. Dingley; *Pdfr.* is "poor dear foolish rogue," Swift. The "little language," as it was called, was baby talk, simple code, and hog-Latin contrivances, the latter so characteristic of prepubertal years. It is possible that the names Yahoo and Houyhnhnm are nonsense words, peculiarly condensing in function, having profoundly to do with Gulliver's efforts to find himself, that is, to achieve some integration of his own identity, and that "Yahoo" signifies "Who are you?" And "Houyhnhnm," the sound of which is so close to "human," contains also suggestions of the pronouns *you, him,* and *who,* in a jumbled hog-Latin fashion. It is on this voyage that Gulliver is forced to admit his attraction to the primitive and dirty, but attempts to save himself through adopting the rationality of the Houyhnhnms, and subsequently suffers a powerful increase in his neurosis.

The family romance has been regarded as occurring in sexually active and imaginative children especially attached to parents toward whom they suffer severe retaliatory resentment, especially in the oedipal relationship, when the parents prohibit the child's sexual practices and the child subsequently recognizes that the parents themselves indulge in the very sexuality they have condemned. The child then repudiates the parents and adopts new, lofty and asexual ones, in a revengeful reversal of the situation. But as Freud remarked in his early paper on the subject, the ennoblement of the adopted parents really represents the original estimate of the child's own parents.

It is my belief that the family romance appears in a severe and sometimes malignant form in those children who not only fulfill the conditions stated but who also have a special distortion and degradation of genitality and the oedipal situation through severe anal fixations, and also in those who have had such overpowering (usually anxious) mothers that the development of the early ego has been possible only through an organization by opposition, resulting in a diffuse negativism. In many instances this early ego-by-opposition combines with the anal fixation in a constitutionally strong and well-endowed child.

Children with emphatic theories of anal birth and with nursery ethics of approval (counterfeit of love) focused on toilet functions frequently utilize their interest in the stool (the visible material dirt) and its smell or gaseous image (thought or memory) as representatives of such opposites as good and bad, dirty and godly, black and white, and low and high. This dichotomizing joins directly with the family romance. The foundling is either the abandoned child of the gypsies or the royal infant stolen by them. Swift rarely wrote or spoke of his father except to remark that the father lived long enough to secure the mother's reputation, a fantasy of bastardy masked by humor. The father had been unsuccessful and had abandoned the family through death and poverty. Neither did Swift write of the nurse, except indirectly as cited. On the other hand, Sir William Temple, ambassador and man of the world, emerges quite clearly as the materialization of the noble, illustrious father, with Swift's grandfather as an earlier, less satisfactory version.

Swift's relationship to his mother, once re-established after its long suspension, remained cordial, and he visited her frequently at considerable expense of effort. The one personal anecdote—her pretending to his landlady that he was her lover—is an indication of her reversed oedipal attachment to him. He rarely mentions her in his writings. But the year of her death, when he was forty-two, marked the beginning of his *Journal to Stella*, with its chronicling of events in the world and its feeling expressed in the "little language" of infancy.

Jane Swift too is very shadowy in the writings of her brother. One of Swift's cousins mentions a chronic hostility between brother and sister, and commends the mother's attitude of fairness. But some fantasied image of the sister, probably from the years of separation following the first year of intimacy, influenced Swift in his selection of and attitudes toward the three women who played such important parts in his life. It is not necessary to repeat the indications that they represented both himself and his sister. He gave them all names of goddesses, and he could not touch them in any intimate way—which to him would clearly have been a despoiling.

Swift showed marked anal characteristics (his extreme personal immaculateness, secretiveness, intense ambition, pleasure in less obvious dirt, stubborn vengefulness in righteous causes), which indicate clearly that early control of the excretory functions was achieved under great stress and perhaps too early. It seems justified to conclude that the kidnapping nurse, however devoted, was in some way overly conscientious and harsh in his early toilet training, and left this stamp of chamber-pot morality forever on his character. That she was also ambitious for his intellectual development is clear as well. He must have been a very special child. A kind of linking of the written or printed word with the excretory functions has already been noted. This seemed to extend further into an animation of the word and its endowment with magic personalized meanings. In this setting, then, the functions of speech, reading, and writing tend to become overly emotional and full of conflicts. In Swift the emotional battleground was shifted largely to the written or printed word—the deposited word, one might say. "I am very angry," wrote Swift to Arbuthnot in 1714; "I have a mind to be very angry and to let my anger break out in some manner that will not please them, at the end of a pen." When Swift was angry but trying hard to please, at Kilkenny and Trinity, he did not break out with a pen, but was compliant and depressed and even thought to be a little dull. Later in life, when he sent his manuscripts to the publisher he disowned them to the extent of having them copied by someone else, and sent them by another —often Charles Ford—to be dropped at night. One gets the feeling that he was acting out both his own birth and early toilet accidents of spite.

That the infant Jonathan lived in such close and continuous bodily intimacy with the nurse as to produce a tendency to over-identify with the woman is strongly indicated; the problem of anatomical differences was never solved in any stable way, but obvious attempts were made to meet the situation by masculinizing the girl. His castration fear of the woman was overwhelming. Every bodily aperture became a threatening vagina-anus. In unconscious or preconscious fantasy Swift tended to phallicize the woman and identify the child, himself, with the female phallus; this is indicated in the passages from the *Travels* already quoted. While we have no knowledge of transvestite tendencies in Swift, it is possible that his accepting the robes of the Anglican priest included such a hidden tendency in an acceptable way that could be integrated into his life.

He was continually obsessed with body imagery which formed the almost too constant backdrop for his moralizing satire. The quotation given by Bullitt (1953) at the beginning of his book on Swift's satire is characteristic:

> To this End I have some time since, with a world of Pains and Art, dissected the carcass of Human Nature and read many useful Lectures upon the several Parts, both containing and contained; till at last it smelt so strong I could preserve it no longer. Upon which I have been at great expense to fit up all the Bones with exact Contexture and in due Symmetry; so that I am ready to show a very compleat Anatomy thereof to all the curious Gentlemen and others.

It is appropriate that Bullitt's book is subtitled *The Anatomy of Satire*. Again Swift wrote satirically to prove that the stomach is the seat of honor.

In the course of the intimacy between the infant Jonathan and the unnamed nurse there was a marked turn for the worse, described rather vividly in the second voyage of Gulliver. He is now no longer the oversized, important, threatening figure, but small, helpless, and endangered among giants. In Brobdingnag the disgusting nurse appears. To quote Gulliver:

> She was carrying a child of a year . . . who immediately spied me and began to squall . . . after the usual oratory of infants, to get me for a plaything. The mother [nurse] out of indulgence, took me up and put me toward the child who presently . . . got my head in his mouth where I roared so loud that the urchin was frighted and let me drop. I should . . . have broken my neck if the mother had not held her apron under me. The nurse . . . was [finally] forced to apply the last remedy of giving it suck. . . . No object ever disgusted me so much as the sight of her monstrous breast. . . . It stood prominent six foot and [was] sixteen in circumference. The nipple was about half the bigness of my head; the hue of that and the dug so

varified with spots, pimples, and freckles that nothing could appear more nauseous: I had a near sight of her, she sitting down . . . and I standing on the table. [I] reflected upon the fair skins of our Irish ladies who appear so beautiful because they are our own size and their defects not to be seen but through a magnifying glass where we find by experiment that the smoothest skins look rough, coarse and ill coloured.

It was after this that he was adopted and protected by the little girl nurse, not yet at puberty, who carried him everywhere with her.

Thus Gulliver bitterly finds the tables turned and himself displaced by the infant who was just the age Swift had been when he was kidnapped, and the age at which in the *Modest Proposal* infants of the poor should be eaten by the rich. The picture of the breast certainly contains elements of awe and envy turned to loathing with the aim of degrading it. It seems likely that the nurse became pregnant after her return to England, and this pregnancy, together with the subsequent suckling of the child, upset the little boy Jonathan and aroused in him intensest jealousy, biting resentment, and cannibalistic feelings toward the infant—projected by Gulliver as felt toward him by the infant.

The image of the nurse's breast carried with it fear and a sense of its similarity to the pregnant abdomen and to an adult phallus. This combined image is then rendered less dangerous by being made into the female phallus and degraded or fecalized. The word *dug* used by Swift in this context is itself close to the word *dung*. Later in the second voyage the bad nurse reappears in male form as the evil kidnapping monkey who carries the small Gulliver as though suckling an infant and does actually cram his mouth full of vile stuff which must be picked out by the amiable little girl nurse. Here we have clearly the turn to the fully homosexual fantasy of fellatio, the reverberation of which appears in Swift's own life in his sickness from "too much stone fruit." In the story the monkey is executed. In the *Travels* two other assaults on the helpless Gulliver are made by male creatures; one by a deformed dwarf encountered in the Queen's garden, who there knocks Gulliver flat by shaking the apple tree so that the fruit falls on his head; and the second by a huge frog which hops into his little boat and, jumping over him, deposits its odious slime upon his face and clothing. Gulliver finally rids himself of this disgusting animal. At about the same time Gulliver seizes a linnet the size of a swan by the neck with both his hands, causing the enraged bird to beat him around the head with its wings until it is finally subdued and ultimately served for dinner.

IV. CONCLUSION

It has been my intention to give the story of Swift based on the known facts and as it is revealed in *Gulliver's Travels*, and not primarily to make a clinical study of Swift's neurosis. Since I begin, however, with references to changes in body image and to fetishism, and since, in the course of presenting the combined biographies of Gulliver and of Swift, I unavoidably include some pertinent clinical data, it seems appropriate to make a few concluding remarks.

Swift does not seem to have been an overt fetishist, although in the structure of his personality there is much that he shares with the fetishist. One gets the impression that the anal fixation was intense and binding, and the genital demands so impaired or limited at best that there was a total retreat from genital sexuality in his early adult life, probably beginning with the unhappy relationship with Jane Waring, the first of the goddesses. After this, Swift never again seems willingly to have considered marriage, and his expressed demands were that the women who were closest to him should be boys. His genital demands were probably partly sublimated through his writings, but these too bear the stamp of a strongly anal character. He did not need a fetish because he resigned from physical genitality. In a sense, converting the women of his choice into "boys" fulfilled his fetishistic need.

Lemuel Gulliver went a step further than his creator. He was a married man, but one who was continually escaping from his marriage which was predominantly disgusting to him, though his periodic sojourns at home sufficed sometimes for the depositing of a child with his wife. The *Travels* seem to be largely the projection into activity of Lemuel's masturbatory fantasies which, like the character of Swift, are closely interwoven with anal problems and ambitions rather than with exclusively genital ones.

The problems of changes in body size (based on phallic functioning) are characteristically reflected onto the total body, and much reinforced by the theme of the reversal of generations. There is much less substitution of different parts of the body for the phallus than is to be found in *Alice's Adventures in Wonderland,* for example; although there are some disguised references in the third voyage, in which the phallic problems are expressed in the medium of thought rather than that of the body itself. A further discussion of the problems of distortions of body image and changes of size will be more fruitful when it can be combined with a study of Alice and Lewis Carroll (see ch. 23).

CHAPTER TWENTY-THREE

"It's My Own Invention": A Special Screen Memory of Mr. Lewis Carroll, Its Form and Its History (1955)

I

It is no news to anyone that Lewis Carroll was preoccupied with dreams. He stated it many times over. Both of the *Alice* books are stated by him to be in dream form.[1] In his extraordinary novel, *Sylvie and Bruno,* he showed a concern with shifts from one level of consciousness to another, which he characterized as (1) real life, (2) the "eerie" stage in which one sees fairies; and (3) the trance in which the body sleeps but the individual does not. The third was not exactly dreaming, although somewhat related to it. These three forms or levels of consciousness were also somewhat based on observations of what analysts know as the conscious, the preconscious, and the unconscious, although here again the comparison cannot be made very precise. It is interesting, however, that the shift from one level of consciousness to another often came about automatically through some *switch* word (a punning word) or when the subject was in a clearly musing or daydreamy

[1] In the preparation of this paper I have drawn on *The Complete Works of Lewis Carroll* (1933), his letters (see Hatch, 1933) and diaries (Green, 1949), and several biographical studies (Hudson, 1954; Green, 1949; Bowman, 1900; Gernsheim, 1949; Taylor, 1952). Additional source material is listed in my book (1955).

state in which free association was likely to take the place of directed thinking, as while looking into the fire, riding on a railway train, looking at a shiny surface, or walking in the depth of the woods.

That Carroll had feelings of unreality in general about life and compared it to a dream was announced also in the poems with which he introduced these major works. In the prefatory poem to *Alice's Adventures in Wonderland,* he writes of the trip on the Isis River with the three little Liddell girls.

> Ah, cruel Three! In such an hour,
>   Beneath such dreamy weather,
> To beg a tale of breath too weak
>   To stir the tiniest feather!
> Yet what can one poor voice avail
>   Against three tongues together?

. . .

> Anon, to sudden silence won,
>   In fancy they pursue
> The dream-child moving through a land
>   Of wonders wild and new,
> In friendly chat with bird or beast—
>   And half believe it true.

. . .

> Alice! A childish story take,
>   And, with a gentle hand,
> Lay it where Childhood's dreams are twined
>   In Memory's mystic band,
> Like pilgrim's wither'd wreath of flowers
>   Pluck'd in a far off land.

Through the Looking Glass, written nine years later, also had its introductory poem. It was now clearly addressed to Alice Liddell, and offered the story as a love gift. At the time it was written, Alice was about seventeen years old and had passed somewhat out of Carroll's life, both by her increasing years and by a degree of alienation between Carroll and the Liddell family. But she is addressed as

> Child of the pure unclouded brow
>   And dreaming eyes of wonder!

and he indicates that he would like to protect her from the stresses of adulthood, by entrancing her with his fairy tale.

> Without, the frost, the blinding snow,
>   The storm-wind's moody madness—
> Within, the firelight's ruddy glow,
>   And childhood's nest of gladness.
> The magic words shall hold thee fast:
> Thou shalt not heed the raving blast.

Just as *Wonderland* opens with Alice attempting to read her sister's book and dropping off into sleepy reverie instead, so at the end of *Looking Glass* Alice is considering whether she has dreamed the story or whether it was really the dream of the Red King who had appeared in the dream. Thus the idea of a dream within a dream, or perhaps a dreamer within a dream, is subtly suggested, only in a bit more complex way than the usual dream within a dream. There is really the question of identity: "who dreamed it?"

At the end of *Looking Glass* there is a closing poem, which clearly takes up the themes of the poem at the beginning of *Wonderland* about the rowing trip on the Isis River. This is recapitulated in the first two stanzas, again emphasizing the dreaminess of the weather, and adds, concerning Alice Liddell,

                    .   .   .

> Still she haunts me, phantomwise,
> Alice moving under skies
> Never seen by waking eyes.
>
> Children yet, the tale to hear,
> Eager eye and willing ear,
> Lovingly shall nestle near.
>
> In a Wonderland they lie,
> Dreaming as the days go by,
> Dreaming as the summers die:

Ever drifting down the stream—
Lingering in the golden gleam—
Life, what is it but a dream?

The initial letters of this poem, only part of which is quoted here, spell out the name Alice Pleasance Liddell. In addition, it should be noted that its author seems to be considering the children yet to come, probably the unborn children who may hear the tale in the future. This theme of the unborn children was even more clearly stated at the end of *Wonderland* when Alice considers how her little sister will ultimately grow up but keep the simple and loving heart of her childhood, and "how she would gather about her other little children, and make *their* eyes bright and eager with many a strange tale, perhaps even with the dream of Wonderland of long ago . . . and find a pleasure in all their simple joys, remembering her own child-life and the happy summer days."

Sylvie and Bruno and *Sylvie and Bruno Concluded* were Carroll's most ambitious works, and were published in 1889 and 1893 respectively, but were made up of shorter stories and sketches which were published at intervals from 1867. These were then pieced together with what their author refers to as "padding" to make them stick into the semblance of a unified fabric. They are not really quite a crazy quilt in design. The repetitive pattern is irregular in outline and rhythm.

The introductory poem for *Sylvie and Bruno* repeats the theme of the dream.

Is all our Life, then, but a dream
Seen faintly in the golden gleam
Athwart Time's dark resistless stream?

Bowed to the earth with bitter woe,
Or laughing at some raree-show,
We flutter idly to and fro.

And in introducing *Sylvie and Bruno Concluded,* Carroll writes:

Dreams, that elude the Waker's frenzied grasp—
Hands, stark and still, on a dead Mother's breast,

Which never more shall render clasp for clasp,
Or deftly soothe a weeping Child to rest—
In suchlike forms me listeth to portray
My Tale, here ended. Thou delicious Fay—
The guardian of a Sprite that lives to tease thee—
Loving in earnest, chiding but in play
The merry mocking Bruno! Who, that sees thee,
Can fail to love thee, Darling, even as I?—
My sweetest Sylvie, we must say 'Good-bye.'

Whereas these writings from his mature years showed Carroll as
one who thought of the world as a place of raving winds and bitter
woe—and that the dreamy state of childhood was the best reasonable protection until death—as a boy he wrote most graphically
of nightmares ("Horrors" [1850] and "As It Fell Upon a Day").
It should be noted too that Bruno, the mocking teasing sprite who
cannot be entirely silenced, is ruled by the loving Sylvie. This
Bruno is the only boy who is treated sympathetically in all of
Carroll's writings. He is five years old, talks cute baby talk, and is
ever under the watchful loving sisterly eye of Sylvie. Sylvie bears
a considerable resemblance to Alice.

II

Lewis Carroll was born Charles Lutwidge Dodgson, the third
child and oldest son in a family of eleven children, seven of whom
were girls. His father was the latest in a line of Anglican clergymen. Carroll and his three brothers all became clergymen, though
he himself was ordained only as a deacon and never as a priest. Of
the entire family, only two brothers and one sister married. Several
of the siblings, including the famous Charles, were stammerers:
some say that all suffered some speech disturbance. Until the boy
was between eleven and twelve (1843) the family lived in a small
farmhouse, which served as a rectory, in an isolated farming area
outside the village of Daresbury, in Cheshire. Here they must have
lived in very limited space, with the family increasing at the rate of
about one child every eighteen months. The eleventh child was
born approximately three years after the family had moved into
a much more prosperous and spacious place, when the father was
given a church at Croft in Yorkshire. Charles went away to school

at twelve or thirteen, first to a nearby school at Richmond, then
to Rugby, and finally to Oxford at nineteen. He was considered
a child who showed genius, was early dedicated to the church, and
had also a special interest in mathematics, a combination of interests which he shared with his father. It was further noted during
his Rugby years that he took uncanny liberties with words and
made them mean what he wanted them to mean. He was probably
lonesome, unhappy, and even depressed during his years at Rugby,
which was a rugged school with great emphasis on physical competitiveness and sportsmanship. He had whooping cough and
mumps during this period, to which a slight later deafness was
attributed. He won honors consistently, but, if anything, they
distressed him. He once wrote, "If I had shot the dean, no more
fuss could have been made about it." It is probable that academic
honors did not improve his standing with the schoolboys. There is
a period unaccounted for—perhaps a year or a little more—between Rugby and the beginning of his residence at Oxford (eighteen to nineteen), when he seems to have been at home. Practically
all that is known of this time is that his mother worried somewhat
about his health but that he gradually grew stronger. During this
time he was writing some of the eeriest and cleverest schoolboy
rhymes and parodies, which he illustrated himself and circulated
as a home journal for his brothers and sisters. His drawings showed
strange body distortions and a hint of combining the sexes.

In the Daresbury days, the children had played much in the
garden where the youthful Charles was the inventor of games and
gadgets, writer of rhymes, maker of toys, and director of a marion-
ette theater. Although this was remembered as a happy period of
his life, and the rectory gardens of Daresbury and Croft were
almost surely the early models for the gardens of the *Wonderland*
and *Looking Glass* worlds, there is some indication that even then
his dreamy separation from life had set in. The scene around the
sundial, portrayed in *Jabberwocky*, probably came from this time.
The preoccupation with manipulating puppets and an unusually
strong tendency to animate inanimate objects and to humanize
animals are indicative of some tendency to withdraw from adulthood. In evaluating these interests, one must recall that Charles
was *not* a lonely child, in need of companionship, but was surrounded by brothers and sisters, overly close to him in age.

In regard to animals, it is reported that he was especially fond of small, slimy ones, and that he was devoted to cats but had a fairly marked fear of dogs. He invented fanciful animals—like his fabulous portmanteau words—which were combinations, condensations, and aggregations of parts or wholes of animals. In his mature years he did not like pets, but played with ideas of animals.

His mother died when he was nineteen, only a few days after his entrance to Christ Church College, Oxford, where he was to remain until his death in January, 1898, approximately forty-seven years. At Oxford he was awarded various scholarships and was presented a teaching studentship in mathematics, which carried with it fair monetary provision, on condition that he remain a celibate and take Holy Orders. He seems not to have developed much as a mathematician, not because of lack of ability, nor lack of contact with the best mathematical minds of the day, but probably because he used his mathematics to keep his thoughts well in compulsive order and could not therefore allow his imagination full reign. Geometry seemed to enclose space rather than to explore it. He continued as a don in mathematics until he was fifty, but his teaching was hampered by his stammer and his stereotypy, and he never gained much pleasure from teaching or research although he showed great skill in the production of mathematical and verbal puzzles.

Charles Dodgson took the pen name, Lewis Carroll, at the age of twenty-four (February, 1856) when he was writing sketches and poems, mostly parodies, for a magazine, *The Train*. For a brief time he had signed his contributions "B.B." His *nom de plume*, Lewis Carroll, he derived consciously from his two first names, Charles and Lutwidge (Ludovici), reversed in order.

The young man, obscure as a mathematics teacher at Oxford, became famous with the publication of *Alice's Adventures in Wonderland*, in July, 1865. This was the written, slightly expanded version of a story which Dodgson had told the three little Liddell girls, daughters of the dean of Christ Church College, on a boat trip on the Isis River on the 4th of July, 1862, where they had been accompanied by another don named Duckworth. It is an interesting fact that all of the members of this little rowing party remember the day as a golden afternoon. Carroll wrote of it many years later (*The Theater*, April, 1887):

Full many a year has slipped away, since that 'golden afternoon' that gave thee birth [i.e., the *Alice story*] but I can call it up almost as clearly as if it were yesterday—the cloudless blue above, the watery mirror below, the boat drifting idly on its way, the tinkle of the drops that fell from the oars, as they waved so sleepily to and fro, and (the one bright gleam of life in all the slumberous scene), the three eager faces, hungry for news of fairyland, and who would not be said 'nay' to: from whose lips 'Tell us a story please' had all the stern immutability of Fate!

Canon Duckworth, in contributing to a memorial fund after Carroll's death, wrote of his memories of "that beautiful summer afternoon in the Long Vacation." Alice, later Mrs. Hargreaves, also remembered the *burning* sun of that July afternoon and wrote (in the *Cornhill Magazine*) of "that blazing summer afternoon with the heat haze shimmering over the meadows where the party landed to shelter for a while in the shadow cast by the haycocks near Godstow."

These recollections by three of the main adventurers on the little trip tally in their description of the brightness of the day— which is, however, *not* corroborated by the records of the meteorological office, where it is indicated that the weather in Oxford on July 4, 1862, was "cool and rather wet"; and that between 10 A.M. on July 4th and 10 A.M. on July 5th 0.17 of an inch of rain fell, mostly after 2 P.M. on July 4th. This discrepancy between memory and factual evidence is very puzzling, especially because of the clear memory of Alice who spoke of the shadows of the haycocks. This matter of the singularly bright and sunny memory which Mr. Carroll could always recall as clearly as though it were only yesterday has this characteristic which it shares with the typical screen memory: the insistent overbrightness. It is entirely possible that it was a memory which served a screening function to all three of these main participants.

In 1871, Carroll published *Through the Looking Glass* and in March, 1876, *The Hunting of the Snark*. By 1882, at the age of fifty, he had resigned from teaching but remained on as Curator of the Common Room, including custody of the wine cellar. He spent his time writing and publishing a rather odd assortment of rhymes, puzzles, brief mathematical treatises, various adaptations of the *Alice* books; and he was much involved with the minutiae of his strangely complicated compulsive systems. He indexed and cross-referenced all his correspondence until he had reached the astounding number of more than 98,000 items. He kept diagrams of all his dinner parties, and records of the menus. He invented numerous gadgets, and made collections of music boxes and fountain pens. Between 1856 and 1880 he was an assiduous and excellent photographer. He devoted himself almost entirely to portrait photography with a special interest in famous people and prepubertal girls. He stopped his photography abruptly without giving any reason. When he died he left directions for the destruction of some of his negatives.

He is not known to have ever loved any woman in the usual sense, but he was passionately devoted to little girls of about eight years of age; in his later years the age rose to eleven or twelve. Some have thought he was in love with Ellen Terry whom he first saw on the stage when she was eight, but he did not meet her until after her marriage at sixteen. Certainly he was fascinated by her. It does not seem to have been more. There was a long succession of little girl friends whom he invited to visit him, who corresponded with him, and whom he photographed—sometimes in fancy dress and, on a few occasions, in the nude. He was a tremendous kisser, both by letter and by mouth.

III

With this very brief sketch of one of the most complicated of men, we shall proceed to investigate a repetitive, perhaps compulsive, screen memory which appears in different versions throughout Carroll's writings.

Through the Looking Glass presents, like *Alice's Adventures in Wonderland,* the story of Alice's entrance into the secret or inner garden. In *Wonderland,* the author is concerned with the general theme of time, announced by Alice's encounter with the White Rabbit who is hurriedly looking at his watch, fearful of being late. In the *Looking Glass,* the initial and dominant theme is space—the other or reversed world which is seen in the looking glass. Time and space play sometimes similar or complementary, and sometimes contrasting, roles in Alice's explorations. Both tales have a general theme of guilt and possible punishment, and end in a grand explosion. In *Wonderland* there is an actual trial going on with the Knave of Hearts being tried for the famous theft of the tarts; but just as the sentence is about to be passed, Alice upsets the whole proceedings by bringing everyone back to reality and announcing that the Royal Family are really just a pack of playing cards. Thereupon the whole pack rises up and flies at her. At this she awakens, finding that leaves have fluttered down on her face and that she has been dreaming.

Through the Looking Glass ends with Alice being inducted into queenship, but just as she arises, actually rising in the air by several inches, to give thanks, everything explodes at the banquet table, the plates and silverware take wings and fly into the air, inanimate things become animate, and pandemonium reigns. Alice finds that the Red Queen is really the black kitten which she is shaking vigorously. As she awakens from the dream the question is posed, to whom does the dream belong: to Alice or to the Red King, and which one was only an actor in the other's dream? "Which do *you* think it was?" is the end of the story.

It is clear from these excerpts that both stories have to do with a little girl not yet at puberty, preparing to be a Queen in her own right, but in a peculiarly dreamy state, in which the phenomena of the shared dream (first with the sister, then with the Red King) and the dream within a dream are noteworthy. Her question, "Whose dream is it? Which is which?" reminds us indeed of the quandary in regard to sexual identity of many prepubertal girls. But her anticipations for the future are clear: there will be future generations of children to hear her dream story.

It is not the dream within a dream, however, but a rather special screen memory in *Through the Looking Glass* that deserves presentation. It is a screen memory within a screen memory within a song within a dream on the other side of the looking glass. There are innumerable wrappings of this memory, and like a mirror image within a mirror image, within a mirror image, etc., it seems to stretch on into infinity and to suggest momentary finite boundaries which stretch and merge endlessly backward into ancestry and forward into posterity, even in a way that Alice seemed to foresee for her sister in her dream within the dream of Wonderland. It certainly has to do with the prepubertal girl pausing for a few moments, not only to ask "Which is which?" but with further bewilderment "Where did I come from?" and "What comes from me?"

The special screen memory, however, is one shared more or less by Alice and the White Knight, and it is presented in a chapter entitled "It's My Own Invention."

> Of all the strange things that Alice saw in her journey Through the Looking-Glass, this was the one that she always remembered most clearly. Years afterward she could bring the whole scene back again, as if it had been only yesterday—the mild blue eyes and kindly smile of the Knight—the setting sun gleaming through his hair and shining on his armor in a blaze of light that quite dazzled her—the horse quietly moving about, with the reins hanging loose on his neck, cropping the grass at her feet—and the black shadows of the forest behind—all this she took in like a picture as, with one hand shading her eyes, she leant against a tree watching the strange pair, and listening, in a half-dream, to the melancholy music of the song.

This picture, which in texture and rhythm is reminiscent of Carroll's own description of the afternoon of the rowing trip on the Isis River, is a perfect description of a screen memory— Alice's—in the making. The feeling, "This I will always remember" (the sense and satisfaction of the screen-memory-hunger together with the command to remember described by Fenichel [1927]), the sense of brightness, of light, of sharpness, of contrast, of darkness and light (like Alice Liddell Hargreaves's description of the shadows of the haycocks), the vividness combined with an apparently prosaic scene and the pervading feeling, "This is overly real, but is it quite real?"—all these are parts of the unconscious determination to conceal the reality. So far the screen memory, *in statu nascendi,* belongs to Mr. Lewis Carroll as Alice, since he wrote it.

At the beginning of the chapter, Alice is troubled about reality, as she is repeatedly throughout her explorations. The hubbub of the fight between the lion and the unicorn has died down and in the ensuing silence Alice becomes alarmed and thinks she must have been dreaming; but seeing evidence of the dreamed scene around her, she considers that maybe she is only a character in a dream. But is it her own dream or that of the Red King?—in which latter case she may disappear when he awakens. Before this can happen, however, she hears the Red Knight clattering down the road, threatening to take her prisoner. He is quickly super-seded by a White Knight who announces himself falteringly as her rescuer. A mock battle for ownership of Alice follows, in which the two Knights joust with each other in a kind of parody of the lion and the unicorn, Haigha and Hatta, or as Alice rather pertinently remarks to herself, very much like Punch and Judy. Curiously, the horses remain quiet and silent and remind her of tables (or perhaps of beds?), as they look so flat. The battle con-tinues until they have both fallen on their heads after which they are satisfied. Alice emerges from this bewildered; she wishes to escape being a prisoner, whether of attacker or of rescuer, and would prefer just to proceed to queenship which will be accom-plished as soon as she crosses the next brook. The Red Knight having galloped away, the White Knight stays with Alice.

The White Knight is a strange fellow, wearing on his shoulders a deal box upside down, the lid hanging open. He explains this as a sandwich box hung upside down to keep the rain out at the expense of not keeping the sandwiches in. He then decides to hang it on a tree to serve as a beehive, since the one hanging from his saddle has remained untenanted, perhaps because of its prox-imity to an equally untenanted mousetrap. The White Knight ponders whether (the thought of) mice would keep the bees out, or (the thought of) bees would keep the mice out, very much as Alice pondered whether cats eat bats or bats eat cats—as she fell down the rabbit hole into Wonderland. (This question as to who does what and whose dream it is anyway seems also to be a motif of all the jousting Punch and Judy battles.) Another of the White Knight's inventions is the horse's anklets devised to protect the steed against the bites of sharks. The White Knight takes Alice's dish for plumcake just in case they should find any, but he gets mixed up as to whether he is the dish or himself and so falls into the bag which he has intended to contain the dish. He describes to Alice some other of his inventions—to wit, a plan to keep hair from falling off or out, by making it creep up a stick, as how can it fall *down* if it is moving upward? (Incidentally Charles Dodgson was fascinated by the idea of hair standing on end. He once took a photograph of a little girl being given an electric shock to deter-mine if hair really stood on end under such circumstances.) But the poor White Knight keeps tumbling head downward from his horse, sometimes in front, sometimes behind, and sometimes sideways and toward Alice. Just as he begins to explain what a really great rider he is, he falls headlong—not once, but twice or thrice. In this state, he is seized with the idea of inventing a way of getting over a gate. He proposes to accomplish this by standing on his head atop the gate and then toppling over. While he is explaining another which-is-what act—in which he has fallen into his own helmet only to have the Red Knight come up and put the helmet on so forcibly that the White Knight is stuck as fast as lightning inside it—he again falls headlong into a ditch from which he is rescued by Alice.

To recapitulate interpretatively the incidents of this strange preparation for Alice's debut as Queen, she is haunted by dreamy memories of primal scene jousting, recurring with obsessional repetitiveness. The differentiation between the sexes and whether there are one or two participants are rather hazy to the little girl, although the essential core of the scene is succinctly grasped by the child who likens these fights to a Punch and Judy show. It seems then that the White Knight, impotent, exhibitionistic, and valiant as he is, falls repeatedly for Alice. He intends to rescue her, but ends by being rescued by her.

There can be little doubt that the White Knight represents Charles Dodgson, the puzzler, the gadgeteer, the puppeteer, the man who traveled with innumberable boxes and valises, and who certainly fell in love in his own strange way with little Alice Liddell before she had crossed the brook to queenship.

The situation that immediately preceded the screen memory is, Carroll-fashion, given at the beginning rather than at the end of the chapter where it occurs. This scene is one in which the White Knight describes how he has such intellectual powers as an inventor that he has invented a new pudding during the meat course. Alice congratulates him on his performance in being in the nick of time to provide the dessert. But having introduced the subject of the pudding, with the boast that his mind keeps on working no matter where his body happens to be, he becomes engaged in a word game of accenting in turn each successive word in a sentence and seeing what different effects are produced (a typical wordplay of both Carroll and Dodgson). In the end it turns out that the pudding is made of blotting paper, sealing wax, and gunpowder. So perhaps the game of words is not irrelevant, and the White Knight may only have been testing the point of explosiveness: whether at the end of the meal or at the end of the story, whether today's, yesterday's or tomorrow's. It is clearly an invention in fantasy only, and in its displacement from body to mind it proclaims the White Knight's ability to work up to an explosive climax, with the danger of getting destructively out of control. This indeed does happen two chapters later, when the banquet celebrating Alice's queenship blows up completely and brings her back to reality.

Alice, being a rather practical little girl, is disappointed that the White Knight does not have a pudding treat to offer her. To console her, he offers her a song, the tune of which, like the pudding, is his own invention. The song is introduced with a play on accents and meaning of words. The White Knight gives the title of the song successively as *Haddocks' Eyes, The Aged Aged Man, Ways and Means,* and it finally emerges as *A-sitting on a Gate.*

The scene which Alice "would always remember" thus begins with the White Knight sitting on his horse, the reins fallen loosely on its neck, and "slowly beating time with one hand, and with a faint smile lighting up his gently foolish face, as if he enjoyed the music of his song." As the White Knight sings, Alice realizes that the tune is not his own invention but that of *I gave thee all, I can no more* (by Thomas Moore). The words too are a parody of the poem, *Resolution and Independence.* The "invention" can hardly be said to belong only to the White Knight, and to be shared with Alice. Mr. Moore and Mr. Wordsworth are now also in the game.

The song is one which must have been evolving in Mr. Carroll's mind, whether in connection with or separate from the body, for some time, for it had appeared in another form entitled *Upon the Lonely Moor,* published when Carroll was just emerging from Dodgson, at twenty-four. World famous as Lewis Carroll, he was forty-one at the time of the publication of *Through the Looking Glass* containing *A-sitting on a Gate.* There is something of a hint of the same theme in *The Storm,* which appeared in *The Rectory Umbrella* when Dodgson was nineteen, in the interval between

Rugby and Oxford. Parts of the tale are to be found also in *A Tale of a Tail* and in "The Headstrong Man" written when he was only twelve or thirteen and had produced *Useful and Instructive Poetry*. In Carroll's mature years we still see reflections and fragments of the same pervasive theme in Father William of *Alice's Adventures in Wonderland,* in the melodiously mad Gardener of *Sylvie and Bruno,* and in the Snark of *The Hunting of the Snark.*

But before we become completely addled by all the facets of this memory as they are drawn into its screen picture or reflect outward new derivatives, let us get back to the White Knight swaying on his horse, while the sun shone on his armor and the black shadows of the forest were in the background on that bright and memorable afternoon. This was *Alice's* screen memory. But the Knight's song as he sat there furnished *his* screen memory. This is our next step. It starts with the White Knight's compulsion to tell.

> I'll tell thee everything I can:
>   There's little to relate.[2]
> I saw an aged aged man,
>   A-sitting on a gate.
> 'Who are you, aged man?' I said.
>   'And how is it you live?'
> And his answer trickled through my head,
>   Like water through a sieve.
>
> He said, 'I look for butterflies
>   That sleep among the wheat:
> I make them into mutton-pies,
>   And sell them in the street.
> I sell them unto men,' he said,
>   'Who sail on stormy seas;
> And that's the way I get my bread—
>   A trifle, if you please.'
>
> But I was thinking of a plan
>   To dye one's whiskers green,
> And always use so large a fan
>   That they could not be seen.

---

2 Cf. the dog's bark in *A Tale of a Tail;* also Moore's, "My Heart and Lute."

So, having no reply to give
  To what the old man said,
I cried, 'Come, tell me how you live!'
  And thumped him on the head.[3]

His accents mild took up the tale:
  He said, 'I go my ways,
And when I find a mountain-rill,
  I set it in a blaze;
And thence they make a stuff they call
  Rowland's Macassar-Oil—
Yet twopence-halfpenny is all
  They give me for my toil.'

But I was thinking of a way
  To feed oneself on batter,
And so go on from day to day
  Getting a little fatter.
I shook him well from side to side,
  Until his face was blue:
'Come, tell me how you live,' I cried,
  'And what it is you do!'

He said, 'I hunt for haddocks' eyes
  Among the heather bright,
And work them into waistcoat-buttons
  In the silent night.
And these I do not sell for gold
  Or coin of silvery shine,
But for a copper halfpenny,
  And that will purchase nine.

'I sometimes dig for buttered rolls,
  Or set limed twigs for crabs:
I sometimes search the grassy knolls
  For wheels of Hansom-cabs.
And that's the way' (he gave a wink)
  'By which I get my wealth—

3 Cf. "The Headstrong Man."

And very gladly will I drink
  Your Honor's noble health.'

I heard him then, for I had just
  Completed my design
To keep the Menai bridge from rust
  By boiling it in wine.
I thanked him much for telling me
  The way he got his wealth,
But chiefly for his wish that he
  Might drink my noble health.[4]
And now, if e'er by chance I put
  My fingers into glue,[5]
Or madly squeeze a right-hand foot
  Into a left-hand shoe,[6]
Or if I drop upon my toe
  A very heavy weight,
I weep, for it reminds me so[7]
Of that old man I used to know—
Whose look was mild, whose speech was slow,
Whose hair was whiter than the snow,
Whose face was very like a crow,
With eyes, like cinders, all aglow,
Who seemed distracted with his woe,
Who rocked his body to and fro,
And muttered mumblingly and low,
As if his mouth were full of dough,

[4] Compare this with Carroll's fantasy about the vampirish nature of drinking health, expressed in his letters to Gertrude Chataway. (*Letters of Lewis Carroll to His Child Friends,* pp. 100-106.)

[5] Compare this with the glue story of the Cats of Finborough Road in the letters to the Hughes children. (*Ibid.,* pp. 64-68.)

[6] When the Croft Rectory was remodeled in 1950, the floor boards of a second floor room, previously used as a nursery, were torn up and gave evidence of having been laid, probably in an earlier renovation in 1843, soon after the Dodgson family moved there when Charles was eleven. In a cache under the floor boards was a collection of childhood relics including a "left-hand shoe," a child's white glove (which makes us think of Mr. W. Rabbit), a thimble (which appears both in the Caucus race of *Wonderland* and in *The Hunting of the Snark*), a lid from a doll's tea set (from the mad tea party or Alice's debut banquet?), a letter from a child's alphabet, and other significant articles. It would seem that the young Dodgsons may already have had some fantasies which were the forerunners of those supposedly spun spontaneously on the rowing trip on the Isis River.

[7] The White Knight had been quite sure that his song would make Alice weep, possibly as the old man a-sitting on a gate made *him* weep.

Who snorted like a buffalo—[8]
That summer evening long ago,
　　A-sitting on a gate.

Before going back over the earlier versions of *The Aged Aged
Man*, it is well to look at the poem *Resolution and Independence*
of which *The Aged Aged Man* was a kind of parody. This was
written by Wordsworth sometime between 1802 and 1807. It is
probable that young Dodgson read this in 1843 or 1844, or at least
by 1849 or 1850, when the clearest parody of it emerged. *The
Rectory Umbrella* of the 1849 to 1850 period contained many
parodies, including one of *The Lady of the Lake*, another of *Lays
of Ancient Rome*. The poem, *The Storm*, of this time is the first
clear parody of the Wordsworth poem. The poems of the thirteen-
year-old period, appearing in *Useful and Instructive Poetry*, have
more the character of expanded nursery rhymes or children's
poems, possibly influenced by Edward Lear, whose rhymes were
then famous.

Wordsworth's poem purports to be an old man's account of himself, as he encountered the poet, who was himself in a somewhat
mystical enraptured state in communion with the calm bright
dawn after a night of wind and rain.

All things that love the sun are out of doors;
The sky rejoices in the morning's birth;
The grass is bright with rain drops;—on the moors
The hare is running races in her mirth;
And with her feet she from the plashy earth
Raises a mist; that, glittering in the sun,
Runs with her all the way, wherever she doth run.

There follows then a statement of the alternating moods:

[8] Three pieces of board in the cache bore pencilled inscriptions. One of them
gave the name of the workmen who laid the floor and the date as June 19, 1843;
the inscription on one was not decipherable; the third bore the words:

　　　　And we'll wander through
　　　　The wide world
　　　　and chase the buffalo.

The Gardener in *Sylvie and Bruno*, who sang so much of the things he thought he
saw, sang:

　　　　He thought he saw a Buffalo
　　　　Upon the chimney-piece.

But, as it sometimes chanceth, from the might
Of joy in minds that can no further go,
As high as we have mounted in delight
In our dejection do we sink as low;
To me that morning did it happen so.

One suspects young Dodgson may at nineteen have responded
greatly to this. Later it would seem the contrasts were between day
and the restless sleepless nights.

.   .   .

Beside a pool bare to the eye of heaven,
I saw a man before me unawares:
The oldest man he seemed that ever wore grey hairs.

As a huge stone is sometimes seen to lie
Couched on the bald top of an eminence;
Wonder to all who do the same espy,
By what means it could thither come, and whence:
So that it seems a thing endued with sense;—
Like a sea-beast crawled forth, that on a shelf
Of rock or sand reposeth, there to sun itself;—

Such seemed this man—not all alive nor dead,
Nor all asleep—in his extreme old age:
His body was bent double, feet and head
Coming together in life's pilgrimage;
As if some dire constraint of pain, or rage
Of sickness felt by him in times long past,
A more than human weight upon his frame had cast.

.   .   .

A gentle answer did the old man make,
In courteous speech which forth he slowly drew:
And him with further words I thus bespake,
'What occupation do you there pursue?
This is a lonesome place for one like you.'
Ere he replied, a flash of mild surprise
Broke from the sable orbs of his yet vivid eyes.

.   .   .

He told, that to these waters he had come
To gather leeches, being old and poor:
Employment hazardous and wearisome!
And he had many hardships to endure:
From pond to pond he roamed, from moor to moor;
Housing, with God's good help, by choice or chance;
And in this way he gained an honest maintenance.

.   .   .

And the whole body of the man did seem
Like one whom I had met with in a dream;
Or like a man from some far region sent,
To give me human strength, by apt admonishment.

My former thoughts returned: the fear that kills
And hope that is unwilling to be fed;
Cold, pain, and labor, and all fleshly ills;
And mighty poets in their misery dead.
—Perplexed, and longing to be comforted,
My question eagerly did I renew,
'How is it that you live, and what is it you do?'

The old man then replies that he is and has been a leech gatherer for many years; but leeches are no longer plentiful and he
finds them where he may. The poet then imagines the lonely
gatherer of leeches who for all his destitute wandering retains a
kind demeanor and stately bearing. He laughs to find so firm a
mind in this decrepit man. "God," he says, "be my help and stay
secure: I'll think of the Leech-gatherer on the lonely moor!"
    Returning to the White Knight's song, it is very clear that the
Aged Aged Man, sitting wobbling on the gate, is a memory to the
White Knight corresponding to himself in Alice's memory. It is
equally clear that he is closely akin to Wordsworth's vision of the
old man who collected bloodsuckers. But the Aged Aged Man's
leeches have become butterflies, haddocks' eyes, buttered rolls,
wheels of hansom cabs—a veritable witches' brew, which with his
batter might permit him to go on from day to day getting a little
fatter.
    The earlier version of the poem, *Upon the Lonely Moor*, pub-
lished in 1856, is not strikingly different. Throughout it, how-

ever, difficulty in hearing takes the place of difficulty in thinking
or understanding, and the reciter of the poem is more outspokenly
aggressive.

> I met an aged, aged man
>   Upon the lonely moor;
> I knew I was a gentleman,
>   And he was but a boor.
> So I stopped and roughly questioned him
>   'Come, tell me how you live!'
> But his words impressed my ear no more[9]
>   Than if it were a sieve.

> . . .

> But I was thinking of a way
>   To multiply by ten,
> And always, in the answer, get
>   The question back again.[10]
> I did not hear a word he said,
>   But kicked that old man calm,
> And said, 'Come, tell me how you live!'
>   And pinched him in the arm.
> But I was thinking of a plan
>   To paint one's gaiters green,
> So much the color of the grass
>   That they could ne'er be seen.
> I gave his ear a sudden box,
>   And questioned him again,
> And tweaked his grey and reverend locks,
>   And put him into pain.

> . . .

In this version of the Aged Aged Man the poem ends not with
the memory of the swaying, snorting, rocking old man with eyes
glowing like cinders—a picture certainly suggestive of sexual

[9] This was written in the period when Dodgson was at home after having mumps
and whooping cough which resulted in slight deafness.

[10] Carroll was not a man to desert an idea after a single usage of it. Here his
mathematical scheme is very similar to a fantasy he had of a traveler's bath so
devised that the water would be conveyed back into the tub as soon as it was
drawn out of it: a closed circle without waste.

excitement—but the reference is a calmer one, suggesting uncertainty, unreliability, or perhaps unreality.

> Or if a statement I aver
>   Of which I am not sure,
> I think of that strange wanderer
>   Upon the lonely moor.

The Storm written for *The Rectory Umbrella* when Dodgson was about eighteen is the first version of the Aged Aged Man which is unmistakably a parody of Wordsworth. Interestingly too, it contains, through a misspelling of *leer* as *lear*, a possible admission of his earlier indebtedness to Edward Lear. *The Storm* is as follows:

> An old man sat anent a clough
>   A grizzled old man an' weird
> Deep were the wrinks in his aged brow
>   An' hoar his snowy beard.
> All tremmed before his glance, I trow
>   Sae savagely he leared.
>
> The rain cloud cam frae out the west,
>   An' spread athwart the sky,
> The crow has cowered in her nest
> She kens the storm is nigh.
> He folds his arms across his breast,
> 'Thunder an' lightning do your best!
>   I will not flinch nor fly!'
>
> Draggles with wet the tall oak tree,
>   Beneath the dashing rain
> The old man sat, an' gloomily
>   He gazed athwart the plain
> Down on the wild and heaving sea,
> Where heavily an' toilsomely
>   Yon vessel ploughs the main.
>
> Above the thunder-cloud frowns black,
>   The dark waves heave below,
> Scarce can she hold along her track
>   Fast rocking to an' fro,

And oft the billow drives her back
And oft her straining timbers crack
   Yet onward she doth go.

The old man gazed without a wink
   An' with a deadly grin:
'I laid a wager she would sink,
   Strong hopes had I to win,
'Twas ten to one, but now I think,
   That Bob will sack the tin'
Then from the precipice's brink
   He plunged head foremost in.

The ending of this poem is strikingly like the end of *The Hunting of the Snark,* and is related, too, to the earlier poem, "The Headstrong Man." The cracking of timbers in the next to the last stanza here resembles the breaking of the branch of the tree in "The Headstrong Man." That this theme was continually preoccupying the young Charles is again brought home to us by "The Poet's Farewell," at the end of *The Rectory Umbrella,* where it appears in another form.

All day he sat without a hat
   The comical old feller,
Shading his form from the driving storm
   With the Rectory Umbrella.[11]
When the storm had passed by, and the ground was dry,
   And the sun shone bright on the plain
He arose from his seat, and he stood on his feet
   And sang a melting strain.

It is probable that Charles Dodgson saw the Wordsworth poem sometime in his teens and that it crystallized for him similar wandering memories of *his* old man seen on a summer evening long ago, and so impelled him to a parody of his memory. The earlier versions, in *Useful and Instructive Poetry,* published at thirteen,

[11] Thus it is clear that the bearded old man with an open umbrella above his head and a closed umbrella worn like a little girl's skirt—which appeared as the frontispiece of *The Rectory Umbrella*—is the version of the Aged Man belonging to this nineteen-year-old time. It is probably the time of the displacement of, or extension of, the castration fears to the head, with only a partial sublimation accomplished.

are not Wordsworthian in form, but the elements of the central experience are there in "The Headstrong Man" and in *A Tale of a Tail*. The former was the second poem in the collection and told of a man who was clearly the prototype of Humpty Dumpty in *Wonderland*.

There was a man who stood on high
  Upon a lofty wall;
And every one who passed him by,
  Called out 'I fear you'll fall.'

Naught heeded he of their advice,
  He was a headstrong youth—
He stood as if fixed in a vice
  Or like a nail forsooth.

While thus he stood the wind began,
  To blow both long and loud
And soon it blew this headstrong man
  Right down among the crowd.

Full many a head was broken then,
  Full many an arm was cracked,
Much they abused the headstrong man
  Who sense and wisdom lacked.

For this mishap he cared naught
  As we shall shortly see,
For the next day, as if in sport
  He mounted in a tree.

The tree was withered, old, and gray[12]
  And propped up with a stake
And all who passed him by did say
  'That branch you're on will break.'

Naught heeded he of their advice,
  He was a headstrong youth,
He stood as if fixed in a vice,
  Or like a nail forsooth.

[12] "Withered, old and gray" is a phrase Carroll twice uses in describing the face of a dead loved one—possibly his mother. In *Stolen Waters* (1862) and *Faces in the Fire* (1860). In: *Complete Works of Lewis Carroll. Loc. cit.*, pp. 962 and 975.

While thus he stood the branch began
    To break, where he did stand,
And soon it dropped this headstrong man
    Into a cart of sand.

The sandman vainly sought for him
    For half an hour or more,
At last he found him in a trim
    He ne'er was in before.

For sand his face did nearly hide
    He was a mass of sand:
Loud laughed the sandman when he spied
    The branch where he did stand.

'Why what a foolish man thou art,
    To stand in such a place!'
Then took some sand from out his cart
    And flung it in his face.

All wrathful then was sandy coat
    Wrath filled his sandy eye
He raised his sandy hand and smote
    The sandman lustily.

Full soon upon the ground he lay,
    Urged by the sandman's fist,
These words were all that he could say,
    For those to hear who list.

Moral:
'If headstrong men *will* stand like me,
    Nor yield to good advice,
All that they can expect will be
    To get sand in their eyes.'

The content of this is strongly suggestive again of a primal scene, but with a preliminary awareness of the excited tumescent state of the man. The idea of the breaking of the branch of the tree that has been mounted is a possible indication of the boy's latent fantasy of the castrating injury occurring to the phallic woman. The ending of the scene in a state of sleepy exhaustion, both for participants and onlookers, is neatly condensed in the sandman stanzas. One must recall that these verses were written just at the age of puberty. This poem seems clearly supplemented by another, also from this period, entitled *A Tale of a Tail* and has to do with a gardener.

> An aged gardener gooseberries picked
>   From off a gooseberry tree
> The thorns they oft his fingers pricked
>   Yet never a word said he.
>
> A dog sat by him with a tail
>   Oh! *such* a tail! I ween,
> That never such in hill or dale
>   Hath hitherto been seen.
>
> It was a tail of desperate length
>   A tail of grizly fur
> A tail of muscle bone and strength
>   Unmeet for such a cur.

The first stanza presents clearly the stoical ideal, the reaction formation against fear of experiencing or seeing suffering which Collingwood was to describe as so marked a characteristic of Charles's adult years. The illustration accompanying the poem shows the gardener with witchlike prominence of nose and chin, but a pitifully ratty tail, apparently the tail to his coat. The next two stanzas describe the dog which appears as an awesome creature with a tail possessing virile qualities out of proportion to the degraded character of its owner. There would appear to be a certain reversal of roles: the dog is a better man than his master.

> Yet of this tail the dog seemed proud.
>   And ever and anon,
> He raised his head and barked so loud
> That though the man seemed *somewhat* cowed
>   Yet still his work went on.
>
> At length in lashing out its tail
>   It twisted it so tight
> Around his legs, 'twas no avail,
>   To pull with all its might.

The gardener scarce could make a guess
    What round his legs had got
Yet he worked on in weariness
    Although his wrath was hot.

'Why, what's the matter?' he did say
    'I can't keep on my feet,
Yet not a glass I've had this day
    Save one, of brandy neat,

'Two quarts of ale, and one good sup
    Of whiskey sweet and strong,
And yet I scarce can now stand up
    I fear that something's wrong.'

There is thus a mutual entanglement between cur and gardener
in which one pulls the other, and produces a state of intoxication,
bewilderment, and confused excitement which reminds us of
Charles Dodgson's horror of convulsions, the idiot boy, and
alcoholism.

His work reluctantly he stopped
    The cause of this to view,
Then quickly seized an axe and chopped
    The guilty tail in two.

When this was done, with mirth he bowed
    Till he was black and blue,[13]
The dog it barked both long and loud
    And with good reason too.

Moral—Don't get drunk.

It would seem here that the dog is associated with or represents
the young boy, as indeed it seems to, in other of Carroll's writings,
especially in *Sylvie and Bruno.* It is to be recalled that while this
book deals with the dog with mercy and respect, and further accepts the five-year-old boy as a charming child in need of taming,
Carroll otherwise developed a strong aversion to dogs as well as
to boys and was especially fearful of being bitten by dogs. In the
entanglement between cur and gardener, subject and object be-

[13] Cf. *The Aged Aged Man.*

come reciprocally confused, and the turmoil ends, not with the customary decapitation, but with decaudation. It may be suspected also that the obvious pun on *tail*, made manifest in *A Tale of a Tail*, indicates further the pressure to tell that was created in the boy as he grew to be a man. This is repetitively expressed in the poem: the tail is *"such* a tail," one of "desperate length"; it is lashed out by the cur (words which also refer to speech), and the dog ends up barking "both long and loud and with good reason, too." This emphasis on telling also occurs at the beginning of the last version of *A-sitting on a Gate:* "I'll tell thee everything I can,/ There's little to relate," which is a more restrained promise than the original by Moore, *"I give thee all, I can no more."* The old Gardener bowing with mirth till he is black and blue reminds one of Father William, the White Knight falling from his horse, the Aged Aged Man swaying on the gate, whom the White Knight shook so "well from side to side, until his face was blue," and of Dodgson himself who felt like rolling on the lawn with horrified laughter after his visit to Bowes where he saw a "mouthing idiot."

Indeed it is remarkable that in *Alice's Adventures in Wonderland, Through the Looking Glass*, and *Sylvie and Bruno*, there are three off-stage characters which are closely related, namely, the Aged Aged Man, Father William, and the mad Gardener. (We suspect that the Snark is here too, only even farther off stage.) All of the three are heard in song or rhyme, but appear scantly or not at all. All are really memories which come to life in their vividness. All are older men, parodies, foolish inferior characters, but merry and glamorously enchanting in their unexpectedly acrobatic behavior and lilting rhythms. In *Wonderland*, Father William appears in the poetry which Alice recites, on the advice of the Caterpillar, to test her memory which she fears is failing. In the *Looking Glass* world the "aged aged man a-sitting on a gate" is in the White Knight's song which he brings out as *his* memory to comfort Alice who in turn thinks she can never forget the scene of the foolish Knight sitting swaying in his saddle as he sings. In *Sylvie and Bruno*, the mad, musical Gardener comes to life out of the reverie of the narrator, "I," as he half sleeps on a railway journey to Elveston, and finds himself automatically conjugating "I thought I saw . . ." as though to test his memory. When he reaches, "He thought he saw . . ." this proves to be the switch phrase which causes a breakthrough of a stanza of the Gardener's song.

> He thought he saw an Elephant,
>   That practiced on a fife:
> He looked again, and saw it was
>   A letter from his wife.
> 'At length, I realize,' he said,
>   'The bitterness of Life!'

At this point the scene shifts to a garden enclosure similar to *Wonderland* and *Looking Glass* worlds. In *The Hunting of the Snark,* a similar but more powerful version of the amazing off-stage character exists in the Snark itself, which does not actually appear though its presence is indicated by the sudden vanishing of the Baker.

The rhyme, *Father William,* is the colloquy between a fat merry old man and a bewildered, timid, lean one. Father William, in spite of hair as white as that of the White Knight or the aged man, insistently stands on his head, balances an eel on the end of his nose, somersaults in the door backward (very much as the White Knight thought of somersaulting over the gate), and defiantly says he intends to "do it again and again," all to the consternation of the younger man. He explains that he has kept his limbs supple with the use of a special ointment which he offers to sell to the young man for a shilling a box; and that since he has reached brainless old age, he no longer fears injuring his brain with his antics as he did in boyhood. He ends by kicking out the anemic youth.

The character of Father William certainly is closely related to that of the aged aged man a-sitting on a gate. The latter is even older, a beggar who is engaged in senseless pursuits, such as chasing butterflies to bake in mutton pies. He also has *his* ointment, Rowland's Macassar-Oil, which he recommends and offers for sale. The place of the lean young man is taken by the White Knight, who sings the song about the aged man and is himself preoccupied with rejuvenation schemes—such as to dye his whiskers green (but hide them behind a fan, thus reminding us of the White Rabbit), and to feed himself on batter and so go on from day to day getting a little fatter. Father William's acrobatics are toned down and the scene is no longer one of defiance but rather

of sad reminiscence which causes the White Knight to weep because it reminds him so

> Of that old man I used to know—
> Whose look was mild, whose speech was slow,
> Whose hair was whiter than the snow,

.   .   .

> Who rocked his body to and fro,
> And muttered mumblingly and low,

.   .   .

The Gardener is the keeper of the door *out* of the garden in
which the fairy children Sylvie and Bruno find themselves from
time to time. He is vigorous, merry, melodious, and mad. He
usually appears first as a song heard from some indefinite place,
and later materializes. There is a description of him only on the
occasion of his first appearance, when he was clearly "mad, madder
and maddest" as he danced his frantic jig and brandished his rake.
His feet were large (like those of the elephant of which he sang)
and were disproportionate to his body which was rather like a
scarecrow deprived of its stuffing. These proportions resemble
those of the lean young man who was amazed by Father William,
or of the White Knight who sang of the aged man whom he had
seen years before, and of the aged man himself. The Gardener too
is the onlooker for he sings repeatedly of the fantastic things
which he has seen which start out appearing to be one thing and
then turn into something extraordinarily and unexpectedly different. His visions and conversation singularly suggest those of the
creatures in the garden in the *Wonderland* and the *Looking Glass*
worlds. Only his exuberant jigging recalls Father William.

That all this is connected with the conception of an older man,
a father, but one who may appear either in a degraded form or
as a beneficent lordly king-father is apparent in the chapters in
Sylvie and Bruno which introduce the mad Gardener. It is the
Gardener who is the keeper of the garden door and permits the
children to go out to give cake to a miserable beggar who then
reveals himself as their father, the Fairy King, who is to teach
them about universal rather than personal love.

The figure appearing sometimes in one guise and sometimes in another, but with his acrobatic swaying, jigging, and snorting rhythm, is, as already noted, a typical dream representation of sexual excitement. It is interesting, therefore, to realize that in the very structure of Carroll's stories, these figures all appear as memories which are represented in dreams. The Gardener's song always comes at the point of a shift from one state to another. The repetitiveness of this excited figure and his constant association with a secret garden, the concern about whether the onlooker's memory is good, and the reciprocal question as to whether the silly old fellow's brain has been injured—whether his behavior is merrily exciting or a comfort to him in a state of distress—lead to the conclusion that there was some actual event as the basis of a repressed memory of the author which was insistently recurring in this hidden form, an observation of excitement which also stirred him, the observer.

The Jabberwock, the Bandersnatch, and the Snark are three other off-stage creatures even less clearly described than Father William, the Aged Aged Man, and the Gardener. They are mysterious frightening animals, having some connection with the excited old men, appearing rather as a second line of even more distorted shadows. The Jabberwock appears only in a poem, read by Alice in a book at the very entrance to the *Looking Glass* world. It is a poem which Carroll composed as part of a rhyme-writing contest at a Dodgson family party, and later incorporated into the *Looking Glass* story. In this way it was like the last stanza of the *Snark* which occurred first to the author and then gradually drew the rest of the poem out after it. The business of *Jabberwocky* occurs at a time when the White King is limp and bewildered after Alice has lifted him from the hearth and dusted him off. He is trying to express his horror, and the fact that he will never be able to forget this incident. (Certainly this is again a variation of the compulsion to remember.) The White Queen then tells him that his memory is so bad that he had best make a memorandum of his experience or he will forget his feelings. Alice interferes with his writing, however, and, guiding the pencil for him, causes him to make involuntarily a factual note concerning the behavior of the White Knight. Thus again a problem of memory is involved, even as it had been in the instances of the excited old men. It would seem too that Alice's interference with the White King produces a memorandum which is strikingly like that of Charles Dodgson's own diary recordings which repress feelings but record facts.

Jabberwocky, possibly the most famous nonsense poem in the English language, contains many arresting portmanteau words, neologisms, which leave us groping and a little tickled at our own stupidity: they sound so natural and reasonable. To enumerate some of them: brillig, slithy, toves, gyre, gimble, wabe, mimsy, borogoves, mome, raths, outgrabe occur in the first stanza. Some of the other stanzas are not so loaded, but all contain two or three. A few are onomatopoeic like "whiffling" and "galumphing" but most are built on other principles. Later, in *Through the Looking Glass,* Humpty Dumpty explains them to Alice, adding that though he is more than a little slow in mathematics, there are few words he can't explain. Like the adolescent Charles Dodgson, he obviously has much fun taking liberties with language. He has conquered words and makes them mean whatever he wants them to, *but* they are troublesome little creatures with tempers all their own and sometimes must be subjugated. This is accomplished by putting them into portmanteau, two or more at a time, subjecting them in this way to extra labor for which they receive extra pay on Saturday nights. Humpty Dumpty explains that "brillig" means four o'clock in the afternoon when things begin to broil for dinner; that "slithy" is a portmanteau treatment of "lithe" and "slimy"; "toves" is a portmanteau combination of ideas containing badgers, lizards, corkscrews, little creatures that live in the grass at the foot of the sundial and feed upon cheese. "Gyre" means to revolve like a gyroscope; the "wabe" is a portmanteau word for the glass plot *way be*hind and *way be*fore the sundial; "mimsy" is "miserable" combined with "flimsy." In "mome" the structure is a little different; it is probably composed fro*m home*. Thus the animated words can be made to combine in different fashions. In the Preface to *The Hunting of the Snark,* Carroll quotes Humpty Dumpty's portmanteau theory with approval; and stating that "frumious" is derived from fuming and furious, explains that the two words might come into collision in the mind and articulation of the speaker whereupon the person with the perfectly balanced mind would say "frumious." It is certainly a just solution and perhaps avoids stammering. We would suspect, however, that frustrated may be somewhere in the portmanteau.

Jabberwocky is the story of a little boy who, warned to beware the Jabberwock, the Jubjub bird, and the Bandersnatch, ventures out into the forest, sword in hand, on a summer afternoon and actually encounters the fabulous Jabberwock, who with eyes aflame comes whiffling and burbling through the wood. He succeeds in beheading the monstrous Jabberwock and returns home to a hero's welcome. The scene sinks again into the hot, bright afternoon in which slithy toves gyre and gimble around the sundial just as they had at the beginning of the poem. The illustration by Tenniel, approved by Carroll, shows a small boy with girlishly long hair manfully striking with a small sword at a gigantic creature, many times his size, that looms over him. The Jabberwock resembles a particularly ugly gryphon but has a long serpentine neck, a fierce face with bared teeth, a tail like a prehistoric reptile, eaglelike claws and oversize rear hoofs. Its wings are spread like a huge bat. It is a gigantic portmanteau creature, indeed! The *first* impression of the Tenniel illustration is of a monstrous octopus, since neck and tail add to the effect of multiple attacking and encircling members. It seems probable that the whole poem presents the drowsy fantasy of a small child in a garden on a summer afternoon, and that the Jabberwock is an enormous enlargement and fusion of the little animals—lizards, worms, and other small creatures—condensed as toves which are first seen on the wabe of the sundial. These are the very animals that the infant Charles was so fond of. Indeed, the story was that as a little boy he had a plan for supplying earthworms with pieces of pipe for weapons and leading them into warfare. The Jabberwock is the momentary enlargement of the tove in the sleepy eyes of the child who indulges then in a dream of glory, slaying the dragon and bringing the trophy home victoriously.

In his later years Charles Dodgson, the Oxford don, played a somewhat similarly fanciful game as he sat in front of his fireplace, the tiles of which contained pictures of these same fabled animals. For the benefit of visiting little girls, he made the creatures have long, amusing conversations.

But the Jabberwock has other meanings too. The encounter

with this monster is certainly related to *The Hunting of the Snark* in which a whole crew participate. The Baker's uncle calls him a "beamish" nephew just as the parent has congratulated his "beamish" son in *Jabberwocky*. The boy looks "uffish" before the appearance of the Jabberwock, and the Bellman has the same "uffish" expression when he hears of the terrors of the Boojum Snark. When the Butcher and the Beaver, comrades in anxiety, hear "a scream, shrill and high" and realize that danger is at hand, they think it is the voice of the Jubjub and begin to count the shrieks. Then the Beaver is so disconcerted that he "outgribes" in despair just as the "mome raths outgrabe" in *Jabberwocky*. ("Outgribing" is described as a sound between bellowing and whistling with a kind of sneeze in the middle. To hear it made one quite content not to hear it again. A "Rath" is a kind of little green pig; and pigs are certainly associated with babies in Wonderland.) The Butcher gives a kind of illicit lesson in Natural History to the Beaver (until recently his enemy) and explains that the Jubjub is a desperate bird as it lives in a state of perpetual passion; it is so very upright and incorruptible that it collects, but does not contribute, at charitable meetings. The grateful Beaver feels he has learned more from the Butcher in ten minutes than he could have learned in seventy years of formal study from books. The bond of their mutual experience with the Jubjub bird cements their friendship forever.

Again it is seen that the land of the Snark is close to that of the Jabberwock, for the Banker in the Snark while hunting finds himself grabbed at by a fear-inspiring Bandersnatch with frumiously snapping jaws and an extensible neck like the Jabberwock's. The poor Banker faints, recovering only after the others have expelled the Bandersnatch; but then he can only stammer in his fright:

> To the horror of all who were present that day,
>   He uprose in full evening dress,
> And with senseless grimaces endeavored to say
>   What his tongue could no longer express.
> Down he sank in a chair—ran his hands through his hair—
>   And chanted in mimsiest tones
> Words whose utter inanity proved his insanity,
>   While he rattled a couple of bones.

It is the Baker, seemingly so inefficient, who becomes the hero of the expedition which is at least in part a would-be bridal journey, as indicated in the verse,

He came as a Baker: but owned, when too late—
    And it drove the poor Bellman half-mad—
He could only bake Bride-cake—for which, I may state,
    No materials were to be had.

It is the Baker too who finally sees the Snark and suffers the fate of instant disappearance, as all must who encounter a Boojum Snark.

It is interesting to note that the excited old men—the Aged Aged Man, Father William, and the mad Gardener—are conspicuous for their motions, swaying, or acrobatics, but their speech is generally clear, although the Aged Aged Man does at the pitch of his excitement snort and talk as though he had dough in his mouth. With the next line of characters—the monstrous forms of Jabberwock, Bandersnatch, and Snark, distorted and oversize in the eyes of the children—terror takes the place of fascination and speech becomes stammering, elided, and confused. Panic seems to have gained control.

While any precise explanation of the nature of the Boojum is evaded by Carroll, some hints are given, not so much in the *Snark* poem itself, as in other writings. "Boo" seems to be derived in part from boo, the frightening syllable which is used to scare children. This ability to frighten was certainly the Boojum Snark's major characteristic. But "boo" is also the first syllable of "*boo*-hoo," a word Carroll used frequently in jests with his little girl-friends. "Jum" is related to *Jam,* which is suggested in the Baker's tale in which jam and judicious advice are offered to the Baker to nerve him from his faint at the mere mention of the Boojum Snark. Thus the word "boojum" contains both the fear and the remedy, the phobia and its counteractant in one word. But "jam" comes around another pair of opposites again, in the pun on the word "jam" in *Sylvie and Bruno* where the word "Boojum" is explained as a kind of elision of sounds for Bootjack and Bootjam, the jack removing the jammed boot. In the same story is the chapter, "Jabbering and Jam," in which Jabber clearly means chatter, talk, and jam, like wine, is the senseless subject talked about with fine distinctions regarding the degrees of sensual enjoyment. "Jabber" in Jabberwock may have this hidden meaning, making a word akin to walky-talky, but it is more manifestly the little boy who goes for a walk and jabs with his sword. The two parts of the word are then somehow similar and opposite.

The Baker tells the assembled crew of the terror of the Boojum Snark as follows:

> I engage with the Snark—every night after dark—
>   In a dreamy delirious fight:
> I serve it with greens in those shadowy scenes,
>   And I use it for striking a light:[14]

He adds that he knows very well that if he ever encounters a Boojum Snark he will vanish—a thought which has caused him to faint at the very word "Boo." The end of *The Hunting of the Snark* portrays the Baker's fate exactly as he, in his anxiety, has predicted it.

> They gazed in delight, while the Butcher exclaimed
>   'He was always a desperate wag!'
> They beheld him—their Baker—their hero unnamed—
>   On the top of a neighboring crag,
>
> Erect and sublime, for one moment of time.
>   In the next, that wild figure they saw
> (As if stung by a spasm) plunge into a chasm,
>   While they waited and listened in awe.

The resemblance of these stanzas to those of *The Storm*, "The Headstrong Man," and *The Aged Aged Man* has already been noted:

> 'It's a Snark!' was the sound that first came to their ears,
>   And seemed almost too good to be true.
> Then followed a torrent of laughter and cheers:
>   And the ominous word 'It's a Boo—'

.   .   .

14 The combination of taking food and taking in the visual stimulation is here apparent.

Then, silence. Some fancied they heard in the air
  A weary and wandering sigh
That sounded like '—jum!' but the others declare
  It was only a breeze that went by.

     . . .

And the concluding stanza is

In the midst of the word he was trying to say,
  In the midst of his laughter and glee,
He had softly and suddenly vanished away—
  For the Snark *was* a Boojum, you see.

Thus it is apparent that the disappearance caused by merely meeting a Boojum Snark is related to fainting, taking leave of one's senses, losing one's head, having a fit or convulsion, being struck dumb or caused to stammer, frightened or awed in the extreme, or falling asleep with sand in the eyes. One form or another of this theme is omnipresent in Carroll's writing.

Many children have some fabled ogre, often in animal form, or some "secret," with which they scare each other and themselves. This is the antithesis of the imaginary companion whose presence is comforting, strengthening or relieving. Psychoanalysis reveals that this is generally some representation of the primal scene in which the sexual images of the parents are fused into a frightening or awe-inspiring single figure. This is probably the significance of *The Hunting of the Snark* in which the last "fit" is an acting out of the primal scene, with the Baker standing "erect and sublime" and then plunging into the chasm between crags. (This inevitably reminds us of the Headstrong Man, who stood "as if fixed in a vice, or like a nail forsooth.") The Jabberwock, too, seems another form of the Snark, but in the hunting of the latter, a whole crew of children participate; i.e., they tell this secret to each other under the leadership of the Baker, who is rather clearly identified as Charles. The part of the poem in which the Butcher gives the docile Beaver a "Lesson in Natural History" is possibly only a thinly disguised picture of a consultation among the little Dodgsons in the Daresbury garden regarding the mysterious life of their awesome parents. It is only the Baker, however, who really knows and suffers.

The screams, which are counted, seem quite possibly to be the clue to that recurrent mystery inevitably becoming sharp reality in the Dodgson household: the births of eight babies after Charles, just as there are eight fits in the poem of An Agony. This, it appears, is the deepest underlying cause of Charles Dodgson's concern about pain, and whether he can bear to see the sufferer if he is helpless to offer relief.

One other connection of this whole picture of the awful fascination and terror of the sexual life of the adults, and the stirring effect of even fantasying about it, is brought out again in *Sylvie and Bruno Concluded* where there is an extraordinary description of an attack of rage, so severe as to have a convulsive quality. This is suffered by Prince Uggug, the loathsome boy, the indulged bad side of Bruno. He is described as prickly and porcupinish, but obviously gets beyond this stage of irritability.

> All along the gallery, that led to the Prince's apartment, an excited crowd was surging to and fro, and the Babel of voices was deafening: against the door of the room three strong men were leaning, vainly trying to shut it—for some great animal inside was constantly bursting it half open, and we had a glimpse . . . of the head of a furious wild beast, with great fiery eyes and gnashing teeth. Its voice was a kind of mixture—there was the roaring of a lion, and the bellowing of a bull, and now and then a scream like a gigantic parrot. "There is no judging by the voice!" the Professor cried in great excitement. "What is it?" he shouted to the men at the door. And a general chorus of voices answered him "Porcupine! Prince Uggug has turned into a Porcupine."

It is then arranged to entice and trap the animalish Uggug into a kind of tunnel made by blankets and a cage like an oversized mousetrap. When the door to this contraption was about to be opened, "the fearful monster threw the door open for itself, and with a yell like the whistle of a steam-engine, rushed into the cage." One sees the probable outline of the primal scene in this, but more too. Bruno watches this odd scene and moralizes complacently that he can never become so porcupinish since he has always been filled with love for Sylvie. It is only a little later that the Professor explains to Bruno that a Boojum is a Bootjack, but remembers vaguely that Boojum had once referred to a creature in a fable, which has almost completely slipped from his memory now. It is possible that this picture of the animal, after a terrible struggle, bursting forth amidst blankets, uttering a yell and then subsiding into a cage, is also a disguised representation of the birth of a baby which is then cradled. But it is also a picture, much closer to consciousness, of rage, the jealous rage of the displaced prince at the birth of another child. And it is a record of the massive overstimulation which results in bursting, exploding, devastating feelings. It is probable that within the cage of extreme reasonableness, intense self-criticism, control to the point of pedantic accuracy and infinite patience of the Christ Church lecturer on Mathematics that was the adult Charles Dodgson, there were old mad memories, like prehistoric monsters, Boojums, which he, like the Professor in *Sylvie and Bruno,* thought he had forgotten.

It appears that the little boy Charles lived too full and exciting a life and was confronted with life's greatest mysteries too emphatically before he could assimilate them. Love and maternal kisses may have quieted, but they did not and could not explain. "Please explain" became Charles's repetitive request. The Boojums finally broke through the restraining bars surrounding them and repeated themselves endlessly in hidden fantasy forms in the games of Charles and the others in the quiet rectory garden, and in the strangely appealing stories of the famous Lewis Carroll. One must remember that the person who has so much difficulty in developing and accepting the satisfaction of adulthood prefers to remain in the fantasy of a beautiful childhood, usually because he is constantly and actively denying, by pretending that childhood has been all beautiful. Charles Dodgson, the Oxford don, did not really like pets or small animals, but he enjoyed fantasies about them and played with the ideas, not the creatures.

IV

I have attempted to trace through the various writings of both Charles Dodgson and Lewis Carroll, the associative connections of the Alice-Carroll-White Knight's screen memory of the Aged Aged Man. This has led to the conclusion that there was a series of interlocking, overlapping, and telescoping screen memories and dreams, which appeared with obsessional repetitiveness throughout the writer's entire life. The themes which appear time and again are the primal scene, fused with the sight of an older and degraded man, perhaps a gardener, in a state of excitement which produced a counterexcitement in a small boy onlooker; all this in turn fused with the awareness of the birth of babies—of the birth cries, and either the very clear fantasy of the event or the actual partial sight of it. The excitement aroused in the passive auditor is both sexualized and aggressive.

The screen memory within the screen memory, and the screen memory within a dream, are, I believe, close to the dream within a dream. Then there is the phenomenon of a series of successive enclosures, one within another, within another, etc. And yet another phenomenon is illustrated by Carroll, the dreamer within the dream, ending in the questions of whose dream it was, and which one exists only in the dream of the other.

Freud (1900) has written, "To include something in 'a dream within a dream' is thus equivalent to wishing that the thing described as a dream had never happened. In other words, if a particular event is inserted into a dream as a dream by the dream-work itself, this implies the most decided confirmation of the reality of the event—the strongest *affirmation* of it. The dream-work makes use of dreaming itself as a form of repudiation" (p. 338). We have all had an opportunity to test this observation of Freud, the importance of which in assaying reconstructions may not have been sufficiently emphasized. Carroll's repetitive memories within memories within dreams present an intensification of this repudiation and represent therefore the force of impact of the original experiences. Even the use of parody in them is not so much an attack on another, as furnishing another form of denial, as though to say, "It is only a parody." Furthermore, at least in some instances, these serially enclosed memories represent the symbolism of the dream form itself, here especially the symbolism of pregnancy and of the series of generations. Certainly with the young Charles Dodgson, before whom there had been several other Charles Dodgsons, and during whose childhood there were eight more little Dodgsons born, there was every reason for such disguised and denied fantasies to arise, to ward off the everlasting succession of hidden realities, of pregnancies becoming babies. This as well as the special fascination with tumescence and de-

tumescence was reflected not only in his dream within dream struc-
tures, but in his preoccupation with changing body sizes and
proportions, ubiquitous in the *Alice* books.

But in the dreamer within the dream there is still another
theme as well as those already mentioned, viz., that of primitive
identification and destruction: which eats the other up; and then
which one exists, the eater or the eaten? This question too is
omnipresent in the *Wonderland* and *Looking Glass* worlds, where
eating and sometimes the combination of eating and looking are
the most frequent forms of identification, as indeed is to be expected where the primary process rules. It is the fixation on the
least sexual form of childhood—the girl child at the age of eight—
which serves best as a fused and castrated version of both sexes,
and the greatest defense against the anxieties of the changing body
forms, whether the phallic boy or the phallic (pregnant) mother.

CHAPTER TWENTY-FOUR

The Childhood of the Artist: Libidinal Phase Development and Giftedness (1957)

This presentation may be somewhat premature. The subject is one about which one thinks slowly and hesitantly, perhaps because genius is always somewhat dazzling and mysterious. Whether the term "giftedness," "creativity," or "marked talent" is used, still the idea of genius is close at hand. The differences in definition as well as nuances in their usage reflect somewhat various ideas of the nature of genius. To my way of thinking, creativity is a special capacity which may or may not be associated with great ability; but it is usually of general significance only when it is part of a constellation of special abilities and drives—which make for the creative individual. Creativity does not seem to have a great deal to do with superior intelligence in terms of quotients, even though excellent intelligence may contribute to the productions of the creative person. In this paper I shall use the term the *artist* as a generic one referring to those possessing unusual creative productivity in any field. My presentation is both schematic and hypothetical, without full documentation and supporting evidence even for some fundamental parts of it, except insofar as occasional illustrations may tend to be of this nature. Neither am I reviewing the work of others who have contributed to this subject. There has been a great deal written that I have not yet had a chance even to read, valuable though it is; nor to reread some articles which I am sure have contributed to my ideas. It has been my intention to use the present formulations as a kind of work sheet, or blueprint of what is to be further investigated and correlated with the work of others.

There is a suspicion that I have been led into this too early presentation by my recent excursion into the field of pathography in the investigation of *Swift and Carroll* (1955)—and that this led like the path of the inebriate into deeper draughts. Before going into the main topic of this paper, I would first like to present a few aspects of the uses and limitations of biography and autobiography in the study of genius. In a naïve way it might seem that the study of autobiography supplemented by biography would be the method *par excellence* of understanding the individual genius. What could be more firsthand and authentic than what a man writes about himself? It is, as it were, from the horse's mouth.

This is of course an illusion. Every analyst knows that the account of his life which a patient insistently gives at the beginning of his treatment, "for the record" as it were, is not only imprecise but often filled with gross distortions and characterized by startling omissions. It is not only that the patient is not on to himself and aware of his deeper motivations, but that the individual memory is a great remaker of events, modeling and remodeling them throughout life with an extraordinary plasticity to make the cloak of remembrance do duty for one occasion after another, to meet both needs and fashions—with all of the skill and less noise than a good tailor.

A rather striking example of this was the case of a patient who had been through more than one period of analysis without revealing the nature or even the fact of having been involved in a tragic family catastrophe early in childhood. The original stunning pain together with the distress that followed and the neurotic guilt investing it had caused it to be left behind in an unused pocket of memory. It was not forgotten and could not be since it involved the sudden death of more than one member of the immediate family. But the ever-changing and increasing complexity of his life focused his vision of himself into a series of changing forms more suitable for the *here* and *now*, and practically bypassed memory of this early tragedy. Nor is this patient's autobiographical statement much more distorted than most of the others. Nicolson (1927) in *The Development of English Biography* remarks, "Creative Biography necessitates something more than diagnosis, it necessitates a scientific autopsy; and this sense of a vigorous post-mortem is just what the autobiographist has always found it impossible to convey" (p. 15).

It must be recognized that autobiography, whether given verbally in the course of treatment or written for publication, is always produced for an audience, and often for an occasion. The audience always consists of at least two sections: the self and "the others"—whoever they may be. These three factors (occasion, self-estimate, and impression on others) combine to make pressures here, expansions there, possible explanations at one time which in further editions are treated as facts; and so it goes. What is true of the autobiography is also true, perhaps often to a lesser extent, of journals and diaries. But here again, journals which are kept very fully generally have, somehow, phantom figures looking over the shoulders of the writers. Otherwise they tend to deteriorate into becoming mere memoranda. Then there are the letters which famous people have written throughout their lifetimes. They certainly are intensely valuable if they are accessible. They too often partake of the journal quality if they are written after the gifted one has attained some recognition or at least after he has recognized his own abilities. They generally have the advantage of being addressed individually to the audience and so present varied and sometimes extreme rather than consistent self-moldings. Further, there is often more spontaneity and immediacy in their writing. But those seemingly insignificant letters and jottings dealing with unimportant affairs are often most fruitful and revealing and yet are frequently lost or edited out of collections. For example, in the earlier publications of Swift's *Journal to Stella* much of Swift's "little language" was omitted as unbefitting a man of fame, even though it gave an understanding of some of the most humanly poignant needs of the great satirist. Consequently in studying any given artist (no matter what the medium), one must draw on all these sources if they are available, and more too.

From my limited experience in studying the lives of artists and saints, I would think that all this is of but limited value unless pondered carefully and correlated with the products of the life-work of the creative person. Here we generally find the less clearly censored dreams of the artist. They too are cut, edited, trimmed down to a beautiful economy if the artist is a good one, and they too are produced for an audience, the collective one of the world at large or even of future generations. But in their emergence they show irrevocably the changing preoccupations, the needs for ex-ternalization, and the searchings for harmony from the artist's own changing and developing life situations. The true artist may be more faithful with deeper inner integrity in his relation to his collective audience than he is with his personal connections.

If all memory, as we ordinarily use the term, would seem to be but a cloak constantly in process of renovation, sometimes with gross additions of new material—in other words, if all memory has a screening function, how else shall we understand the man within it? Certainly we must examine the cloak and know that it reveals much of the man within and is genuinely a part of him, but neither mistake it for the man within, nor discard it as of no value because it is not he. There are many critics of psychoanalysis and many psychoanalytic patients who protest, "But why should she (or he) put much stock in all this, when there is no clear memory of these things." There is often a note of triumph in such protests. Or, if our work has been able to go a bit deeper, there may be the addition, "I only feel as though this might have been so, but how can I tell?" If this attitude persists greatly, it must itself be analyzed. It generally indicates a rather special need of the patient to see himself as some kind of formal figure on the stage of life, rather than to feel himself as the growing, working, changing individual he is and has been. In my experience, recon-structions, if they are done painstakingly and with an almost sacred regard for the endless forms in which old experiences are emerging, become a working part of the individual, which under optimum conditions are assimilated and used without so much self-awareness. But reconstructions which are forced insistently represent the analyst's image of his patient or of himself, and are worn with increasing distress or discarded by the patient according to the degree of misfit. In studying the psychic life of the artist, it is probably necessary to use the methods of reconstruction of the analyst, in which the artist's production takes the place of many analytic hours. But there are limitations and temptations, for the artist analysand cannot talk back. If all memory is a screening process, so may this be true of official history.

I am indebted to Ernst Kris for directing me to Misch's *History of Autobiography in Antiquity* (1951) and to David Beres for Nicolson's *Development of English Biography* (1927). But especially invaluable is Kris's own book, *Psychoanalytic Explorations in Art* (1952). It is impossible for me to determine how much I have taken over from him in my own terms, for it is not the sort of situation in which I can quote specifically this and that passage, but rather, like a good analysis, it has worked upon me against my own considerable resistances, in ways that I have assimilated without being clearly aware of how and when. In the chapter on "The Image of the Artist: A Study of the Role of Tradition in Ancient Biographies," Kris presents in a much more specific and detailed form the story of the distortions of biographies of Italian Renaissance painters, to fit a family romance pattern in which the artist is biographized as a shepherd boy whose talent is accidentally discovered by an older already renowned artist, who becomes his genius father and patron. Kris points out that this was given a specific form in commentators on Dante's *Divine Comedy* who made the construction from a scant reference of Dante's and gave rise to the tradition that Giotto was a shepherd boy who was so discovered by Cimabue, the then established master, whom Giotto subsequently surpassed. Kris points out that there is little factual evidence for this story, but that it was the crystallization of a tradition which became fixed for some time as the appropriate biographical account of painters of genius. Its connection with the Christ story is obvious. It seems, however, that the family romance problem is inherent in unusually deep imprint in the lives of artists. We no longer demand that the official biography shall be literally cast along these lines. But reading the lives of various writers has led me to think that the family romance constellation has an intrinsically strong place in their psychology and probably in that of the creative person in any field.

Before deserting the subject of the biography or even autobiography of the artist, we might emphasize certain changes in what might be called "biographical perspective" in the fairly recent past. I am not a sufficiently serious student of history, history of literature, or history of the development of science to present this in any accurate detail. It is apparent to the naked eye, such as mine, however, that a change in the accepted demand of biography appeared in English literature after the First World War and was clearly announced in the biographies of Lytton Strachey in the early 20's. This began to be called, in this country at any rate, the debunking method of biography. It sometimes became as fanciful and as faulty as the bad historical novel has become, and represented the hauling down of heroes. It sometimes contained, however, a new growing respect for life as it is, and not as it is glorified to appear. Something similar had already been appearing in a gradual way in changes in English literature. Only in the first half of the nineteenth century could a heroine in an English novel be homely—a feat scarcely yet achieved by the American cinema. It is conspicuous that since the beginning of the twentieth century there has been an increase in interest in the childhood of many great people. This interest is reflected in many fields and is certainly apparent in changes in education, in literature, in social legislation as well as in many other ways. In my own mind I always think of the possible influence in this country as well as in England of the novels of Charles Dickens nearly half a century before such interest crept definitely into biography and autobiography. Certainly this interest in childhood antedated psychoanalysis, which gave it, however, new depths and perspectives with an enormous interest in artistic productions as well as in the artist's estimate of himself. Having recently read such autobiographical accounts of present-day writers as Sean O'Casey (1956), Herbert Read (1940), Richard Church (1956), Osbert Sitwell (1952), Stephen Spender (1951), C. S. Lewis (1955), Christopher Isherwood (1947), and a few others, I have been impressed with the willingness of many writers of today to reveal much of their early emotional life and problems, and in a few instances to view themselves self-consciously much in terms of analytic patients or as they conceive analytic patients to be. All this deserves more than this extremely hasty account, but will have to wait for more careful study in the future.

II

This second section of the paper consists of a series of tentative formulations and questions regarding the effect of marked talent or potential talent or giftedness on the early childhood of the artist. I have used the term "talent" rather than the more exalted one of "genius," although I believe that the same questions and problems would be true in both conditions, which may differ only in degree. I am aware again that some would consider talent and genius of quite different quality and that talent is often used to mean simple unusual brightness or special skill, without regard for the element of originality. In this present paper, however, I shall not differentiate talent from genius except in the matter of degree. *Talent* is defined by the *Oxford Dictionary* as "Mental endowment, natural ability," from the parable of talents (Matt. XXV, 14-30), and further as "Power or ability of mind or body viewed as something divinely entrusted to a person for use and improvement"; while the term genius has much more the connotation of spirit or the visitation of the God-power himself, alternately described as extraordinary capacity for imaginative creation, original thought, invention or discovery. In the sense in which I am using the term talent, it is necessary to differentiate it from brightness or appearance of brightness, whose development is the result largely of enforced practice or drill.

What then are the basic characteristics of creative talent? Are they inborn? Both questions seem difficult to answer. From the subjective accounts of creatively talented people writing of their own work and lives, and especially from some descriptions of the creative process itself by those gifted ones who were experiencing it (Ghiselin, 1955), it seems possible to describe the basic characteristics under four headings: first, greater sensitivity to sensory stimulation; second, unusual capacity for awareness of relations between various stimuli; third, predisposition to an empathy of wider range and deeper vibration than usual; and fourth, intactness of sufficient sensorimotor equipment to allow the building up of projective motor discharges for expressive functions. The unusual capacity for awareness of relations between various stimuli must involve sensibility of subtle similarities and differences, an earlier and greater reactivity to form and rhythm—thus a greater sense of actual or potential organization, perhaps a greater sense of gestalt. It has been said that the creatively talented person sees three dots at once, not as three separate points, but as constituting different line and triangle forms (Gerard, 1946). The increased empathy associated with creative talent would seemingly depend on the sensory responsiveness to the individual's own body state as well as to the external object, and appears as a peculiar degree of empathetic animation of inanimate objects as well as a heightened responsiveness and anthropomorphizing of living objects. The difference between empathy and sympathy here is especially conspicuous. Such animation of the inanimate and anthropomorphizing ordinarily is lost after early childhood, but in gifted individuals remains active either in its own right or appears in the form of the ease and wealth of symbolization.

Next as to the question of whether talents are inborn, this may be further subdivided into questions whether they are inherited according to definite biological laws or whether they are otherwise congenital, i.e., potentially present at birth but due rather to a sport appearance. Obviously, genius or marked talent has, through the ages, been thought to be the gift of the Gods, as the very definition of the word implies. Galton's early study of *Hereditary Genius*, first published in 1869 and revised in 1892, strongly supported the idea of inherited genius. When one reads this today, however, it is singularly unconvincing in certain respects. There is doubtless much to be learned from biologists on this point. But I know of no decisive study.

It is also apparent that it is difficult if not impossible to differentiate potentially talented infants from less gifted ones. Not only is there the problem of how much any difference is already operative to a degree to show in behavioral responses in infancy, but further that temporary variations of general bodily conditions or of external environmental ones may obscure or heighten the degree of responsiveness of a more ordinarily endowed infant, as well as that of the gifted one at a time when inherent differences are not yet decisively projected in performance. Especially may it be true that a potentially gifted infant with oversensitivity in sensory responsiveness, either in general or in some special sense, may be at first more than usually overwhelmed by the onrush of stimulation and in the extreme react less rather than more. In all of this, it seems one must be aware of the limitations of direct observation even though study of such observations as part of the development of life studies may ultimately lead to the most valuable results.

There are also dangers of overemphasizing heredity. Identification plays a very important role in the selection and zeal for a field of development of talent. Particularly is one aware of the complete disregard or ignorance of such possibilities in a study like Galton's, important as that was for its time. The problem of identification simulating inheritance is probably as great in the development of talent as it is in the appearance of certain neuroses in successive generations. In the latter case it may appear as though the neurosis were inherited when more thorough scrutiny shows clearly that it is passed on by contact, direct or indirect, through subtle processes of identification. (The influence of identification even with legendary parental figures is seen strikingly in the case of the tragic poet, Thomas Chatterton, who wrote phenomenally good poetry when under the influence of identification with a fifteenth-century "father," but otherwise, under his own aegis, showed much less talent.) It is also particularly tempting to ascribe genius to heredity when it appears in a member of a family possessing other members who are unusually bright. Undoubtedly intellectual brightness, e.g., involving excellent memory and quickness of response, is a help to greater productiveness and enhances creative imagination but cannot substitute for it. Observation of many of the "quiz" shows of current television programs is sufficient to indicate the striking difference between the accomplishments of unusual memory (piling up impressive stores of factual information, possibly of neurotic defense value) and the flowering of really creative imagination.

Further, it may be useful here to consider certain questions regarding the development of the child prodigy and even those extraordinary cases of pseudoprodigy or skill development against a background of generally undistinguished or even inferior intelligence—the peculiar prodigy known as the idiot savant. This condition sometimes occurs in childhood, less frequently in adult life. There are some people of genius who have shown a prodigious development early and whose mature genius appears as a fairly continuous outgrowth from the promises of childhood. There are also a number of others whose genius does not become evident until adolescence or young manhood; and still an appreciable few whose genius flowers only in the middle age or later. Conversely it is true that some spectacular prodigies peter out and develop into humdrum, rather undifferentiated individuals doing routine work. Others become bright and effective individuals but not seemingly possessed of remarkable talent or genius.

It appears that child prodigies may be divided into three groups. *First* are those in whom the precocious development appears as a spontaneous, rapid unfolding of the inner demanding pressure for unusual growth in some way inherent in the child himself. *Second* are those in whom the prodigy performance is mainly the result of demands of adults, usually the parents who push the child, using him as an extension of themselves in an attempt to realize some expansive ambitions in which they have felt themselves frustrated. One sees this not uncommonly in the field of athletic prowess and physical skill as well as in intellectual and artistic endeavors. A very restrained but moving account of the problems engendered or accentuated in such a child is given in the autobiographical account of Norbert Wiener (1953), indubitably an extraordinarily brilliant boy but so pushed by an ambitious father as to limit his spontaneity and his confidence in spite of his considerable attainment. *Third* are those in whom the remarkable performance is the result of neurotic conflict with the development of special achievement usually on a somewhat compulsive basis as part of an effort to overcome or counteract a masturbation addiction which is heavily charged with anal problems. From a recent review of some of the clinical reports on lightening calculators as this condition developed in imbecilic as well as in well-endowed individuals, it seemed rather indicated that the apparent facility at calculation resulted from an extension of counting compulsions. This is of some interest since the propulsive force of fantasies first associated with and then detached from masturbation appears to be of considerable importance in gifted individuals as well as in these retarded ones. But skill on a compulsive basis as a substitute for masturbation is limited by the span of the memory and the continuation of practice; whereas skill in a gifted individual is but part of the unfolding of the imagination which may originally gain impetus in connection with masturbatory activity but becomes liberated from it.

It is striking that some of these skilled but untalented individuals appear to be sensitive to gestalt configurations of numbers. Further scrutiny of the accounts of their performances suggests, however, that such awareness of patterned relationship of figures and groups of figures is not flexible or general, but restricted to a set of ritualistic performances, possibly derived from some elements in the situation in which the counting calculation was originally developed. It partakes rather of a rigid and empty, though superficially spectacular mnemonic scheme of narrow applicability.

In discussing the relationship between potential talent and libidinal phase development, I would wish to make clear that while recognizing the difficulties in making direct observations on infants and in determining the presence of potential genius at birth, I am myself largely convinced that genius is a "gift of the Gods," and is already laid down at birth, probably as a sport development which finds especially favorable soil for its evolution in families where there is also a good inheritance of intellect and a favorable background for identification.

If we think then of the potentially gifted infant as possessing a conspicuously greater than average sensitivity to sensory stimulation, this might mean both an intensification of the experience and also a widening of it to include not only the primary object which is focused on but more peripheral objects which are related in some degree or fashion to the primary one in their ability to arouse somewhat similar sensory responses. To illustrate this with a hypothetical example: we might conceive that the potentially gifted infant would react to the mother's breast with an intensity of the impression of warmth, smell, moisture, the feel of the texture of the skin, and the vision of the roundness of form, according to the time and the situation of the experience—but more than might be true in the less potentially gifted infant. Such an infant would also react more widely and more intensely to any similar smells, touch or taste sensations or visions of rounded form which might come his way. Thus we can conceive of the fact that for the potentially gifted infant the primary object which stimulates certain sensory responses to it is invested with a greater field of related experiences than would be true for the infant of lesser endowment. As part of this reaction, too, there would inevitably be a greater vibration and need for harmonizing the inner object relationships (as the perception of the object reacts on and combines with other body sensations) and the world of sensory impingement. In an effort to clarify this in my mind, I have adopted the phrase "collective alternates" to describe this range of extended experience which may surround or become attached to the main focus of object relationships. I am not sure that this is a good term, but I have not been able to think of a better one and for the sake of economy shall continue to use it in the present discussion.

In this connection it seems to me that this may be the beginning of the love affair with the world which appears to be an obligatory condition in the development of great talent or genius. From the study of lives of artists and from such analytic experience as I have had with them, it seems that the artist invariably has some kind of genuine collective love affair. "Writing is an act of love" says an epigrammist, "If it isn't that, it is handwriting" (Cocteau, 1956). I believe that this collective love affair has too often been considered largely as the narcissism of the artist, whereas it partakes more of an object relationship, though a collective one, than has been considered. It seems unlikely that the artistic performance or creative product is ever undertaken purely for the gratification of the self, but rather that there is always some fantasy of a collective audience or recipient, whether this is a real audience, as for the stage, or the unseen audience of the writer or painter; whether this be contemporary or extend into the limitless future. The artistic product has rather universally the character of a love gift, to be brought as near perfection as possible and to be presented with pride and misgiving.

Such love affairs with the world (appearing sometimes, of course, in their converse forms as colossal disappointments) occupy various relationships with individual love relationships, sometimes one being at the expense of the other; at other times, or in other individuals, appearing as quite separate or as complementary attachments. But generally the more powerfully demanding one is that of the world. Further, it is possible that in the libidinal phases of development of the infantile years, the presence of such collective alternate relationships permits diminution of the effect of critical situations involving the individual object relationships— critical situations which would otherwise tend to limit or temper the dominance of any given phase in the process of or at the height of maturing. Again to illustrate this with a hypothetical example: such a gifted child, on being forced to exert control of his bowels, may the more readily turn to play with mud or fecal substitutes, which he begins to fashion according to his current imaginative playful wishes toward his own bowel movements. He will do this more readily and more extensively than the less gifted child, and will submit to bowel training which at the same time may have less meaning to him than it would to the more average child. This has some bearing on problems of sublimation. It is my opinion that the observations of early childhood play, both as to the richness of content and the relationship to current pressure in the young child's life, may give important clues to the presence of potential creative ability (see chs. 20 and 27).

Especially is this true in the oedipal phase which may normally, in the male child at least, end relatively abruptly—to be reinvoked in a new version at puberty and thereafter. In the gifted one, however, the individual object may be only apparently relinquished, to appear rather in a glorified collective form which becomes the object of the love for a time. The ideals seem to be extended even more than the prohibitive conscience is developed, as the oedipal wishes are expanded, apparently desexualized by their deflection from a personal genital aim, but not renounced. The castration fears remain active and may invade the functioning toward the collective alternates, but their force is usually somewhat less focused. It is usually intensely strong and vivid, however, in the individual object relationship, where it does not produce an abandonment of the oedipal object but only a bypassing of this in favor of the larger collective, more powerful one. It seems that gifted children may solve their oedipal problems less decisively than more average children do. The apparent desexualization of the love object may be due as much in the postoedipal phase to the biological lessening of sexual pressure at this time as to the reaction of the castration fear which is further overcome by also heightened identification with collective power.

Indeed, the conditions of the latency period generally appear as a paradigm of the development of talent. It is conspicuous then that under the lessening of sexual pressure and the relinquishment of the oedipal aims, a period of actual heightened physical growth sets in normally in which aggressive drives are used much in the service of mastery, of learning, exploring, and experimenting. Even in nongifted children the latency period may be a time of great artistic interest and development. Especially if the incomplete closure of the oedipal phase has permitted the extension of some sexual interest, the explorations and drives toward creative productions seem propelled and colored by the conflict. Under such circumstances there may be the appearance of seeming talent, and the expectation arises in others that the child will mature as an artist. Commonly, however, except in the presence of inherent gift, this flowering of the latency period goes into eclipse with the onset of puberty and reappears scantily, if at all, as "interests" and hobbies thereafter. In such latency development of artistic interest, the content of the productions is sometimes discernible as derivatives of masturbation fantasies, either extended from or detached from masturbation itself and presented in projected and disguised forms.

In the libidinal phase development of the child of potentially great talent or genius, there is then an even less decisive than ordinary progression of the phases which overlap and communicate with one another in a way which more closely resembles the libidinal organization of the perverse individual than that of the neurotic. At the same time it is coupled with an intensity of all experience which may be disconcerting as it is revived in later life. Talented people are not immune from neurotic and psychotic developments under all conditions, but neither is there an intrinsic connection between talent and neurosis, except insofar as this kind of incomplete organization of libidinal structure may predispose to intense episodes of dissociation, which are, however, of less ominous prognostic significance than would be true in the less gifted person.

In the perverse individual the overlapping, fusion, or at best too great communication between different phase drives, results in too easy substitution of one for another or sometimes in chaotic disorganization. Problems resulting from these states are frequently played out on the own body. In the talented person or one of genius such confusion may be obviated by the discharge through channels of developed or developing talent. In this situation there may be a full play at different times of the different preoedipal drives, continued even with or accessory to an oedipal re-enactment in the formation of the love gift of the creative product. In studying the creative process, however, as it is described by various people of genius, one is struck by the imprint of the pregenital patterns.

The question of the choice of the form of creativity—the area of expression of talent—also demands consideration: the problem of *why* there is the universal genius such as Leonardo or the more frequent development of talent in one or at most two directions. Indeed in people of small gift, the stimulation to work in more than one direction sometimes seems to produce distraction and limitation of development. It is possible that the universal genius may have been more frequent in past centuries and during times when the mass of technical knowledge was not so great. Certainly too the direction of development of creativity may conceivably be influenced by the needs of the surrounding world and the way in which this is indirectly transmitted to the developing child. It is also conceivable that the direction of expression of genius may be determined by special gifts, transmitted by inheritance or in some way determined before birth in which some sensorimotor functional constellation is especially superior and becomes the dominant channel of reception and production. In general, however, we are more impressed with the probability that a potential genius has polymorphous possibilities, some of which may be inhibited by special circumstances of early development; but more conspicuously that direction of development of geniuses or talent is largely determined by identifications.

The experience of awe in childhood, the forerunner of the mystical experience, is described with special intensity by creatively gifted ones. That this belongs to the two periods of special sensations of exhilaration and upsurges of intense animation, characteristic of the latter part of the second year and to the fourth-fifth year (the phallic phase), has seemed to me evident in many clinical studies of less gifted individuals, as well as in the autobiographical statements of artists (see ch. 6). It may be that the identification with a father—or with a specially powerful godlike father—begins at this time and is felt rather regularly due to the combination of the sharpness of the body sensation with the intensity of the sensory sensitivity to the outer world. Whether this image of the father is then retained as a God or put in other terms remains largely determined by the tradition of the time and place. Kris (1935), in discussing this same problem, remarks, "A young sculptor, in whose life the idea of being 'discovered' could play a considerable role, associated the fantasy of the sudden un-folding of his talent with the idea, disclosed in his dreams, of being given a real, i.e., a fully grown, penis by the father image of the discoverer. The matrix from which this fantasy evolved was the old competition with the patient's real father who had been successful in the same branch of art" (pp. 70f.).

It would appear to me that this description takes very much into account the phenomenon which I have described as penis awe, dependent in most individuals on the actual seeing of the adult tumescent penis at a time when the child himself is in a particularly sensitive state. It is possible that in children of po-tential genius this inner state of awareness of tumescent feeling may be especially strongly pervasive. Combining with the sensitive perception of external objects, it may give rise to sensations of invigoration, inspiration, and awe. These depend not so much on the actual sight of the penis as on a communion with outer forms which reflect inner feelings in a way which I have tried to describe under the title *collective alternates*. It seems to me also that under such conditions the development of the family romance in espe-cially strong form is inevitable. Such a child must develop an early attitude of glorification of the parents in accordance with the peculiar vibrancy and capacity for near ecstasy derived from his own body states. Fortunate is such a child if the own father fulfills the need for the model with which then to identify. It is my sus-picion, however, that in some instances where this is not true, the child carries the ideal with him as though it were the real father, and that subsequent identification may be made and the development of direction of talent determined in part at least by the chance encounter with some individual or even some experi-ence which strikes a decisive harmonizing note with a part of the hidden image of the father, belonging to the original experience of infantile inspiration. I am not sure that with children of potential genius the contact with an actual individual may be required for the crystallization of the identification with the idealized image.

Certainly the family romance in exaggerated form is present in many writers, and may be ubiquitous in artists of all sorts. It is readily decipherable in many of the *nom de plumes* of writers as well as in the search for and expectation of finding the patron, which seems part of the apparent naïve dependency and unworldliness of many gifted people.

All of this leads to questions of the relation of creativity to the process of sublimation and allied problems in less talented people. I see these questions in slightly different perspectives than those recently presented (Hartmann, 1955; Kris, 1955). I would not limit the term aggression to hostile aggression—certainly not to the expression of a force always hostile in its aims. An army which enters a territory to improve it and make new constructions is still an aggressive force and its energy may be turned with varying degrees of rapidity from benevolent to hostile aims. Hostility seems further to have some implication of motivation. I would think of the aggressions of life as shows of force in whatever direction. The expansive aggression of growth of one organism may be destructive to another without being hostile.

During the first months of life there is not a clear differentiation of the sexual drives from the general energetic aggressive ones. This condition gradually changes during the first two to three years. A great deal of the energy endowment of the young infant is still used in the process of growth—in the actual increase in the size of the infant and in the unfolding of his functioning. This utilization in growth is even more extreme in the prenatal period when the increase in size and organization from a single fertilized cell to the fantastically complicated and developed infant at birth is a demonstration of a force which would really overwhelm the universe very shortly if it were not slowed down. Such slowing down in rate of size is reached in late adolescence. That the process of growth involves aggressive force was brought vividly home to me by the remark of my friend, Susanna Haigh, who said: "When I see the crocuses and the snowdrops pushing their way through the frozen earth at the end of winter, I am appalled at the fierceness of the tender shoots. It would take a swing of a pickax to do as good a job." Incidentally, the use of the word "shoots" for these

early growths is a significant recognition of their force. This is
the fierceness of expanding development and not of hostility. It
is in this process of growth and its slowing down lest it explode
the organism that I would see the basis of the death instinct;
granted that this evolution from the beginning of life to death is
at a different level than we conceive of instincts biologically. It
more nearly approaches a cosmic rhythm, which affects inanimate
as well as animate organizations. Personally I can no more conceive of life without an intrinsic movement toward death—the
death instinct, so-called—than I can conceive of perpetual motion.

But to get back to the human species, the baby of five to six
months extending his legs and pushing with his feet against the
lap of the mother does so from the aggression of developmental
force, not from the aggression of hostility. Later on, however,
derivatives of this same force may be used in hostile attacks against
the mother or others who stand in his way or interfere with the
attainment of some goal or desire. Hostile aggression implies a
sufficient degree of individuation for there to be a sense of the
self and the other(s) against whom activity is directed.

Further, in this early little differentiated stage of the drive development, the libidinal aspects of activity must consist in the
state of gratification and comfort (or lack of it) achieved in the
course of any activity, whether this is accomplished as a result of
the patterned inherited instinctual pressure or in a more diffuse
pleasure when performance itself fulfills the needs of expanding
growth. To attempt an illustration: the gratification of the infant
in nursing not only may be the attainment of a sufficient supply of
warm milk for the satisfaction of hunger (and so indirectly for the
further growth of the body), nor the passive comfort of warmth
of contact with the mother's body, but it probably also contains
the satisfaction of the use of the special neuromuscular equipment
engaged in sucking, i.e., the satisfaction of the discharge of a
developmental tension.

I would understand the unfolding growth pressures as they become organized, partly through maturation and partly through
experience, and are increasingly capable of working in some sort
of relative harmony as forming the somatic nucleus of the beginning development of the primary autonomous ego. There follows
then a further development of libidinal (sexual) drives and the

capacity of hostile aggressive ones in the service of self-defense or positive attack. The maturing of the central nervous system means the development of the psychophysical equipment for the more economical control and direction of the forces of the body. It seems probable that the aggression of the first months of the infant's life is expressed both in the endogenous processes of autonomous growth as well as in object- and goal-directed activities arising from such organismic growth. Insofar as these activities are directed against the environment—in meeting the infant's needs, they may *appear* to be destructive or hostile, but no true hostility is possible without the existence of object relatedness.

This may be of some importance in understanding special conditions of early ego development and of sublimation in creative people. These may in turn contribute something to the understanding of sublimation in more ordinarily endowed ones. It is also possible that in very gifted people a process comparable to sublimation in those of more average endowment does not occur, inasmuch as they possess much more mobility of libidinal energy, and change of aim and object is achieved with greater flexibility, although often accompanied by outer displays of disturbance. I want to make clear, however, that I am not here attempting any comprehensive statement but only making a few tentative suggestions regarding some problems which need much more careful study.

If the conception of libidinal phase development (under conditions of potential creative giftedness) which I have presented has any merit, it may be considered further that this early sensory oversensitivity together with the greater reactivity to rhythm and gestalt relationships of form would bring the infant into a wider range of awareness of his own body and of the surroundings as well.[1] How early and in what way this might operate would of course depend on other early circumstances as well, including special birth conditions, the presence of any defects in development, and the nature and immediacy of the relationship to the mother. It may also be that such an intensification and extension of the field of reactivity would form the anlage for the development of a greater richness of capacity for symbolization, which is

[1] The role of the capacity to form illusions in the gifted person's heightened sensitivity and responsiveness is discussed further in ch. 19.

so characteristic of creative people, and for the continued exigent demands of the primary process later in life.

Under most conditions such an infant would probably develop an intense and demanding relationship to the mother and to other early personal objects. The reactivity to the peripheral field might at first be largely extensions of these. Subsequently (I would conceive it roughly as from the latter half of the first year on) a powerful libidinal investment in the areas of the collective alternates, either in general or in some chosen part, might arise coexistent with that to the personal objects. The relationship between the forces of the individual personal object cathexes and those of the collective alternate ones would appear to exist in varying balances depending on a complexity of factors which cannot now be gone into.

What I would want to emphasize, however, is that this balance would influence very much the outline and organization of the incipient ego development; especially the growth of any self-image or self-representation; and even of perceptions as well of the self. It is conceivable that under what are generally considered favorable conditions of infancy, the primary (personal) self-representation would be at first the dominant and might always remain the firmer or more solid one. But in the course of time there may precipitate some rival or accessory self-image, again partly determined by the contact with some accessory adult idealized figure, who condenses and consolidates some area of the collective alternates through furnishing special sources of identification. Fortunate is that creative child or youth who has available within his own family individuals suitable for these identifications and reinforcements of his own creative needs.

Indeed, I do not believe that this is a mere whimsy of mine. It is evident in studying the lives of markedly creative people that such splits in the self-representation, going over into even a split in the sense of identity, do occur and relatively frequently—sometimes developing along parallel lines and sometimes alternating, one emerging from cover of the other. This division into the two or more selves may be experienced in childhood with some distress and with the wish to deny the creative self in favor of the social stereotype, which exerts so much constricting pressure during the school years. The creative self is then felt as freakish, abnormal, and to be fought. Under many circumstances, this struggle continues into adult life, when the more conventional self may be more or less guardian or enemy of the creative self. In the latter instance one may see the literal escape from one to the other. All this, it would appear, must also contribute to the ubiquitous and specially strong family romance among creative people.

Under conditions of frustration and disappointment in the personal object the creative individual may turn to the collective one(s); or the movement may be in the opposite direction. Under still other circumstances frustration in one area may lead to reciprocal inhibition in the other. Clinical illustrations may be developed in some later paper. These are matters determined by —among other factors—the degree and fashion in which the collectively determined creative function has been used too much in the service of the personal defense mechanisms, i.e., has been subjected to the burden of displacements, the effect of which depends on the amount, form, and location of the libidinization. In the extremely gifted individual, however, there may be a sufficient margin in the development of the artist self to overcome all but the most sweeping displacements of this kind. It also means that among some creative people, the rhythm of personal disappointment giving rise to renewed efforts of realization through artistic endeavors has become established early and sets a pattern which causes them to fear even the illusion of a well-developed personal life, lest it deprive them of the impetus for creative production.

At this point I would want to make clear that my own conviction is that creative activity is highly libidinized and that without this libidinal charge it could come to naught. I would even suspect that it may carry the whole gamut of mixed libidinal phase pressures, genital and pregenital, more diffused and with wider and deeper range than is true in the less gifted person, but discernible in the form and nature of the creative process and in the artist's relation to his own creative product. It may be that the capacity to turn emotional drive to artistic creation is determined not only by the amount of gift endowment, but as part of this by the ease, mobility, and plasticity of the communication between the individual (personal) emotional interests and those of the general outer world, of collective significance. Further, the creative activity of the artist seems to me also highly aggressive, but with aggression allocated to special growth developments, to extents probably much greater but not wholly different from the situation of sublimation in those of lesser talents. The problem of ego syntonicity in the artist is further complicated by the degree of acceptance or denial of the creative talent by the total individual and not merely by some competent part of the self.

What I have said here crudely and in first draft may not differ greatly in some essentials from others' views, even though terms may have been used somewhat differently. My formulation indicates, however, why I find the term *neutralization* so difficult in this connection. To me *neutralization,* borrowed presumably from chemistry, has the natural connotation of something which has been rendered inert, or at least temporarily ineffective. I would think of the need for a specific process to produce neutralization and a somewhat similar but reversed one again to produce deneutralization before a new direction of force or activity might arise. It is not that borrowing a chemical term is in itself objectionable. "Sublimation" itself and "valence" are such borrowed terms. But sublimation seems a more apt and condensed metaphor for it implies change in physical form—through diffusion as a gas and reprecipitation as a solid—without change of chemical structure. This is, however, accomplished by changes in temperature. Sublimation also has the connotation inevitably—though without chemical foundation—of conversion into a higher form. With "neutralization" the comparison fits less well. If by neutralization one meant a stage of busy and productive peace such as neutral nations are supposed to have, then the metaphor would seem more appropriate. Parenthetically I have thought the limitation of the term "aggression" to mean "hostility" may have been reinforced in recent years by the emphasis on the culpability of the aggressor nations.

There is one way, however, in which the energy passing from individual to the collective objects might seem to me to approach something like a neutral state. That is in relation to specific masculine or feminine differentiated direction. In other words, I would think of some degree of loss or diminution of sexual polarity; love of mankind, fervid but both diffuse and intense, expressed very much in the creative love gift, may take the place of or be in communication with the love of a man or of a woman. Perhaps this is the more possible in those gifted ones, the artists, who by the very nature of their early libidinal phase development must have not only a higher capacity for bisexuality, but a greater fluidity in changes of emphasis between the various libidinal phase drives. The reaction of the artist to the collective object(s) also involves utilization of the most primitive but acute empathic responses to an extent greater than is true in relation to the personal object. It is the force of the amalgamation of this dominant primitive empathy with the summation of experiences of the total span of life which acts then in a depolarized sexual way in the struggle for harmony of which the creative product, the love gift, is the outcome. This struggle for harmony takes the place of some (much or little) of what might otherwise go into the personal love relationships of a polarized sexual nature. When the polarity of the personal sexual investment is not appreciably diminished and displacement has occurred too massively, then the collective love affair also assumes (by this direct displacement or by the rigidity of reaction formation) too much of the personal conflict. It is then subject to the same hazards, usually derived from the castration conflict, which have existed in the personal sphere. The site and nature of the displacement will further determine the character of the symptomatic invasion of the creative activity.

One may examine these matters sometimes in the situations of slightly or only moderately gifted people in whom, through early overtraumatization, a sensitivity and flux of libidinal phase development has occurred. Here one sees a much simpler situation, complex though it is. Though the analysis of such patients is extremely difficult and arduous, one sees the gradual liberation of the bound energy to produce a greater possibility of dominantly genital-sexual love, but the constitution remains susceptible and the personal sexual love relationship may be sustained only insofar as it may be supplemented by libidinized interests of a nonpolarized type. That such a person may not become a good creative artist depends rather on the mediocrity or at least lack of superiority of the basic endowment; and on the fact that his sensitivity, the result of unfortunate early conditions rather than of special gifts of nature, has not had the same range of reactivity, nor produced the same compelling need for seeking harmony. I must reiterate, however, that I have not carried these ideas into repeated and carefully checked extensive application to clinical cases, nor tested them out in the study of famous people. In any event, they may need both correction and refinement.

Some few rather less important observations may be discussed before closing this paper, certain special problems and difficulties of people of marked talent. If the talent is very great, there is indeed a sense of pressure, an obligatory quality to the expansion of development. If, while this is still in a state of potentiality, for any reason channels of outlet are blocked, states of frustration and blind frenzy with very slight provocation may arise. The best description I know of this is in Helen Keller's autobiography, in which she gives a picture of her inner explosiveness before her need to communicate could be channeled expressively after the illness which cut off both her sight and hearing.

It was probably an intuitive awareness of this obligatory creative pressure as well as his enthusiasm for a biological genetic classification of people that led Galton to conclude that genius always asserts itself: that it will not remain hidden. Indeed, the compelling drive of creativeness, sometimes contrary to the conscious wishes of its possessor, may give the creative activity the semblance of a special kind of addiction for which there is no cure. Galton considered that three qualities of "ability—combined with zeal, and the capacity for hard labor" are essential to genius and are inherited. Again he says, "If a man is gifted with vast intellectual ability, eagerness to work, and the power of working, I cannot comprehend how such a man should be repressed." Once more he took an emphatic stand:

> People seem to have an idea that the way to eminence is one of great self-denial from which there are hourly temptations to diverge; in which a man can be kept in his boyhood only by a schoolmaster's severity or a parent's incessant watchfulness and in after-life by the attractions of fortunate friendships and favourable circumstances. This is true enough of the great majority of men, but it is simply not true of the generality of those who have gained great reputations. Such men—biographies show to have been haunted and driven by an incessant craving for intellectual work. If forcibly withdrawn from the path that leads towards eminence, they will

find their way back to it as surely as a lover finds his mistress. They do not work for the sake of eminence, but to satisfy a natural craving for brain work, just as athletes cannot endure repose on account of their muscular irritability, which insists upon exercise. It is very unlikely that any conjunction of circumstances should supply a stimulation to brain work commensurate with what these men carry in their own constitutions. . . . [The natural disposition of genius] keeps a man ever employed,—now wrestling with his difficulties, now brooding over his immature ideas, and renders him a quick and eager listener to innumerable almost inaudible teachings, that others less keenly on the watch, are sure to miss.

Thus Galton makes quite clear his appreciation of the difference between superior skill attained through demanded practice and that achievement which derives chiefly from the inner pressure of essential endowment. While his insistence on the constitutional elements in genius, or as he sometimes refers to it as "great eminence," led him to emphasize inheritance in ways which we might now question, he brings out some interesting peripheral observations and assumptions. In accordance with his belief in the inheritance of genius and its appearance, he may rather have ignored the instances in which genius became manifest and obligatory late in life. From the analyst's angle, the study of such men would be most illuminating.

I would interpolate a few of Galton's observations—aside from his emphasis on inheritance—because they are interesting and because they show that, in spite of his conscious focusing on inheritance and insistence that it alone was responsible for the appearance of genius, he inevitably came upon other determining factors. Although he concluded generally that the "female influence is inferior to that of the male in conveying ability," he realized that this might not be entirely due to hereditary factors, and added cautiously at a later time, "I think there is reason to believe the influence of females but little inferior to that of males in transmitting judicial ability," and that such influence might not be wholly due to inheritance is tacitly admitted in his discussion of men of science. Here he states that the fathers of the ablest men in science have frequently been unscientific; and elsewhere states, "It therefore appears very important to success in science that a man should have an able mother. I believe the reason to be that a child so circumstanced has the good fortune to be delivered from the ordinary narrowing, partisan influence of home education . . ." and again indicates that the sons of the most gifted men in science have themselves become distinguished in science only if they have also truth-loving mothers.

Another interesting conclusion arrived at by Galton was that in general men of genius were more often of good physical constitution than otherwise and he added, "I do not deny that many men of extraordinary mental gifts have had wretched constitutions, but deny them to be an essential or even a usual accompaniment." From studying the mortality of his men of genius, he concluded "that among the gifted men, there is a small group who have weak and excitable constitutions, who are destined to early death, but that the remainder consists of men likely to enjoy a vigorous old age." This was true in the group of artists and distinctly so in that of poets, but it came out in most startling definition in the cases of men noted for their remarkable precocity. The mortality curve was normal only in those who did not appear to have been eminently precocious. Scientific men lived the longest and the number of early deaths among them was decidedly less than in any other groups. All this is interesting and provocative and deserves much more careful study. I have quoted Galton's work, for though first published nearly a century ago, it was one of the most comprehensive studies of men of genius ever attempted. Incidentally, in my hesitation to psychoanalyze the dead artist, I found some amused comfort in the discovery that in recent years, the psychologist, Terman (1917) did postmortem tests on Galton and decided that in his childhood Galton's IQ had been 200.[2]

---

[2] A paper on "The Early Years of the Gifted Child: A Psychoanalytic Interpretation" (1962a) deals with the same topic in less technical language. To avoid duplication it has not been included here.

CHAPTER TWENTY-FIVE

The Family Romance
of the Artist (1958)

I

The present paper is a continuation of preoccupations giving rise
to preliminary investigative studies, finally brought to some focus
in "The Childhood of the Artist" (ch. 24). The subject of creativity had not, previously been in the arena of my clinical research
interests and I had never expected to tackle it. Perhaps I was in-
timidated by a latent interest which might become too engrossing.
At any rate, it was through the stimulation—even the persistent
prodding—of the late Ernst Kris that my concern with the subject
was brought into the daylight. Now I am grateful for this gift—
surprising to me at the time and hesitatingly accepted. His friendship was immensely enriching; and I am glad of this opportunity
to contribute to an occasion in his honor and memory.

The study of the creative artist presents, from the analyst's angle,
a particularly difficult set of obstacles. First, not many very creative
people come to analysts—at least they do not come to me; second,
they present peculiarly difficult problems in analysis; third, the
publication of clinical material from their analyses contains
unique hazards. The study of the analyses of moderately gifted
people is of great help, but I found that I had to have contact
with the patient of marked gift before I adequately appreciated
and used fully the depths of those of slight or moderate gift, in

collecting my observations and translating them into the beginnings of theory. I turn then, in order to supplement my own clinical observations, to the study of creative artists of the past, whose lives are moderately well known and whose artistic products are also available. As this requires an enormous amount of investigation, any such study proceeds very slowly. Further, it launches one at once into the subject of biography and autobiography: what functions they have served throughout history; to what extent they are molded by the "myth-in-the-making" demands of the group; and to what extent is the unique individuality of the artist preserved.

Perhaps at no time so much as at present has there been such an active interest in the specific influences of childhood on the development of the man. This emphasis, originating before Freud, has been given enormous impetus and implementation by the work of psychoanalysis, even in the hands of those who believe themselves opposed to psychoanalytic theory. Consequently, at present it is somewhat exceptional to find a contemporary biographical or autobiographical study which does not include some kind of a detailed account, either direct or implied, of the early years.

I would emphasize that in using the term *artist* I designate the creative individual no matter what the medium of his artistic expression be—i.e., the person whose work-product shows not only the skill due to learning and practice, but also unusual capacity for imaginative creation, original thought, invention or discovery. While much of my reading has been in the biographies, autobiographies, and letters of writers, since they are unusually articulate and have more frequently left direct records of themselves, it has not been confined to them. I would further include among artists those prophets, religious leaders, and scientists whose philosophies and discoveries have influenced the course of their times and left an imprint on history.

After reading a great many accounts of artists, I was struck with the prominence of the family romance in their lives. The germ of the family romance is ubiquitous in the hankering of growing children for a return to the real or fancied conditions at or before the dawn of conscious memory when adults were Olympians and the child shared their special privileges and unconditional love without special efforts being demanded. Family romance fantasies of a well-organized nature seem to emerge most clearly in the early latency period; are indicative of a marked degree of ambivalence to the parents, especially due to grossly unresolved oedipal problems. This ambivalence seems reinforced by the ambivalence of the anal period to which good and bad, applied to the self and to the parents, appear like black and white twins in so many relationships. One has only to talk to a number of institutionalized children to see how fact and experience are counterbalanced by fantasy born of longing, and their own parents, though disappointing and sometimes overtly cruel, become ideal, powerful, and magnanimous, once they are out of sight for a time. But in the artist there seem to be some special ingredients to the family romance.

If what I have postulated in my earlier paper is true—namely, that the artist has an inborn heightened perceptiveness of the outer world (including intensified and precocious awareness of form and rhythm) and that this leads to the development of the background of "collective alternates" (ultimately cosmic emotional conceptions) which invest the main personal relationships of life—then it may be seen that the child who is the potential artist starts out with different materials for his sense of his parents and his developing sense of himself from what is true in the less gifted child. The fact of the development may then depend in some measure on the sort of relationship which is maintained between the personal parental figures and the cosmic ones. If one or the other actual parent (more often the father) is able in sufficient degree to qualify for the mantle of greatness in any sustained way in the postoedipal period and at the same time to keep a warm relationship with the child, or even if one or the other parent (without greatness) maintains a warm, sustained belief in the unusual potentialities of the child, then I think that child has much greater chance of fulfilling somewhat his creative destiny than if neither of these conditions is true. In the one instance, the child gets the reinforcement for himself from the postoedipal identification with the father; in the other, from the acceptance by the parent of the increasing power within himself. Yet the developing gifted child, even in very untoward circumstances, will sometimes be able to find a temporary personal adult substitute or even to extract from a cosmic conception some useful personalized god conception on which to project his necessary ideal for his father and himself to enable him to develop further.

Kris, in his paper on "The Image of the Artist: A Study of the Role of Tradition in Ancient Biographies" (1935), presents the family romance pattern which became the accepted traditional biography of the Renaissance. According to this pattern, the artist of genius was a poor boy; often a shepherd boy, whose talent developed in his solitude and was accidentally discovered by an older established artist who then became his patron and his genius father.[1] Kris further indicated that the emergence of this patterned story was given a definite form and in a sense authorized by commentators on Dante's *Divine Comedy*, who constructed this account from scant references of Dante's and developed the tradition that Giotto was a shepherd boy thus discovered by Cimabue, the master, whom Giotto then surpassed. Actually, there was little or no factual evidence for this beautiful oedipal fable; but for some time it became the accepted story in one way or another of the development of the genius of the Italian Renaissance. It obviously had an earlier version in the Christ story, and one may suspect that it was much affected by the way in which the monastic Christian life had held the hope and the learning of the Dark Ages, and then came to furnish the content of the Renaissance painting, while the fierce, cruel aspects which are inevitable in any organized religion first found expression in the frightful religious wars and finally in the Inquisition.

This shepherd boy tradition is in distinct contrast to the opinion of Galton (1869), who concluded that relatively few geniuses came from families who had not been well-established people of distinction for generations. He was himself probably of genius caliber, a member of a well-established family, and made his study in the middle of the nineteenth century, when class-conscious England felt itself secure and mighty. His methods of selection of genius for study reveal thoroughly the pitfalls of statistical methods of this kind. Since his selection was made on the stated assumption that "high reputation is a pretty accurate test of high ability," necessarily supplemented by his subsequent conviction that the

---

[1] A degraded form of this story appeared in the juvenile American literature of this country during the Victorian period—in such boy's books as the Henty stories.

power of genius is so great that it will always mature sufficiently to make itself well known (i.e., that the pressures of genius are so great as to overcome all obstacles), he had to use many different channels in trying to arrive at criteria for judging "high reputation." It was quite striking that he felt on safer statistical ground when he was making his study of genius in judges, statesmen, and military men, in whom attainment might be recognized by rank, while publicized position and renown were generally achieved in the man's own lifetime, than when the study concerned literary men, poets, musicians, painters or even scientists. In all of these latter fields full recognition of superior achievement is often not accorded during the artist's lifetime and attainment is only rarely stamped by an official designation or title. Galton concluded that genius was hereditary and invested in certain leading families. Although his study is fascinating in his suggestons regarding certain essential qualities of genius, it is unconvincing in many of the respects in which he felt it to be most assuredly sound.

II

I shall attempt in the present paper to discuss the family romance as it is evident in the lives of five men of genius: one was a religious leader in Italy in the twelfth and thirteenth centuries; one an English poet of the eighteenth century; one a writer of plays and fiction in Russia in the first half of the nineteenth century; one a Welsh-American explorer of the second half of the nineteenth century; and one a Czech poet whose life spanned the last quarter of the nineteenth century and the first quarter of the twentieth. Their lives thus cover a considerable range of time, of space, of experience, and of interests. The choice of these men is not a symmetrically balanced one, nor is it entirely random. It springs probably from personal interests of my own, for I picked them from a number of biographical or autobiographical accounts which I have read in the last few years, when a former interest in biography was revived. They are all men whom I had meant to read more about some time, because the vague snatches of information I had about them somehow invited me. But I had not studied the lives of any of them until recently. First is St. Francis of Assisi, the founder of the Franciscan Order of the Catholic

Church; next I refer to Thomas Chatterton who committed suicide before his eighteenth birthday, yet reached posthumous fame
as one of the greatest English poets of his century. Third is Nikolai
Gogol, whose *Dead Souls* is considered by many the great prose
classic of Russia and its author the beginner of the Russian novel.
Fourth is the fabulous American explorer, Henry M. Stanley, who
was born John Rowlands in North Wales and died Sir Henry
Stanley in London, in 1904. The last is Rainer Maria Rilke, perhaps the most complex of those I have mentioned and the one of
whom I can say least in this paper, although he deserves much
more.[2]

Chatterton

Perhaps the most gifted and most tragic of them all is Thomas
Chatterton, the English boy poet from Bristol who committed
suicide before he was eighteen. Not only did he reach posthumous
fame, but he was himself a posthumous child, born three months
after his father's death in 1752. From a simple family background,
the son of a schoolmaster of a family who through generations had
furnished a sexton to the Church of St. Mary Redcliffe, in Bristol,
in his infant years he was cared for by his mother, a hard-working
woman of barely twenty years, who ran a needlework school to
gain a livelihood for him, his sister two years older, and the
paternal grandmother who lived with them. The boy Thomas
always seemed strange, had an unusually large head and a condition which caused one eye to seem to light up with excitement
more than the other. He was a dull-appearing, sullen child, given
to violent tempers and infantile depressions. In his sixth year he
was dismissed from school as too dull, after a few months' trial.
The school, interestingly, was the one in which his father had been
master. The character of the father is not definitively known:
teacher and singer in the church choir, he was said by some to be
honest and worthy, but there are also reports of extreme violence
and half-concealed dissipations.

2 St. Francis of Assisi was born Giovanni Bernardone in Assisi in 1182 and died
there in October, 1226. Thomas Chatterton was born in Bristol, England in 1752
and died in London in 1770. Gogol was born in a Ukrainian village in 1808 and
died in Moscow in 1852. Henry M. Stanley was born John Rowlands in Denbigh,
Wales, probably in 1840 or 1841 and died in London in May, 1904. Rainer Maria
Rilke was born René Maria Rilke in Prague in December, 1875 and died in
Switzerland in December, 1926.

A few weeks after his dismissal from school, a miracle happened to Thomas: the little boy fell in love (these were the mother's words) with the Gothic script in a songbook which lay about the house and about which his mother had remarked that it belonged to his father. The infatuation continued into a sustained love affair in which the child learned the letters, then the words and was presently reading, in a way that showed extreme precocity and absorption. Some ten years later another observer caught him in another love affair, this time with the Church of St. Mary Redcliffe. Of him it was said, "He was fond of walking in the fields, particularly the Redcliffe meadows, and of talking of his manuscripts and sometimes reading them there. There was one spot in particular in full in view of the Church in which he seemed to take peculiar delight. He would lay himself down, fix his eyes upon the Church and seem as if he were in a kind of trance. Then of a sudden he would tell me, 'That steeple was burnt down by lightning: that was the place where they formerly acted plays' " (Masson, 1856). This imaginary cosmic primal scene furnishes much for an understanding of the preoccupation and the disaster of Thomas Chatterton.

The little boy had a weird sense of his own power and greatness and made bizarre suggestions regarding the illustriousness of his future. A further attempt at school, in an endowed boarding school formerly attended by his father, lasted several years, but seemed sterile and disappointing. By ten years he was writing verse, and soon he had a poem published, entitled "On the Last Epiphany or Christ's Coming to Judgment." Again he lampooned the churchwarden who proposed to level the churchyard and cart off excess earth and clay—a desecration in the eyes of the infatuated child. At fourteen he was writing to the local pewterer, telling of old manuscripts he had located which gave evidence of the noble ancestry of this gentleman, the pedigree dating back to the time of the Norman Conquest. And soon he unearthed a number of poems dating back to the fifteenth century, written by a monk Rowley, who was part of a group around the great Canynge, fifteenth-century Mayor of Bristol and donor of funds for the Cathedral of St. Mary Redcliffe.

The connecting links between these events and his inspiration by the Gothic letters in the old songbook of his father at the age of five is a fantastic contribution to the understanding of genius. Some years before the birth of Thomas Chatterton, his father's brother, John, sexton of St. Mary's, had been present at the opening of some old coffers used as storage places for old documents of the church. One of these reputedly contained valuable papers concerning Mr. William Canynge, five times Mayor of the city in the fifteenth century. The others were full of unimportant records to be cleaned out and disposed of. Sexton John took some of these home with him and gave some to his brother, the schoolteacher, who used the old parchments to cover schoolbooks for the children. Some of this was still on hand, and Thomas's mother used bits of it on which to wind her thread.

The little boy's love affair seemed now to have extended itself from the songbook to the church and the parchments. It seems probable that his fantasies carried him back, in his own genealogy, in the fashion similar to what he had offered the pewterer. Gradually he constructed a group of men whom he asserted were contemporaries of Canynge and brought them to life in his imagination with extraordinary vividness. It seems possible that this was going on during the period of his prodigious reading when he was attending the unsatisfying school. Now he was in an equally unsatisfying position—after the age of fifteen—apprenticed as a scrivener to a local attorney where his hours were rigid and his work light, so that he had ample time for thoughts and pursuits of his own. The medieval manuscripts which emerged, many of which contained poems by the monk Rowley, were welcomed by the local surgeon Barrett, who was writing a history of the city. Chatterton also repudiated orthodox religion, drew up his own articles of faith which he carried always with him, and became an adolescent freethinker.

Presently seeking wider fields he sent a manuscript by this Thomas Rowley, concerning the "Ryse of Peyncteyne in Englande," to Horace Walpole and received an encouraging and cordial reply. But with naïve lack of shrewdness, he presently sent a supplement along with a description of his own situation, and a hint that he needed help. By now he was seventeen years old and dreaming of establishing himself as a writer in London. Walpole's suspicions were now aroused and presently confirmed by those to whom he sent the manuscripts—that they were a hoax and a forgery. He wrote in this vein to Chatterton and in his reaction to having been almost taken in by a charlatan, he paid little heed to the poems themselves. Chatterton was at first apologetic, gradually worked himself into a grievance, furthered by Walpole's dilatoriness in returning the manuscripts, and soon was assuming a somewhat boastful, arrogantly defensive attitude, which covered inadequately his moods of depression with suicidal threats. These probably caused him to be dismissed from his position.

He next set out for London, with scant financial backing and exaggeratedly optimistic expectations of trying his hand in political writing. It was obvious that he expected much from obtaining an interview with the Mayor of London, who may have been a present-day version, in his feeling, of the good father Canynge of Bristol. Things went from bad to worse; his employment was scant and irregular, and the sudden death of the Mayor almost on the eve of the interview was a final blow. He seemed gradually to disintegrate. It was only four months after his arrival in London that his death from arsenic poisoning occurred in August, 1770. Samuel Johnson and Oliver Goldsmith, back in London after a summer away, saw an elegy published in his memory in a journal to which he had been an occasional contributor, obtained the Rowley manuscripts, and saw that the writing was that of a genius. Most interesting, however, is the fact that the Rowley poems were infinitely superior to anything which he wrote in his own name. One suspects that in the character of Thomas Rowley, the priest, Thomas Chatterton lived.

Stanley

The Autobiography of Sir Henry Morton Stanley (1909) is an impressive document in the sense of restraint, of personal dignity, of the apparent wish to be accurate in a factual way, in spite of the abuse and ridicule which he had suffered. It is a massive volume and gives an impression of granite texture. He is undoubtedly not wholly accurate in his presentation of himself as a human being and it may represent rather his image of himself as a historical figure—actually symbolically represented after his death in a huge natural monolith marking his grave. A recent biography, *Dr. Livingstone, I Presume* (1957), written by an Englishman, Ian Anstruther, forms an interesting contrast to the autobiography, as it illustrates well the varyingly slanted selection of material and the indelible imprint of the writer. The author plays down the importance in the life of Stanley of the search for Livingstone, saying that most biographers make no more than a passing mention of it. The title itself is chosen as an illustration of the banality of the Victorian era—a banality forever associated embarrassingly with Stanley. It casts a bright light on many of the events of life which Stanley had himself deleted or trimmed down, in his official version which he had himself come to believe. Stanley suffered in some measure from the need for a personal myth, of which Ernst Kris wrote so recently (1956). Anstruther seems to have as little understanding of Stanley's poignant story and less of the real genius of the man than Stanley himself had. He presents Stanley as an American whose harsh voice and pronunciation grated badly on English ears, while his lack of humor and resiliency, his pomposity and gaucherie always made him slightly ridiculous to any well-educated Englishman. That he happened to have been born in Wales, and to have spent the first fifteen or seventeen years of his life in the British Isles is also described by this author; but still by the time he was thirty and found Livingstone (1871), he was indubitably an American in the eyes of the English public. It is probable that consciously and for unconscious reasons he promoted this idea and suffered from it. Incidentally I was first interested in reading more carefully concerning Stanley when I read a brief, not very reliable account which presented him as the proverbial shepherd boy, ultimately rescued by a patron who established him.

John Rowlands, the future Henry Stanley, was born in February, 1841. The father died a few weeks after the birth of his son and before he had gotten around to marrying the mother. The child, however, bore the father's name. The mother promptly left the child in the care of her father, a man in his early eighties, with whom John lived until six years. The grandfather was a stern, reliable, and respected man and may have contributed something to the tenacity of the small boy, who never knew either of his parents and can hardly have had a very favorable picture of them. He next spent some months, perhaps a year or more, being boarded with an elderly couple, where he was filled with stories of ghosts and devils. Then under the pretext of taking him to his

Aunt Mary's, he was actually deposited in the local workhouse "which housed poor people and superfluous children." This was a nightmarish place, in the charge of a teacher, an ex-miner whose chief qualification to teach was that he could no longer be a miner because of the loss of a leg. He was a chronically enraged man who later became psychotic. Here the boy remained until after ten years he could no longer stand it, and thrashing the headmaster and fearing at first he had committed murder, he lit out in search for his own family and a home. In spite of his unhappiness young Rowlands had succeeded in gaining recognition as the outstanding student in the school, but perhaps because of the very content of the conflict, he was unable to accept the outward signs of this, for when he was selected to represent the school at a National Welsh Festival, he promptly fell ill. The same thing happened forty years later when he was scheduled to speak at such a gathering; this time he broke his leg at the eleventh hour.

The period at the poor farm had several significant crises. At twelve to thirteen one of the boys died, with the suspicion that he had been flogged to death by the headmaster. John Rowlands, recovering from an illness in which he was semidelirious, had fears of ghosts and devils, reminiscent of the period of his grandfather's death (which according to his memory had occurred after the grandfather, enraged at some apparent vandalism of the five-year-old boy, had threatened to punish him). The boy fortified himself with an intense friendship with another boy, at the same time constructing an image of a Personal Guardian Angel, who represented God and protected him. In this same era (at the age of twelve), his mother visited the poor farm, not so much to visit him as to deposit another child, a half-sister, there. There was still another child, a boy, who accompanied her, but whom she took back with her. All three children were illegitimate. She was probably a habitually delinquent woman, though coming from a rather sturdy background of farmers. Although the sister remained at the school, John Rowlands apparently saw little of her.

It is interesting that by the time he left the poor farm, the critical pattern of life seemed well set for this boy. At the turning point of each epoch in his life, the oedipal crime seemed reenacted and initiated a new period of wandering in search of the good, protective, forgiving father—the God-father, the patron. In the weeks that followed his leaving the workhouse school, he did find some temporary protection at Aunt Mary's, the same to whom he supposedly was going when he left his grandfather's home. And at this time he did actually work as a shepherd boy for some little time. But he did not find his patron for some months and many misfortunes later.

After several other attempts to gain an independent footing he shipped as a cabin boy on a boat going to New Orleans. But life aboard ship was so cruel and uncertain that he jumped ship in this new world rather than return to the mistreatments aboard the vessel. Here the frightened and unworldly boy had his first experience with a prostitute and around the same time discovered to his wonder and dismay that the sailor boy with whom he shared a bed in a sailors' rooming house had bumps on his chest and was really a transvestite girl. Presently, looking for a job to give him food and pocket money, he sought out a commission house which had advertised for help, and advancing on the middle-aged gentleman sitting near the door asked: "Do you want a boy, sir?" This was the forerunner of "Dr. Livingstone, I Presume," which was later to impress the British with its awkward banality. But here it was different—the gentleman was Henry M. Stanley, who apparently was very much in need of a boy. Stanley was a former clergyman, turned broker, looking to trade and commerce to develop the lower Mississippi Valley, where organized religion had failed. Mr. Stanley evidently did want a boy, employed this one, spent much time training him in a kind of apprentice relationship, and finally adopted him and gave him his name. This followed a period when Mrs. Stanley was ill and died during an epidemic while Stanley was away in Cuba, and young John Rowlands had done what he could to help and comfort her. The account in Stanley's *Autobiography* would indicate that the boy went through some sort of rebirth at this time in which he relinquished the personal paternal God on whom he had depended, and gave the place more satisfactorily to the earthly Stanley. One sees in this account an indication of real growth, a development from an anal-phallic emphasis on people as tangible possession to an awareness of an object love with personal ideals and desired positive influences—to resemble rather than to mimic, an art in which he had shown some talent. It was a period of temper outbursts without the expected punishments. Father and son explored the Mississippi Valley in a way which was a strange precursor of the Congo and the Nile explorations, which were to follow in a few years. Then a temporary separation, due to the elder Stanley's obligation to go to his brother in Cuba, proved permanent, for Stanley Sr. died only a few weeks before his expected return.

In the meantime this twice-orphaned Welsh boy, now named Henry Stanley, had become as fascinated as a Hudson with the wild forest country, and his writing of this time, though clumsy, showed a poetic responsiveness to the new country where he found himself. The next years, from twenty to twenty-seven saw him drawn into the Civil War, fighting first for one side and then on the other, in a way which showed a complete confusion of loyalties and values, which was certainly also involved with his struggle to maintain his new identity as Henry M. Stanley, son of a worthy Southern gentleman. That his deepest sympathy was with the black man there can be little doubt, though expressed in faltering and sometimes ambivalent ways. At one time in this period he made his way back to the Welsh village of his birth, obviously with the fantasy of presenting himself to a welcoming mother. If he had sought a father for a reinforcement of his masculinity, the complete bisexuality of his nature is apparent in his Journals of this time; for he sought his mother for help in his depleted feminine state. In November, 1862 he wrote: "Like a bride arraying herself in her best for her lover, I had arranged my story to please one who would at last, I hoped, prove an affectionate mother! But I found no affection and I never again sought for or expected what I discovered had never existed."

The years immediately after the Civil War were spent exploring the West, where he acted as a reporter for various news publications. By 1868 his reputation as an intrepid and colorful reporter brought him contact with the powerful and garishly inventive James Gordon Bennett of *The New York Herald,* who commissioned him to report on the Abyssinian Campaign, then on the building of the Suez Canal, and finally sent him on the mission to find Dr. Livingstone, the Scotch missionary doctor explorer who seemed lost or overlooked by the British in the heart of Africa. That this was less an act of science or of mercy than a news coup is apparent. Yet to Stanley this man was inevitably a reincarnation of the God-father, a superior version even of Henry M. Stanley, Sr., whom he had known so briefly in his teens. He was only twenty-seven when he started on this mission and thirty when he accomplished it. Again he was to greet this father, stay with him briefly, and part from him forever. One suspects that the grandfather, Moses Parry, was the original God-father, and that in the mission to find Livingstone, there was an unconscious Savior quality which was to undo the deaths of father, grandfather, and foster father. The tragedy was that he had again to abandon and in a sense to be abandoned by the old man who elected to stay in Africa where he died less than a year later.

The mission to Africa also served for a reworking of his attitude toward slavery. Stanley knew well what it was like to be in the servile position of an outcast. He was a hardened man with a violent temper, curbed but frightening; and he believed thoroughly in thrashing helpers whom he could not control otherwise. But he had great reverence for Livingstone's gentler methods. All of this was played out in another version of his family romance, in his adoption of a native African boy, Kalulu, whom he attempted to educate in England, and later took on further explorations in Africa. On one occasion after the boy had deserted, he was whipped by Stanley's orders. Not long after this he was drowned when his canoe failed "to make" the falls. Stanley's grief was extreme. He subsequently wrote a fictional account of the boy entitled *My Kalulu, Prince, King, and Slave* (1874). He explained that the book was intended to describe the evils of the slave trade in Africa.

Stanley was a man of small stature, a fact which one would hardly learn from his *Autobiography*. He was sensitive, vain, and hungry for recognition and applause, which he had been led to expect would come to him after his successful finding of Livingstone. The Livingstone expedition was a complex affair, since the British had sent out a rival expedition on hearing of Stanley's efforts, and they were, to say the least, begrudgingly cautious in their attitude toward him; and he was not only ridiculed for his banal greeting of Livingstone, but he was denied recognition and considered an impostor by the British Geographical Society, one of whose recent presidents was Sir Francis Galton. When he returned to England no one was there to greet him except one or two of his now unwelcome relatives from Wales. He became bitter and withdrawn, nor was this really much relieved by belated English apologies, or by a raucous American reception when he came to this country. Ultimately he was to return to England and to head the work of exploring and developing the region of the Congo—an international project resulting in the founding of the Congo Free State. Again England became his home, but he was really identified with Africa, of which he wrote, "It is like looking at the face of a promising child: though we find naught in it but innocence, we fondly imagine that we see the germs of a future genius, perhaps a legislator, a savant, a warrior, or a poet."

Stanley died in 1904—Sir Henry Stanley, a man of renown throughout the world. He had been an unhappy member of Parliament where he suffered a kind of claustrophobia and felt a degradation in being one of a number herded around like a flock of sheep. He married late. His only child, a son, was born in 1896. He wrote to his wife then, "Denzel is now inseparable from you— and you from him. Together you complete the once vague figure of what I wished; and now the secret of my utmost thoughts is realized, a pre-natal vision, embodied in actual existence."

Gogol

Both Gogol and Rilke were the sons of extremely devoted, solicitous mothers, probably warm but fantastically exaggerated in their adoration, while the fathers were sterner, older, and sought to masculinize their sons with discipline. Neither father inspired the son greatly or aroused any desire for emulation, though Gogol's father was a raconteur and a writer of plays for amateur theatricals and may have influenced his son somewhat. Gogol's mother was fourteen when she married and only eighteen when Nikolai was born. Two children born before him had died soon after birth, and his survival, which for a time seemed precarious, was attributed by his mother to her prayers to Saint Nicholas for whom the child was named. There were twelve children, only five of whom survived. One of these, a brother, Ivan, died when Nikolai was ten. The effect on this sensitive boy of almost endless succession of deaths of siblings has never been especially noted by his biographers, and the fact that he himself did not mention it is certainly no indication that it was not powerful, and may have been one factor in promoting his aversion to marriage. His mother was a naïve, silly, and improvident woman (Magarschak, 1957), who believed that God worked always for her good no matter through what channels, and bored or amazed her friends by her similar faith in her son, maintaining "that railway engines, steamers and what not had been invented by her Nikolai" and drove her son to the limits of irritation by her coyly suggesting that he was the author of any trashy novel that came her way (Nabokov, 1947). The father died when the boy was sixteen, and within a few days he was writing to his mother of his intentions to become a writer. One biographer, Lavin (1951), remarked that Maria Gogol used her son as a fetish.

Within three years he was making efforts to get away from her and fled from his Ukrainian homeland to St. Petersburg, and in a few months, disappointed at the failure to win acclaim immediately, he was moving on further. Embezzling a sum of money sent him by his mother for another purpose, he wrote her that he must travel because of a chest ailment. (He had been a delicate and scrofulous chlid and always remained hypochondriacal.) Soon forgetting this, however, he wrote her again, now giving the story of a *femme fatale* whom he had a compulsion to follow wherever she went (Lavin, 1951). He also wrote sententiously of his awareness of God and his need to work for the welfare of the world (Nabokov, 1947). These letters, callow, pompous, insincere sounding, might incline one to think of their author as a prankish schoolboy outwitting his mother and exploiting her gullibility by writing to her this sort of exaggerated unreliable statement that he was used to getting from her. Yet from the further course of his life, in which he seemed never to form a sexual or deep emotional relationship to any women, it seems that the maneuvers of this period were an oedipally determined flight from his mother and led to an overt outcropping of the family romance. Communion with God and his Muse and a real sense of compelling destiny were embedded in the flamboyant symptoms of his individual and severely neurotic character. Certainly his sense of obligation to do something for the welfare of mankind, expressed early, was later praised by the serious-minded and his *The Inspector General, Dead Souls,* and *The Overcoat* were considered documents of social protest against the Russian bureaucracy. It has been suggested, however, that

Gogol had no conscious aim of campaigning for reform, but rather that he wrote with comic tenderness and touching absurdity of all the little men's aspirations in a "world of utter futility [in which] the highest degree that passion, desire and creative urge can attain is the new cloak which both tailors and customers adore on their knees" (Lavin, 1951). That he was pursued by his oedipal fears and ambitions was apparent at the end of his life when he felt sure he would die because he was at the age at which his father had died. He had returned in torment to the kind of super-stition-invested God with whom his mother had been on such intimate terms and whom for years he had abandoned and ridiculed.

Gogol was himself a little man, in stature almost a dwarf. His face was dominated by an enormous beak of a nose which also was the source of the greatest sensual pleasure (Magarschak, 1957), as he wrote in one of his letters.[3] And in one of his stories a nose got loose from its owner, a certain military man, who then met it walking on the street in a military uniform. This was considered a satire directed against officialdom. It is interesting, too, that liter-ary censorship would not permit the detached nose to visit Kazan Cathedral as Gogol would have it, so that he had to relegate it to a shopping trip instead (Magarschak, 1957). One can understand in this nose story, however, the depth of Gogol's fears and fantasies and his inability to have any physical relationship with a woman.

At twenty-two his literary success had begun with the publica-tion of a collection of Ukrainian ghost stories. He met Pushkin, who, ten years older and established as a writer, served somewhat as a patron to the younger man. This friendship had already be-come attenuated at the time of Pushkin's death in 1837. But this coincided with the beginning of a critical time for Gogol. Then living in Paris, he apparently was now passionately attached to a former schoolmate, and following the death of his friend's mother (June, 1838) he broke out into a violent assertion of his claims. The friend was unresponsive and furthermore seemed to have

[3] He wrote in April, 1838 from Rome, "What air! When you breathe it, it is just as though seven hundred angels flew into your nose. A wonderful spring! The whole of Rome is covered with roses, but sweeter still is the scent of the flowers which have just begun to bloom and whose name I have forgotten. . . . I know you won't believe me, but I am often overcome by a mad desire to be turned into one enormous nose—to have nothing else, no eyes, no hands, no feet, except one huge nose with nostrils the size of large buckets so that I could inhale as much fragrance of spring as possible."

turned in the direction of a woman. Gogol begged his friend's walking stick as a memento of their past love (Magarschak, 1957). He is said at sixteen to have responded to the death of his father with a euphoria (Ermakov, 1924[4]), and with a sense of liberation. Pushkin's death and the defection of his friend seemed to begin a period of disastrous confusion involving a sense of personal contact with a supervising God as well as the identification with the collective God-force of the creative artist.

There was a period of frantic flight from place to place during which he wrote several of his best satires,[5] but this was followed by a long period of restless movement without literary production and with a gradual increase in his paranoid sensitivity,[6] and in his personal religiosity, culminating in his conversion to Catholicism under the tutelage of a vigorously exorcising priest, who admonished him (1852): "Renounce Pushkin. He was a sinner and a Pagan." After a period of self-starvation, he burned his manuscripts, including the second and third parts of *Dead Souls,* and on March 4, 1852, he died at the age of forty-three.

Rilke

A recent biography of Rilke by W. L. Graff (1956) presents a valuable study of the Czech poet. He was a premature baby, born with proverbial distinction just at midnight on December 4, 1875 in the city of Prague. Both parents wanted a girl, and since December 4, Saturday, was the day of the Holy Mary, he was given, among other names, that of Maria. His first name was René, which he bore until his young manhood, when with the supporting influence of Lou Andreas-Salomé, he changed it to Rainer. It was felt that René was too readily confused with Renée, and emphasized too much the wishes of the parents for a girl. Like Gogol's mother, Phia Rilke was an immature buoyantly imaginative woman given to excesses of play-acting the grand lady, in some fantasied continuation of her own girlhood, which had been spent in the comfort and distinction of a well-to-do home. But as the wife of a railway employee, living in cramped, drab quarters, she still managed an occasional great party. At such times the child, René, had to give

---

4 I am indebted to Dr. Alexander Bromley for translating this work.
5 Between 1838-1839 he wrote *Dead Souls,* followed by *Overcoat.*
6 This has recently been dealt with by Mark Kanzer (1955).

up his sleeping quarters to add to the sweep of the party rooms and was secreted in his crib behind a large embroidered screen, on the other side of which the party continued. Whether or not this was actually true or only a primal scene screen memory is difficult to determine. Phobically anxious and oversolicitous, she rationed nearly everything he did. He is reported to have had twenty-four nurses during his first year. Yet she is supposed to have shown genuine warmth and devotion, though Rilke himself did not think so. He was dressed and played with as a girl until his fifth year. At this time he presented himself as of two characters, Ismene, the good little girl, and René, the good-for-nothing boy.

While Gogol was described as being his mother's fetish, Rilke is said to have become his mother's glamorous show child. The mother showed a colorful religiosity too, perhaps greater even than that of Maria Gogol, in which she immersed the small child.

The father bore some resemblance to Gogol's father, too. Brought up in the expectation of becoming an army officer, he could not realize this because of ill health and was reduced to the position of a civil clerk in railway offices. For a time he attempted to escape by becoming the manager of a country estate, but failed in this venture. He had a strong sense of social decorum and bore himself in a military fashion even in civilian life. He was devoted to his son, wished him to develop as a boy, and attempted to instill in him a wish for virile exercise and military training. Already by the age of ten to twelve, however, the boy's independent genius had begun to show itself, he had begun to write poetry and to paint pictures. These latter are described as of two types, those emphasizing space and movement and caricatures.

He too had a rather unhappy adolescence in a military school, which his father recommended and his mother railed against, the two having been divorced when Rilke was nine. An open identification with Christ appeared in his letters. When unable to stand up to the fighting of the other cadets, he wrote, "I suffer it because Christ suffered it, silently and without complaint, and while you were hitting me I prayed my good God to forgive you," although at other times he daydreamed of becoming a great military leader. He left military school under a cloud because of "an affair of morals" and reacted with a mild elation—which reminds us again of Gogol's elation following his father's death at about the same time. Following this, however, he made an attempt again to comply with family wishes and enter the University to study law, but this, too, petered out, possibly forced out by his stronger compulsion to be a poet, even at the expense of chronic estrangement from his parents and other relatives. Insistently rebellious against bourgeois life and values, he also maintained then and later that he was of noble descent.

He had already begun to write poetry in the military school days and even earlier, and he was progressively preoccupied with his relation to God, not at all in the phobic and compulsive sense of the religiosity of his silly mother, nor seemingly with a feeling toward a stern commanding paternal God, but with his own direct relationship to the cosmos, drawn over and over again into personal and sensual forms. At the outset of his career he was tempted to try for personal applause, but abandoning this quickly, wrote that he would rather "be endured by God than idolized by the mob." In a poem written at thirty-two on Capri, he wonders whether the rush of blood to his ears has suddenly become louder or whether he actually hears the voices of the cloistered nuns in the latticed choir of the church nearby. A single voice detaches itself, "A pale, a light, a small voice clinging to God's ear like the hollow of a shell." At forty-five or so, while staying at the Castle of Bergam Irchel in Switzerland, he wrote a number of poems, supposedly dictated to him by a fictitious ancestor of the Estate, Count C.W., in which many childhood memories appear.

There is evident a constant vibration and need for harmony between an inner sensual reality (based, I believe, on the internalized collective alternate experiences of infancy) and the ever-changing new experiences with similar aurae. These may be condensed incompletely, intensely and usually unsatisfactorily in various personal relationships, but come to full expression only in his poetry. Graff defines this well when he says, "It is in this layer of inner sensual reality, not in any abstract ideal world, that we must eventually look for Rilke's angel of the *Elegies*, for the maidens and women of his poems, for his Prodigal Son, for his *Weltinnenraum* (Inner Cosmic Space), and last but not least, for his longed-for childhood." Throughout all his writing there is, in various forms, an insistent identification with the family of God. Perhaps the strongly feminine part of his nature was expressed in his preoccupation with growth, with slow creative change, transition from day to night and night to day, changes of the seasons, development from infancy to childhood and finally to maturity. But the demon of work which possessed him always may have been more masculine in form, and at times was given angelic form. Rilke's own expression in regard to God was: "O mere direction of the heart, an unfinished, a future God, for the creation and realization of whom the artist has a special mission."

It is a temptation to continue further, but for the purposes of this paper it is probably better to sacrifice this in the interest of further clinical example. I would turn then next to another creative man of extremely different background and experiences.

St. Francis of Assisi

It is said that there is no saint about whom more has been written than St. Francis of Assisi,[7] partly because the Franciscans are the most widespread institution in the Church; yet it is not only the Catholics who write of him (Sabatier, 1908). The *Poverello* has the appeal of a universal poetic myth. He is the Stigmatized Saint, the most perfect imitation of Jesus.[8]

The child of Pietro and Madonna Pica Bernardone was born in Assisi in 1181 or 1182, while his father, a prosperous and energetic cloth merchant, was away in France. He was first called Giovanni. There is a pretty story that when the father returned home and unpacked his cloth, he named the boy Francis in memory of the land where he had so recently been—which also meant the land of his wife. It is remarked that the father had probably had a prosperous trip and struck good bargains, but it is also said that Pica was of Provencal origin and possibly of noble birth (Mrs. Oliphant, 1907), in which the good bargain could mean his marriage as well, which had brought him this son. It is not clear whether he was the oldest child, but it seems likely. Some accounts refer to two brothers as though they were younger.

---

[7] See Tamassia (1905), Chesterton (1923), Mrs. Oliphant (1907), Sabatier (1908), Engelbert (1950), Jörgensen (1912).

[8] It was a picture of St. Francis receiving the stigmata painted by Fra Angelico which first fascinated me, at a time when I had become vaguely interested in the relation of art to fetishism. The composition of the picture, together with its content, was so directly an expression of the forces of fetishism, that I thought again that the miraculous charm of religion must have some relation to the function of art and the more mundane service of the fetish in the less gifted individual.

Of his youth it is reported that he was carefree and extravagant and aped the young nobles of the town with whom he associated. His earliest biographer, Thomas of Celano, described him as being given to the vilest excesses. But this may be a feat of ecclesiastical bookkeeping, for Thomas of Celano was an official biographer and such an account increases the value of his subsequent redemption. Another story is that, in spite of merriment, dandyism, and prankishness, he was "a model in all that related to the opposite sex" (Jörgensen, 1947); and that like "all the pure of heart, Francis had great reverence for the mysteries of life." Either side of the coin is quite possible and he has become so long established as a myth that it would be impossible to say which of these opposites was predominantly true. He is described even during his golden gay days as phobic, fearful of disease, especially of bad odors, and inordinately afraid of hurting anyone by violence. In contrast to his father, he was both self-indulgent and impulsively generous; and spontaneous and vivid in his response to the natural beauties of the countryside.

At about nineteen to twenty he was imprisoned for a few months during an outbreak of war between Assisi and the neighboring town of Perugia. Here he was classed with the local nobility, and seemed to have quite a jolly time. At twenty-three, following a dream in which the cloth of his father's business was replaced by spears, he decided to participate in another war to the south of Assisi, and started out with dreams of glory and avowed intentions of returning as a conquering prince. But he fell sick only a few miles from Assisi, and gave up the enterprise before it was fairly begun. Whether from shame or illness, his high spirits were reduced and he entered a period of indecision and uneasiness, finally relieved by his miraculous conversion, which occurred gradually and amid much difficulty. He forced himself to overcome his fear of illness and took especial care of the lepers. He attempted under direct guidance to rebuild the crumbling church of San Domiano, and for this purpose stole the goods from his father's shop, during the father's absence, and sold it in the market place, giving to the priest this money to be used in the restoration. In return he was permitted to live in the church and began his religious life.

The rest of the story of his conflict with his father sounds not so unlike clinical accounts of many a young man's acute illness, in the special struggle between father and son. In this, the father returned, received the ill-gotten money back from the priest; had the young man seized and shut up in a cellar to cool down and recover his senses. The father then went on another business trip and the devoted and indulgent mother liberated her son and provided him with money. The father next sued to banish his son and recover the money. The lawyers withdrew from the case, perhaps when they found that the young man had already received the lower order of the Church, and the quarrel between father and son was then pursued by the representatives of the Church. Reacting to the reproaches from his father who said he had given his son the only clothes and money which Francis possessed, the young man tore off his clothes, returned them defiantly to his father whom he disowned: "I shall not say 'Father Pietro di Bernardone, but Our Father who art in Heaven.' " The sympathy of the crowd turned in Francis's direction, and his life as an apostle and Evangelist began. As one reads further the account of the teachings of Francis, the spectacular growth of the order, the self-denial so rigidly and absolutely applied, it impresses one as the ultimate in a control of rage.

But although Francis was seemingly fearful of women, two were so bold as to enter his life: Clara Seifi, daughter of the most prominent family of Assisi, and Jacoba de Settisoli, the widow of a Roman nobleman. Jacoba was a woman of manly character, for which he named her "Brother Jacoba." Clara Seifi was sixteen when she fell in love with him and his preaching, thereby escaping a marriage which had been planned for her. She became the founder of the order of St. Clare. It was the manly Jacoba who cared for him when he visited Rome and nursed him when he was sick. In return he gave her a present of a lamb, which may have been the prototype of the lamb of Mary in the nursery rhyme, for it followed her to Church, slept while she prayed, and called her to awake and attend to her devotions by butting her with its horns and bleating in her ear (Tasmassia, 1905).

III

These case histories are samples taken from a large number of biographies and autobiographies read in the course of trying to study other problems of the character of the artist. All of these show, in dramatic overdetermination, the outlines of the family romance. In three, Chatterton, Stanley, and Gogol, the circumstances of birth already contributed to the sense of specialness, and added to the coloring of the story, thus giving in fact what tradition demands in any case.

There are conditions further which make the family romance more durable in an almost obligatory way in the life of the artist. If the tentative formulation of my earlier paper is correct—that in the artist exist certain inborn qualities of greater sensory responsiveness, greater capacity to organize sensory impressions into related engrams with special sensitivity to rhythm and form—then personal relationships in the gifted individual may also have a heightened intensity; further, an extension of empathy may occur with animation of related inanimate peripheral objects. It is this widened area of responsiveness, with the inclusion of peripheral highlighted objects that I have referred to as the field of the collective alternates. The effect of this would be to promote preconscious development and diminish the boundaries between libidinal phases. Naturally, the oedipal phase would thus also be prematurely developed with an increase in intensity, but with a diminished probability of its achieving even the ordinary degree of relinquishment of oedipal strivings, since these can instead remain attached as well to the collective alternate objects of the outer world. Further, the heightened sensitivity to bodily sensations and rhythms, as well as to the outer world, causes a continual searching for a harmony of balance between the two. States of imbalance may then be played out in disturbance of body sensations (hypochondria) as well as in disturbances of perception of the outer world and of emotional relationships to other human beings.

The tendency to ambivalence and the splitting of images into good and bad parts proceeds not only from the unresolved oedipal complex but from the heightened capacity for ambivalence of the anal phase, and especially from masturbatory fantasies associated with strong phallic pressures. These disturbances are not so much regressive in character as in a neurosis, but arise more from an unusual degree of fusion of phase pressures, with shifts of emphasis from one instinctual drive to another, and often with the coalescence of certain part reactions from different phase drives reinforcing each other.

Another source of the disturbance of family identification as seen in the family romance appears in the latency period, still under unusual sway of oedipal fantasies. This is the sense of difference which the child then feels when confronted by the social group. Whether unusual precocity has developed or the reverse picture of blocking and pseudostupidity is uppermost, in either case the child of great potential creativeness often feels different and strange among his colleagues, and at a time when, as in adolescence, there is a strong wish to conform, the family romance furnishes a further rationalization for this sense of difference and is reinforced by it.

The ambivalence of the anal phase and its association with masturbatory fantasies are especially important. Not only is the stool valued so predominantly as good and bad, but there is concomitantly a sense of heightened and mysterious sensation in the phallus. And the smell derived from the stool lends itself further to growing concepts of air movement, flying, communion and communication without touch, an increasing sense of life and death, of thought and spirit, i.e., a nontangible representation of the self and others. Even in the not especially gifted child this is a period of great vitalization. In the potentially creative one this sense of phallic pressure begins earlier, but still reaches its height at the phallic age. From the few unusual creative patients I have known, I have thought that such children were erotized early and if subjected to extreme frustration, sickness or bad handling got readily into states of frenzied masturbation, sometimes of a compulsive sort. Whereas the "free" masturbation, i.e., of a noncompulsive type, was transitory and associated with feelings of well-being and positive feelings of power and capacity for inventiveness, the compulsive masturbation took the place of anger or rage. In the latter case the fantasies were colored by sadistic wishes, sometimes leading to feelings of destructive inventiveness of great proportions. Thus the compulsive perfection drive later derived from these is still a further masked sadism, which may be one of the main obstacles in loosening the full power of the creative drive. The other aspect of the wish for perfection is essentially a need for harmony as part of creativity. The attitude expressed in these two types of masturbatory fantasies may be reflected in the family romance.

Consideration of the God identification of the artist and of the shepherd boy story will close this paper. In all of the individuals studied here, some identification with God was prominent—experiences connected with deep religious feeling. In Chatterton and Stanley, there was the adoption of a concept of a God-father in the actual absence of the personal father, and this God-father had some worldly form in myth or in fact. In Gogol, the God-father was contaminated by the mother's conceptions passed on to the child, with subsequent attempts to discard or overcome them, but with a final self-destructive submission.

But the inner side of these stories is not so vivid or so easily decipherable but basically more important; namely, the obligatory identification of the artist with God and Nature, or with Nature as God, through the force of the own body feelings which respond to and cause a kind of amalgamation of body imagery with outer forms in the world. The thrust of such body feelings usually reaches a first crescendo in the phallic-oedipal period, but it carries with it some influence from the whole gamut of the earlier development. This peak of the thrust toward and incorporation of the world reappears in some special degree and forms in the later experience of inspiration. These can be dealt with more profitably in the consideration of the creative process. But it is important that the extraordinary strength of the body sensitivity and the pressure of developmental feelings are so much greater in the artist than in less gifted people, and may be more compelling to the individual than the actual personal experiences which reinforce and give secondary molding and content. It is very striking how many creative people describe memories of experiences of revelation, awe or some kind of transcendental states in childhood and how regularly this is placed at the age of four to five. But there is another component of religious feelings from early childhood which involves not so much of sharp ecstasy, in which fear gives some special intensity, but rather a sense of fusion with the outer world in a state of mutual permeability, sometimes described as an *oceanic feeling*. This latter state seems derived from re-aroused infantile experiences of nursing. A sense of special light-ness or airiness may pervade either of these subjective states producing an illusion of flying or of floating.

Now to return to the shepherd boy and his sheep: I do not believe that this figure is so limited to the traditional image of the Italian Renaissance artist as Kris's early paper (1935) suggested, although at that time with the special connection of art with the Christian Church, it was given an especially firm and generally accepted form. The same imagery of the shepherd boy becoming the great leader and influencer of men reappears time and again, somewhat molded and reshaped in the stories of the lives of great men. It is so often that of the lonely or isolated youth, with scant human contact, who turns to animals for companionship which supplements his world of dreams. But the shepherd boy with his sheep was for many centuries a singularly good symbolic picture. Anyone who has really seen the shepherd and his sheep realizes how physically filthy, isolated, and monotonous such a life must often be. The black side of the shepherd boy story is the develop-ment of bestiality and perversion. That it provides, however, a culture ground for the split between the sense of hopelessness and degradation and the fantasies involved in the hope for salvation is apparent. It is a parable of the anal-phallic period. The sheep (of which we recently heard that there are a fifth as many in the world as humans) and the proverbially docile animals, to be herded and led like a hypnotized mob; on the other hand, they have in ages past, more than any other domesticated animal, supplied man's essential needs to an extraordinary degree, with their wool, their flesh, and their skin. It is interesting too that the word "sheepskin" is still used as an idiom for a diploma, marking at-tainment, presumably, of ambition. But the sheep, in its softness, in its smelliness, in its pliable docility, i.e., a quality of dumb reliability, has possessed more fetishistic qualities than most other domestic animals. The fetish, it seems, has a peculiar significance in both religion and art.

Further, the child of potential genius is inevitably a lonely child, no matter how many people surround him. For he is a child who senses his own difference, feels isolated and inferior thereby: or, if he becomes aware of his gift, is still isolated, finding the greater sustenance in fantasy until his ability begins to be realized in some definite expression. I believe that this realization of ability is often of great relief to extremely talented people, not so much because of the narcissistic gratification of recognition and not because of realization of balance and harmony, but because of the temporary interruption of essential loneliness. But this sense of difference, whether it seems to be by special ability or is felt, as it must often be in childhood, as purely social inferiority, is probably a reinforcing factor to the development of the family romance.

CHAPTER TWENTY-SIX

The Relation of the Impostor
to the Artist (1958)

Many artists feel as though they were impostors, especially at the beginning of their careers. The possession of extraordinary gift is apparently not easily taken for granted. The performances of many impostors, especially of those seemingly dedicated ones, in whom the works of imposture form the main core of existence, impress others as having the quality of artistic achievement. The ability of the impostor to put on convincing acts of impersonation, including facsimilar reproductions of special skills (such as usually involve considerable preliminary training, knowledge, and practice), may seem to be almost miraculous and inspired. Indeed, the impostor may bring his latent fantasies into a vivid living form in the assumption of his impostured character so far surpassing in interest and apparent ability his ordinary "other self" that one is tempted to say that he is his own work of art.

The artist too is at least two people, the personal self and the collectively stimulated and responsively creative self. These two selves are sometimes nearly as separate as they are in the impostor —the division not infrequently recognized in the use of different names. Further, the character of the impostor seems especially to intrigue the artist, and the subjects of changing identities and the nature of imposture are ever-recurrent themes of myths, fairy tales, and of all literature. On his journey to the Hebrides, Samuel Johnson showed a ruthless fascination in visiting those remote

Highlanders who were the alleged sources of information to James Macpherson in his perpetration of the great hoax of the Ossian poetry. On the other hand, Johnson was happily impressed by another impostor, George Psalmanazar, who, presenting himself as a Japanese, invented a history, geography, alphabet and language for the Island of Formosa, and was so successful in his masquerade that his private name and facts of his own birth were never definitely known. Johnson admiringly said he would rather be Psalmanazar than anyone else he knew (see ch. 7). Goethe became so interested in the background of the impostor Count Cagliostro that he sought out the humble Sicilian family of the Count, visiting Palermo to do so; and while doing this, himself used a false name and false credentials (Brandeis, 1925), and made a pretense of bringing the mother a letter from her son. Later he sent money to the old mother of Cagliostro, thus making good the defaulted promise of the notorious "Count."

Fritz Kreisler, beginning at the age of eighteen, launched a series of at least somewhat impostorously announced compositions —a fact which he did not reveal directly until the occasion of his sixtieth birthday. According to his own account, under pressure of the need for usable concert material, he composed a number of pieces and attributed them to certain little known composers of the past—Vivaldi, Pugnani, Francoeur, Couperin, and others. To be sure, he listed himself as the editor of these original works and stated that in his editing there was a free treatment of the original; also that if these works were played in public, his name must be mentioned in the program! Yet it was not generally suspected that he was author, not editor. He made no effort actually to copy the work of those men whose names he took. "Everything was pure Kreisler," he admitted at sixty. When, on a few occasions, he was asked about these compositions, he either evaded the questions or gave the explanation that he had found the manuscripts in old libraries, an explanation very similar to that of Macpherson in regard to the Ossian poetry, or Thomas Chatterton's in regard to the poems of Rowley. At sixty, Kreisler recognized and stated that he had done this at a time when he was still uncertain what he wanted to do or be. He had already sampled training in medicine and in art, and had entered training for a military career as well. He did not wish to become known as a composer, and believed it would be unacceptably arrogant to have his name on the program as composer of several different pieces. Furthermore, it seems that he had not yet settled what identity he would assume or fully accepted his talent. He might have felt like an impostor to show himself in the full array of his ability; so he felt better when he hid behind the borrowed names of older men. It is the very typical story of an impostorous episode, but the untalented impostor (who is on the way to making a career of imposture) seemingly produces better work under the stimulus of the assumed name and character than he can under his own. This does not seem to have been true with Kreisler (Biancolli, 1951).

It is necessary to summarize briefly certain observations regarding the development of the impostor, which are presented in my paper on "The Impostor," since these form the basis of the comparative observations in the present paper. The material there contains observations from patients of my own who had had episodes of imposture of varying magnitude and severity in the course of their lives. In none was the imposture of major proportions. For reasons of discretion it is difficult to give very full case histories of these analytic cases. The detailed study of these cases, however, was supplemented by the study of several cases of famous impostors of the past.

There are many different forms and degrees of imposture, a fact especially emphasized by Helene Deutsch (1955). It is frequently related to and associated with other forms of swindling, forgery, counterfeiting, the assertion of divine or miraculous power; and in the past, the gift of alchemy and of divining the presence of buried treasure.

Count Cagliostro, whose name will always be associated with the affair of the diamond necklace at the time of the French Revolution,[1] was probably the son of a poor Sicilian widow named Balsamo. His impostorous career began in his adolescence when he left the Brotherhood of Misericordia after learning a smattering of pharmacy and launched on a period of alchemy and quest for buried treasure. In the course of this he organized "magical" demoniac robberies, the description of which suggests Ku Klux Klan

---

[1] Cagliostro was not directly involved in this, although he was the main figure in a court of tawdrily glamorous scoundrels of the French Court, and in a sense was the most inspired one. See Frinck-Brentano (1902).

activities. Next in Rome he became a copyist of drawings and
etchings of old masters, a forger of old documents, and obtained
some protection from the church. He married a beautiful young
woman who became his companion, ally, and stooge in all his later
activities. Proceeding northward, picking up money by forging
legal documents, the couple became again migrant pilgrims so-
liciting and distributing alms in Robin Hood fashion. (This period
is described by both Goethe and Casanova.)

In London about 1772, their abilities took a new turn with the
practice of the badger game, reputedly the more spectacular since
it was carried out in a group of Quakers by whom they were be-
friended. It was during this period that there was the first assumption of a noble title, that of Marquis of Balsamo (thus probably
indicating a continued attachment to the name of the impostor's
birth). Only a few years later (1775) he took the title of Marquis
Pellegrino, in this also retaining some connection with the past
since he met his young wife on Pellegrini Street during his first
period in Rome. This title was later supplanted by Count Cagliostro, which he then retained throughout his life.[2]

As Cagliostro he became successively astrologer in London; a
swindler in Russia and Poland; a drug-dispensing prophet in
Strasbourg; a physician with miraculous cures in Bordeaux; and
finally in Lyons (1784) began his career as the founder of the
Egyptian Masonic Lodges. The career of this one arch impostor
includes many of the accessory disturbances of behavior which often accompany imposture in less florid array. In addition, it should
be noted that imposture is often related to paranoid conditions
(especially evident if one studies the lives of the founders of
religious cults) and to overt perversions, notably those involving
transvestitism.

The present paper will, however, restrict itself to the comparison
of the nuclear findings which are characteristic of the major impostor with those of the creative individual, the artist. While
some impostors seem to feel their unusual drive only after reach-

2 It is interesting that Cagliostro is said to be the name of a maternal great uncle,
and originally the name of a small town near Messina. One suspects that this great
uncle may have played the role of the mythical father in Cagliostro's childhood,
being then a smaller version of Chatterton's Rowley and Macpherson's Ossian. Indeed, just as Rowley was the priest scribe to the fifteenth-century mayor of Bristol,
and Ossian, the blind son of the great tribal father Fingal, so also was Count
Cagliostro's ancestor the factor of the Prince of Villafranca.

ing maturity, as in the case of the Tichborne Claimant, the com-
moner story seems to be that the special impostorous craving and
ability manifest themselves around puberty; although in some
cases, as in the patient reported by Abraham (1925), some degree
of definite impostorous behavior was reported as early as the age
of five.[3]

The well-developed career impostor appears to suffer from an
incompleted development of the ego, involving grave defects in
the ability to form object relationships, along with special disturbances in the sense of identity and reality. A preponderance of
imitative tendencies, arising at an early pregenital level, invades
the process of identification and precludes the development of
sound and well-anchored ego ideals of the postoedipal period.
Inevitably then there is a deformation of the superego, with the
absence of well-internalized standards and values. Vision plays a
larger than ordinary part in all processes of identification and
showmanship substitutes largely for real achievement. The measure of the immediate response of the public to the impostored
performance completes the spurious gauge of reality.

The nature of the oedipal conflict appears very characteristic
and conspicuous. Ego defects derived from strong pregenital fixations cause a thin but dramatic enactment of the oedipal conflict,
which is constantly re-enacted in each imposture. It is conspicuous
that the imposture itself is most often the assumption of the
identity of a father or an older brother, on the scale of the family
romance: a distinguished noble or famous person, who is symbolically killed by the imposture and robbed of his greatest treasures
—his fame, his wealth, his achievements. Further scrutiny shows,
however, how much this extraordinary struggle is devoid of any
true libidinal investments, and consists rather of an overthrowing
of the king-father and an assumption of his mantle in a real or illusory assumption of power. There is really no effort to do this
in order to gain or to retain the mother's attention and indulgence,
which in actuality may have been excessive or, conversely, eternally and teasingly promised but never really experienced. It can
readily be seen that the libidinal development of the impostor is
always infantile and rarely reaches a true genital and hetero-

3 The case of the Tichborne Claimant as well as that reported by Abraham are
discussed in ch. 7.

sexual level, although in some few instances a pseudogenitality with singularly little real pleasure takes the place of a truer genital relationship. Perversions are rife. In terms of the body image, there is commonly a real or fancied sense of defective development of the genitals. Imposture, of any well-developed proportions, is characteristically limited to males. From what I have attempted to sketch here, it may also be seen why the impostor frequently feels incomplete, anxious, and fearful when he is not engaged in imposture, but is subjectively fulfilled and unanxious in the very acts of imposture, although they may involve considerable reality danger and risk of severe punishment as well.

In my earlier paper on "The Impostor" I have attempted to give a more detailed picture of the clinical development of the impostor as it can be deciphered in the histories of famous impostors of the past. I would furthermore emphasize that successful imposture also involves a social element—in the cooperation of its victims. Consequently, a large-scale imposture is most successful in times of disturbed or near-revolutionary social conditions, when people are looking for panaceas and a savior, and are uncritical and overly ready to believe. In terms of the genetic development, such conditions permit first a kind of new version of the parents' (most often mother's) early indulgent or erratically provocative attitude toward the child of two or three, and second a falsification of the social ideals in the struggle for approval which the child has experienced in the postoedipal extension of family relationships into the community.

It would be a naïve simplification to attempt to "type" the character structure of the creative artist, in such protean outlines and with such a diversified combination of forces is it cast. In "The Childhood of the Artist" (ch. 24), I made an attempt to present my ideas concerning the libidinal phase development of the creative individual, emphasizing there that the innate increased sensitivity and perceptivity of the potential artist permit or enforce a vast extension of the area of responsiveness from early infancy onward. This means that the child may react to the external world in the direct personal way of the maturational forces of the ordinary child and that his libidinal attachments develop in the direction of the object relationship in ways comparable to his less gifted brother. But further, with his greater perceptive response to both form and rhythm, the personal objects of his immediate human environment may be invested with a greater range of other outer (often inanimate) object perceptions, which are related to the animate personal objects by similarities in form or in active and passive movement and rhythm. This increased range and deepened sensitivity include heightened reactions to the own body sensations as well as to the outer world. I have referred to this increased range of outer objects as the field of the collective alternates—"alternates" because they may on occasion substitute for the warmer personal human objects, if for any reason these latter are temporarily unavailable. This means that all object relationships may be felt and expressed with a vast increase in their symbolic representations and that the tendency to anthropomorphism in observation and thought is increased and usually lasts throughout life. These characteristics constitute the access to primary process thinking, the retention of which into adult life is noteworthy in the artist.

It is interesting in this connection that this capacity for anthropomorphism in thinking may be encountered in the creative scientist as well as in the poet, novelist, and painter, where it is conspicuous. Both William Harvey, the discoverer of the circulation of the blood (Chauvois, 1957), and Ramón y Cajal, the great Spanish neurologist (Cannon, 1949), have described most beautifully their persistent anthropomorphizing perceptions of the material with which they worked, and their belief that this was of great help to them in the production of original thought and theory.[4]

---

[4] I quote from a memoir of Dr. Ramón y Cajal, written by Sir Charles Sherrington. In this recollection, the unique animation of the surroundings of the creative artist is so well described, as well as certain qualities of innocence, directness, and passionate responsiveness (see Cannon, 1949):

"He was strikingly simple in several ways. At dinner one evening whitebait was served. He could not be persuaded to eat the tiny fish whole although he saw the rest of us doing so. But he persisted in trying to dissect out the backbone of each one. We were delighted to find that at meals he would often manage to follow the general drift of talk at table and that he did not let the language disability deter him from joining in. . . . The climax he would emphasize with a final dramatic gesture for which his left hand had been preparing. That hand had been busily crumbling the bread beside his dinner plate. It would gather the crumbs into a high pyramidal heap and then, to stress his closing words, sweep them with cupped hand from the table to the carpet, accompanied by a challenging look round, to the dismay of the maid servant. . . .

"A trait very noticeable in him was that in describing what the microscope

It is my belief, however, that because the collective outer world does offer alternates for the specific objects of the human object relationships and frequently is invested to a greater extent with fantasy, it may furnish a retreat from the exigencies of personal pressures and permit a less decisive dealing with their problems. This together with the fact that the gifted child is, in his very

---

showed, he spoke habitually as though it were a living scene. This was the more striking because not only were his preparations all dead and fixed, but they were to all appearances roughly made and rudely treated, no cover glass, and as many as half a dozen tiny scraps of tissue set in one large blob of balsam and left to dry. . . . Such scanty illustration as he vouchsafed for the preparations he demonstrated were a few slight rapid sketches of points taken here and there, depicted, however, by a master's hand.

"The intense anthropomorphism of his descriptions of what the preparations showed was at first startling to accept. He treated the microscopic scene as though it were alive and inhabited by beings which felt and hoped and tried even as we do. It was a personification of natural forces as unlimited as that of Goethe's Faust, Part II. We must, if we would enter adequately into Cajal's thought in this field, suppose his entrance through his microscope, into a world populated by tiny beings actuated by motives and strivings and satisfactions not very remotely different from our own. He would envisage the sperm cells as activated by a sort of passionate urge in the rivalry for penetration into the ovum cell. Listening to him I asked myself how far this capacity for anthropomorphizing might not contribute to his success as an investigator. . . . [Sherrington also describes with considerable poignancy Cajal's consuming love of country, not to praise or boast of it, but often to muse upon and regret some defect which he detected in Spain as contrasted with elsewhere. Cajal's love of the world had as its foreimage his native Spain.] This solicitude for his country's repute deserves explicit mention here, it was perhaps the most powerful driving force in the make-up of his whole scientific character. It lifted him altogether above all personal vanity. His science was first and foremost an offering to Spain, a spiritual motive which added to the privilege of knowing the man." Such was Sherrington's estimate.

And what manner of childhood did this man have? Born the oldest child of a father who was bright, ambitious, persistent, and obdurate, and a mother of whom little is said except that she was extremely beautiful and that none of her children inherited her beauty, he saw life first in a tiny isolated mountain village in the north of Spain. The father, who had a passionate ambition to become a doctor, was still hardly beyond the stage of being a barber and bloodletter when his son was born, but with great sacrifice of himself and deprivations to his growing family succeeded soon in obtaining real training.

There is little information of the babyhood, but the young child was certainly harassed by recurrent disturbances—for three younger children were born by the time he was eight, and with each child the struggling young country doctor moved from one village to a bigger one. From four to six, the child showed precocity in learning to read and write and already aroused great expectations. In the early part of the latency period, he became prankish and mischievous with boundless energy and curiosity, wandering the countryside exploring flora, fauna, and topographical curiosities with what was described as an inborn sensitivity to natural beauty and what Cajal himself was to describe as his exploration of "nature's gaudy festivals." I think we can see this same vivid, expectant, animated and animating attitude transferred years later to his anthropomorphizing of his explorations of the human brain.

But the age of eight was a turning point, the year when his youngest sibling was

nature, subject to possible overstimulation may conceivably predispose to an earlier stimulation of the developing libidinal phases,
resulting in a less clear hierarchy in the phase progression. This
is particularly obvious in the fate of the oedipal conflict which is
rarely solved as well as in the less gifted individual.

In addition, the incorporation of the field of the collective

---

born, when a move to still another village confronted him with a new and larger
group of schoolboys to be won or conquered, and when Spain emerged from a
long period of despair and celebrated glorious conquests in Morocco, reminiscent
to the discouraged Spaniards of other past power. The little boy reacted to all this
vividly—as his later productions were to show. But what is even more interesting
is that two cataclysmic events appeared to shake his predominantly happy, though
shy, naturalistic preoccupation: there was an eclipse of the sun, and a severe
electrical storm struck the school, shattering it and electrocuting the village priest
who was caught in the belfry by the lightning bolt and his body left dangling
almost in midair. These events which one suspects at once as being screening
experiences (I might even say—collective cosmic experiences) cover some of the
fantasies or experiences connected with the other natural events—the births of the
younger children. At any rate, these events seemed to initiate two trends of new
activity, one of bursting "delinquent" behavior, stealing, leading a gang of youthful
marauders in countryside depredations—and the other, the emergence of a need
to sketch, draw and paint. This in itself also took on the semblance of rebellion,
since it was considered useless, frivolous, and wasteful by the child's stern father.
What the mother's attitude was is unstated. But a kind of oedipal warfare, expanded to the community and the teachers, continued throughout latency, in
which there was very destructive behavior, with secret learning, experimenting,
writing, and painting. One gets the impression that these creative but secret pursuits
were partly sublimated and "neutralized" masturbatory substitutes, but that he was
pressured more by the innate creative ability and not so much by the real solution
of a conflict. This state of affairs continued during late latency, resulting in the
boy's being sent away to different schools but with worsening rather than improvement. Finally at eleven and twelve, his inventiveness and destructiveness reached a
pitch in his construction of a homemade cannon which when ignited blew up the
neighbor's garden and garden gate. The boy who was to become Spain's greatest
scientist was lodged in the local jail as the only place strong enough to hold him.
    Cajal's war with his father continued even through adolescence, with a partial
capitulation to the father's demands when the younger man began the study of
medicine; but his rebellion flared again when the father tried to induce him to
enter into practice with him. Cajal's dramatic development as Spain's greatest
scientist and one of the greatest anatomists of his day was essentially an outcome
of his oedipal struggle and ultimate victory. But it was not the first choice of
creative channel for him.
    I have given this illustration of a man who already can be accepted as a person
of superior creative ability because I think it speaks for me regarding the intermingling of the personal and the collective attachments and problems in which
the collective may both merge with and be a retreat from the personal. I want to
make clear, however, that this outline of the forces at work in young Cajal presents
a structure of relationship between creative and personal lives (and communication)
which is only one of a number of different constellations of forces seen in different
creative individuals.
    The above material first appeared in my paper on the psychology of creativity
(1962b, pp. 134-137. Other parts of this paper have not been included in this
volume.)

alternates with its enormous enrichment of all reactions then causes a peculiar development of the primary narcissism in a less clearly delineated relationship with the outer world, in which rich fantasy and seemingly mystical elements develop. This is, however, a true object relationship, albeit of a different order than the more usual personal family object relationships of the ungifted child. Inevitably the artist must have a special texture of his sense of reality. Behavior which, when viewed on phenomenological grounds only, would resemble a state of regression in the more ordinary individual may actually be rather the continued libidinized object relationships to the collective world of the artist. It should be noted, too, that with the fusion of phases and the capacity to bypass many of the decisive conflicts of early childhood by constant recourse to the collective outer world, a sharp delimitation of the primary from the secondary process cannot occur.

It has already been noted that every artist is at least two people, the personally oriented self and the artistic one. The relationship between these two (or more) people in one body varies enormously. Sometimes they are on good speaking terms with each other; sometimes the identities are relatively separate, and in extreme cases may be quite dissociated one from the other. How much the personally oriented self resembles the "ordinary citizen" must depend largely on the nature of the pressures, personal attachments, and especially the identifications of early childhood. In the matter of identification both the character of the person(s) who furnish the models for identification and the mechanisms through which it is achieved are important. Even where a fairly secure beginning of ordinary-citizenship development is established early, one finds then the creative pressures asserting themselves in rebellious attacks against ordinary order in the blind search for liberation. Quite as frequently the creative pressure achieves early some room for itself, whether or not its nature is recognized and appreciated. It then may still infiltrate and upset the ordinary course of development, producing seemingly unreliable or even chaotic behavior which is likely to be regarded only as perverse or psychopathic until the strength of the artistic demands have brought about some definite fruitions.

As the capacity for artistic creation emerges, develops, and is accepted into the individual's life, it is not unusual for some kind of pattern of rhythm in the creative work to be established. The interplay between the aggression of creative activity and compulsive controls would be a subject worthy of study. Many creative people produce their best work in a kind of quiet, inspired, compulsive brooding. In others this takes on the intensity of a frenzy, in which libidinal and aggressive components are grossly evident. Between spurts of creative activity, some fall back to monotonously compulsive interests which seem to offer a neutral resting and reorganization period until the need for new creative effort gathers force. Yet others seek relief from what has been felt as the bondage of the creative work by abandoning themselves temporarily to indulgent excesses. It is interesting to note how many poets, painters, and imaginative prose writers have held humdrum civil service jobs, or their like, concurrently with their artistic activities or in intervals between special epochs of creative production. One gets the impression that at least in some instances, these seemingly tiresome daily demands have really furnished an organized scaffolding for life as well as a minimal sustenance. It has been a ballast and tethered the person to "ordinary life," permitting his fantasy to seethe and boil, and reassuring him against the fear of being engulfed by it. The variety of patterns involving the forces of creative productivity and compulsive controls is not surprising when one considers the probable influences of the complex instinctual understructure. The pressures of anal productivity and aggression combine and merge into the creative genital drive with its own strong aggressive components.

Nearly always there are conflicts and often confusions between the aims, ideals, and love objects of personal life and those of the collective interests. The sweetheart becomes temporarily the Muse, even when the incompatibility between the two would seem glaringly apparent. The love life of creative individuals seems to be conspicuously unstable, varied, and inconstant—sometimes with rather amazing periods of absence of personal love relationships, or even of erotic interests. Those marriages which seem most enduring are not infrequently least genitally erotically based. The drives seem intense and mobile and, according to ordinary standards, not well controlled by reality testing.

It is a truism that the possession of the extraordinary gift of genius is a source of peculiar satisfaction and a burden sometimes of overwhelming weight. It may give pleasure and progress to all mankind, but at the expense of personal trials and suffering and an agonizing sort of gratification to its individual possessor. The Greek myth of Prometheus makes this exquisitely clear. Prometheus, with his brother, Epimetheus (afterthought), was to create man and give all animals, as well, faculties which would insure their self-preservation. Epimetheus agreed to do the task and let Prometheus be the overseer. But Epimetheus proceeded with more orderliness than vision, and soon distributed all the gifts at his disposal to the animals present, without regard for man—much like Alice in Wonderland handing out the prizes to the participants in the impromptu race. Like Alice, he came out short in the end, and had no special gifts left with which to endow man, who lay still unfinished and barely emerged from primordial slime by the earlier help of Prometheus. Whether sibling rivalry had a hand in Epimetheus's oversight, or whether it was only the lack of foresight, Prometheus had again to come to the rescue and in order to enliven and inspirit the inert clay form of man, he lighted his torch at the chariot of the sun and brought down the fire from Heaven. Not only did this give man imagination and hence creativity, but it furnished him with the practical means for working on the durable materials of earth, giving permanent form to tools and weapons. According to the Greek version, Jupiter was jealous and fashioned the beautiful Pandora, to distract and disrupt the godlike progress of the two brothers. Again the short-sighted Epimetheus accepted her unconditionally. The beautiful Pandora was unable to resist the temptation to open the Box of Secrets (whether of good or evil nature, according to the one account or the other) in which hope alone remained behind when the others had fled. It would seem that this story of the two sons of the Titans presents rather succinctly our picture of the two men in one—of the creative artist: Epimetheus, the more work-a-day ordinary citizen, and Prometheus with the daring to obtain, some said to steal, the gift of fire.

It may be worth noting that in the Norse version of this tale, Loki, the satanic god of mischief and fraud, also was the thief of fire. He seemed, however, to combine in a fraudulent version, some of the characteristics of Prometheus and Pandora. He too was the son of a giant, but one who presided, like Charon, over the entrance to the dead. According to some stories, he spawned three evil children, a wolf so destructive that he had to be held in check by mystical fetters (made of the Norse cat's footfalls, the beards of women, the roots of stone, the breath of fish, the spittle of birds, and the sensibilities of bears); a serpent who encompassed the world with his tail; and a third—a female Death who lived daintily and monstrously on the brains and marrow of men. According to another version, it was Loki himself, rather than this wolf-son, who was chained to the rock after he, by trickery, accomplished the death of Balder, the god of peace, by using misteltoe for the lethal arrow. In this story we see hints of the dark impostorous character which accompanies, like a shadow, the tread of genius.

Finally, it is worth examining the theme of artist-and-impostor, or at least of artist-swindler, which appears with so repetitive a beat throughout the fiction of Thomas Mann as to announce itself as one of his main preoccupations. Mann wrote of himself in his slight *Sketch of my Life* (1930), "The truth is that every piece of work is a realization, fragmentary but complete in itself, of our individuality; and this kind of realization is the sole and painful way we have of getting the particular experience—no wonder then that the process is attended by surprises!" As to the impostor, one thinks immediately of Mann's *Felix Krull, Confidence Man*, which appeared first in an abbreviated and unfinished form (1911), presenting only the boyhood of the swindler (see Mann, 1936). Mann was then thirty-six years old, married for six years, and the father of a daughter and a son. It was forty-three years before *Felix Krull, Confidence Man* was to reappear as a full-length novel (1954), and even then the story carried its hero only to a climactic event in the early part of the young man's first major imposture. Between the publications of the two versions of *Felix Krull,* the two infant children had grown to womanhood and manhood with a fascinating and tragic beauty and closeness, seemingly an intensity of brother-sister relationship which is one of the chief motifs of Mann's novels.[5] In 1954, Mann was nearly eighty years old and had passed, by almost a decade, the age at which he had expected to die; i.e., his mother's age at the time of death (1930). His own death was

---

[5] This theme reappears in other of Mann's stories, sometimes fused with the oedipal theme as it is in *Felix Krull,* the novel. (See also footnote 9 below.)

to occur within the next two years, and the extended version of *Krull* was one of his last literary productions. In one of those extraordinary compliances, produced apparently by Fate, but made rather by powerfully strong though not easily discernible strands of intrafamily identifications, he had lost his son to death even as his mother had lost her daughter—the one who was closest to Thomas in age.

While *Felix Krull* is manifestly Mann's greatest story of the swindler, the theme of the phony, the pretender, the charlatan, the occultist, the masquerader emerges in many of his early stories as well as in some of the later novels, other than *Felix Krull*. It appears in "Disillusionment" (1896), "The Dilettante" (1897), "The Infant Prodigy" (1903), "Tonio Kröger" (1903), "Mario and the Magician" (1929)[6] as well as in the novels *Royal Highness* (1909), *The Holy Sinner* (1951), and *Doctor Faustus* (1947). The engrossment in this theme is further apparent in many short passages in his stories, as in the description of the beautiful and inspiring deceptions of nature as seen by Felix Krull on his visit to the Lisbon Museum of Natural History, presided over by the erudite starry-eyed Professor Kuckuck (whose name is so alliteratively close to our American slang coo-coo and is also probably related to the idea of the swindling bird which lays its eggs in another's nest). Or again it appears in the contemplations of the young Adrian in *Doctor Faustus,* when his religious but biologically minded father reveals to him the protective illusory color and configuration of certain plants and butterflies.[7] Here the emphasis is on protection through achieving invisibility or through reflecting color only from others. "And so, it is all a cheat!" says Adrian's mother, the literal-minded and practical, with the same mental

6 These stories are collected in Mann (1936).

7 It is interesting here that Mann describes Adrian's father, Jonathan Leverkuhn, as having a "veiled effort in his gaze, a certain sensitiveness at the temples" which "a physician might have attributed to migraine"; and adds that Jonathan "did suffer from headaches, moderately, and not oftener than once a month." Besides his natural history readings, this worthy man spent much time in studying the Bible. (Here the association of ideas suggests the configuration of my own clinical study, "Vision, Headache, and the Halo" [1947].)

Compare Edmund Gosse's account (1934) of his own bewilderingly revelatory experience with his father, a botanist and rigid member of the Plymouth Brethren. There the story is told in reverse: the son's imaginative and unconscious rebellion and almost discovery of the wonders of nature which the father's constricted gaze could not see except as problems of plant morphology.

cadence as Zouzou, Professor Kuckuck's forthright daughter when she answered, "Stuff and nonsense" to Felix Krull's attempted seductions. There are passages, too, in which the two-facedness of charm is portrayed—the very word *charm* condensing to itself the ideas of pleasant and delicately unfocused seductiveness; of good and bad magic; and of bauble or dangling adornment.

In his autobiographical sketch of 1930, Mann described how he wrote "Tonio Kröger" as a kind of intermission in his struggle in the production of the *Buddenbrooks*—although he did not publish it until later. Both were clearly autobiographical, although written in the third person, in contrast to some of his short stories and later novels. (It is perhaps noteworthy that in these latter the theme of deceptions or illusions of identity are most striking.)

"Tonio Kröger," more than any of his other writings, is tender in its picturing of the fledgling artist, bewildered, unsure, and frightened by the intimations of his artistic ability and the urgencies of his own expanding growth—envying the commonplace and standard against which he, however, constantly rebelled; and suspecting himself as an impostor in his attempt to accept his creative power. At the end of the story, he is, of course, actually detained by the police as a suspected impostor when he visits incognito his old home which has been turned into a library since the death of his father and the liquidation of the family business. Of this story, Mann (1930) was to say, "Of all I have written, perhaps still dearest to my heart today [i.e., at fifty-five] and still beloved of the young . . . is 'Tonio Kröger.' "

The novel *Felix Krull, Confidence Man* has always impressed me as having some flaw which kept it from being a really good exposition of the impostor. Although it was enthusiastically hailed by many colleagues whose judgment I very much respect, I still felt that there was something false: that it did not ring true. I then read a number of biographies and autobiographies of impostors and similar accounts of many artists, and came back finally to several rereadings of the two versions of *Felix Krull*. Further, I began to consider it in the light of other works of its gifted author, and especially of what he has written of himself, both in the autobiographical sketch already alluded to, and in the less self-conscious statements in the prefaces of several of his books. I began to understand my dilemma in regard to it.

The result of all this is that I have come to the conclusion that the novel gives, in an almost marvelous way, descriptions of the feelings and inner workings of the life of a swindler, in which imposture is one of the polymorphous possibilities of activity. Still, these descriptions are given with a precision of insight and an accuracy of expression which is *not* characteristic of the impostor, or even of the swindler with his whole bag of tricks. The impostor often deals in verbalisms rather than in accurate language. Like Humpty Dumpty in *Alice Through the Looking Glass,* he makes words do what he wants them to do—perform tricks at his bidding. The fact that the story is told in the first person vitiates its effectiveness and, for me at least, interferes with its ring of genuineness. The swindler may do these things or related things, and for the very reasons and with the complex feelings that Mann so artfully depicts. But he is not aware that he does them for these reasons or in these ways.

Some very intelligent swindlers may be somewhat aware of their own reactions, and especially in that type of swindle which involves complicated scheming, planning, and thoughtful outwitting of the enemy, the other(s). This is a type of disturbance which is closely related to that of the spy, whose activities are justified as for the fatherland or the motherland in time of crisis—or to the paranoid character in less disturbed times. It is more closely allied to the activity of a Van Meegeren who with painstaking self-discipline impostured Vermeer, although never careful enough or thoughtful enough about all details; or to the pursuits of forgers in other media. *Felix Krull* is rather the impure account of an impostoring swindler—impure because it is contaminated by the imprint of genuine artistic talent. If the account were not written in the first person, the discrepancy would not be so great. But it is really the high degree and nature of the insight which causes the significant incongruity.

It is worth noting, too, that there is a revision or a transformation of the language—the *taste* of the vocabulary between the two versions of *Felix Krull.* I doubt whether this is the result only of different translators. For it coincides rather with certain other changes which the author has made in format and even in the names of some of the characters of this place of fiction. The short version (1911) is written in the warm fluid manner of an author definitely and yet subtly emotionally involved in the story he is writing: it is more in the taste or tone of "Tonio Kröger," of which it is, in its way, a darker shadow. The second version of *Felix Krull*—"Felix Krull, Sr.," one might call it—coming when the writer's life was clearly mostly behind him, is in the stilted, pompous style which might be befitting to an impostorous writer or one at any rate who fancied himself much beyond his actual literary merits. This was certainly not Thomas Mann himself, but rather evidence of his attempt to lend his style more, to counterfeit it, to match the character who was telling the story in the first person—the impostor himself. But it is in this second version that there is the greatest development of the psychological insight, which corresponds in many respects with what I have written in the earlier part of this paper.

But what does Thomas Mann himself say of "Felix Krull," who remained with him, repeatedly active, in the various recesses of his mind, over so much of his lifetime? For anyone who wishes to understand "Felix Krull" (1911) even in a rudimentary way, it is important to read Mann's autobiographical sketch, so close does the childhood of the one follow, like a distorted and caricaturing shadow, even the outlines of the events of childhood up to late adolescence. He writes here (1930) of his play *Fiorenze* (1904) that "part of it is personal and primordial: the youthful lyric love of fame and the fear of fame, in one early involved in her toils. 'O world! O deep delight. O love-dream of power, so sweet, consuming! One may not possess. Yearning is giant power, possession unmans.' " In these words he betrays one of the basic conflicts of the artist whose love of the world turns too far to love of the world's—applause and power, a situation inevitable in the true impostor, not because he is diverted by conflict from real love of world or of individual, but because the inadequacies of his own development make it impossible for him ever to love at all, and the craving for applause, recognition, and power must fill the void.

Soon after his marriage, Mann wrote first *Royal Highness* (1909),[8] and finishing this turned to "Felix Krull." The idea for

[8] This story he regarded as the first fruit of his married state. It was an attempt to come to terms, as a writer, with his own happiness. Of himself he says, "A young man recently married here explored, by means of a fable, the possibility of reconciling the claims of society and the solitary: of harmonizing form and life" (1930).

this came shortly after, or at least took definite form after the suicide of his sister, Carla, which occurred on the eve of her expected marriage. An actress, but not a born one, she had since childhood been physically delicate and had always been preoccupied with the macabre. In the end, however, her death was sudden, unexpected, and shocking. (It may be recalled here that in *Felix Krull*, later version, Felix's only sister, Olympia, is about to be married when the father kills himself and the girl remains then with her mother.) The idea of writing "Felix Krull" came ostensibly from Mann's reading of the memoirs of Manolescu (a Rumanian rogue), a fact which was recognized by many readers of this first story. Mann saw here—or so he thought—something new to the artist and his art: the psychology of the unreal, the illusionary form of existence, while stylistically he was intrigued with the autobiographic form, which he had not previously tried. He found, he reported, "a fantastic intellectual charm in the burlesque idea of taking a much loved tradition—self-portraiture in the Goethe manner, the introspective 'Confessions' of the born artistocrat [i.e., genius]—and transferring it to the criminal sphere." He considered that it had great comic possibilities. Thus the first version of "Felix Krull," the childhood chapters,. was written in the manner of the artist, was well received, and was considered by many the best thing which he had till then written.

In 1936, in a Preface to a collection of his short stories, Thomas Mann wrote that he was apparently "not destined" to return to "Felix Krull" and he described it as "like *Royal Highness*—in essence the story of an artist; in it the element of the unreal and illusional passes frankly over into the criminal." It is here, I believe, that he betrays the crux of a severe neurotic problem, and one which in a less talented person might have caused more destructive consequences. He referred to the early "Felix Krull" as having been written with great zest, and considered it to be the most personal of anything he had written. But he found "writing the Krull memoirs a difficult feat of equilibrium" and turned to "Death in Venice" (1911) as an interlude after which he would return to "Krull." One interlude followed another and it was only after forty-three years that the novel *Felix Krull* was brought out. It is clear, however, that in Mann's mind, Felix Krull is more artist than impostor and it is in this fact that I find the "contamination" which keeps it from being as good a picture of the imposture as it might be. It was apparently neurotically obligatory, however, that he write in autobiographical form.

One final topic must be reintroduced before closing this part of the paper—viz., a return to the discussion of the oedipal struggle in the impostor and in Felix Krull. Mann (1954) pictures his hero as bound by the fascination of a brother-sister intimacy, more alluring than anything else on earth.[9] The adolescent Felix Krull, a sidewalk idler in Frankfurt, is intoxicated by seeing a lovely brother and sister as they appeared for a few minutes on the balcony of a hotel:

> Dreams of love, dreams of delight and a longing for union—I cannot name them otherwise, though they concerned not a single image but a double creature, a pair fleetingly but profoundly glimpsed, a brother and sister—representative of my own sex and of the other, the fair one. But the beauty here lay in the duality, in the charming doubleness, and if it seems more than doubtful that the appearance of youth alone on the balcony would have inflamed me in the slightest, apart perhaps from the pearl in his shirt; I am almost equally sure that the image of the girl alone, without her fraternal complement, would never have lapped my spirit in such sweet dreams. Dreams of love, dreams that I loved precisely because—I firmly believe—they were of primal indivisibility and indeterminateness, double; which really means that only then is there a significant whole blessedly embracing what is beguilingly human in both sexes.
>
> [And somewhat later he writes]: Let it be said right now, however, that divorcing myself from the spectator's role, I sought and found a personal relationship to that world to which I was drawn by nature,

evidently referring to the period when he assumes the character and identity of Loulou (note the almost mirror image in name to Zouzou), the young Marquis de Venosta.

Later on when traveling as Loulou he arrived in Lisbon, he experienced a somewhat comparable but even greater ecstasy on seeing two women together; a young girl of eighteen and her austerely handsome mother:

9 This theme of the tender incestuous brother-sister relationship is the central theme of *The Holy Sinner* (1951) and appears in other of Mann's writings. Its definite relation to the oedipal struggle is beautifully presented in the short story "Disorder and Early Sorrow" (1925).

The connoisseur of humanity will be interested in the way my penchant for twofold enthusiasms, for being enchanted by the double-but-dissimilar, was called into play in this case by mother-and-daughter instead of brother-and-sister. I, at all events, find it very interesting. I will just add, however, that my fascination was soon enhanced by a sudden suspicion that coincidence was here engaged in an extraordinary game.

The reader will indeed agree that coincidence is on a rampage, for not only has Felix, masquerading as Loulou, the Marquis, thus chanced upon Zouzou and her mother, daughter and wife of the starry-eyed Professor Kuckuck, whom Loulou had already met by chance on the train to Lisbon, but Zouzou also resembles in name (not only Loulou but also) Zaza, the actress—loved one of the real Loulou, who has remained in Paris with her. Further, Zouzou is described as appearing less impostorous than Zaza, whose beauty is too *frou-frou* to be real, while the daughter of Professor Kuckuck is so direct and forthright that Loulou, the impostor, in Lisbon, wonders whether she is real or whether he had dreamed her because he wanted so much to see her.[10]

But the denouement of the tale comes presently. After the Professor's family and Loulou have returned from a particularly fascinating bullfight, Zouzou finally weakens and agrees to meet Loulou secretly to obtain some sketches she believes he had drawn of her and which she claims as belonging rightfully to herself. These are really sketches of Zaza in the nude, drawn by the real Loulou, to which the false one has added Zouzou's curls. She is so delighted with them, thinking them of herself, that she tears them to bits and, releasing these to the breeze, gives herself up to Loulou's embrace. Thus the young couple are, when suddenly the austere señora, Zouzou's mother, appears before them, dismisses her daughter, and berates the treacherous Marquis, and accuses him of childish stupidity in thus turning a young girl's head. Quick to make amends, he soon sees the beauty of the angry woman, and consequently feels and acts like a man; for the scene and the novel end in a whirlwind of primordial forces.

10 Stated in these terms, the intrinsic burlesque of the presentation is exaggeratedly clear. One sees its relation on the one hand to Shakespeare's *Comedy of Errors*, and on the other to Lewis Carroll's *Sylvie and Bruno*. Indeed, I am beginning to suspect that everything is done with mirrors and sound effects and that nothing is in the least real.

To turn, however, from this exciting burlesque—to catch our breaths as it were—it is necessary to consider the scientific aspects of the oedipal conflict (here to be perpetuated doubtlessly by the successful consummation of the oedipal wish) and the way in which it is manifested in the artist and in the impostor. The splitting of the oedipal drive between mother and sister (here appearing as mother and daughter) is seemingly of a particularly resistant nature, perhaps because it is the more likely to have been lived out in incestuous play in childhood. But in any event, the relation between brother and sister is the more burdened with sharp envies and rivalries which amalgamate with and increase the oedipal jealousies. Only insofar as it increases these problems, and contributes to the vividness of the madonna and prostitute fantasies—the unreachable and the bought—does it seem to give much to impostorous tendencies. It would seem that its peculiar prominence in *Felix Krull* is due to some special intrapsychic situation in Thomas Mann (and written into his other stories as well) rather than belonging essentially to either artist or impostor.

To be sure it seems that the artist falls short one way and another in his attempt at solving or sidestepping his oedipal strivings. This has already been discussed early in the paper. But the major, the "dedicated" impostor without artistic talent appears always to be striving toward an oedipal realization, although in a peculiarly lopsided and makeshift way. Real love for the mother is lacking, but is supplanted by the narcissistic wish for power and applause, to be gained through pleasing. The dreams of "primal indivisibility," spoken of by Felix Krull on seeing the brother and sister on the balcony, are not only primal scene derivatives. More importantly, they represent the wish for union by primary identification, which may be mistaken for love in the perverse, and which exists in a more restrained and less exigent form in the heightened empathy of the artist.

In concluding, it is interesting to quote a passage from "Tonio Kröger" which, written in regard to the artist, might, with only few changes, apply equally well to the impostor. "It begins by your feeling yourself set apart, in a curious sort of opposition to the nice, regular people; there is a gulf of ironic sensibility, of knowledge, skepticism, disagreement between you and the others; it grows deeper and deeper, you are alone; and from then on any rapprochement is simply hopeless!" We might add, unless, as an impostor, you find a new character for yourself. Thomas Mann's thought obviously also turned in this way, for a few sentences further on he remarks again, through the mouth of the young Tonio, "I once knew an actor, a man of genius, who had to struggle with a morbid self-consciousness and instability. When he had no role to play, nothing to represent, this man, consummate artist but impoverished human being, was overcome by an exaggerated consciousness of his ego. A genuine artist—not one who has taken up art as a profession like another, but artist foreordained and damned—you can pick out." In both creative artist on the brink of a new surge of creativity and in the impostor, between periods of imposture, there is a sense of ego hunger and a need for completion—in the one, of the artistic self; in the other, of a satisfying identity in the world.

CHAPTER TWENTY-SEVEN

Play in Relation to Creative Imagination (1959)

This paper makes no attempt to cover the whole area of play, and not at all to explore the full reaches of creative imagination, but only to present certain special characteristics of the functioning of play in the service of creative imagination. I believe that play may work somewhat differently in conjunction with creativity than it does, for example, in the service of the neuroses.

Here one may note that the very juxtaposition of the words play and work suggests the seeming paradox—when is play only play and when is it work? Again this is in an area with which I cannot adequately deal. I suspect that the two are never to be completely dissociated and that the superficial distinction that work is for a definite and useful goal and play has no such utilitarian aim *is* a superficial distinction. It is based on recognition of conscious goals alone and does not take into consideration the highly useful but unconscious goals of much play. I also shall not speak of organized play in the sense of competitive games and their function in education and in neuroses, but only of play which is essentially solitary and takes part—often seemingly a small part—in creative work.

One more caution and limitation: I should like to make a preliminary distinction between *creativity* and *productivity*. I am aware that in many theses, perhaps those especially of educational psychologists, the term creative activity is used to describe an activity in which a definite achievement, usually of a tangible nature, is the result. This is in contrast to random, unproductive, or even destructive activity. I use the term creativity in a somewhat different sense, as I have in earlier papers, to mean the capacity for or activity of making something new, original or inventive, no matter in what field. It is not merely the making of a product, even a good product, but of one which has the characteristic of originality. No absolute dividing line between creativity and productivity can be made. The different meaning between the two extremes—the copied product and the new invention—is clear enough and is important in this presentation, and might become of greater significance in considering the blocks to creativity. There it becomes apparent that the interference may be in the creative process itself or in the subsidiary executive functions involved in productivity. Furthermore, I use the term "the artist" to mean the markedly creative person, even including the creative scientist and the prophet.

Play seems to be a rather general accompaniment of life. Animals as well as humans play. Young creatures seem to play more than older ones. At least among animals the play of the mature ones may be somewhat more allocated to courting and to becoming readily involved in frankly aggressive competitions, while the play of young ones seems to be concerned more with general motor activities of agility and strength. But I am not a biologist and am fearful of extrapolating too uncritically from animal life, even though it is tempting to make comparisons with humans. One thinks generally of lightness, movement, and a feeling of pleasure associated with play. Even inanimate objects of organisms not capable of independent motion may, metaphorically, seem to play, as grasses that *play* in the wind, or light that *plays* across the sky. Here of course there is a bit of anthropomorphizing, but other than that, it is the quality of playfulness which is emphasized, a quality which invests most play, but I do not believe is synonymous with it.

A derived but frequent meaning of *play* contains the notion of make-believe or even imitative action, as children who are *playing* at being grown up, or actors *playing* on the stage; and the term play is certainly not limited to that which is amusing, lighthearted, spontaneous and aimless, although these are the ingredients of playfulness. We speak of play, especially when one gets beyond the reach of early childhood, as recreative, i.e., renewing or reviving. I shall compare the play related to creativity with the play of young children and solitary play, or at least play which is "made up" by one player with whom the other participants comply. An attempt will be made to differentiate between the play which is in the service of a developing neurosis and play which is akin to that of the creative individual, and takes part in creative activity.

Before getting down further to the core of this discussion, it is necessary to consider briefly another attribute of human behavior, namely, the tendency to repetitive activity. This might at first seem to be in contrast to the freedom, spontaneity, and lightness of play, or at least to the quality of playfulness. To a limited extent this contrast may be accepted. Repetition implies some degree of organization, and hence some restraint. This does not refer to the kind of repetition that appears as the result of externally applied forces which bring about automatic conditioned responses or habits, as a part of compulsory training, but to repetitive behavior according to internal tendencies or impulses. This may in one sense be quite spontaneous, although subject to internally imposed limitations, which are, however, unconscious.

Freud (1920a) developed a conception that this inner pressure to repeat significant and disturbing experiences is an important factor at the heart of neurotic developments, and used the term *repetition compulsion* to describe this state of affairs. The concept probably began with the idea of the need to *re-experience* the trauma in neurosis, but was gradually extended to other meanings.[1] We might more accurately speak of repetitive tendencies of which the repetition compulsion is one form.

Fenichel (1945a, 1945b)[2] has described these tendencies under three categories: first, repetitive behavior due to natural peri-

[1] Kubie (1939, 1941) took issue with the concept of the repetition compulsion, pointing out that the repetitive tendencies were not uniform in their nature and not genuinely compulsive. The term "compulsion" (in repetition compulsion) is used in a somewhat different sense than in speaking of a compulsion neurosis; still it has been so generally used and any ambiguity has interfered so little in the understanding of it, that it is retained.

[2] Fenichel's (1945a, 1945b) organization of the repetitive tendencies into three different categories provides a useful clarification of some of the inconsistencies which had been pointed out in Kubie's articles.

odicity of instincts rooted in their physical sources. While these are basically somatic problems, or at least contain basic somatic components, profound psychological consequences are derived from them. The periodicity of the instinct may then set in motion the neurotic behavior involved in the psychological derivatives. This is conspicuous, for example, in the extreme repetitiveness of certain disturbances of behavior associated with the menstrual rhythm. Second, repetitions which are due to the constantly recurring struggle between the repressed impulses and the repressing forces. As the wish for gratification of the impulse manifests itself either through the inherent strength of the instinct or as the result of new stimulations, anxiety again arises and there is a repetition of the already established defensive measures which have proved more or less effective earlier. Third, repetitions of traumatic experiences for the purpose of achieving a belated mastery. He considers that this type of repetition is seen most clearly in children's play, in dreams, and in the attacks of patients suffering from traumatic neuroses. It is then stated that the attitude of the ego is ambivalent. The repetition is desired to relieve the painful tension resulting from the overwhelming of the organism by the traumatic stimulation. But because the repetition *is* painful, the individual simultaneously wishes to avoid it. A compromise may be the result; the repetition is on a smaller scale or under somewhat more favorable conditions, i.e., in play.

The attempted solution by repetition of the disturbing experience as in the traumatic neurotic is not only characteristic of the play of children, but also to a certain extent of the repetitive behavior of the second type, viz., the neurotic struggle between the repressed impulse seeking gratification and the repressing forces. There is then not infrequently a further attempt to attain gratification through the illusion that the new situation is different and thereby more favorable and that now everything will be all right. But the change is expected in the external situation, whereas it is the inner one which is usually more important. In children's play, the more favorable condition lies especially in the fact that the play apparently *is* under the control of the child. Further reassurance is formed in the reversal of roles, the child often in imagination or in acted-out play taking the powerful part and assigning the weaker, more passive, or more suffering role to a toy, a pet, or another child, thereby re-enacting, in an active way what he has previously experienced passively.

But the second and third types of repetitive behavior may not be as clearly demarcated as Fenichel's categories present them. For in the constant repetitive struggle for gratification of the repressed instinct, what may be seen as a more favorable situation through the use of rationalizing self-deception may actually prove to be less favorable. New and powerful elements from the outside may complicate the repetition of the experience so that it becomes a further traumatic one, and this in itself tends again to increase the tendency to repeat it.

Still another source of repetitive tendencies is to be considered, although little attention has generally been paid to it in this connection, viz., the necessity for repetition of experience in establishing the sense of reality. While this is obviously important in infancy, it enters into many situations in later life as well. Any experience which is so strange that there is little in the individual's life to which he can relate it is felt as inimical, alien, and overwhelming. On the other hand, an experience which is only somewhat or a little bit new is pleasantly exciting. In the first instance, the individual is prompted to go back and take another look to verify reality again and again until familiarity is established. Then fear gives way to triumph of recognition. This need to establish familiarity is strikingly apparent in the play of young children.

Freud's several early statements concerning play brought forth the idea that fantasy and play, much of which in human beings consists of acted-out fantasy, serve the dual functions of trial behavior and gratification of the wish that all will turn out well. This is especially clearly stated in "Creative Writers and Day-Dreaming" (1908), but it is also indicated in *Beyond the Pleasure Principle* (1920a). In the former article, he considers not merely the play of childhood, but play and fantasy of the specially creative person, the poet. Play was considered to be in the service of the child's growing up and the need to meet strain and uncertainty about his abilities in contrast to those of older children or of adults. Play, said Freud, occurs under the influence of the powerful wish to grow up. This conception, *the wish to grow up*, may be seen to have two component parts which are more or less fused: first, the inner maturation pressures, the wish in terms of organic *need* or obligatory demand to grow up, i.e., the spontaneous unfolding due to growth; and second, the wish to be "grown up" as this is experienced psychically through the observation of others by the child. Between these two forces, the one pushing and the other pulling, the child finds his way in play. In these terms, play may appear as a kind of paradoxical make-believe reality testing—a reality testing, however, in which the child holds the joker through the fact that much of play *is* make-believe even when expressed in overt action. It is not then "real reality."

In 1932, Robert Waelder reviewed the observations of children's play and integrated these findings into current psychoanalytic theory. Utilizing the further understanding of the role of anxiety which Freud (1926a) had meanwhile formulated, he indicated that play was the child's way of attempting to allay the anxiety by overcoming and mastering those situations which had caused it. Play then would have something in common with counterphobic behavior. The anxiety-provoking problems of today in the child's life then become the subjects of the play of tomorrow, whether or not these problems have apparently risen from or even are much involved with maturational needs. There is certainly a difference in emphasis from Freud's earlier statements which stressed the anticipatory aspects of play and gave less prominence to the already experienced discomfiture. Freud (1908) had spoken of "unhappiness," to be sure. This is particularly interesting in view of the reluctance of many artists to part with their disturbing morbidities and anxieties unless these are of crippling proportions. It seems to me, however, that there is a difference between the role of anxiety in relation to the creative product in which play takes some part in the highly creative individual from that in the less talented, more everyday person. In Freud's early statements, we have a picture of play as a kind of dress rehearsal for the future in respects in which the child has already felt himself to be "insecure," to be compared with the "unhappiness" of the poet, and emphasized further in the "anxiety" of the later formulation. Play, being under the child's own direction, can represent fragments and bits of reality according to his needs and wishes. Thus he can dose himself with larger or smaller bits and need not bring the whole overwhelming situation down on himself at one time, even in played-out form. An understanding of all this is at the heart of play techniques of child therapy and the understanding of children's drawings and writings.

Although Waelder explicitly stated that his theory of play did not cover the entire range of play functions, its great clinical usefulness has made it the center of a large number of the psychoanalytic discussions of play in later years. (This central place is more or less implied by the very title "The Psychoanalytic Theory of Play.") In summary he stated: "the psychoanalytic contributions to the problem of play may be indicated by the following phrases: instinct of mastery; with fulfilment; assimilation of overpowering experiences according to the mechanism of the repetition compulsion; transformation from passivity to activity; leave of absence from reality and from the super-ego; fantasies about real objects." This summary will be referred to again later.

Waelder accepts the existence of *functional pleasure* in play (a term especially used by K. Bühler) in the sense of pleasure experienced in pure performance without regard to the success of the specific activity, although he states that functional pleasure obviously cannot be considered the *main* factor underlying all play; and further that what might appear as functional pleasure may be due rather to the psychic content of the activity which gratifies the child insofar as, for example, he may seem in the play activity to be bigger and stronger than he actually is. But Waelder grants the possibility of a truer, not illusory, functional pleasure (satisfaction inherent in the use of developing function) and states that this may play a role "particularly during the period of growth of the organism, that is to say, in childhood." It is this "truer functional pleasure" with which I am especially concerned: this is what I have referred to as *satisfaction of maturational pressures*. Since, after the first weeks of life, such pressures must be expressed further through psychic content of varying degrees of complexity, it is easy to overlook or discredit their importance. This may be the case with Fenichel (1945a, p. 543), who sees the functional pleasure of play as due only to the relief of anxiety.

Since Waelder's article there have been a number of other studies of play, including those of Hendrick (1942, 1943a, 1945b), Bally (1945), Erikson (1937, 1940, 1951), K. Menninger (1938,

1942a, 1942b), K. and J. L. Menninger (1942), and J. L. Menninger (1942), Peller's article (1954) which surveys the various characteristic forms of play as they are correlated with libidinal phases and certain aspects of ego development, Kardos and Peto (1956), and finally a recent article by Alexander (1958). There is of course an enormous literature on play therapy with children, and many articles, especially those of Menninger and his associates, on play in connection with hospital treatment of psychotic and severely neurotic patients. I shall only refer specifically to those articles which have a direct bearing on my present subject—the special relation of play to creative imagination.

Waelder's use of the term "instinct of mastery" in the summary of his article appears somewhat ambiguous, or at least not clearly enough defined in relation to the rest of the content of his study. He wrote consistently of play being used to reduce the discomfort produced by specific recent experience in which the child has felt overwhelmed. At the same time he also made it clear that in the mastery of the original experience through playing it out, there is not a mastery through the development of a skill or of a function in reality but rather by the use of fantasy about the original overt reality. He believed that in a state in which reality and fantasy are not clearly differentiated there can be an abreaction of the original discomforting experience and thereby a reduction of anxiety. He and Fenichel both asserted that the repetitions in play *may* lead over to practice and learning but do not fundamentally and explicitly contain a need and pressure to learn.

That play does serve to diminish anxiety after trauma seems definite, but it may be doubted whether the anxiety is so thoroughly and generally reduced, and the originally disturbing experience so nearly mastered as Waelder's theory suggested. It seems to me that frequently some residue of the anxiety contributes to the fun and excitement of play; and that this is made tolerable not by the fusion of fantasy and reality, and an abreaction through this, but rather by the opposite, the child's ability to separate fantasy and reality and his tacit realization that his play is not real reality after all. It may be that when he has familiarized himself with some of the elements of the disturbing experience in the representational way of play, only then a truer mastery can occur through dealing again with the real situation or ones closely allied to it.

One must realize, however, that Waelder's theory was produced some time before Anna Freud's *The Ego and the Mechanisms of Defense* (1936), and that the very characteristics of play which he enumerated as operating in the service of mastery are essentially defensive mechanisms. It may be questioned then whether the beneficial effect of play in childhood is not rather a reduction of any severe degree of anxiety through illusory mastery sufficiently to permit further maturational development to occur and give opportunity to meet similar disturbing experiences in reality later. In other instances, however, repetitions in play may not be so helpful, but rather take part in establishing overly strong neurotic defenses and constitute a stage in the development of a potential neurosis.

Especially may this be true in situations in which there was no therapy connected with the play, i.e., no interpretation of its significance. The same result may occur in unskillful therapy in which the therapist joins too consistently in the play without critique, thereby verifying rather than relieving, much in the fashion of a contaminated transference relation in adult life.[3]

Hendrick's articles on "Instinct and the Ego during Infancy" (1942) and on "Work and the Pleasure Principle" (1943b) develop further a concept of an instinct to master. The terms *instinct of mastery* and *instinct to master,* used respectively by Waelder and Hendrick, appear to stress different aims of mastering, in the one a mastering of the feeling of helplessness in regard to a specific and often complex situation; in the other, the achievement of mastery of a function or group of functions leading to the perfection of a definite skill. The concept of an instinct to master in the sense of Hendrick arouses in me a doubt whether there is a universal drive for perfection of skill and attainment, in any appreciable degree, separate from identification and rivalry. Hendrick's studies, however, contain much which is important for an understanding of the functional pleasure of play: not merely pleasure as the relief of anxiety, but in the truer sense of pleasure in functioning, i.e., satisfaction of maturational potentials.

This seems indeed to be part of the repetitive oscillation be-

3 I am indebted to Dr. Nelly Tibout for discussing situations of this kind with me.

tween progression and regression which occurs rather generally in the young organism during periods of its greatest growth. It seems that maturational forces push the organism onward, first with increasing special sensorimotor responsiveness based on somatic developments, the milder increases of excitation appear in enlivening and playful behavior with signs of pleasure. But further progressive excursion means increased excitation and strain. Then a regression to the familiar and restful sets in before the next progressive forward push.

Functional pleasure may be seen in its simplest form in the early months of life when the psychic structure is most primitive. Observing a baby four to six months old, kicking with his legs, making movements as though to push or to stretch, while he gurgles as though in a comfortably happy state, one cannot avoid the impression that there is some enjoyment in motion itself, not merely a release from anxiety and fear. Later during the latter part of the second year and again in the fourth year, there appear similar but more complicated heightenings of pleasure in movement with minimal external stimulations to such a degree as to give the impression of strong endogenous elements at work in producing the reaction.

It may be noteworthy that during even such mild strain as that of prolonged nursing, many babies develop rhythmical playful movements which accompany the nursing. Thus the baby, simultaneously with sucking at the breast or bottle, may play with his hands over the mother's breast or clothing, may later develop a rhythmic touching of his own cheek or pulling at the lobe of his own ear, or touching a lock of his hair, or the edge of the blanket. This seems to be an early manifestation of the use of the transitional object which is both *me* and *not me* (Winnicott, 1953). What I would emphasize now is not especially the intermediate quality of the object but the playful comforting rhythmic use of it which is also significant. Further, that even rhythmic oscillation of movement or behavior, whether occurring as part of or parallel to the main stream of activity, is in itself comforting as it involves a repetitive return to the familiar. This is an ingredient in much play.[4]

Hendrick saw this repetitive regression to the normal stage of

4 The function of play is discussed further in chs. 19 and 20.

an unlearned function as occurring whenever a function is blocked or obstructed from reaching its goal. I see it as occurring regularly as part of the maturational development but focused in content according to the libidinal stage, especially influenced by the impact of untoward external events. When mental memory and thoughtful imagery are developed in contrast to the sort of memory of purely somatic responses and physical conditioning; when rational thinking has begun—in short, when the secondary process has begun to be established, then indeed we have the beginning of both imagination and anxiety. Then time begins to have some significance and memory can be projected forward as expectation. Play can now become more diversified in form and in function. It is in regard to this period that Freud's (1908) second meaning of play can be considered, viz., the wish of the child to be grown up. Imitative responsiveness gives way to definite wishes to be like another person, child or adult. Differences in size are more clearly comprehended. Play may now be carried on individually and privately in fantasy or expressed in action, either in acting out of preconceived fantasy often of an imitative type, or in the repetition of various versions of previously disturbing experiences. Now with the development of imagination, between the two forces of maturational pressures expressed through extensive mental picturings combined with somatic sensations and the pull of definite wishes to be grown up (to be in control rather than relatively helpless), the child begins to find ways either to achieve mastery through reality testing and practice if the task is not too great, or to win an illusory mastery in play.[5]

Finally, I refer to a recent article by Alexander, "A Contribution to the Theory of Play" (1958), since he also deals somewhat with the relation of play to creativity. He presents a point of view which is quite the opposite of Waelder's, stressing in his conclusion that "in true playfulness the solution of a problem is not imperative." He seems to imply that play can be clearly differentiated from work in all instances, and he does not differentiate between the quality of playfulness and play itself. Alexander states that play comes from surplus energy, by which he means all energy which is not necessary for the bare maintenance of the body. This

---

[5] The development of play, speech, and thought, and their impact on the gifted are discussed further in chs. 19 and 20.

surplus energy is the source of all sexual activity. This schematiza-
tion seems to me not to do justice to the total situation, however
beguiling its simplicity makes it. He considers that through this
"free play" the child discovers new uses for his organs and exer-
cises them until mastery is achieved, and their different functions
become integrated in a utilitarian fashion for independent existence. He also states that the utility of this play is entirely a
secondary effect and has no motivational significance. I seem here
to hear the echo of a behaviorist bell, which has scant place for the
unconscious.

Alexander mentions the strong affinity between play and creativity, yet he does so without reference to unconscious motivations
or fantasy. He considers the creative aspect of play to lie in an increased, almost unlimited freedom of choice which lends to play
an experimental connotation. In this he contrasts play with adaptive behavior which, with its nose to the grindstone, is restricted
to its goal, viz., the problem it must solve. He speaks of repetitions
in play only as serving to make useful functions automatic and so
save energy. In further defining the relationship of play to creativity, he states: "Complex play activities, such as artistic creation,
may be highly organized in themselves but pursue their own intrinsic aims, as expressed in *l'art pour l'art*. Probably creativity in
art and in 'pure' science consists in the complex organization of
these nonutilitarian motivational forces, 'surplus energies', for
autonomous expression" (p. 186, n.). This point of view appears,
more by implication than by direct statement, to disregard the
deep (and not necessarily immediately recognizable) but powerful
service of art in expressing in nonlogical terms and in endlessly
new forms the collective problems of the group, or even of
mankind.

Moreover, art has its roots in unconscious reactions and processes of the artist, even including basic somatic ones. There are
many indications of the influence of somatic processes on fantasy
and therefore on art. The delicate but intense sense of rhythm,
which is an essential quality in any artist, is basically of somatic
origin. This subject, i.e., the somatic substructure of fantasy, is
discussed by Susan Isaacs in "The Nature and Function of Phantasy" (1948).

An incident in the life of Edward Lear (1907), English painter and nonsense poet, is rather striking. Lear was an overly sensitive, shy man subject to the most extreme inhibition of aggression which may then have found a discharge in his occasional epileptic attacks. On one of his numerous travels into remote regions he began to complain, in his journal and in letters to a friend, about his sufferings from the noises and invasions of his privacy by native children. Gradually definite cannibalistic fantasies emerged, of which he wrote with nonsensical relish. Some days later, however, he was reporting his surprise on discovering the eruption of a couple of teeth on his upper jaw, although he was past forty. He noted no connection between the teeth and the cannibalistic urges, but there was no further mention of these fantasies in later letters or journal notes. The possible connection seems plausible, however, as Lear was a man who lived always in contact both with reason and with primary process imagery and seemed repeatedly involved in primitive introjection and projection mechanisms.[6]

Art generally touches the feeling-imagery rather than the rational, somewhat detached intellectual thoughts of others. It clarifies by stimulating a unique set of feeling responses in each of its recipients, whether or not there is much conscious intellectual content resulting. Each artistic product is the delivery into an externalized and communicable form of an economically organized piece of the artist's interaction with the world around him. In doing this, the creative artist expresses more than he is aware that he knows.

Thomas Mann stated this when he wrote of himself (1930): "The truth is that every piece of work is a realization, fragmentary but complete in itself, of our individuality; and this kind of realization is the sole and painful way we have of getting the particular experience, no wonder that the process is attended by surprises" (p. 41). There is something in this which is not identical with, but seems related to, the expression of maturational pressures in childhood.

The relation in the artistic product between the total (collective) and the specific personal problems and experiences of the artist's life must vary greatly. The inevitable imprint of the specific and conscious personal problems may be either great or slight,

6 Other aspects of Edward Lear are discussed in ch. 29.

but the enduring and widely serviceable creative product is generally not so explicitly restricted to the personal.

This brings us back to further questions of the relation of play to creative imagination. It is clear that much complex play is acted-out fantasy; and that fantasy of special quality is the stuff of which creative productions are made. It is likely, however, that the original, the new (whether in form or content) will be derived from fantasy or play which is less rather than more bound by the repetition compulsion. As already noted, too, the markedly creative person generally progresses in his artistic development insofar as he is not tied to the repetition of his own explicit experiences. The writer must get beyond the confines of the "one story," his own story, which every writer and every person perhaps is said to have the urge at first to write.[7]

Growth and development of creative power is undoubtedly sometimes aided by the loosening up of personal conflicts and the liberation of energy which is then available for less restricted productions. But I doubt whether development through sublimation comprises the major growth of creative abilities in all, or even perhaps in most artists. Neither do I think that creativity of an impressive degree develops from random play and empirical experimentation, no matter how wide the field may be, as described by Alexander.

Artists do not seem to abreact a great deal through what they produce. Neither does it always seem to help them to gain distance from their individual dilemmas. Occasionally it may help to establish personal defensive measures, but then I believe there is a danger of inroads into artistic integrity.

Artists are notoriously playful people, who make the profoundest commitments to life through their art, yet may be quite irresponsible and unstable in their personal lives. Their behavior is frequently quite paradoxical, and does not regularly improve with artistic success. Viewed from a phenomenological angle, their behavior might lead them to be considered neurotic, psychopathic, or at time psychotic. It cannot be said either that creative production

---

[7] There may be exceptions: to be sure, Eugene O'Neill, one of America's greatest dramatists, seems to be endlessly writing his own story in a frenzied agony. Powerful as some of his plays are, partly by their stark primitive quality, they nonetheless appear to me to suffer from the lack of any distance on the part of their author.

appears regularly as the result of mitigation of the individual instability; or conversely that lasting alleviation of instabilities is achieved through satisfying creative work. This may be true in some instances, and in some people, but it is by no means even a general rule. In my other papers (see chs. 24 and 26) I have presented the view that the artist's sense of reality is different from that of the less gifted person, and that his emotional make-up is more complicated and paradoxical by virtue of his usually having severe problems of identity with conflicts of varying intensity between the personal and the artistic selves.

Markedly creative people seem to be not only playful but restless and responsive to the new to an unusual degree. They frequently make the world their home. They are innocent and even childish along with great width of experience and sophistication. Their sexual activities are varied, not infrequently with suggestions or the open appearance of perversity. Yet in many there are unusual periods of sexual inactivity and continence. From a limited experience in analyzing a few creative people, I would also think that the energy utilized in creative activity often is not well "neutralized," but is associated quite frequently with sexual excitement and aggressive feelings, amounting almost to frenzy. Love relationships, like other interests, may be intense, but impermanent, overlapping, and complicated. It seems that in the choice of love objects there is a much greater variety of type of choice than is true in less gifted people who so often show a compulsive repetition in their choices. There is the capacity for the most intense and absorbing cathexis, coupled with the opposite characteristic, viz., a peculiar cathectic mobility with quick withdrawal and equally quick reinvestment in a new object or interest if the first cathected object or interest is actively interfered with or spent. I must make it clear, however, that I present these generalizations with reservation, since such characteristics are only frequent and not universal. Yet I believe them to be significant. Further, they do not harmonize with our ideas of sublimation, which possibly may be of greater import in less creative people.

As has already been stated, it seems that much of early play is alternately stimulating and comforting in a rhythmic pattern. In this sense it is repetitive. It must be recognized, however, that the content of such rhythmic playful activity may vary considerably and increasingly with the unfolding and complexity of psychological experiences. It may be that not enough attention has been paid to the differences between content and underlying drive in play. Content too may be repetitive and reassuring, in the fashion of the repetition compulsion; or in some instances the playful acting out may get the upper hand.

The mental play of the artist with the alternation of expansive experimental stimulation and withdrawal for testing is beautifully compared to the play of a young cat toying with a mouse in the following poem, written on the margin of an eighth-century psalter in an Irish monastery (Chauvire, 1952)

> I and Pangur Ban, my cat,
> 'Tis a like task we are at;
> Hunting Mice is his delight,
> Hunting words I sit all night.
>
> 'Tis a merry thing to see
> At our tasks how glad are we,
> When at home we sit and find
> Entertainment to our mind.
>
> 'Gainst the wall he sets his eye
> Full and fierce and sharp and sly;
> 'Gainst the wall of knowledge I
> All my little wisdom try.
>
> When a mouse darts from its den
> Oh how glad is Pangur then!
> Oh what gladness do I prove
> When I solve the doubts I love!
>
> So in peace our tasks we ply.
> Pangur Ban, my cat, and I;
> In our arts we find our bliss,
> I have mine and he has his.

> Practice every day has made
> Pangur perfect in his trade;
> I get wisdom day and night,
> Turning darkness into light.[8]

It must be remarked that the testing accomplished by the poet-monk's play with words and phrases is not merely a testing of external reality, in any empirical fashion. It is rather the putting forth of word or phrase into clear conscious form, whether written or spoken, making a mouse of it, in terms of the poetic metaphor, in order the more clearly to test its euphony and potential harmony in uniting external reality with the inner preconscious or partly conscious fantasy in the poet's mind. This is, I suspect, one of the main functions of play in connection with creative imagination. It aids in delivering the unconscious fantasy and harmonizing it with the external world. By momentarily changing places from subjective creator to objective audience (listener or viewer) the artist so crosses the bridges back and forth, and the externalizable form, the creative product, grows.

The play of the creative person may even seem to be performed at random; to involve pure chance; or to be really free, in the sense of not being determined by any choice on his part. It may even appear to have the empirical quality described by Alexander. But this appearance is misleading. The artist's persistent access to primary process thinking and imagery means that he possesses a wider variety of symbols and of related perceptions, which in turn make more choices of expression available to him than is true in the less gifted person. In addition, the special quality of his sensitivity, the inevitable polymorphous character of his perceptiveness, and the capacity for synesthesias enormously enrich the very matrix of his experience. Even so in some situations where the playful act may seem to be one of pure chance, this too may be utilized as the means of delivery of the inner preconscious fantasy. (We here approach the problems of inspirational experience, which I shall not make any attempt to discuss.)

A famous story comes to mind in this connection, concerning Leonardo da Vinci in a state of restless incipient creative produc-

---

[8] Robin Flowers's translation. This poem has also been translated by Walter de la Mare.

tivity. When the inner fantasy had not yet sufficiently emerged for him to begin the work of externalization and yet he felt the strong urge to do so, it is said that he would crumple a piece of paper, toss it on the floor, and then sit staring at it until some form began to emerge in his vision, from its wrinkled, seemingly meaningless shape. It would thus appear as a kind of self-created and self-administered Rorschach test. In this way he might begin the delivery of an inner imagery. Whether or not the story is apocryphal, it or similar methods are familiar to and used by many artists. Play in this way too would help to engage and to bring into some externalization preconscious fantasy which for one reason or another was slow in emerging by itself.

There is only one other aspect of our subject which I would attempt to touch on in this paper and that very briefly, viz., the varying role of anxiety in relation to creative productivity. I have been rather impressed, in treating creative people and in seeing a number more in consultation, that unless the anxiety is utterly overwhelming, many of them do not wish to be relieved of it. In fact, they sometimes fear that it will be lost in the course of treatment, and that they will thereby be deprived of creative urge and so indirectly of creative productivity. This might seem to be a direct confirmation of the applicability of Waelder's theory of play. But it frequently does not work at all in this way, for the period of creative work which has been provoked or initiated by the bout of anxiety has often very little content related to the source of anxiety. There may then be no abreaction at all through the creative work, sometimes only a partial abandonment through the identification of the self with and the absorption in life on a larger collective scale. That is to say, the individual is able to take leave of the individual self and go to the other collective one. The anxiety is never thoroughly silenced in this way, and I have sometimes thought that it added to the excitement and gave a special tang to the satisfaction of the realization of the creative productivity itself. Undoubtedly in some instances the preliminary suffering also is a kind of penance which permits the creative artist, who is guilty for the possession of this superior ability, to claim it and possess it at least for the time being. Sometimes in fact, the content of the creative product *is* in some relation to the underlying personal conflict, but is transformed into collective terms and may add to or interfere with the effectiveness of the creative production. It may be paradoxically true then that the artist himself gains less in his personal life from this creative work than do the others who receive it. (This seems, for example, to have been repeatedly the situation in the case of Jonathan Swift.)

In the transformation from the personal to the collective understanding, there is less chance for any degree of abreaction than may be true in the more explicit terms of some play of childhood.

An example of a situation in which writing did serve to reduce anxiety through abreaction is given in the recently published *Autobiography of Mark Van Doren* (1958). When, in December, 1918, Van Doren was twenty-four years old and had just been discharged from army service, he was amazed to find himself with an aching void, missing army life, and unable to let any other life take its place so that he thought he must die of loneliness. He cured himself by writing a factual but infinitely detailed account of all that he could recall of people and events occupying the nineteen months of army service. He drew maps and diagrams, made lists of names, in all an encyclopedic record of nearly 300 pages. After working unceasingly for a week he found himself cured of his unease. There was no attempt to fictionalize or to convert into poetry, but the expression of a stark need to preserve and yet gain distance from his experiences by this detailed accounting. This piece of work was certainly a part of the process of mourning. The young man was then able to return to his interrupted work, the study of Dryden, and to resume his contact with the university life, from which he had been temporarily alienated.

I can only emphasize that the role of anxiety in connection with the artistic product varies according to the special nature of the interlocking relationships between the personal self and the artistic self in each creative individual. The problems of the invasions of creative work by the anxieties arising in the personal life and appearing as a block rather than as open anxiety should be the subject of further study.

In concluding this paper, I again emphasize that I use the term *creative* imagination to imply a capacity for originality and inventiveness, rather than creative in the sense merely of ability to synthesize to reach a product. The service of play in the artist in introducing more executive work in materializing the creative product does not depend on clear visual or auditory imagery even when it is carried on in fantasy and not played out overtly. It involves the whole spectrum of sensory modalities and corresponding responses, e.g., visceral as well as outer-body-rind reactions such as tactile and kinesthetic stimulations and responses. It may include the gamut of primary and secondary process activities. The beloved "doubt" of the Irish monk is not to be confused with obsessional doubt, but rather to be likened to the *evenly suspended attention* of the analyst to the patient's productions (Freud, 1912). But in the artist's playful thinking or trial activity, this suspended attention is to himself. This permits various harmonious elements of his psychic content to slip into place as though by good luck.

CHAPTER TWENTY-EIGHT

Woman as Artist (1960)

It is readily apparent that special creativity in the arts and sciences, including inventiveness, appears to be less frequent in women than in men. Only the most fanatical feminist would strive to deny this fact. Certainly there are, and have been, competent and distinguished women writers and painters, not as many of the latter as of the former; and the light of an occasional outstanding woman scientist shines the more brightly because of its relative isolation. Women as noteworthy musicians are almost as rare as women scientists and seem to be largely interpreters. It is difficult to think of a single woman composer of note. In a recent *Dictionary of Art and Artists* (painters and sculptors) the names of only five women appear among a total of over seven hundred; and two of the five were not of sufficient note to appear in the last edition of the *Encyclopedia Britannica*. This dictionary, intended as an informational handbook for visitors to the museums of the Western world, restricts itself to Western artists of the seven centuries preceding Picasso. Just why the authors (L. & P. Murray, 1959) hit upon this particular limit is their secret which I have not attempted to fathom. Another history of art includes three thousand names, only forty of which are those of women (MacFall, 1911).

At any rate, such compilations are inevitably limited to those individuals whose creative products have won the kind of acclaim which has placed their work in museums. This obviously is a practical, but not necessarily an accurate gauge of actual merit. Although time does do something to sort out the really great from the merely competent and fashionable, it is by no means a reliably just and accurate judge and only occasionally delivers up "lost work" which has not previously had some recognition. But it must also be noted that especially among painters the height of their fame is often not reached until some time after death. Any appraisal of creative work based largely on the degree of recognition must risk grave inaccuracy. Perhaps nowhere is this more obvious than in Sir Francis Galton's study of genius, which floundered so badly in the estimate of artists and writers (as compared to military and civic leaders) even though he otherwise gave some valuable hints. There has similarly been a serious fault in the studies of many later geneticists who based their estimates of ability almost exclusively on recognition in *Who's Who* and similar compilations.

In spite of all these reservations and the inadequacy of such compilations, it certainly must be recognized that there is a great discrepancy between the number of men and the number of women who realize outstanding creative talent in producing lasting work.

We are faced then with the question why this discrepancy between the sexes in the realization of artistic creative potential exists. Does it, for one set of reasons or another, lie in the area of ability to achieve this externalization? Are women more inhibited than men in this respect? Or may there be more basically, or even in addition, a difference in fundamental capacity? Before we proceed further it is desirable to emphasize too that in this present discussion, the word *artistic* will be used for any creative ability involving not only skill, but originality and vision. We would differentiate it on the one hand from mere skill perfected by practice, and on the other from a more limited kind of creative productivity involving adeptness in synthesizing design but without marked originality. The term *artist* is used here in the same sense in which I used it in earlier papers (see chs. 24, 26, 27).

Robert Graves is reported to have said that when a woman has a baby her artistic creativity ceases. I seem also to remember that Freda Kirchwey, writing in *The Nation* some years ago, said somewhat wryly that women might not be such productive artists as men because they lacked the ability to abstract themselves, and were always worrying about whether the potatoes were burning. These two homely statements clearly face up to the opposition of the forces of biological and artistic creativity. Certainly, common observation bears this out. A woman's part in biological creativity is much more prolonged, more physically involving and emotionally committing than that of man. The very facts that she carries the baby as a part of her own body for the better part of a year and that there are further years of his relative helplessness in which her concern, activity, and direct physical ministration are generally called upon naturally cause her all-around practical absorption in the young child to be greater than that of man. Certainly there is superb artistic creativity involved in the sound rearing of a child, a fact recently emphasized again by Ernest Jones (1956) in his Freud centennial lecture, and the woman must here play the primary role. But the canvas is so large, and the span of time and the intricacies of development so great, that even the artistry of a talented and dedicated mother may fail, be interfered with, or lost sight of.

In studying the conditions which may be the basis of woman's lesser productivity in the arts than man's, we shall deal with the problems under two general headings: (1) Are there differences between the sexes in constitutional equipment and functioning which have bearing in this special sphere? (2) What, if any, neurotic interferences with the processes involved in the externalization of creative forces may be greater in women than in men? These do not necessarily involve inherent differences in potential creative capacity, but rather interferences in the executive work of expressing these creative powers. This distinction may become clearer as we progress. As the genetic point of view influences much of the thought of this paper, material will be presented largely from this angle. Other approaches, however, are certainly possible—as the topographical. For example, Kubie's recent lectures (1958) deal essentially with disturbances due to neuroses affecting preconscious activity, which may be so important a stage in the development of creative work. It would be a mistake, however, to consider the *creative process* as synonymous with *creativity*, or with creative ability. While Kubie's presentation is valuable and provocative, focusing clearly on one of the most vulnerable areas involved in creative work, it does not deal with some of the other neurotic and general problems of creativity with which this paper will concern itself.

Creativity seems to me to rest on a basis of certain fundamental biological potentials, probably inborn but not necessarily hereditary. They may develop well or little according to the vicissitudes of the individual life which promote or impede their flowering. Important in these potentials are an especial range and intensity of sensory responsiveness present from the first months onward, including marked kinesthetic as well as other sensory responsiveness to rhythm and an innate capacity or tendency to feel sensory responses in gestalt or patterned ways but with great flexibility and variability. This permits the sensing of a wide variety of similarities and differences and promotes richness and persistence of formation and utilization of symbols. All this is enhanced by good intellect and good memory, but marked superiority in these latter respects is not intrinsic in creative ability itself. In earlier chapters (e.g., 24, 26, 27) I have presented my own ideas that these special capacities draw the potential artist into an early relationship with collective figures and forms in nature (both animate and inanimate) which are related to the objects of the personal relationship, for which they may readily be substituted; hence they are referred to as *collective alternates*.

Such a capacity for substitution also means that when the relationship to the personal object is disturbed, the young child may turn away to the collective substitute object and there gratify his wishes in actuality or in fantasy. Consequently, in my estimation, there is the possibility of a less clear resolution of the problems of the libidinal phase development in some potentially gifted young children than there might be in less gifted children. This is reflected in the high degree of pregenital neurotic elements in the later lives of many artists—apparent in failure to make stable adult object relationships, relative ease of dissociation, and even a seemingly high incidence of outcroppings of perverse tendencies. The "instability" of the artist and his right to a different sort of life from that of the ordinary citizen is generally recognized by the public (Kris, 1935). This right may be granted as a special privilege to those touched with divine inspiration, or may cause them to be devaluated—according to the nature and stage of the culture at any given time. It probably also contributes to the idea that creative talent is akin to psychosis, a conception on which psychiatrists of the past spent so much time (Kris, 1952). It must be definitely understood, however, that such interferences with or deviations in libidinal phase development are not *obligatorily* inherent in the development of creatively gifted children. Under specially favorable conditions a good development of libidinal phases and resolution of their problems, leading to a sound oedipal development, may occur. There are accordingly many different interrelationships possible between the personal relationships and those of the collective alternates.

The material of this paper is drawn very largely from my own analytic practice. To be sure I have attempted to increase my knowledge by as much reading as possible about the lives of many women artists—for the most part writers; but the study of the more detailed or even microscopic structure of the development of creativity in women and the interferences with its full fruition are the result of my own analytic work. There has recently been some good-humored reproach to me concerning my articles on creativity, expressed in recent reviews with statements of regret that clinical illustrations have been drawn too exclusively from biographies of famous people and not sufficiently from my own analytic practice. I shall, however, still maintain caution about presenting case material very specifically, to avoid possible harmful effects on patients when it is impossible sufficiently to preserve their anonymity, an especially difficult task when one is dealing with gifted patients. Consequently the pleasure of giving vivid clinical illustrations must be sacrificed no matter how much they would increase the effectiveness of this presentation.

Attention is next turned to the consideration of *constitutional differences between the sexes in anatomical structure and function* which might influence artistic productivity, that it, the capacity to bring to external form the conceptions coming from true creative ability. There seems to be no sufficient way at present of ascertaining clearly whether there is any innate difference between boys and girls in the properties of sensory sensitivity, response to rhythm, and the spontaneous tendency to gestalt or patterned organization of perceptions. But there are differences in other respects—in the influence of anatomical structure and functioning —which can readily be seen to shape and channel the unfolding of these capacities, and it is to an examination of these influences that I would now turn.

In a comprehensive and imperative sense, women's absorption in childbearing and child rearing occupies the center of the stage. Does this mean more than the crowding out of the fulfillment of one set of talents by the realization of another, such as might be implied in the remarks of Miss Kirchwey and Mr. Graves? Certainly, the jostling for position in the choice of one talent or medium of expression at the expense of another may be seen in many people who are gifted in more than one direction. Woman has the fateful biological gift of childbearing. It is conspicuous when one studies the lives of a number of women writers and painters who on the whole are not a very biologically prolific lot; nor are they conspicuously successful mothers. When nevertheless they forego or limit the realization of this natural destiny, not many women seem to achieve great pre-eminence in the arts. It is desirable to look as well at the other and less massive determinants in the situation.

One may look then at the shaping pressures on creative productivity which may differ in the two sexes; first, in accordance with the inherent influence of differences in general body build and structure; second, in the specific awareness of and reaction to the sexual parts which are so uniquely contrasted in the two sexes. There is only a moderate contrast in general body structure and configuration between male and female affecting direction and utilization of energy; but these differences seem to contribute to fundamental differences in secondary attitudes. The male, with greater muscular development of extremities and of shoulder girdle, is built more for an active and mobile muscular life, perhaps determined originally by fitness for the fight and the chase. The female, with greater pelvic girdle development and lesser strength in the extremities, is clearly more destined for conservation and endurance rather than for immediate and forceful thrust of energetic response. While analysts are used to contrasting male and female as respectively active and passive, one might emphasize receptivity rather than any extreme of passivity in the female. To some extent there are characteristic centrifugal energetic responses in the one sex, and centripetal ones in the other. Clearly, giving birth is an exception, being a climactic, energetic, centrifugal, and aggressive female response.

Characteristically the girl baby talks earlier than the boy, but he precedes her slightly in walking. Even in quite young nursery school children the girl's greater preoccupation with personal relationships and the boy's with muscular activities is noticeable. While children of both sexes show great capacity for imaginative games in the period of latency, the boy generally shows a greater interest in adventure and physical aggression, in experimentation, manual activity, reality testing, and what might be called executive expansion. His acquisition of skill in bodily performance with emphasis on precision and logic is conspicuous. In the girl, imaginative fantasy seems characteristically less linked with experimentation. It is involved more with romanticizing on the basis of personal emotional involvements. Externalization of fantasy appears often in the form of playing a role or dramatization. Frequently there is more secretiveness regarding her fantasy, with a lesser need to test or act it out openly. These differences are not so great as to exclude a very considerable overlapping of interests between the sexes, which seems especially conspicuous in the prepuberty years and may extend well into adolescence, whenever it is reinforced by strong special identifications with the opposite sex.

Still, by and large, it seems that the male characteristics of need for externalization, of testing, of development of precision, may greatly promote male superiority in artistic creative *productivity*, and may contribute further to the choice of certain areas for development of special giftedness. Thus the boy conspicuously excels in science and in mathematics more frequently than does his sister. Woman's creative work seems stamped with attributes resembling her biologically creative functions, as it is most often involved in problems of human relationship and interpretation, and rarely shows a high degree of originality in other respects. This may be the basis of the fact that women are frequently skilled as musical interpreters but are rarely great composers, because composition demands the precise skill of a creative engineer as well as the emotional response to and auditory "vision" of the total sound picture. Similarly among painters, those women who have gained some eminence have been concerned much with portraits and illustrating. We can include here also the excellence of women in the performing arts of the theater and other entertainments.

The psychological importance of these basic differences lies not only in the direct selection of certain activities by men, and others by women, but in their tendency to lend patterns, and subtly to stamp other characteristics and attitudes which are not primarily based on them.

In considering next the influences of the awareness of the differences between the sexes with respect to their genitals, such secondary effects on character, interests, and attitudes are, I believe, more conspicuous, even as the contrast in the sexual organs is more striking. The external exposed position of the boy's genitals means that from earliest infancy he becomes aware of them to a much greater degree than can be true in the girl. They are visible, they are touchable, and the penis becomes early involved in the acquisition of a skill in controlling and accurately directing the urinary flow, which in turn means focus and precision. The boy further tends to have an earlier, more frequent, and more extensive external genital stimulation than does the girl. This takes place first by the external frictions of cleansing and clothing and later in compliance with endogenously arising internal sensations. This obligatory externalization of genital awareness and sensation in the male, in contrast to the female, and the clear implications of genital thrust and power long before maturity seem to reinforce the masculine characteristics associated with the body build, the greater manual and bodily dexterity evident in competitive games.

The girl's genitals, being almost completely invaginated, are hidden from her view. They are ordinarily almost "silent" in early sensation except for the clitoris and the mucous membranes around the vaginal orifice. While the clitoris is the site of strong infantile genital sensations, it is not readily seen by the girl, is sufficiently variable in size and degree of embedding as not always to be readily located manually by her, and her ideas of its location and function are frequently confused. Her early sexuality then must be much more mysterious and uncertain, and under most conditions lacks those specific, precise, and organizing qualities which are so characteristic of the male.

While the exposure of the male genitals promotes their stimulability, it also heightens the direct threat and fear of injury to the organs; but the whole problem is a focused one. The castration problem of the girl, with its devious explanations and its excess of hypothetical guilt, is linked with her envy and confusion due to her awareness of the difference from the boy and her inability to see her own organs clearly. It gives rise to a type of competitiveness which cannot be met directly with reality testing and so must depend on displacement, rationalization, and fantasy. The girl's resolution of her envy of the boy's phallus, with the realization that she will later be able to have a child, contains so great a deferment that its acceptance cannot be achieved until she has reached the degree of maturity to tolerate this postponement. In addition, it is an unusual woman who attains so nearly complete an acceptance of her own intrinsic feminine role as to include a full object relationship to the child—an acceptance of the child as different and separate from rather than an extension of herself. The marked dependence of the child on the physical care of the mother certainly increases and prolongs the inner attitude in the mother that the child is essentially still a part of herself. Child-bearing remains in feminine psychology heavily stamped with a tacit attitude of considering it essentially a substitute, although possibly a superior recompense, for the original inferiority in her presumed genital deficiency. A more nearly complete acceptance of herself by the woman, and of the child as a separate individual, is sometimes accomplished only after parenthood has actually been experienced, but it is relatively infrequent even then.

The effect of the body build and of the relationship to one's own genitals thus tends to combine with and emphasize different character traits in the sexes which apparently in turn promote a greater artistic productivity in the man than in the woman, largely through a greater concern with and development of precise externalization. Here I would again emphasize that productivity as such is the channel of delivery of creativity, but is not the index of the inherent creative potential itself.

We come now to the question of *neurotic interferences with creative productivity*. Up to this point, consideration has been focused on problems arising from inherent natural sexual differences, present throughout all mankind. It is necessary to examine specifically those problems uniquely adherent to remarkable giftedness, and to attempt to elucidate the ways in which the possession of a remarkable endowment of artistic creativity in a woman

tends, paradoxically, to increase her vulnerability to certain blocking neurotic developments which interfere with its fulfillment.

In my earlier papers, the view is stated that many gifted people
develop at least two and sometimes more than two self-images with
more or less separate identities—that of the ordinary citizen and
that of the artist. In many creative people there is a considerable
struggle between these self-images. I am aware that some colleagues
do not accept at all this point of view, but to me it seems clear that
this is true at least in a very considerable number of artists, is rather vividly described by some, and is frequently reflected in the
use of different names for different identities. It is also reflected in
the titles of many autobiographies. Not only is there a struggle
between the different identities, but there are various degrees of
fusion and interaction between them, with unevenness in their
development. Consequently, problems existing in the personal
life and identity may invade the development of the artist's life
(which is proceeding in the same body and environment), or in
some instances there is flight from one identity to the other. Inevitably the invasion of the artistic work is greatest when the
personal life is the dominant one or when the two are fused. As
has been suggested, there may be a greater tendency for such fusion to occur in women than in men because of the absorption of
the girl child in, and her generally progressive commitment to, the
enveloping life of childbearing and child rearing; but there are
other influences too which are at work.

Clinical observations based on the analyses of a few very gifted
people—both men and women—have led me to the conclusion
that the greatest blocking in realization of talent arises from disturbances at the anal and oedipal levels. In the former it arises
in connection with anal functioning which is the prototype of
productivity in general. This is a chapter in itself but probably
does not show an extreme contrast between the two sexes. Susceptibility to such blocking due to anal problems may possibly be
greater in women than in men due to the tendency to identify the
vagina with the anus. The disturbances due to castration fears on
the genital or oedipal levels may interfere with the work of truly
artistic conception, in contrast to that of production alone. These
problems may be neurotically devastating to the personal life,
but when the two identities are relatively discrete, the artist some-

times takes flight from personal into creative activity, the beginnings of which may seem to be enhanced rather than blocked by personal exigencies. It may be because of this latter apparent gain in incentive to launch into creative work that many gifted individuals fear the loss of anxiety by analysis and sometimes fear a "successful" analysis.

Because of the inborn heightened sensitivity and general responsiveness of creatively gifted people, they may suffer from overstimulation even in infancy. The world may rush upon them with seemingly greater intensity than is the case in the less gifted. One of the most striking findings in the autobiographical accounts of artists concerning their early years (as well as in the analyses of gifted patients) is the regular appearance of especially strong exhilarating, inspiring, or even frightening experiences, felt as transcendental implications and occurring in the preoedipal years. Frequently their occurrence is rather precisely placed at the age of four, i.e., at the height of the phallic phase. Sometimes they are even earlier. They are characterized by generally strong sensations of all sorts, but especially of brilliant light, and also of body lightness. They may readily be recognized as screen memories or even screening experiences. They may arise as part of the invigoration of the total body as well as from the localized genital sensations of the phallic phase (see ch. 6).

Sometimes the intensity of stimulation is overwhelmingly terrifying and produces a blocking or a susceptibility to inhibition rather than an exhilaration. An illustration of this is given in the opening pages of the autobiography of Ellen Glasgow (1954), a competent though not a great writer. She was aptly described by her Negro mammy as having been born without a skin. Of her first recollection she says:

> Moving forward and backward, as contented and mindless as an amoeba, submerged in the vast fog of existence, I open my eyes and look at the top windowpanes. . . . In the midst of a red glow, I see a face without a body staring in at me, a vacant face, round, pallid, grotesque, malevolent. Terror—or was it merely sensation?—stabbed me into consciousness. Terror of the sinking sun? Or terror of the formless, the unknown, the mystery, the terror of life, of the world, of nothing or everything? Convulsions seized me, a spasm of dumb agony. One minute, I was not: the next minute, I was. I felt. I was

separate. I could be hurt. I had discovered too the universe apart from myself. . . . I cannot now divide the outgrowth from the apparition, distorted, unreal, yet more real to me than either myself or the world. . . . What, I wondered long afterwards, could have caused the illusion? What had I seen or imagined before I could make myself understood? What unknown terror had startled my consciousness or my senses awake? . . . Why should that one instant, that one vision, pierce through my covering of unawareness, and pin me to life as a pin fixes a butterfly? . . . .

Miss Glasgow fixes this experience as occurring probably during her second year. From other memories which she gives, it may be surmised that the nucleus of this startling vision from the second-year period—which is so characteristically and generally linked with the phallic period (Loewenstein, 1950)—has been used as a condensing screen for later memories which were then projected backward onto it. It is of interest here too that at another time Miss Glasgow refers to her mother as "the sun in my universe" in a benevolent sense, but was from her earliest recollections frightened by her austere and threatening father, whose cruelty to animals made a dark impression on her entire life. The essentially castrating and castrated effect of the evil, glowing, bodyless head is impressive.

It is also noteworthy that although Miss Glasgow makes a strong point in her autobiography of the fact that she was never in the least aware of any maternal instinct and believed herself to be "born without it," she did not recognize that her passionate love of animals and her intense resentment of her father's interference with this had all the earmarks of being the substitute for the lacking demand for maternity. She seems also to have been influenced by her mother's life of self-abnegation and individual lostness as the head of a very large family, of whom the child, Ellen, was next to the youngest member.

It is a common clinical observation that a high degree of bisexuality exists in creative artists. The forces of bisexual identifications may be actively felt in states of inspiration and in the working of the creative process in which there is a personal surrender to the forces of the artist's creative power. This is not surprising if we are correct in our view of the extreme sensitivity of the potential artist even in earliest infancy; for this means a wider and a deeper capacity for universal empathy during the period of incomplete differentiation of the sexual identity. This extraordinary empathic capacity is retained throughout life, since in the artist the barrier between primary and secondary process thinking is conspicuously slight.

Among girls especially, the combination of this strong bisexual empathy with increased, often precocious, genital sensations gives rise to special problems. From this tendency to early genitalization, which results from the prolonged and strong sensory overstimulation that is inevitable in the gifted child, an unusual degree of clitoral pressure develops. While this arises probably endogenously, the degree to which it becomes sharply focused may also depend upon the extent of the exposure of the clitoris and consequently its availability for external stimulation, whether this be from contact with clothing, active seduction, or by self-manipulation. In any event this makes the gifted girl child unduly susceptible to the formation of a fantasied or illusory phallus, and further increases her bisexuality. In this excessive stimulation there may also be some early development of vaginal awareness, partly borrowed from rectal and anal tensions, and partly by displacement from disturbed conditions of the clitoris. If the clitoris is well developed and actually stimulated from without in response to an endogenously aroused appetite, the illusory phallus may assume considerable durability. It is this phenomenon, in turn, which seems from the analyses of especially gifted women, to have played so much havoc in interfering with both personal and artistically creative lives.

The presence of giftedness often arouses in those who possess it—whether men or women—the inner questions: "By what right do I have this? Why is it bestowed on me?" and even, "Does it really belong to me?" These implicit questions may otherwise appear in the form of a feeling of guilt, as though the special ability had been stolen, and the realization of it then involves the feeling of being fraudulent. In the girl the sense of a special gift may utilize the illusory phallus as its representative and either be highly prized or give rise to a wish to repudiate it in conformity with the wish to be a "regular woman" and have the fullest experience of woman's life.

I have found in analyzing very talented women who were

blocked in the realization of their abilities that this bisexual conflict was strong indeed, based fundamentally on the two body
images—the one arising from the realistic knowledge of their own
feminine bodies and the identification, by comparison, with others
of their own sex; and the other, that of the phallic girl or woman
with the mysterious unseen phallus, subjectively experienced as
real because of the early insistent clitoral-phallic pressure. Wherever such a degree of phallic illusion exists (in those of lesser as
well as in those of greater giftedness), the young woman after
puberty suffers an extreme and often incapacitating set of castration problems, compounded of both masculine and feminine elements. But if the specially gifted young woman has associated her
talent with the illusory phallus, the realization of her talent may
become impossible whenever the definitely feminine aims or
obligatory evidences of femininity are in the ascendancy—as with
the onset of menstruation or the experience of pregnancy. There
may be short bursts of creative interest and activity, but without
sufficient ability to sustain them to bring the experience of organic
growth and development into realization.

There may, furthermore, develop a definite fear of her imagination, since this means unconsciously the possible re-establishment
of the illusory phallus and the repetitive excruciating re-enactment
of the castration experience with each menstruation. Such women
—if they cross the bridge to achieve maternity—may in turn devote
themselves to the child with a possessiveness and excluding intensity which risks much for the future of the child. More commonly, I believe, the realization of artistic creativity in the girl
child takes one of the following courses. (1) It may go into
eclipse at puberty as she gives up the imaginary phallic world in
favor of the more regular feminine goals and aims. (2) She regresses
to the anal level, depending on the earlier vicissitudes of this
period, and develops a restraining compulsiveness. (3) She aban-
dons her feminine identification largely or almost completely in
her official life, although it still teams up with the phallic identification in the bisexual activity of her artistically creative work.

Inhibition of artistic interest to the extent of its actual suspension seems particularly likely to occur if the parents, especially
the father, react with disfavor toward this interest of the daughter.
In other words, the push of creative drive can hardly be sustained

against the full force of the oedipal attachment. On the other hand, the father's approval and encouragement, particularly if he is himself an artist, may permit the girl to develop a predominantly positive oedipal relationship, together with a limited identification with him, in such a way as to salvage or even free her artistic interests. This appears possibly to have been true in two —and perhaps three—of the five women artists listed among the seven hundred in the *Dictionary of Art and Artists* mentioned at the beginning of this paper.[1]

On the whole women artists—in whatever medium—do not seem to have been conspicuously excellent mothers. There are undoubtedly exceptions, but as one thinks of the various women writers of note in the past (in a field in which women have produced more than in any other) it seems that there are some who married rather late and had no children, a number who never married at all, and others who, though sometimes marrying early, had one or two children whom they treated with a combination of neglect and narcissistic devotion, to the detriment of the child. It is not an easy subject to study and one on which I have done an inadequate amount of research to speak further with explicit conviction.

There are some women artists who, as already noted, abandon their positions as women, assume very largely roles of masculine identification, and follow much more the path of the man in their artistic creativity. I have never analyzed such a woman, but from reading biographies I have thought I could decipher this probable outline in the cases of several illustrious women. Here I must speak with caution, but for the sake of illustration I will confide my surmise that such a one was Gertrude Stein, who despite this attempt at simplification of life's problems by abandonment of most of the goals of womanhood, seemed never sure of her own sexual identity and was continually preoccupied with this quandary, as most of her writing testifies. She seemed at first to be almost in the relationship of a *doppelgänger* with her brother; then assuming the ascendancy she parted from him (at the expense

1 These five were Rosalba Carriera (1675-1757); Mary Cassatt (1845-1926); Barbara Hepworth (1903-   ); Angelica Kauffman (1761-1807); Louise Elizabeth Vigee-Lebrun (1755-1842). These last two were child prodigies, and also were the children of painter fathers. The first of the five had a sister who was also a painter, and came of a family much concerned with art.

of an alienation lasting the rest of her life), and presently she established herself with a woman in a relationship which lasted the rest of her life. It is interesting that in the four autobiographies which Miss Stein wrote, none was simply the autobiography of Gertrude Stein. One was called *Two—Gertrude Stein and Her Brother* (1951); another was entitled *The Making of Americans* (1934). It must be noted that Gertrude Stein, who boasted that American doughboys mistook her for the American flag, could nevertheless maintain her identity as an American only by remaining consistently an expatriate. Her third autobiography was entitled *The Autobiography of Alice B. Toklas* (1933), written as though by Miss Toklas; the fourth was *Everybody's Autobiography* (1937).[2] There are other woman artists who play out bisexual roles dramatically, as seems to have been true in the cases of George Sand and Madame de Staël. The latter became repeatedly the center of a bisexually oriented circle whose members seemed constantly driven by the interplay of their jealousies.

The most prolific woman composer whose life has come to my awareness was Dame Ethel Smyth. She attained considerable recognition as a composer and conductor in late Victorian England, and believed herself to be one of "the great" who suffered from incomplete recognition because of her sex. A cooler judgment indicates that her fame was possibly enhanced by her sex. She seems to have had a very strong masculine identification, as her extensive autobiography and memoirs (1946) reveal; and her conducting was early characterized by an exuberance which was sometimes an interference.

There is one aspect of the oedipal problem of women which tends to focus their creative activity on an emotionally interpretative role rather than on courageous originality, and which I have thus far overlooked. This has to do with the peculiarly intricate development of the little girl's oedipus complex. It is a well-recognized fact that the girl child develops an early and bisexually complicated oedipal stage, due perhaps to her early castration problems and to her need to separate herself from too overwhelming an identifying attachment to the mother, combined with the natural stimulation of awareness of the difference from the father.

2 See Brinnin (1959) and Sprigge (1957).

The oneness with the mother may be engulfingly comforting; and by the same token, the difference from the father is stimulating and exciting. This means that in the ascendancy of the oedipal attachment to the father the girl has to maintain herself in a practical dependence on her mother for her physical care and direct nutrition at the very same time that there is a growing hostility and rivalry. Hence, there is a complexity in the little girl's emotional development, in contrast to the more nearly straight-line course of her brother. It means an early development of caution growing out of ambivalence—the forerunner of tact—the need for careful balance and infantile diplomacy. This in turn restricts the full expansiveness of creative originality.

SUMMARY

It appears that in general fewer women than men realize substantial artistic creative talent. This paper limits itself to a consideration of early genetic factors, which may restrict the female's later development of adequate capacity for externalization of artistic creativity. It does not seek to examine evidence of differences between the two sexes in intrinsic creative potentialities; nor does it deal at all with special neurotic interferences in the creative process. Differences in anatomical structure between the sexes which tend to make for a lesser degree of precise externalization seem to contribute to the lesser artistic productivity of women. The obligatory differences in attitude toward their own genitals pattern different attitudes toward, and content of, the fantasy involved in artistic creativity. In girls, fantasy is much more concerned with emotional and personal relationships and less with impersonal or abstract constructions than in boys. Girls appear to be more readily blocked in materializing artistic creativity than boys, both through the nature of the castration complex and the special exigencies of the oedipal conflict. In specially talented girls, both areas of conflict are hazardous due fundamentally to the increased bisexual elements among creative individuals.

CHAPTER TWENTY-NINE

On Nonsense (1966)

I

This paper will deal with nonsense and its relation to aggression and anxiety. It draws largely on the study of the nonsense of Lewis Carroll's *Wonderland* and *Looking Glass* countries, and somewhat less on that of the nonsense rhymes of Edward Lear. But before discussing the nonsense of these two authors we must first approach the question of what we mean by nonsense anyway. Very many definitions of nonsense have been given by the various critics of this field of literature. Of these only a few will be mentioned.

Emile Cammaerts (1925) points out that the general opinion of nonsense is that it consists of anything which displeases you or any statement with which you emphatically disagree, and that there are as many different nonsenses as there are individual opinions, so that it would be a hopeless task to distinguish between them, or to attempt to draw up a list of them. He argues further that what is nonsense for one person is very often sense for another—similar to the situation of one man's meat being another man's poison. Someone else has remarked in regard to science fiction and scientific theory that yesterday's scientific nonsense becomes today's scientific sense. Be that as it may, Cammaerts introduces this view of multiple nonsense with a quotation from H. G. Wells's *Christina Alberta's Father*, which describes Mrs. Preemby's nonsense thus: "She said it was nonsense. And when your dear mother said it was nonsense, it only made things disagreeable if you agreed it was anything else."

Cammaerts then proceeds to give his own version of poetical nonsense, seeing it as arising from the same matrix as nursery rhymes, viz., the "innocent exuberance of childhood." He believes that writers of nonsense, referring especially to Lear, Carroll, and Kipling (and here it seems he stretches a point to include the *Just So Stories*), wrote their nonsense out of memory of this joyously restless state of childhood and to please child friends of later life. This point of view would certainly oppose the theory that many of the Mother Goose rhymes originated as slyly disguised political satires which only later were incorporated into the lore of childhood. But there is at least some disagreement from another angle, and I would point out that Lear did not have a happy childhood and felt burdened by the obligation to teach children later—gradually becoming somewhat irritable toward them. In his adult life their noise almost literally set his teeth on edge. And Carroll's friendly relationship to children, almost exclusively to little girls—for he had an open aversion to little boys—was an exceedingly complex one. "Stuff and Nonsense," or "Fiddlesticks," has a considerable excluding aggression in it, like Mrs. Preemby's declaration of nonsense. It is an attitude which may become playfully elaborated when it has gone through another stage of development, achieving some degree of emotional detachment. But Mrs. Preemby could never achieve this and so was always stuck with an argument.

Another writer, Elizabeth Sewall, an English philosopher dealing with the *Field of Nonsense* (1952), goes to considerable length to show that nonsense is an intellectual game with its own rules, and is really a manifestation of the mind's force toward order, and the establishment of order over a counterpull to disorder. Having a stance just the opposite of Mrs. Preemby's, she seems to take nonsense entirely away from any emotional connections. She sees in the extraordinary meticulousness of both Lear and Carroll only an indication of their spontaneous pleasure in "being that way," since they were not compelled by *external* events to behave in this fashion. She seems to see mental health and balance in terms of derangement or no derangement, and scouts the idea that there was emotional disturbance of any importance in either man, ignoring the painfully disturbing symptoms associated with Lear's severe epilepsy during his adult life, and his constant anxiety about money. The fact that neither man married or was known to have a sexual interest in any adult woman appears to her insignificant.[1] The nonsense of these men, she says, represents their sanity and reason. I shall return to look at this from a little different angle later.

Max Eastman (1936), looking at nonsense more from the angle of the effect of the finished product than from that of the process, says that nonsense is effective only if it pretends to make sense, i.e., if in some way it gives the illusion of being sensible. It appears, then, that part of its effectiveness has an element of the practical joke in it; one laughs at oneself for reaching for something that isn't there. Koestler (1964), who quotes Eastman and himself writes only briefly of nonsense, turns his attention at once then to tickling; and it seems possible that there is a connecting link between the two: both are threats that were only play after all.

This discussion will deal chiefly with the nonsense of Carroll in the *Alice* books, but will rely also on *The Hunting of the Snark* and the songs of the mad Gardener in *Sylvie and Bruno*. No one can talk about nonsense in any serious, sensible way, however, without considering the nonsense rhymes in the *Book of Nonsense* and *More Nonsense* by the master, Edward Lear. These two, Lear and Carroll, are certainly the outstanding professors and practitioners of nonsense. But here may we add the name of another literary man whose work would not generally be considered nonsensical at all, but only gruesome, eerie, and nightmarish. Yet his writings, especially *Metamorphosis*, *Amerika*, and *The Trial*,

---

[1] Lear's ideas about marriage seemed to be part of his whimsey. According to Holbrook Jackson (who edited the 1950 edition of the complete works of Lear), Lear "puzzled over the problem of marriage in much the way he puzzled over so many things that are not quite obvious." At forty-one, thinking of marriage in the abstract at a time when he felt a renewal of energy and spirit after cutting two new teeth, he reflected that if he married he was sure he would paint less well, and besides the idea of an infant a year would make him frantic. He felt that he saw few happy marriages around him, and that marriage could not even be relied upon to be a corrective to the loneliness of old age. In Corfu at fifty he was wishing that he were married to a clever, good, nice, fat little Greek girl, and had twenty-five olive trees, some goats, and a house. And again he said that if he went to heaven, he would ask the polite angels to leave him alone, but after he had become established in the course of a million or two years, he might have an angel for a wife. In fact, he had the same man servant for thirty years, and the same cat for seventeen.

contain many of the ingredients of nonsense, without the detachment which permits comical effectiveness. I refer to Franz Kafka.

What do *we* mean by nonsense? Obviously, the word means no
sense, i.e., without sense. This would seem to be clear enough.
But *sense* is not so clear-cut in meaning as one might at first think.
Sense at once suggests the intellect and reason, and nonsense
would then consist in words or actions which convey an absurd
meaning or no meaning at all. But sense also refers to the ability
to receive and to respond to stimuli. The senses considered as a
total bodily function are distinguished from intellect and movement. Thus the word *senseless* may mean unconscious, or it may
refer to something unreasonable, foolish, and apparently meaningless in content. My scrutiny of the nonsense of Lear and Carroll
will encompass both meanings of the word *sense,* for it seems to
me that the intellect and reason emerge developmentally from the
hinterland of the bodily senses, and that the separation of the two
areas of functioning is never complete. This becomes more obvious with the examination of the content of the nonsense productions which critics like the philosophically minded Sewall
would rule out of the field altogether.

It is an interesting fact that the term nonsense, except when said
in a very emphatic tone of voice, is rarely applied to production
without some qualifying adjective. There is "just nonsense,"
"mere nonsense," "utter nonsense," "sheer nonsense," or, in the
extreme, "absolute nonsense." These qualifying adjectives convey
the subjective judgment of the spectator or listener, and go all the
way from a relatively mild feeling: "I don't understand what you
are talking about (or doing). It does not seem reasonable to me,"
to the extreme judgment of "absolute nonsense," implying:
"What you are saying is so unheard of, so generally incomprehensi-
ble, that it disturbs me unbearably unless I think that no one can
be expected to understand it." Now, absolute nonsense, with the
meaning of a complete elimination of any kind of coherence or
even cohesiveness of content, and associated with an inability to
receive or respond to stimuli from others—the elimination of any
degree of relationship whatsoever would mean such a state of disorganization and psychophysical disintegration as to be scarcely
compatible with life itself. Like its extreme opposite, absolute
perfection, it then becomes static, isolated, and approaches lifeless-

ness. When Lear speaks of his rhymes as "absolute and pure non-sense"—as he does in the introduction to the book *More Nonsense* (1872)—he is using the phrase not to indicate the degree of nonsensical quality, but rather to indicate that his nonsense does not contain any hidden attack on any specific individuals or any sly political satire.

II

In studying nonsense from the productions of Lear and Carroll, we have to realize further that neither of these men could possibly have come very close to absolute nonsense, not only because of the practical inaccessibility of that chaotic, disorganized, anarchic state except for a babbling idiot incapable of writing or of definite language formation, but also because both Lear and Carroll were gifted men, perhaps men of genius. This in itself gives an obligatory inner organization with some extra capacity for rhythm and patterning both in awareness and in execution. Absolute nonsense is incapable of representing itself.

The garden variety of judgment of nonsense may represent the frame of mind of the spectator or listener rather than having much to do with the product itself. Thus, as in Mrs. Preemby's case, it may show rather the antipathy of prejudice with an *accompanying* aggressive wish to rid oneself of the disquieting intrusion. The aggression then may be largely on the part of the spectator, although it is felt by him as a justified reaction to the aggressively nonsensical intruder who must be banished. But with Lear and Carroll, the object of the nonsense and the subjective audience are essentially the same person—the author of it. The public is only taken in by accident, as it were.

Lear was a painter of considerable ability, and Carroll was a mathematician and an Oxford don, although trained to be a clergyman. Neither made the writing of nonsense his primary profession, and both were puzzled or even annoyed at winning fame more through their nonsense than through their serious professions. Charles L. Dodgson, the Oxford don, was so annoyed, in fact, that at one time he disclaimed knowledge of Lewis Carroll and refused to receive mail directed to Carroll at his, Mr. Dodgson's, address. Carroll's nonsense works have been translated into some thirty to forty different languages, and it is reported that in English-speaking countries the *Alice* books rank next to the Bible in the frequency with which they are quoted. Almost the whole world knows some, at least, of Lear's rhymes, though relatively few know anything of his painting.

III

The form of the work of the two men is rather different, although the ingredients of nonsense contained in it are strikingly similar. Lear was probably best known for his rhymes in the *Book of Nonsense* and *More Nonsense*. In these books the rhymes were entirely in the limerick form, in which there is usually a single verse consisting of five lines, rhyming *aabba,* with the third and fourth lines half the length of the others. This verse form, usually facetious in content, and at least in some way related to doggeral, anagrams, punning riddles, and even charades, had originated in England about 1820, i.e., when Lear was eight years old, and had a certain vogue in his young manhood. The continued popularity of the limerick seems to have been sustained, however, by Lear's indefatigable productions. The term *Limerick* was not applied until 1898, ten years after Lear's death.

Lear wrote some songs not in limerick form, of which *The Owl and the Pussycat* is probably the best known. He also wrote a few very short stories for children and several nonsense alphabets. All of these were greatly enhanced by his own illustrations, which are more captivating than his words. At thirty-four (1846) he published his *Book of Nonsense* containing 112 nonsense verses. These show a certain uniformity of structure and content. In all of them the third and fourth lines are combined into a single line contracting the verse to a four-line outline. The last line is generally an actual or approximate repetition of the first. This has a soothing, letting-down effect rather than the stimulating effect of the punch line so common in limericks. Many of the verses begin: "There was an old man of Crete . . ." (or some other place). Proper names of individuals are never intruded; it appears as though the person were hardly an individual, but only to be seen as part of the place. Most of the rhymes are mildly comforting in content, in that they offer nonsensical answers to ridiculous dilemmas or infirmities (which are understated or overstated, but not presented in reasonable proportions). The last line goes back to a repetition of the first, as though to say: "Well, that's the way it was anyway." For example:

> There was an old Person of Annerley
> Whose conduct was strange and unmannerly;
> He rushed down the Strand, with a Pig in each hand,
> But returned in the evening to Annerley.

or:

> There was an old Person of Spain,
> Who hated all trouble and pain;
> So he sat in a chair with his feet in the air,
> That umbrageous Old Person of Spain.

One has meandered a bit, but after all nothing has changed.

In 84 of the 112 rhymes in the *Book of Nonsense,* the rhymes have to do with old men who are generally (57 of the 84 times) referred to as "There was an old man of . . . ," but in 27 the central character is referred to only as an "Old Person," and the rest of the limerick shows him to be an old man. Never once does he make a young man or a boy the main character of a rhyme. In 28 of the 84 limericks, the central figure is female, who (in 21 of these 28 verses) is referred to gallantly as a "Young Lady," and in two as a "Young Person." Once he introduces a "Young Girl," and there is one Old Person who turns out to be female rather than male. There are three Old Ladies in the galaxy. His gallantry toward the female sex is in his words rather than in his drawings, which show many of them as misshapen old creatures. All of his characters, male and female, tend to be restless persons, as he himself was, and seem to be dashing about with their elongated arms and legs so flung out that they seem in danger of becoming detached from the body. On the other hand, there is not the same emphasis on the cutting off or spontaneous loss of a body part as occurs in the *Alice* books of Carroll, and is seen in purest culture in the German *Struwwelpeter.* One young lady loses her head and one male loses his thumbs. Lear's ladies often have big noses and sharp chins, like the one of the rhyme:

> There was a young lady whose chin,
> Resembled the point of a pin;
> So she made it sharp, and purchased a harp
> And played several tunes with her chin.

And they do not often redeem themselves by their behavior. Daughters especially seem to be trials or at least irritations rather than comforts to their parents.

Lear became known for his *Book of Nonsense,* which is supposed to have been written for the children of the Earl of Derby into whose household Lear came as an illustrator for the Earl's considerable ornithological collection. But the Earl and then the whole family of the House of Derby served as Lear's patrons, so that during his long life Lear was to know the benefit of patronage of four generations of Earls. A dedication dated 1862 is to the great-grandchildren, grandnephews, and grandnieces of Edward, 13th Earl of Derby, but he puts in parentheses: "The greater part of which were originally composed for their parents." This is a slightly ambiguous statement, and Lear's relationship to children was complicated by his pathological sensitivity to the noise from which he was frequently trying to escape. While in Corfu, he wrote that he was much distressed by people next door who had twin babies and played the violin, but one of the twins died and the other had eaten the fiddle—so peace was again established. His sensitive nerves were always aroused by young women practicing singing or violin playing, and in those nonsense rhymes which do deal with young ladies, there is the repetition of the young lady playing on a harp with sufficient frequency to make one wonder whether one of his many sisters intruded on him in this way in his childhood.

In 1871, twenty-five years after the *Book of Nonsense* first appeared, Lear published, at the age of fifty-nine, *Nonsense Songs, Stories, Botany and Alphabets;* and in the next years, *More Nonsense, Pictures, Rhymes, Botany etc.* In 1877, at sixty-five, he brought out *Laughable Lyrics, a Fourth Book of Nonsense Poems, Songs, Botany and Music, etc.;* while in 1895, seven years after his death, *Nonsense Songs and Stories* appeared. It would seem that as he grew older he became more reconciled to or philosophical about being famous as a writer of nonsense rather than as a painter.

When one examines the "one hundred nonsense pictures and rhymes" of the *More Nonsense* volume, it turns out that there are only 96 of the nonsense rhymes. The rhymes are limericks having much the same, almost stereotyped form as the first batch had had twenty-five years earlier. No young men and no girls appear in this *More Nonsense* group. Men are not designated as "Old Man" as often (only 33 out of 96 possibilities) but are referred to as "Old Person" (42 out of the 96), who is shown to be mad by the rest of the rhyme and the drawing. "Old Person" is also applied more frequently to his female characters and fewer of the latter are dubbed "Young Lady" (only 5 in the 96 verses; as in contrast to 21 out of the 112 in the first series). On the other hand, "Young Person" is the designation for 10 young women and is not used at all for young men. If we can draw any conclusions at all from this kind of analysis, it would be to say that as he got older Lear tended to think of those around him even more as persons than as male and female.

In his limericks in general, even though they were dedicated to children, he did not deal with children but with adults. His appeal to children was not through presenting pictures of their adventures or antics, but rather through lampooning adults—often thinly disguised versions of himself—for the children, and making the lampooning foolish or nonsensical enough to take the sting out of any irritability he may have felt toward them. He thought of himself as "an old cove," and once referred to himself as a frisky and energetic old cove. He once confessed that with few exceptions he found all human beings awful idiots. But one gets the impression from his journals and his letters that at least some adults could be quiet and this he appreciated. Here one remembers that Lear was the next to the youngest of twenty-one children and must really have been subjected to a great amount of varied stimulation. It has seemed to me that Lear may never have felt quite at home in the world—as a child feeling like an older person and as a man feeling like a child. I cannot quite agree with Holbrook Jackson (1950) that his rhymes and his drawings are sexless. The drawings especially show rather the perpetual preoccupation with sex in one who feels shut out from its enjoyment.

Lear's underlying sensitivity was very great indeed and may have been part of his creativity as well as associated with his epilepsy and possibly secondarily with his severe and chronic asthma. He was conscious of being influenced to an extreme by everything in natural and physical life, i.e., atmosphere, light, shadow, and all the varieties of day and night. He wondered whether it was a blessing or the contrary, but decided that "things must be as they may and the best is to make the best of what happens." One feels that this is what he is unconsciously aiming at in his nonsense limericks—temporarily and repetitively to insensitize himself by laughing at his infirmities so that he may get back to his real work of painting. The lack of real joyousness in Lear's limericks is conspicuous. It is only when he deals with animals or with inanimate objects which he animates that he can let go in joyous fun rather than in the fun of the comic in his nonsense. The latter tends to have a reduction and an attack in it —surely often primarily against himself—*even* though he over and over again attains a kind of recovery through bringing the last line back to the first. If one compares the mood of the nonsense limericks with the joyousness of the love affair of the owl and the pussycat or the flirtatious walk of the table and the chair who danced on their heads till they toddled to their beds, one realizes that something was probably felt as dangerous in the relations between human beings.

Lear's stories are relatively few, are short, and do contain children as characters. The chief one is the story of four little children who went around the world. They are personalized to the extent of having names and definite sexes: Violet, Slingsby, Guy, and Lionel. There is a certain amount of play with reversals as in the case of an island of water surrounded by earth and a great gulf stream that runs over evanescent isthmuses. There is some play with alliterative and rhyming words and a few coined words, but the whole story is more at the level of the absurd than the nonsensical.

The vehicle of Carroll's nonsense is quite different from Lear's, for Carroll was known primarily for his stories, especially the *Alice* stories. These are interlarded with rhymes and nonsense poetry, but he seldom uses the single verse, except for the songs of the mad Gardener in *Sylvie and Bruno,* and he does not use the *aabba* form (the limerick) as Lear did. Many of his poems are parodies and all abound in original word forms—for Carroll was a master at these bumptious creations and has contributed more to the English language than even Lear did. His verses are more elaborate, more sprightly, and do not show any of Lear's tendency to stick to one form in an almost stereotyped way.

In each of the *Alice* stories there is a central theme, though it is almost lost sight of in the nonsensical meanderings of its pursuits. According to Carroll, Alice is a little girl of seven and a half, though she talks and acts more like a prepuberty child of nine. The aim of Alice's adventures in the first book is to find a secret subterreanean garden, toward which she has been led by her curiosity in following a white rabbit, dressed as a gentleman, whom she sees as he disappears into a hole in the ground. In the pursuit of this goal she wanders through a wonderland confused and bewildered. She is never quite sure who she is and time itself is quite mixed up and runs one way and another. In fact, nothing, not even ideas and knowledge, remains reliable. She thinks of bats in connection with rats and mice and then finds herself in a confused doubting "Do rats eat bats? Do bats eat cats?" and a little later she is wondering whether she is herself or Ada who has ringlets or Mabel who is rather stupid. She is constantly growing up or shrinking down and is fearful that she may go out like the flame of a candle, but what is the flame like after it is out? She encounters animals who behave like human beings and human beings who behave like savages. Her hands and feet grow so large and distant that they seem to have identities separate from her own, and she considers sending a letter in order to communicate with her right foot, but realizes that she is talking nonsense. Her voice is so strangely hoarse that it too hardly belongs to her. There are many tears in Wonderland, and once the diminutive Alice nearly drowns in a pool of tears wept by Alice the Great. In general, however, she maintains a somewhat addled philosophical poise through all the faultfinding and threats of open savagery. Decapitation is the favorite threat of those in power.

No one laughs much. But the Cheshire Cat grins in his superior fashion since he can withstand decapitation by allowing his own body to disappear leaving his grinning head, which in turn fades with the grin, the last part to go. The story begins by Alice being bored at the book her sister is reading to her until she drops to sleep, and dropping to sleep with boredom, even in the thick of an argument, remains one of the retreats of minor characters in the tale. At one point, when with a spurt of growth Alice finds herself so large that the room will no longer contain her and she is pressed against all its sides, she considers that when she is (really) grown up she will write a book about herself describing all this. This evidently is the task undertaken then by Lewis Carroll, even though Alice herself could not decide whether it was better to risk growing up to old womanhood or remaining young and doing other people's bidding, even that of cats and rabbits. Then again in a diminished phase when she is very small indeed, she gets into an argument with a caterpillar who, seated on a toadstool smoking a hookah, defends the idea that metamorphous changes need not be upsetting. He admonishes her to curb her temper and directs her to recite that erotically suggestive rhyme about Father William. Soon she is growing so big again that a wandering pigeon mistakes her elongated neck for a serpent.

In her protest that she is only a little girl (and she has jiggled herself small again) she continues to look for the secret garden, and then comes to a diminutive house in the wood. Here she encounters a grotesque version of maternity, in a ferocious duchess who is impatiently nursing her baby while she sings "Speak roughly to your little boy . . ." as she is anxious to be off to a croquet game with the Queen. Complete pandemonium soon reigns. The baby's nose is cut off by a flying saucepan hurled by an enraged cook. The baby himself is thrown into Alice's arms, but quickly turns into a pig and runs off into the woods. The Cheshire Cat appears or disappears, as the case may be, and directs Alice to the Mad Hatter, who quickly lands her in the Mad Tea Party, all of whose members are male. She is no better off here, for all her remarks are turned around and used against her until she doesn't know the meaning of anything she has said. The Hatter's remarks seemed to have no sort of meaning at all and yet certainly were in English. (Here Alice certainly seems to agree with Max Eastman's views about effective nonsense.) Confusion is piled on confusion. Time and size are mixed up individually and together. Alice is accused of having beaten Time in her music lessons, and the Hatter is threatened with decapitation for having murdered Time. But in the end Alice does find the door to the secret garden and enters.

This, the royal garden, is as chaotically angry a place as the Duchess's kitchen had been. A rampageous croquet game is in progress. All humans, regardless of sex, age, or rank, look exactly alike from the rear, as they are really animated playing cards. The balls and the mallets, however, are animals who contribute to the general anarchy by doing whatever they please while the Queen threatens decapitation to anyone who displeases her. The Cheshire Cat materializes out of his grin and escapes execution, though the King argues that anything that has a head can be beheaded, and the Queen threatens to execute everyone unless a way can be found to execute the cat. The game ends with everyone, even the wickets, being taken into custody, leaving Alice alone with the King and Queen while the King whispers a pardon to all whom the Queen has executed or imprisoned. Alice is taken in charge by the Gryphon, a hideous composite of lion, eagle, and dragon, who explains to her that the executions are only the Queen's fancy. "They never execute anybody you know." After an interlude of a satirical and whimsically nonsensical discussion of education with the Gryphon and the Mock Turtle (who suffers from sorrow which is only a fancy since he is only a *mock* turtle and the source of Mock turtle soup), the messily confused day ends in a trial. The King with the Queen by his side is an uneasy judge fearful lest his own crown may fall off. The Knave of Hearts is being tried for stealing tarts. But execution is threatened to nervous witnesses and then for good measure to nonnervous ones as well. A general atmosphere of execution prevails.

Alice feels herself suddenly growing up, getting too big for all this nonsense. When she at last is called as a witness she has so far outgrown any trepidation that she tips over the jury box with the edge of her skirt and has to pick up the spilled jurors and return them to the box for the trial to go on. Alice's testimony that she knew nothing whatsoever about the business is considered important or unimportant, as the case may be, until an argument arises about it, and Alice herself is ordered out of the court as being too high and mighty. But before she leaves, an incriminating bit of evidence against the knave is discovered in an unsigned set of verses not in the knave's handwriting which proves beyond the shadow of a doubt that the knave is a dishonest man. For why else would he have not signed his name and further gone to the trouble of imitating someone else's handwriting! Alice declares that the verses have not one atom of meaning in them, but the Queen demands the sentence first and the evidence later, while the King thinks that he detects some meaning somewhere. Alice, now full size, declares the whole thing stuff and nonsense, while the Queen shrieks, "Off with her head," and Alice retorts, "Who cares for you, you are nothing but a pack of cards!" Whereupon they all rise up in the air and come flying down at her. She wakes to find her sister brushing away dead leaves that have fluttered into her face. And in the epilogue, when Alice tells her sister the dream, she herself begins to dream Alice's dream and then, half awake, muses that this little sister of hers will soon be a grown woman with children of her own.

I shall not go to as much length in describing *Alice Through the Looking Glass.* It is a less spontaneous production and seems more consciously contrived than *Wonderland,* almost as though Alice herself had become a little more settled. It too is played against the background of a game involving a royal family, the game of chess in which the characters are now three- rather than two-dimensional, and the sexes can be distinguished even from the rear. Alice's aim in this game is to become a queen. There is not quite as much riotous confusion as in *Wonderland,* but the bipolarity of constant doubt is paramount. Many experiences appear in opposites, and many characters are in pairs: Alice and her mirror image, the black kitten and the white one, the Red King and Queen, and the White King and Queen, Tweedledum and Tweedledee, Haigha and Hatta, etc. Alice's size does not change so much as was true in *Wonderland,* but the creatures around her are often outsized, especially the insects; and space and time have a way of extending and contracting themselves that is bewildering

In the end Alice does find a crown on her head, but her maturity is at once challenged by the Red and White Queens, who then succumb to the fatigue of their own arguments and fall asleep on her shoulder. In the last scene, a coronation banquet is given for Alice who arrives late and is scolded like a bad child. Nothing can be eaten, however, as the food is all animated, and the various dishes behave like guests as soon as they are introduced to Alice. The whole party ends in a riot with the White Queen disappearing into the soup tureen, while the mutton sits in a chair. Alice and all the plates and the candles fly up in the air while the guests lie down in the remaining dishes. Alice completes the destruction by pulling the tablecloth off and dumping everything left onto the floor. She again awoke to find it all a dream.

The Red Queen whom she thought she was scolding for having instigated the mischief turned out to be the Black Kitten whom she had been admonishing for tangling up the yarn at the time she had gone to sleep. In talking to the Black Kitten (alias the Red Queen) Alice gives a valuable clue to the meaning of all this nonsense, when she says, "Let us consider, who it was dreamed it all. You see Kitty, it must have been either me or the Red King. He was part of my dream—but then I was part of his dream too. *Was* it the Red King, Kitty? You were his wife, my dear, so you ought to know—*do* help to settle it!" It may be worth noting, too, that in *Wonderland,* Dinah (Alice's cat) does not actually appear unless we are to consider her reincarnated as the Cheshire Cat— and there is no mention of kittens. In the *Looking Glass* world, it is Alice's play with the kittens that initiates her adventurous exploration. Perhaps we may guess that the kittens or the thoughts of kittens have arrived in Alice's life between *Wonderland* and *Looking Glass.* But I shall have more to say of content later.

Carroll's nonsense rhymes are quite different from Lear's in form. They are generally interspersed through his stories, and many among them are parodies. He did not use the *aabba* rhyme form;[2] and his single-verse rhymes, appearing mostly as the songs of the mad Gardener in *Sylvie and Bruno,* achieve a comical effect largely through the utter incongruity of the fused pictures and ideas presented.

---

[2] There is one exception to this—a verse addressed to one of his little girl favorites, Miss Vera Beringer. It runs as follows:

> There was a young lady of station,
> "I love man" was her sole exclamation;
> But when men cried, "You flatter,"
> She replied, "Oh! no matter
> Isle of Man is the true explanation."

Here the punch is obviously in the last line in contrast to Lear's form.

It is interesting to see that in the *Complete Works of Lewis Carroll,* introduction by Alexander Woollcott (1936), this is headed "A Limerick." According to other authorities, the term *limerick* did not come into use until 1898, and Carroll died on January 14, 1898. The limerick form *aabba* had been popular, however, since the early nineteenth century.

Thus the rhymes (from *Sylvie and Bruno*):

> He thought he saw an Elephant,
>   That practiced on a fife;
> He looked again, and found it was
>   A letter from his wife.
> 'At length, I realize,' he said,
>   'The bitterness of Life!'
>
> He thought he saw an Argument
>   That proved he was the Pope:
> He looked again and found it was
>   A bar of Mottled Soap.
> 'A fact so dread,' he faintly said
>   'Extinguishes all hope!'

These rhymes spoof the dilemma, critical though it may be, by making it ridiculous, and the rhythm and utter absurdity of the solution have a stimulating, almost staccato effect. This form is different from the returning monotony of Lear's last lines in his limericks and is also in contrast to the word distortions and creations of new words which reach their height in the *Jabberwocky*. This is not only written backward in mirror writing, but it contains twenty-six newly coined words in its five stanzas.

IV

What are the ingredients in the picture of nonsense? The feeling of nonsense materialized by Lear and Carroll has a general background of confusion against which a central bewildered explorer struggles with the problems of life. One aspect of the main problem is that of maintaining a sense of his own identity. With this in jeopardy, there can be no definite decision about which course to take, what road to pursue, or even whether to move forward, go backward, or attempt to stay where he is. This uncertainty of the identity is felt variously not only concerning the self and the own body, but also about all the elements (animate and inanimate) of the environment, which are generally anthropomorphized as well. Activity is the order of every situation, as is shown endlessly in Lear's drawings and in Carroll's prose. This multiplies the confusion since no one—whether Alice or the animals she meets or the path she travels—seems able to keep straight who or what he is; is supposed to be doing; or how it can be done. Even the words get out of hand and cannot be relied upon. A variety of verbal switches are utilized with punning based on klang associations, alliterations, spoonerisms, malapropisms, portmanteau condensations, neologisms, etc. Humpty-Dumpty tries to master words by making them mean whatever he wants them to, but very often, in the struggle, the words themselves win out and seem to go their own way.[3] In other words, even words lose their identity in losing their uniqueness of form and meaning, and seem to run off in various directions. Sometimes the word self-consciously maintains two opposite meanings (as indeed may be the case even with well-behaved words), but in the *Looking Glass* especially, opposites seem like nearly identical twins who are bound in an eternal wrangle as in the case of Tweedledum and Tweedledee.

The *portmanteau word* is a descriptive phrase originating with Carroll, who applies it to a combination of a number of words in one single one which contains at least the remnants of them all. Thus just as the *snark* is a monstrous combination of animals, so the word itself, like a composite photograph, contains snake, shark, snail, and probably many others. *Jabberwocky*, too, is such a portmanteau word, designating a terrifying animal composed of several others. There is one word play used by both Carroll and Lear which has never been given a special name. It consists in the snapping off the end of one word and adding it to the word next to it. Thus in *Jabberwocky*, the "slithy toves did gyre and gimble in the wabe." As it is explained later, *wabe* comes from *"way-before"* and *"way-behind"* the sundial in the garden. Lear spoke of a "sill kankerchief," "a nempty stomach," etc. But he was in any case an inveterate tamperer with words, combining phonetic spelling with colloquialism in a way which may make sense to the ear but is grotesquely unfamiliar, when printed, to greet the eye.[4]

---

3 Humpty-Dumpty would also take liberties with body configurations; it is he who suggests to Alice that she cannot be distinguished from others, as her features are arranged like everyone else's; "Now, if you had the two eyes on the same side of the nose for instance—or the mouth at the top—that would be some help in identifying you."

4 Further examples are discussed in ch. 23.

A certain compulsiveness appears in Lear's punning, for his journals and letters are heavy with it. To me, at least, it becomes tiresome in its monotonous cuteness, as though it were a repetitive plea not to be taken seriously, and not to be held responsible. In *Looking Glass* in which accusation and trial seem always in the air (and the trial has actually taken place in *Wonderland*), the compulsive nature of the punning is clearly indicated. While Alice finds herself riding in a railroad carriage over the chess-board of life with a variety of animals dressed as humans, as fellow travelers, she hears a hoarse voice down the car a way and thinks to herself that it sounds like a horse. At the same time a very small voice close to her ear says, "You might make a joke of that—something about 'horse' and 'hoarse' you know." When presently she wishes that she could go back to the wood she has just left, the same little voice echoed, "You might make a joke on *that,* something about 'you would if you could, you know.' " It was a gnat that had lodged in her ear and was directing her travels punwise. And just as a bee she had seen only a while ago had become an elephant diving into enormous flowers with his great proboscis, so the gnat flew into a tree and became the size of a chicken.

Tampered-with words resulting in distortions of their form and meaning are obviously closely bound up with problems of their identity, whether these have to do with flora,[5] fauna, or the human species, and involve in turn changes in size and apparent distortions of part or all of the body. Gross changes in size overtake Alice and many of the animals whom she encounters. But since these change individually rather than in an epidemic wave, there are many discrepancies and incongruities. In Lear's rhymes and stories there are more distortions of body shape with accentuation or a practical loss of some body part than changes which involve the entire body. There is not the same fluidity of form as occurs in Carroll's productions. In Lear indeed the body distortions are much more apparent in the drawings than in the rhymes.

[5] Lear's *Nonsense Botany*, illustrated, includes "small tooth-combia Domestica," "Phatfacia Stupendia," "Many peeplia Upidownia" as well as other rare flowers; while the Garden of Live Flowers in the *Looking Glass* world is guarded by a tree which has a protective bark and whose branches are called *bough-woughs*. Both Lear and Carroll have a playful time with snapdragons and tiger lilies. Insects seem to loom large to both, and both have the experience of seeing dishes and tableware rise up in the air in sportive love or anger. And so it goes.

The basic sexual identity of the characters is maintained at least in outline by both nonsense writers. Alice does not change into a boy, nor does she behave like a boy; and there is no frank change from one sex to the other as there is in Thorne Smith's stories or in *Orlando*. But there is a thinly disguised set of sexual problems in Alice's quest for the secret garden and for queenship. Her dilemma is rather: "What does it mean to grow up, be a woman and have children? How do the two sexes really get together? Is it after all an enviable state to be grown up?" At times it is as though she were saying, "What is happening to my body anyway? It is getting out of hand in its demands on me, and I can't stop it, or can I?" Older people whether men or women are, on the whole, unappetizing and as unpredictable as children in Alice's worlds. But one must remember that Carroll was next to the oldest of eleven children, and a crowded parsonage may well have been tempestuous. In Lear's drawings, many of the men have enormous heads and large bellies, but spindly arms and legs that wave like banners in the breeze. His women are nearly always thin, board-like creatures with sharp noses, chins, and long pointed toes.

Lear much more openly than Carroll indicated his feeling of inadequacy as a man. Carroll seemed to sidestep masculine goals in many ways and identify with the prepuberty girl who was doubtful but inquisitive about growing up.[6] In some of Lear's rhymes, one about a man is followed by one about a woman, with very obvious comparisons, but clear-cut contrasts are evaded. For example:

> There was an Old Man with a beard
> Who said, 'It is just as I feared!—
> Two Owls and a Hen, four Larks and a Wren
> Have all built their nests in my beard!'

and:

> There was a Young Lady whose bonnet
> Came untied when the birds sat upon it;
> But she said 'I don't care! All the birds in the air
> Are welcome to sit on my bonnet.'

6 In my book on *Swift and Carroll* (1955) I have examined the life story and concluded that Carroll probably had an unusually close relationship and identification with his sister, Louisa.

A last major ingredient of the nonsense picture, and one which is also part of the identity complex, has to do with the loss of body parts, either in actual fact or threatened as accident or punishment. In Lear's rhymes this is a less frequent occurrence than it is in Carroll's writings. Lear describes the Old Man of the Nile who loses his thumbs as the result of sharpening his nails with a file, and another old man who just escapes catastrophe when he is offered a hatchet with which to kill a flea that is biting him sorely. Then there is the famous Pobble that has no toes, as well as one young person who loses her head by its being fanned off by a too-attentive uncle. Lear also works this theme of loss in reverse in his accentuation or enlargement of body parts and members. It is perhaps most dramatic in his nonsense song of the Dong who fell in love with a Jumbly girl and so grieved when she sailed away and left him that what little sense he had in his head also left him. Consequently, as he wandered disconsolately over the world hunting her, to light his way at night he made an artificial nose with a luminous light on its end, which served as a beacon. He became celebrated then as the Dong with the Luminous Nose.

Lear's "nonsense" pictures of body mutilations and compensatory exaggerations are readily recognizable by anyone familiar with the psychology of the unconscious as expressions of severe castration fear which is being expressed directly or in an extreme form of denial.

In the *Alice* books, this is presented differently. Decapitation and extinction by fading out are more frequent threats than those of damage to or loss of a body part. To be sure the baby does lose its nose, sliced off by a flying pan; and the extinction of the Cheshire Cat proceeds bit by bit rather than through a massive fading. Decapitation in a less corporeal form is suggested too by Alice's recurrent fear of loss of memory even of her own name and whereabouts, so that she is frequently testing her own mental functioning.

V

It is not my intention to go into a very extensive or detailed interpretation of the thematic content of the nonsense productions of Carroll and Lear. I have attempted this somewhat, for Carroll's stories and nonsense poems in an earlier work (1955). The thread of the stories in the *Alice* books shows quite clearly the major crises of growing up, with attempts to solve the problems of sexual identity and identification. But the fears of castration and annihilation are so vivid and repetitive as to suggest chronic anxiety of panic proportions. All this is in the general setting of oedipal guilt; but is complicated by the persistence of infantile rage in the case of Carroll,[7] and by real epileptic attacks in Lear. What is striking, however, is that the situations which might produce panic are presented in so exaggerated and confused a way as to appear ridiculous. The panic is quickly muted. The beheading is anticipated on the scale of the French Revolution or worse, only actually "They never behead anyone," and it is all in the Queen's mind anyway. Certainly the sadistic aggression, which is a component of all anxiety and especially of that arising in anticipation of cruelty, is then compounded and directed against the self in guilt—the conscience is on a veritable rampage, until the voice of reason steps in and says, "This is all mental, a dream, a game." In this sense Sewall is right—that with the ability to get some distance, the force of reason prevails over the destructive forces. This control by the rarified counteraggression of reason—the superiority of the mind over primitive instincts—is personified by the Cheshire Cat sitting aloft, grinning a superior (rather than a merry) grin, which is the last to go.

But there may be another determinant in the fear of beheadment, to be found in the nature of extreme rage. The enraged person then "loses his head"—he loses his sense of direction and becomes disorganized. He acts, we say, like a chicken with its head cut off. Some think indeed that the epileptic convulsion is in-

---

[7] About the time of puberty or early adolescence, the boy Charles Dodgson began writing a small family newspaper in which he was already developing some skill at humorous verse writing. Among these early verses are some dealing with the *First Ear Ring*. This was a pun for "ringing in the ears" following a severe box on the ears. The story was that this had been admnistered by a father who had lost patience with his son and in his counteranger had boxed the child's ears so severely as to impair his hearing slightly but permanently. The young Charles seemed to get some of his talent for nonsense from this same father. Derek Hudson, in his life of Lewis Carroll, reproduces a letter from the father written apparently in the hope of counteracting the angry disappointed outburst he anticipated from his young son when he was unable to bring the child certain ardently desired things which the father had promised on a shopping trip in a nearby town. This letter contains elements of the same sort of nonsense which Charles was later to use so effectively in the *Alice books*.

trinsically related to and represents repressed rage. This is a state very close to absolute nonsense. But the ability to write, or to paint, or to reproduce this in a communicable form saves the person—here Lear or Carroll—from being devastated by it. It is my suspicion that communicating nonsense always requires considerable talent. This is a way of saying that talent provides ways of leaving the purely individual personal experiences, pains, and pressures of life; and through channels of empathic association not open to the less gifted, talent permits the maintenance of a distance from which to hear the collective or even the cosmic beat or see the outlines of organization and feel relationships in that which would otherwise be personally devastating. Communicated nonsense is a defense against destructive forces. But it may be more than a defense in that its very ability to maintain an equilibrium against such odds contains a constructive force offering, at the very least, continuity of existence rather than complete annihilation or disintegration. One might liken it to the expectation of rebirth which sometimes accompanies the intention of suicide.

Earlier in this discussion I have mentioned that some of the stories of Franz Kafka contain many of the ingredients present in the nonsense rhymes and stories, and especially in the full-length productions of Carroll. There is the same feeling of bewilderment and questioning, both about the self and the surroundings, the distortions of and changes in the body form and functioning, the becoming too small to cope with the people in the environment, the almost constant awareness of senseless frustration and of being unreasonably held responsible for all manner of happenings, of being threatened with punishment, and ultimately having to stand trial. But in the *Alice* books these are presented in what may be called a focus of absurdity with all manner of diverting incongruous detail; whereas in Kafka's stories the nightmare scenes are recounted with the most meticulously realistic details, especially in regard to the subjective feelings and perceptions of the central character.

If we compare, for example, Kafka's description of the opening of the door of his room by the cockroach who used to be Gregor Samsa with Alice's various attempts to open the door into the little garden, the contrast is striking. In Alice there is nothing to compare with the exquisite horror of the cockroach's attempts to turn the key in the lock of his door: first using his tiny legs with their sticky exudate to give some purchase on the wall, then turning the key in the lock with his mouth with such effort that a brown saliva covers the key and drops to the floor—in the meantime circling round and round the lock, holding on with his mouth, pushing on the key as required or pulling it down again with all the weight of his body until the lock yields.

With Kafka, there are symptoms of chronic panic from guilt, probably largely in relation to his father. He seems as though caught in the eddy of hostile aggressive feelings with the hostility absorbed into a sadistic conscience turning it mercilessly and eternally toward himself. Several times in Kafka's stories, the central character tells himself that these monstrous events must be nonsense, but is unconvinced and unrelieved. I shall not attempt any detailed analysis or interpretation of Kafka or his works, but I would point out that Kafka comes as close perhaps as is possible to presenting .the destructiveness that actual nonsense is, whereas Carroll and Lear use the sense of nonsense in a defensive way to allay panic. The sadism is then diluted but is to be detected again in the triumph of the comic, the persistent grin of the Cheshire Cat which disappears last of all. Rage and panic can in the extreme reach a state approaching annihilation of reason.

Kafka would seem to be a man doomed to slow self-destruction and indeed he died at forty-one (1924). Yet he seems to me somehow more of a piece even in his endless struggles and his profound chronic depression than Carroll or perhaps Lear. Carroll seemed to take leave of his masculinity and to present rather the clinical picture of a negative fetishism through his identification with a little prepuberty girl. There was in fact some indication of perversion in his great absorption in photographing little girls of nine or ten either in the nude or as close to it as a Victorian setting permitted.

While the typical fetishist has always to have an object which will be a phallic representative for him if he is to function sexually at all, there is no evidence that Carroll had any sexual interest in any woman, except his lost mother. But just as the fetishist must have his fetish not only for sexual adequacy but for the narcissistic completion of his body image, so Carroll, I suspect, in his voyeurism and intensive interest in prepuberty girls was repetitively confirming his identification with them, thus denying his need for masculine genital adequacy. But this very denial could not help but contribute to a sense of unreality and alienation from his actual body and from the pursuits of family life which constitute so much of the emotional foundation for most of us. It permitted, however, the development of a defensive critical distance in which a sense of nonsense could develop and flourish. It is interesting, too, that whereas Kafka remained painfully faithful to his interest in writing and is known for the scrupulosity of his writing, which won him posthumous fame, both Lear and Carroll have become renowned for their nonsense writing, and were less productive and attained less recognition in the fields in which their major interest presumably was involved.

Part III

PSYCHOANALYTIC THERAPY
AND TRAINING

CHAPTER THIRTY

Evaluation of Therapeutic Results: Contributions to a Symposium (1948)

I

The question of *methods* of evaluating therapeutic results of psychoanalytic treatment is an extraordinarily complicated one. I confess that it frightens me somewhat, especially as it seems to me almost as broad, and perhaps as staggering, as the question of evaluating surgical treatment, for example, and I doubt very much whether anyone would attempt that. At the risk of repeating what Dr. Oberndorf has said, I want to emphasize certain general considerations.

The degree of difficulty in evaluating the results of any sort of therapy seems to me to depend on two sets of general factors: (1) the complexity and specificity of the pathological process(es) involved, and (2) the complexity and/or specificity of the methods used. It is obviously necessary to determine the state of the patient after treatment, both immediately and from a long-term range, and to attempt to assay the extent to which any improvement or worsening of the patient's condition was due to the specific treatment used and not to some external factors.

Since the psychoanalyst is not generally dealing with a specifically circumscribed disease process in the patient, but with a number of interweaving disturbed functions embedded in or consisting of the very fabric of the patient's existence, and since psychoanalytic treatment involves a relatively complicated set of techniques applied over a long period of time, with the additional variable of the human administration of these techniques and the peculiarly important role of the transference which is in itself an interaction between patient and analyst—because of all these we become aware of, and I said, frightened by the enormous intricacies of the job. If there is added to this the need to establish criteria of judgment of improvement and the question of immediate or ultimate outcome and consideration of all the questions of the multiplicity of factors influencing differences between the immediate and the later condition of the patient, we, or I at least, begin to suffer from an overload of precision. Yet, if critical precision is relaxed on any one of these counts, there is grave danger of distortion of evaluation.

The time element alone seems to me exceedingly important. In order to determine the effects of treatment on any patient, it is necessary to see not only whether his symptoms disappear, but more importantly whether his total functioning in life is better; and further whether such improvement is sustained. This means practically that psychiatrists and psychoanalysts should have longer lives than others in order to get an adequate vision of their work.

I have myself had two periods of work which gave me direct experience bearing somewhat on these problems of evaluating treatment. About 1924 I was asked to submit a plan for the investigation of the clinical results of a certain program of treatment then being carried on in one of the state hospitals of one of our nearby states. The statistical reports of improvement and recovery had risen so very markedly—reaching, I think, a phenomenal height of 85 percent of all admissions—and because this high rate seemed to have resulted from a steady progressive rise in the recovery rate since the inception of this particular set of treatment procedures, the members of the state board of supervisors had become impressed and asked for a survey of the work before extending the use of these methods into other hospitals in that state. During the year 1925-26, I took charge of this clinical investigation, and in order to minimize the differences in judgment entailed if more workers had been involved and also to carry the responsibility directly, I personally examined all of the patients in certain designated groups, even though this meant, in many instances, paying home visits in outlying districts as well as going into many hospitals. It is not necessary to go into the exact ways in which this clinical investigation was set up, but I mention it in order to bring out certain conclusions which I found impressive.

If my judgment was anywhere near being correct, the survey showed not a genuine sustained improvement after these therapeutic procedures, but paradoxically that patients who had been systematically treated were less well after a lapse of five years than they had been at the time of their first admissions and showed fewer remissions or recoveries than a control group of patients who had received only custodial care. The program of treatment had included surgery, and it was very striking that in many instances there had been a dramatic symptomatic improvement after the surgical operation even though the ultimate result was bad. Most impressive, however, was the influence of the therapeutic wish, ambition, and enthusiasm of the director of the hospital on the majority of his staff members who were devoted to and identified with him. The place hummed with pleasant inspiration. There was no doubt of their essential integrity, but their wishes fantastically clouded their vision, and I, an outsider, was somewhat in the position of the child in the story of the Emperor's new clothes.

The other period of work to which I referred consisted in an attempt to set up a comprehensive file of cases treated in a psychiatric clinic over a period of years. The aim of this was to make clinical material available to staff members and thereby to aid clinical research. With a zeal undoubtedly born of compulsiveness, I set about to do a thorough job of it, including not only a cross-filing of the contents of case records, but a system of following up patients after discharge and an attempt to evaluate not therapeutic results, but simply the degree of recovery in each case, i.e., the postdischarge conditions. I gradually became convinced of the futility of my project, and I am inclined to believe that I was probably the only person who profited much from my efforts. I am sure that it very much broadened and deepened my clinical experience to read over those hundreds of case records, but I doubt whether the file was very much used by my colleagues who probably got more by verbal communications with each other,

and located old cases on this basis too, than from use of my painstakingly and amateurishly set-up system. This was due, I believe,
to the fact that it was too complex to be really plastic, and at the
same time it was not really comprehensive enough to have any
genuine statistical value. I am glad to contribute the account of
this relative failure for whatever it is worth in a reconsidering of
these problems in a different setting now.

Before discussing specifically anything about methods as such,
it seems wise to consider also whether there are any disadvantages
in setting up systems of examination of case material primarily
from the angle of therapeutic efficacy or failure.

Freud always sensed the danger of too great therapeutic zeal
in the analyst, and his warning appeared again and again in his
writings. In the Postscript to *The Question of Lay Analysis*
(1926b), in his *Autobiographical Study* (1925), and especially in
the *New Introductory Lectures* (1933a, p. 151f.) he referred to
these problems at some length. He repeatedly indicated that
marked therapeutic zeal on the part of the analyst was frequently
an indication of underlying sadism, and there is of course the
corollary that a pressure of this kind brings about an excessive and
distorting reaction formation operating from the therapist onto
the patient or onto the consideration of the case material as such.
I would further like to stress a derivative of the sadism which also
seemed to me to play an important part in too great and destructive therapeutic zeal in psychiatrists and psychoanalysts—and that
is personal ambition. Under these circumstances the analyst forms
a peculiarly intense and ambivalent countertransference to his
patient, who becomes too much the means of unhealthy narcissistic gain to the analyst. In other words, the analyst has too great
a stake in the patient's recovery, not actually for the patient's sake
but for the analyst's own comfort, either for prestige gain or even
for the feeling of power in curing. When, as so often happens, the
analyst really demands too much of his patient, the patient inevitably disappoints him, and not infrequently the negative side
of the countertransference becomes quite apparent. Freud emphasized that his own interest in the truth, in his case, his original
interest in the "living pathology" of the patient, was the greatest
therapeutic safeguard to the patient; and this seems to me so
basic and so sound that I think we should consider it in setting

up or planning to set up any system involving a review of results of treatment. I shall return to this point later in the discussion of specific plans. It seems to be so simply true as to be elusive that the worker whose goal is the essential verity of his scientific work may in some instances take unnecessary detours of exploration, but by and large will contribute most to the science and to his patient.

There are two other aspects of this problem of therapeutic zeal and goal in the analyst which Freud touches on, and which I would like to develop a bit further: (1) the naïve expectation that the neuroses *can be* completely cured, and (2) the question of the nature and intensity of the positive countertransference which furnishes a good and essential part of the psychoanalytic work. Freud deals somewhat with the first of these in his *New Introductory Lectures* when he states (p. 153): "The expectation that every neurotic phenomenon can be cured may, I suspect, be derived from the layman's belief that the neuroses are something quite unnecessary which have no right whatever to exist" and then refers to their constitutional determination. He touches on the second in his obituary for Ferenczi (1933b), in which he remarks that this great scientific worker did, toward the end of his life, probably attempt the impossible, i.e., to *give love* to his patients.

It seems to me that we must remind ourselves very definitely of the first of these considerations, namely, the danger of expecting that neuroses can be completely cured, and yet not slip into the pitfall of using this as a rationalization for our failures. I have thought of—what is at least translated as *constitutional* in Freud's paper—as not only "constitutional" in the more limited sense in which the word is generally used, but as the genetic neurotic elements which must be present in every individual, due to the discrepancies between the slow processes of inner biological change and the sometimes more rapid changes in environmental demands. I am inclined to believe that in disregarding these, the psychoanalyst not only reverts to the naïve lay attitude, but that this too is part of a narcissistic need to seek or to have omnipotence.

In regard to the second question, i.e., what degree and kind of positive countertransference is desirable and even an essential part of the psychoanalytic work, it is certainly obvious that no analyst can exactly legislate or ration his own countertransference to conform to a demand for the optimum. The best he can probably do is to exercise some broad general principles in the selection of patients and to proceed with the analysis with a sensitive finger upon his own pulse, as well as giving his attention to his patient throughout his work. Still it may be worth considering what, from a detached point of view, constitutes the best countertransference atmosphere for the psychoanalysis to proceed. I think that we would all agree that it is unwise to accept patients toward whom we feel in the first hours a definite antipathy. This is the negative side of our question. I do not believe that it is possible, or even desirable, for us to be completely neutral, and that some positive attitude of the analyst toward the patient is a *sine qua non* for progress. I doubt whether we ever teach or learn in an emotional vacuum, and this is as true for the special kind of learning of the analytic process as it is in the classroom. I would think, however, that in analytic work, especially, the best kind of liking for the patient and the optimum emotional temperature for the work occur when the positive feeling is largely a zest for the integrity of the work involved and includes, rather than being primarily directed by, a personal interest in the patient.

As I have thought over the question whether and what systems of evaluating results of psychoanalytic treatment might be set up, I found that I doubted the wisdom of focusing on this particular area in making any plans; but if one is to do it at all, one should make some plan whereby clinical material would be available and therapeutic results might be studied as part of the broader questions involved, whether of suitability of certain clinical groups for treatment, efficacy of certain techniques, or other points of investigation. In this connection certainly the consideration of therapeutic results forms an integral part, but it is not the primary end of the critical study.

My own proposals are hesitant, but would be along two lines: (1) The planning for some uniform scheme of filing of case records in the various psychoanalytic clinics of the country so that ultimately there might be the opportunity for genuine statistical evaluation, rather than the pseudostatistical small group compilation of cases which we must depend upon if we are limited only to our own patients. (2) Some very simple flexible scheme of case filing in each clinic for the use of its own workers, for the enrichment of their clinical experience, and to give them the opportunity to locate cases similar to their own. My impression is that this is of greatest value when it leads to mutual discussion of cases rather than merely to an examination of dead records, which can again so readily be unconsciously distorted by the reader who has a clinical cause to support.

As to the overall statistical approach which I mentioned first, such a scheme would have to be worked out by a biological statistician, someone like the late Raymond Pearl or perhaps a man like Lazarsfeld, in careful consultation with analysts.

Again I would return to Freud's discussion of the statistics on therapeutic results in the Berlin clinic (1933a, p. 152): "But statistics of that kind are in general uninstructive; the material worked upon is so heterogeneous that only very large numbers would show anything. *It is wiser to examine one's individual experiences.* And here I would like to add that I do not think our cures can compete with those of Lourdes."

There is one other aspect of this whole problem of method of evaluation which I would mention and which may represent an oversensitivity on my part, and that is whether psychoanalysis has yet reached a degree of general acceptance in which it is wise to have files of case records; whether the dangers of betrayal of confidence, either actual or feared, may not introduce a new element into psychoanalytic clinic work which would possibly impair the work itself. The fear of the clinic patient of being exposed is generally so great anyway and while it has been diminished somewhat by the newer clinic setups eliminating common waiting rooms, etc., it is still a subtle but appreciable interference in treatment.

In summary, I am constrained to remark that while you have asked me to speak of methods of evaluating the results of psychoanalytic treatment, I am afraid I have been unable to comply, but rather to indicate why I think that a primary focusing on therapeutic results is unwise and not especially productive. It appears to me to shift the center of investigation in such a way as to risk causing a distorted perspective of the field. If, however, it may be possible to set up a system for a genuinely inclusive statistical survey, applicable to all psychoanalytic clinics, and including secondarily results of treatment, then it seems to me this might give valuable data by itself, as well as offering a sound stimulus to the individual analyst to scrutinize his work and especially to weigh his failures.

II

In the first place I am happy to see in the discussion today a shift from the emphasis on scrutiny of therapeutic results to a scrutiny of the therapeutic process. This was less definite in the discussion last night. Part of my own emphasis was that focusing on results divorced from consideration of the case as a whole would run the risk of emphasis on therapy to a point approaching a dangerous therapeutic zeal or at least encouraging it. I would want to make clear that I am quite in accord that it behoves us all to look at our results and to make a distinction between zeal and interest.

This afternoon's discussion brought out a cooperative interest and study rather than the tendency to bipolarity of points of view, which can occur rather spontaneously and then tends to make us overstate ourselves. So often we tend to think in terms of "either-or," in an effort to be definitive, and this may take the place of a more appropriate "and." In addition, the emphasis on a study of the countertransference seems to me both very important and very difficult. We pay too little attention to that. We think in terms of the patient, often overlooking the constant interplay between doctor and patient.

In regard to a remark of Dr. Bandler's concerning the discrepancy between the real cause of improvement in a patient and the things to which he attributes it. There is often a considerable discrepancy and sometimes in a reverse direction from that indicated by Dr. Bandler. One has to be exceedingly careful, critical, and sometimes uncertain in assaying the fundamental pivots of improvement. In my own follow-up studies, made more than twenty years ago, I occasionally found that patients seemed to have profited quite fundamentally from treatment but would attribute their improvement to something quite trivial. There was, then, however, much more shyness and concealment of psychiatric treatment generally—which may have influenced this effort to minimize it officially.

CHAPTER THIRTY-ONE

The Role of Transference: Practical Considerations in Relation to Psychoanalytic Therapy (1954)

It is my intention to discuss some of the practical considerations in psychoanalytic treatment in their relationship to the role of the transference. I shall not enter into any extensive technical or historical survey but shall confine myself to a few problems expressed in nontechnical terms, and without benefit of quotation. I shall deal with these problems in the following order: (1) a discussion of the essentials of the transference relationship; (2) a brief outline of two different points of view regarding the utilization of the transference in therapy; and (3) a discussion of practical arrangements as they are determined by the transference.

I

First as to the nature of the transference relationship itself: If two people are repeatedly alone together, some sort of emotional bond will develop between them. Even though they may be strangers engaged in relatively neutral occupations, not directed by one or the other for or against the "other one," it will probably not be long before a predominantly friendly or predominantly unfriendly tone will develop between them. The speed and the intensity of this development will be enhanced by the frequency of the periods in each other's company.

Human beings do not thrive well in isolation, being sustained then mostly by memories and hopes, even to the point of hallucination, or by reaching out to nonhuman living things (like Mendel and the beans). This need for sensory contact, basically the contact of warm touch of another body but secondarily experienced in the other senses as well (even the word "contact" is significant), probably comes from the long period of care which the human infant must have before he is able to sustain himself. Lonely infants fed and cared for regularly and with sterile impersonal efficiency do not often live to childhood.

Even if the periods of repeated contact between two individuals do not comprise a major part of their time, still such an emotional bond develops and does so more quickly and more sensitively if the two persons are *alone* together; i.e., the more the spontaneous currents and emanations of feeling must be concentrated the one upon the other and not shared, divided, or reflected among members of a group. I have already indicated that I believe the matrix of this *is* a veritable matrix; i.e., comes largely from the original mother-infant quasi-union of the first months of life. This I consider the basic transference; or one might call it the primary transference, or some part of primitive social instinct.

Now if both people are adults but one is troubled and the other is versed in the ways of trouble and will endeavor to put the torchlight of his understanding at the disposal of the troubled one, to lend it to him that he may find his way more expeditiously, the situation more nearly approximates that of the analytic relationship. The analyst then acts like an extra function, or set of functions, which is lent to the analysand for the latter's temporary use and benefit.

Since this relationship may, in its most primitive aspects, be based on the mother-child relationship and since the patient is a troubled person seeking help, one can see at once that the relationship will not be one of equal mutual warming, but that there will be a tendency for the patient to develop an attitude of expectant dependent receptiveness toward the physician. It is the aim of treatment, however, to increase the patient's maturity, to realize his capacity for self-direction, his "self-possession" (in the deeper sense of the word); and *not* to augment his state of help-lessness and dependence, with which he in his neurotic suffering is already burdened.

How then is the patient's autonomy to be safeguarded and strengthened, in the very situation which might seem to favor its depletion? The chief safeguard is the analyst's sticking to the work of actually analyzing, and not serving as guide, model, or teacher, no matter how luring these roles may be. He must there-fore genuinely leave matters of decision in the patient's own hands without guiding interference. We all know that the work of analy-sis consists very largely in helping the patient to rid himself of the tensions, patterned attitudes, and expectations which have arisen in the vicissitudes of the past and are impinging unhelpfully upon current situations, so much so that they actually distort his appre-ciation of and his reactive possibilities to the present problems of his life; and that this help of riddance is carried out through a mutual exploration of the forgotten past, using mainly the special techniques of free association and dream analysis.

The analytic relationship is used entirely for the benefit of the patient. Analysis is the profession of the therapist and he sets his fee and makes his time arrangements with his patient in advance; and thereafter attempts to keep these constant except when extra-ordinary reality conditions intrude to force a dislocation of these elements of the reality framework. The analyst does not intrude his life, his point of view—moral, political or religious or any other—into his responses to his patient. His aim rather is to listen, to clarify, and to communicate step by step an understanding of the patient's current dilemmas in relation to the intrusion into them of inappropriate emotional attitudes and action tendencies having their origin in the past. This sounds too mechanistic and too simple, but will be considered again in dealing further with the transference development. In the very neutrality and constancy of the physical arrangements of treatment, in their noncontamina-tion by contributions from the analyst's own life, and in the essentially research and nondirective attitude of the analyst, many forces which might diminish the patient's autonomy are avoided.

It is quite apparent that in nonanalytic relationships, in just everyday give-and-take contacts, we react not merely on the basis of the realistic current elements of the situation but as these influence us additionally in accordance with their stirring memories of past experiences, whether or not these are available to direct recall. Indeed we seem to be more influenced when the memory is not available, and we mistake the feeling aroused by the past for one belonging intrinsically to the present. In each life situation, whole series of memory reactions of more or less related situations are re-evoked, and it is certainly not merely the present but a composite of past experiences which is influencing the attitudes and actions of the individual at any given time.

Now in the artificial situation of the analytic relationship, there develops early a firm basic transference, derived from the mother-child relationship but expressed in the confidence in the knowledge and integrity of the analyst and the helpfulness of the method; but, in addition, the nonparticipation of the analyst in a personal way in the relationship creates a "tilted" emotional relationship, a kind of psychic suction in which many of the past attitudes, specific experiences and fantasies of the patient are re-enacted in fragments or sometimes in surprisingly well-organized dramas with the analyst as the main figure of significance to the patient. This revival of past experiences, with their full emotional accompaniment focused upon the analyst, is not only more possible but can be more easily seen, understood, and interpreted if the psychic field is not already cluttered with personal bits from the analyst's life. This of course is the work with the neurotic symptoms and patterns as they occur in the transference, i.e., projected directly upon the analyst. Many times it is the most convincing medium of demonstration and interpretation to the patient and permits a greater degree of relief, probably because the memories are thus being actually experienced with their *full* emotional resonance, and not merely being reported and talked about with a *partial* reliving. One should recall that even in the matter of a confession, more relief is obtained if the events are specifically told, than if simply the recognition of wrongdoing is admitted in general terms.

So much time has been spent on these very elementary conditions for analysis because recently there has been a tendency to disregard them somewhat, and sometimes to ignore—on the basis that they are unnecessary, cumbersome or just so much rigid ritual anyway—the restrictions and to resent the deprivations which, admittedly artificial, are designed to promote the development of the full display of neurotic manifestations in the transference.

II

In regard to the role of the transference development, it seems that two fundamental and divergent points of view are represented more and more clearly among us. The one sees the transference relationship in its full development (permitting and even emphasizing the repetition in the transference of older, nuclear experiences) as the most delicate, subtle, and precious medium of work and considers that its development should be furthered, its existence safeguarded, and its content analyzed. The other (with which I am less familiar) regards the basic positive transference in the form of mutual respect and confidence as essential for the best progress of the work, very much as it is in any other therapeutic or cooperative working relationship, but considers intensity of transference relationship beyond this as largely a dependency reaction which should be diluted or dispersed as expeditiously as possible, by indicating to the patient that his reactions *are* those of different varieties of dependency, belonging to his childhood rather than to adulthood, and by encouraging him as quickly as possible to change his actions in the outer world, to undertake new experiences which will then, with the emotional support of the analyst, be of a different nature and configuration than those which he has experienced in the past. It is even said that transference reactions needing specific interpretation should be avoided, and the relationship with the analyst is used for its emotional leverage in the enticement, direction or persuasion of the patient to his new undertakings. Thus, hopefully, the patient will not remain dependent on the analyst because he will be throughout engaging himself in new and beneficial experiences in reality, although he is at the same time depending on the analyst's explanatory encouragement. Guided and suggested or at least supported by the analyst, he enters the "corrective experience," and is supposed to break the habitual neurotic constellation which has previously held him. This appears to be little more than the old-fashioned habit training with especially strong suggestive influencing. Or it might be compared to the reconditioning experiences in which the approval of the analyst is the reward for running the new maze.

The contrast of these two points of view is summarized as, first, one which encourages, develops, and utilizes the full transference reaction as a medium of re-experience and interpretation; and second, one which utilizes only the basic transference, avoids the intensity of the full transference development, directs by interpreting dynamic lines and relationships rather than eliciting and interpreting specific past experiences, and encourages and promotes new experiences per se during the analytic work, often as quickly as possible. In the former there is a considerable reliance on the "working through" process, utilizing the analyst as an essential focus; in the latter, a considerable reliance on the "working out" process, carrying into reality activity new behavior patterns under the suggestion and support of the analyst, and sometimes even with his stage management. The aim in the "working through" is a loosening of the neurotic tendencies at their source, since deepest emotional tensions are invested in the specific experiences; while in the "working out," counteracting, neutralizing or freshly coating experiences are relied upon to coerce the emotions into new patterns without paying too much specific attention to the old. One is a method of detailed analysis; the other of survey and forward propulsion with the aid of the strong suggestion of personal attachment, which will, however, presumably and paradoxically be without increased dependency. If we keep in mind these two divergent points of view, I think we may understand different emphases in technique and even in the maintenance of practical arrangements.

III

Much has been said in the recent past concerning the rules and rituals of analysis, the worshipful obedience which our organization is said to exact of its devotees. The magic numbers three, four, and five seem to recur. But rules are the implementation of principles, i.e., the forms of their specific application; and no rule is very significant except as it represents the general practice of a desirable principle. In addition, there is no rule which may not have to be modified. It is from this angle of principles that practical procedures will be discussed here.

In the sort of psychoanalysis with which I am dealing, *the full transference relationship is accepted,* its establishment promoted and safeguarded, and its content examined and selectively interpreted. To the end of its speedy establishment, it is well to have analytic sessions spaced sufficiently close together that a sense of continuity of relationship (between analyst and analysand) and of content of material produced may be sustained. It would seem then that as nearly as possible a daily contact avoiding frequent or long gaps in treatment is desirable. In the setting of the organization of most lives, the analysis takes its place in the work of the week and accordingly five or six sessions are allocated to it. Later in many analyses it may be desirable to reduce the number of sessions, after the relationship between analyst and analysand has been consolidated, and the analyst has been able to determine the analysand's reactions to interruptions, first apparent in the reactions to weekends. If the analysand carries over a day's interruption well, without the relationship cooling off too much and the content being lost sight of, then it may be possible to carry the analysis on a three- or four-session-a-week basis, keeping a good rhythm of work with the patient. The desirability of this, however, can only be determined after the analyst has had a chance to gauge the patient's natural tempo and needs and the character of his important defenses; and this must vary from patient to patient. This initial period is generally at least a year, and more often longer.

There are three additional unfavorable factors here, however, which are seldom mentioned: (1) the actual prolongation of the treatment by spreading or infrequent spacing of sessions, in analytic work as well as in other psychotherapeutic approaches. If this prolongation is great, there is that much longer impact on other arrangements of the patient's life. "Brief psychotherapies" are sometimes paradoxically extended over very long times indeed, being repeatedly ended and reopened, because little was consolidated in the treatment and all sorts of extraneous and unnecessary interferences entered. (2) The larger the number of analytic patients possible at any given time when sessions per patient are less frequent, the greater the tax on the analyst in keeping at his mental fingertips the full range of facts and reactions belonging to each patient. The monetary recompense may, however, be greatly increased. Here again the feasibility of spacing must depend on some factors belonging to the analyst's special equipment and demands, combined with the patient's ability to "carry over," and there will inevitably be considerable variability in these. (3) The less frequent the therapeutic sessions the greater may be the risk of inadequate analysis of the negative transference. Especially with those patients where hours are made less frequent because the patient is thought by the analyst to be "wasting the hour" by what appears to be unproductive talk or by silence, or where the analyst fears that the patient is feeling guilty over his silences, it has sometimes been recommended that the patient be given a vacation from treatment or that sessions be made less frequent. From my experience in the reanalysis of a number of patients, it has seemed to me rather that many of these periods are due to the patient's difficulty in expressing hostile or erotic feelings. It is about these feelings, rather than about his silence, that he feels guilty. Too often if he is given a rest or hours are made infrequent, these emotional attitudes are never brought out to be analyzed, and appear later on in disturbing forms. I am further impressed with the fact that those analysts who talk most about the dangers of dependence seem rarely to consider the reciprocal relationship between tenacious dependency and unanalyzed negative transference. Insofar as negative attitudes toward the analyst are not analyzed or even expressed, the need of the patient to be reassured of the love and protection of the analyst becomes enormously increased and demanding. The analyst may see only this side of the picture and erroneously attempt to deal with it by greater spacing of contacts.

The length of the hour is, as a matter of practice, generally maintained at forty-five to sixty minutes. Certainly it is desirable that a sufficient span of time be permitted for a kind of natural organic pattern of productivity to occur during many of the sessions. The hour is our time unit in general use, perhaps because it does involve some kind of natural span of this kind, and it is a feasible unit fitting into the working day. While there have been many experiments of speeding up the analytic sessions to two a day or increasing the length to two hours at one session, no such practice has generally taken hold. It is my belief, however, that a regular allotment of time—the same duration and so far as possible on a prearranged and constant week-by-week schedule (in contrast to varying spans of time in sessions at irregular periods not expected in advance)—generally aids in the rhythm and continuity of the work and minimizes utilization of external situations as resistance by the patients.

The idea has been advanced by some that it would be wiser, when feasible, to have so flexible a schedule that it would be possible to see patients according to their sense of need, a kind of on-demand feeding program; or such resiliency that hours could be lengthened or shortened according to the seeming current emotional state of the patient. While I have little doubt that this may be desirable in some open psychotic conditions, I do doubt its benefit in other conditions. I believe that in neurotic and even in many borderline states, patients gain a sense of strength in relation to reality and growing inner capacity in the ability to carry on regular work, tolerating some discomforts and anxieties, knowing that these will be worked with at a regular time and have actually a lesser degree of (oral) dependency than where appointments are made on demand. This does not mean, however, that in situations of crisis from inner or outer reasons, extra appointments should necessarily be denied.

No discussion of practical arrangements for psychoanalytic therapy would be complete without paying one's respects to the question of whether the couch or the chair is to be used by the analysand during his treatment session. Indeed, to many lay people, the use of the couch became the main or only index of whether the treatment was psychoanalytic or a discussion method. Couch meant psychoanalysis; chair meant no psychoanalysis. With the increased popularity of psychoanalysis, unfortunately some young psychiatrists became analysts through the purchase of a couch and the reading of the dream book; and with the increased interest in recent years in the hypnotic and drug and electroshock therapies, the couch is more or less routine equipment and no longer a mark of distinction. Although its use was originally probably derived from the hypnotic therapy with which analysis originated, it was retained—not as a residual organ—but because it was of service in inducing a state of mild relaxation and limiting gross movement in the analysand, a condition favorable for attention to the flow of associative thought so necessary for the exploration of unconscious connections. Furthermore, with the analyst sitting at the head of the couch, the patient is not distracted by watching the analyst's facial expression and attempting to read it and accommodate to it, while the analyst can rest his face the more by not having to be looked at all day long and to inhibit or control the unconscious blend of reaction and reflection in his facial expression. As every analyst knows, there are some patients in marginal relationship with reality who find it very difficult to talk unless communication is maintained through visual as well as through spoken contact. Such patients naturally require to be treated vis-à-vis, but generally require other marked changes in analytic technique as well. Many analysts make a considerable distinction between what is said before the patient gets on the couch and immediately after he arises from it, from that which is couch born. Certainly there may be considerable significance in the difference in his postural relationship to the analyst and its connection with his utterances. One notices these things rather naturally with each patient and quite as naturally determines what importance to put upon them. Only a very compulsive analyst will want to determine an inexorable precision of rule of interpretation about these matters, or to prescribe every detail of the analyst's office. The general principle is to keep the physical arrangements of the office substantially the same throughout the treatment. Certainly this aids in limiting diverting influences and intrusions.

The safeguarding of the transference relationship is of prime importance. The relationship is an artificial one, arranged and maintained for the definite purpose of drawing the neurotic reactions into a sharp focus and reflecting them upon the analyst and the analytic situation. It is therefore just as necessary to keep the field pure for the clear reflection of the memories emerging from the past, as it is not to contaminate a field of surgical operation, or to avoid getting extraneous dirt onto a microscopic slide, which will blur or obscure the important findings, create artifacts, and confuse interpretive understanding.

The two sets of considerations in safeguarding the transference field of work which seem most important to me are the strict maintenance of the confidences of the patient and, second, the elimination of other avenues of relationship with the patient than that of analysis. Both of these are difficult to maintain, but only by keeping the principles continually in mind, training oneself to respect safeguarding rules, and closely examining any times in which violations occur, can an analyst really do justice to his work; and only if he is willing to maintain this degree of respect for his patient, himself, and his work, is he genuinely up to the job in hand. I cannot in the least agree with the remark of a quite eminent analyst, repeated to me several times, that so many analysts overstep the boundaries of the transference—even in grossly sexual ways—that therefore the best thing to do is to say nothing about these incidents. It is only by discussing these possibilities (rather than by punishing the offenders) and by emphasizing their dangers to students and among ourselves that we can really develop our science to the research precision which must be aimed at in each clinical case.

In regard to maintaining the confidence of the patient, all would probably agree on the unwisdom of gossiping about patients, although even here, where should a person draw the line? It is not always easy to say where professional discussion ends and anecdotal interest starts. Further than this, seemingly less hazardous but in my opinion even more seriously endangering analytic work, is the giving and receiving of information directly about the patient to and from relatives, sincerely interested friends and even physicians. Here there is the danger not only of the breach of the patient's confidence, but the breakdown of the analyst's own integrity of work with the patient, his tendency to become prejudiced, seemingly paradoxically, by the supposed objective facts obtained from other sources. While it is undoubtedly true that an analyst's vision of the total situation may at certain points be seriously impaired by his need to stick to the microscopy of his work or by an overidentification with the patient, still it seems that this is in the long run less distorting—in that it leaves the autonomy of the patient intact and "objectivity" is obtained through the patient's changing activities and reality testing in the world—than if the analyst succumbs to the pressure of outside information, which is sometimes not in the least objective, and begins insidiously to exert "corrective" influential pressure in the analysis, sometimes without the analyst even being aware that he is doing so. Therefore it is a better principle to seek or to give specific information about a patient only with the patient's definite knowledge, understanding, and wish.

It is almost self-evident that the same problems of breach of confidence, of insidious therapeutic pressure, and of the enormous complication of the changing transference identity of the analyst militate against sound analytic work in the simultaneous analysis of married couples or of those in close emotional relationships. While this may occasionally seem necessary under very extraordinary circumstances, it is at best a precarious proceeding. Recently it has sometimes been justified on the basis of the wealth of factual background available to the analyst and the greater skill possible in handling the situation. That greater skill is demanded is evident; that that degree of skill is frequently possible seems dubious. In the reanalysis of analysts in my own practice, I have sometimes found that such a strong wish on the part of the analyst represented rather an unusual degree of unresolved primal scene scoptophilia in the analyst himself.

The need to avoid violation of the transference field by the establishment of other avenues of relationship with the patient demands a high degree of restraint and sacrifice on the part of the analyst. It demands, among other things, the sacrifice on the part of the analyst of conspicuous public participation even in very worthy social and political "causes" to which he may lend his name or his activities. For insofar as the analyst is thrown into so active, even though general, a pressure role outside the analysis, his situation is the more complicated inside the analysis. It may be impossible for him to detect this if it then means that the patient just automatically does not dare to think of certain things which he unconsciously feels would cause him to be unacceptable to this particular analyst. Such deletions from the analysis only turn up on reanalysis or in the negative transference reactions which crop up after the termination of an analysis. The analyst must forego the privilege of eliciting the patient's admiration for his personal exploits.

Another form of contamination of the transference occurs when the analyst asks special favors, even seemingly minor ones, from the patient. This is frequently done and justified on the basis that the request is only a minor one; or, on the opposite basis, that the external situation is so important as to warrant breaking the rule;

or that the analyst's skill is so great and his knowledge of his patient's inner situation so nearly perfect that he can afford to do so with impunity; or even that he is really doing it for the benefit of the patient; yet it may be followed by very severe disturbance. This rule about not entering into other relationships with the analysand is one which always deserves our most careful and respectful scrutiny.

This leads back again to consideration of that grosser overstepping of the transference limits in the establishment of a sexual relationship between analyst and analysand either during the analysis or relatively soon after it is officially terminated. That this is not so infrequent as one would wish to think becomes apparent to anyone who does many reanalyses. That its occurrence is often denied and the situation rather quickly explained by involved analysts as due to a hysterical fantasy on the part of the patient (indeed one knows how universal and necessary such fantasies are) is an indication of how great is the temptation. It would seem that there is a factor in this which is one of the not immediately observable implications of the setup of the analytic consulting room, with the patient in a passive-receptive position, and the whole situation one of intimacy and shutting out of the external world. Certainly such a situation is most provocative to a male analyst and a female patient.

It is my contention, however, that an equally distorting but not so obvious invasion of the transference relationship may occur with the female analyst, who may be drawn unconsciously into an overly protective, essentially maternal nursing attitude toward the suffering patient, whether man or woman. One must remember in considering the effects of such transgressions that the analytic situation is an artificial, tilted one; that there is none other in life that it really reproduces. In this very fact is its enormous force and capacity for utilization as a medium for establishing new integration. It is one which more nearly reproduces the demand of the child for a perfectly understanding parent than any parent-child relationship can possibly approach, and it is the only one in life in which no emotional counterdemand is to be expected. It is produced for the purpose of drawing these infantile and childish reactions into a new life for the sake of their being understood and newly assimilated by the suffering adult whom the child has become. For this very reason, the carrying through into a relationship in life of the incestuous fantasy of the patient may be more grave in its subsequent distortion of the patient's life than any actual incestuous seduction in childhood has been.

Psychoanalysis is a hard taskmaster. Even in its practice it demands the accuracy, the fidelity, and the devotion of the true research worker. It is not something to be played with or even to be too lightly experimented with. The power of the unconscious is such that it "gets back" at those who work with it and treat it too lightly. There are some unfortunate sides to the markedly increased popularity of psychoanalysis since the last World War. Perhaps chief among these is the fact that because its importance, in its derived forms, was seen clearly under war conditions and attracted the attention of physicians and psychiatrists rather generally, the demand for training became so great that a growing temptation arose for the substitution of some of the therapies derived from psychoanalysis for psychoanalysis itself, at the risk of expediency being rationalized as tested theory.

CHAPTER THIRTY-TWO

Re-evaluation of the Process of Working Through (1956)

The process of *working through* has held positions of varying importance and significance in the development of psychoanalytic therapy. Just at present one hears it referred to relatively little, and as a specific principle in technique it does not attract very much attention. Indeed, students rarely use the term, and sometimes seem uncertain as to its meaning. This may be due in part to the fact that the process of *working through* is now largely subsumed in other technical procedures. But there may also be some lessening in emphasis on its value. There are certain cases, however, and some situations in many cases in which a sound and thorough working through is essential for a sustained therapeutic result. A consideration of these is the topic for discussion at present.

In the early days of psychoanalytic treatment, when it was still within nodding distance of hypnotic therapy, the aims of therapy were especially the recovery of infantile traumatic memories and their abreaction through repetition, first in the hypnotic, subsequently in the psychoanalytic relationship. It was observed that the specific reliving of the disturbing experience relieved the associated conflict-bound emotional tension more than educative discussions concerning disturbed feelings could possibly do. Certainly in the reliving, the patient may more nearly admit the full emotional resonance to consciousness, whereas in discussions dealing with the disturbance in general or in incompletely specific terms, some degree of defensive distance may be maintained. In these early days, neurotic disturbances were thought to be due largely to actual experiences producing disturbing traumatic effects. In this setting, then, *working through* seemed to have two functions: first, it was a progressive and repetitive overcoming of resistances, which uncovered the repressed instinctual demands and showed their power to the patient; and second, it was a *working to* the supposed traumatic memories which were considered the nuclei of the neurosis. In his paper on technique (1914a), Freud warned of its necessity and its arduousness.

With the realization that many of the events described by the early patients were not actual happenings at all, but consisted rather of strong and insistent fantasies, growing out of developmental conflicts, more intense but otherwise not generally different from the ubiquitous neurotic pressures of early childhood, the emphasis on actual events was eliminated and the theory of traumatic etiology was discarded. There then grew up a greater emphasis on the nature of the fantasies associated with the different stages of infantile development, with a consideration of conditions which influenced the special forms and intensities of such fantasies, and on investigations of their sequelae. In this setting, then, the deduction was drawn that it was not the event but the fantasy that was of primary importance. Stated with a little different emphasis, this was put in the practical form: that it makes little or no difference whether an event has actually happened or has been fantasied and believed by the patient to have happened: it is the subjective experience that is of etiological significance. This belief is still held by many therapists, who make little distinction between the fantasied event and that actually experienced. This problem will be discussed below.

At present, however, it is desirable to point out different combinations of subjective and objective experience which may occur. The typical fantasies of the infantile years, arising from the genetic stages of development, do not appear in the genetic form alone. Certainly this is usually recognizable, but it is subject to infinite unique variations producing combinations of the products of the basic genetic drives with special individual conditions in reality which mold or transform the fantasies even at their source. Such reality conditions modifying the form of generic fantasies are seen, for example, in the effect of the loss of one or other parent in infancy, and especially the time and situation in which such a traumátic happening occurs; the timing of the birth of siblings; the sex of siblings, etc. We take such events for granted in their reality, and see their effect on the evolution of the infantile theories and wishes. Further, we know, but often forget, that specific "fantasies" which persist until adult life are rarely *only* "typical" fantasies, common to all infantile development, but rather those typical ones which have been given a special strength, form, and pressure for repetition through having been confirmed by external events. These reality confirmations may have been incipiently instigated by the child or more rarely have been almost purely coincidental—in that sense, accidents which affected the child little or much according to how well they fitted in with, substantiated, or elaborated and extended the fantasies which were emerging in any case. It should be realized that the unique *specific* (in contrast to the generic) elaborations of infantile memories are for the most part assembled from realities—either in small pieces, taken magpielike from a number of different impinging related actual experiences and woven into the fantasy; or determined largely from a single (or very few) actual events of life. They represent in either case some combination of the infantile wishes with the reactions of other people in the outer world. If the reinforcement has been much influenced by a single disturbing experience, verifying the infantile fantasy and making it powerfully real, the organizing effect of such an event is very great and the fantasy behind it gains much force. This predisposes to later repetition in acting out.

It was early recognized that if the infantile memories were recovered too quickly, or were *acted out* in the transference and not adequately interpreted, the abreaction at the time might be appreciable, but had no lasting effect. In such instances, the working through had not seemed necessary for the recovery of the memory, but now became essential to sustain any therapeutic effect—not to diminish the resistance and *reach* the memory (Fenichel, 1934), but to demonstrate again and again to the patient the working of instinctual trends in various situations in life (Fenichel, 1935). In other words, the defensive conflict remained somewhat structured unless worked with repetitively and in connection with its effect in various situations, and was not relieved by the momentary abreaction of the central situation (Fenichel, 1945a, 1945b).

This aspect of *working through* was stressed as essentially of an educative value and was likened to the work of mourning in the gradual and progressive detachment of the individual libido from the organized tensions and aims which permeated the later life (Alexander, 1925; Lewin, 1950).[1] Fundamental and valuable as this conception was, it possibly became one nucleus in the tendency away from recognizing the importance of the infantile years —and furnished an ingredient for what was to appear more as a *working out,* with repetitive scrutiny of multiple current situations and reactions. Finally it led over to the emergence of the conception (in certain diluted or revised forms of psychoanalysis) of the *corrective experience.* This might occur in the transference and be considered to require there the active participation of analyst and analysand; or, propelled by the encouragement of the basic transference relationship, the patient might be encouraged specifically to undertake new, different, and presumably more favorable experiences in actual life. It is not my purpose here to enter directly into the question of the therapeutic effectiveness of such procedures, but rather to emphasize their tendency to draw therapy more and more into a manipulative and role-playing participation of the analyst and gradually to divorce it from the consideration of the genetic basis of neuroses and character disturbances with which psychoanalysis has traditionally worked.

The rise of ego psychology has meant the recognition of the need for consistent work with the patterns of defense, as they appear both in the current situations of the patient and are recognized in his memories of the past. This has taken over much of what would previously have been referred to as *working through.* But it has tended to be exploited by some groups of psychoanalysts who do not go much beyond or below the descriptive analysis of current defenses and depend largely on repetition of interpretations of this kind and the manipulative methods as already indicated. In their most degraded form these repeated interpretations appear much like the slogans of an individual propagandist. From my experience in reanalyzing patients who have been treated in this

[1] Fenichel attributes this statement to Rado, but it is not contained in the article he refers to (1925). It was, however, stated by Alexander in that same year.

way, I would conclude that the immediate symptomatic effectiveness may depend very much on a transference bondage to the analyst rather than on real understanding.

The emphasis on analyzing current defensive patterns has in some instances been further diverted and used in the service of the culturists who would tend to ignore the biological structure of psychic development and see it largely in terms of social reactions. Against this background, then, I would discuss briefly special situations in which the importance of *working through* is preeminent.

There are patients, however, who during repeated analyses by competent therapists seem to work well on their therapeutic tasks and to have made consistent improvements thereby, only to be drawn back subsequently into the former neurotic tensions, pressures, and symptoms. This sometimes occurs even without there being any very marked external events to precipitate the relapse, which more frequently occurs rather insidiously. The effect is as though the neurosis acted like a quicksand which treacherously re-engulfed the individual who had not quite sufficiently freed himself. Further analysis revealed in a few of these cases at least that the adhesiveness of the neurosis seemed to be due to the persistent effect of severe organizing experiences of childhood, such as have already been referred to. These occurred in patients with markedly disturbed and grossly unresolved oedipal relationships, whether due to preoedipal deforming pressures or to essential interferences in the oedipal period itself. What impressed me especially, however, was that such reality experiences occurred most often in the latency period; and that in spite of the relative lateness of these events, they had been almost completely repressed from memory and their contents projected backward onto the infantile years, where they enhanced the brightness of and added elaborations to the early screen memories.

In some cases, at the very beginning of the analysis, the patient had had little memory of any of his childhood until puberty or prepuberty. But when the amnesic gaps began to be filled in, the memories of the infantile years could be more readily reconstructed than those of some silent period of latency. I gradually came to understand that what had happened had been that, still under unduly strong infantile pressures, the child had entered latency with a special cargo for the intense outward exploratory drives of these years. Under these conditions, he had succeeded, during the acting out of his fantasies, in precipitating experiences in reality which sometimes were almost exact reproductions of his earlier fantasies. These were thus corroborated for him, but might involve even more extensive, bizarre, and painful ingredients than those of his infantile fantasy or experience.

Indeed, the severity of the effect might be due to the fantasy seemingly having got out of control, by the additions to it through the participation of others, frequently adults. In some instances, the experiences may seem to validate magic thinking and feelings of omnipotence, which have been incompletely renounced, and its memory has been warded off out of fear, or has bent itself to attempts to deny differences between reality and fantasy. It is striking, however, that under most circumstances, recall of such experiences is repressed with an immediacy and a force which approximates a denial. I have had a few chances to observe this probably as it occurred, when consulted by pediatricians about young patients who had experienced seduction or rape or been present in peculiarly violent scenes of suicide. They seemed sometimes almost immediately to ignore and then to forget the event.[2]

Yet the fact that the event had been experienced in reality seems to add to the strength of its later impression and to the tendency for it to be unconsciously acted out in part or *in toto* subsequently; thereby furnishing a wellspring for neurotic revivals. It appears that the force of the repression may be due to the fact that the experience has occurred during a time when the superego is well developed and some degree of shame or humiliation is frequently involved. There is probably more guilt involved anyway in acts in reality than in those done in fantasy.

This was particularly evident, in its reverse form, in a small group of cases which I studied some years ago and described in a paper on "The Prepuberty Trauma in Girls" (1950a).[3] Among the patients there described, traumatic experience in prepuberty

---

[2] This is illustrated in fictional form in the story *The Innocent Voyage*, by Richard Hughes (London & New York: Harper, 1929).

[3] The title of this paper is somewhat misleading. The situation probably occurs about equally in boys and girls. At the time of my writing the article, I had encountered it mostly in girls, and thought that it might be more frequent in them than in boys.

was especially remembered and announced at the very beginning of the analysis. It was offered as an unfortunate event which had befallen the young girl, and subsequent disturbances were attributed to it. Memories of earlier events were blanched or lacking. It proved a very effective barrier at the outset of analytic work, because it readily permitted the dodging of feelings of responsibility and diminished the sense of autonomy of the patient, who considered herself victimized. It was of particular interest, however, that this prepuberty trauma could be retained and cherished in consciousness, because it repeated similar experiences of the early oedipal period which had been more severe and more clearly accomplished on the child's own initiative. Consequently in these cases the *later* memory was the retained one, with a brilliant screening and stubbornly defensive function.

There is another group of cases in which the organizing event is of equal importance—viz., those severe neurotic disturbances usually with definite affective coloring which tend to appear in recurrent attacks. I refer especially to neurotic depressions, some phobic and obsessional states, usually with depressive admixtures, and some recurrent states of overactivity, probably essentially neurotic hypomanic states. These "attack" disturbances, particularly after the first attack, may come on rather abruptly, and seemingly with even less than ordinary provocation in the current situation. They may repeat themselves with an almost photographic fidelity in their course and constellation of symptoms. It is my experience that in some of these cases the hidden organizing and sensitizing experience is exceedingly important as furnishing a trigger area, which after the initial breakthrough needs barely to be touched to set off the series of symptomatic events which follow. Sometimes these can be understood as expanded and disguised repetitions of the childhood experience, which have been endowed with special force because of the preoedipal components which are also invested in them. I doubt whether the susceptibility to recurrence of these states is effectively diminished by reconstruction of the earliest infantile problems and fantasies (even though attacks may be less severe), unless there is also a thorough *working through* of any traumatic events which have organized the earlier preoedipal disturbances—whether this has occurred in early childhood or in the latency period. The outline of such experiences may sometimes be retrospectively deciphered in the nature of the events which have precipitated the breakthrough of the initial attack. Unless thorough treatment occurs in this setting, subsequent attacks may occur with less provocation, the disturbance being set off by anniversaries or even assuming the appearance of seasonal variations in susceptibility.

This may be a particularly difficult group of patients, since in the severity of their disturbances they may readily seduce the analyst into too active participation in the therapy, and to manipulative or supportive measures, or to interferences which then vitiate the cleanness of the transference relationship necessary for the *working through* process. It may happen further that such experiences, having been touched on or partly worked with but not thoroughly understood by the analyst and patient, have thereby been more activated by the analysis and appear even in circumscribed symptomatic behavior after the analysis is over and the basic transference relationship has become attenuated.

It appears then that the process of *working through* is of particular importance in cases in which infantile neurotic drives have been carried over into actual experience in reality, in whatever way or at whatever time this has occurred. The detection of evidence of such experience is, however, not easy, especially if there has been an almost complete amnesia for the experience itself. But there is always some bland representation of it or some vacuole of memory which is a warning, and which may be brought up incongruously again and again when certain fantasies or experiences of the infantile years are being considered. In addition, the repetitive appearance in dreams or free associations of some specific age or place seemingly inappropriately but insistently associated with events belonging to another period; the special repetition and content of the dream within a dream; the frequent appearance of dreams which exactly reproduce reality events, but seem at first barren of other associations; the occurrence of isolated and peculiar delusions or hallucinations in the setting of a generally sound sense of reality; the repetition through a series of dreams (or similarly through a series of symptomatic acts) of some apparently unimportant but realistically embellishing detail; all these are indications of the reality of some experience which is being worked with in the unconscious.

Illustration of some of these clues may help. First regarding the vacuole in memory:

A patient came for his second analysis, a period of a few years having elapsed since his first analysis, which had been helpful to him and had brought many changes into his life. His main symptoms, modified but not fundamentally changed, had gradually reasserted themselves, and he felt miserable and discouraged. I noticed during the first months of our work that there was one member of his family, a brother, whom he did not mention except for infrequent, casual, laughing, and slightly derogatory references. This was the more striking since in the initial consultation he had made it clear that this brother suffered from a disturbance in many ways similar to his own. When after some time I mentioned to him the peculiarity of his apparent blandness to the brother, he laughed off the discrepancy with easy but stubborn rationalizations, and then would revert always to very early primal scene experiences as though offering these instead. Only the most persistent efforts brought the material of the latency period, in which this brother was primarily involved, into focus so that it could be worked through.

Further, in regard to the incongruous repetitive appearances of certain age periods:

A patient, in his consultation interview with me, reported that he had been much disturbed by having been aware of an abortion which his mother had had when he was eight, and during which she had thought she was dying. I was somewhat surprised, as he had already made clear that his father and mother had been separated and his father had lived in another country from the time the patient was three until he was ten. Later on, when the subject of the abortion came up in the analysis, he always referred to it as having occurred when he was eleven, after his father's return. I noticed, however, that frequently, when this subject came up, the number eight would appear somewhere in the associations. In the end, it developed that the mother had had a lover at this time, and had also an intimate woman friend who had an abortion. But what was most important was that connected with the stimulation of these events the patient had made sexual approaches to his sister with extremely guilty fears of having impregnated and injured her. Thus there was a deflection of the oedipal problem onto these events and a complete amnesia for them.

The dream within a dream (or its equivalent—the play, or the memory, or the joke within a dream) appears especially significant when it is repetitive in content as well as in its appearance. I have illustrated this in a study of the works of Lewis Carroll (see ch. 23). Finally, in regard to the insistent and peculiar delusions or hallucinatory experience, two clinical examples may illustrate:

1. A patient whose obstinately firm sense of reality somewhat stunted his imaginative ability had nonetheless a recurrent hallucination of a hair in the mouth. This generally appeared during the analytic hour, and was very vivid and uncomfortable. Only after a very long analysis was an especially disturbing fellatio experience of the latency period uncovered. This man had always been ready to bring up his attachment to his mother and his interest in the breast (which was undoubtedly part of the basis of this later experience), but the hallucination of the hair was the telltale symptom which could not be so disposed of. Fundamental relief did not come until the working through of this later experience.

2. A woman patient had a screen memory that as a child she had been punished by being aroused from sleep at night, brought downstairs, forced to kneel before a punishment chair, and to eat asparagus from a platter placed on the seat of the chair. What was striking was not only the bizarreness of this improbable memory, but the patient's complete conviction that it had occurred exactly as she related it. This screen memory was a remarkable piece of condensation, involving several experiences in reality, and was based on the patient's observations of sexual activities between her mother and her psychotic father; and her own re-enactment of these with cousins. Her insistence on the reality of the memory not only bore testimony to the reality of the experiences, but may have been the greater because of her guilty terror of having behaved in a crazy fashion like her father.

These instances are probably sufficient to give some picture of the way in which such *working through* problems may emerge.

It is through alertness to clues such as these that the work of reconstruction and the concomitant process of *working through* is accomplished in patients of these special groups.[4]

---

[4] Additional aspects of working through are discussed in chs. 33 and 36.

CHAPTER THIRTY-THREE

Certain Technical Problems in the Transference Relationship (1959)

In the conduct of an analysis, once treatment is established, the relationship of the analysand to the analyst is traditionally thought of as consisting of two main areas. The first is that of the verbal and other communication of the patient to the analyst, gradually revealing neurotic attitudes and behavior not only as these appear in current and past activity, but as they are reproduced, sometimes with additions, in the special attitudes and behavior toward the analyst himself. This is traditionally spoken of as the area of the transference neurosis. The other is the area of margin, frequently peripheral to this central area of communication; it consists of the relatively intact part of the ego which is depended upon to cooperate with the analyst in scrutinizing, understanding, and working over and through the communications of the first area. This has been spoken of as the area of the therapeutic alliance, and was clearly described by Richard Sterba in 1929. It is through the work in the therapeutic alliance that interpretation assumes dynamic therapeutic force. This paper will emphasize especially the changing relationships within and between these two areas of contact between patient and analyst. Some questions may be raised; and it is probable that not many will be answered.

The so-called transference neurosis varies markedly in texture— the neurotic representations in the transference appearing (1) in direct behavior and attitudes, experienced toward the analyst as though they were objectively determined; (2) in less massively projected and recognizable forms in the dreams and dream associations of the patient; and (3) in the frequent associative references connecting the analyst with events and people of the past and present. While the experienced analyst can usually detect according to what transference role or composite of roles the patient's relationship to him is being cast at any given time, the intensity, clarity, and availability of this for use with the patient is not as easily defined.

Fenichel (1941) described the handling of the interpretation of the transference as presenting "no special problem; everything that has been said of interpretation in general, holds true for analysis of the transference: the surface first of all, the defense before the instinct—the interpretation must be timely, not too deep and not too superficial; particularly necessary, preceding the interpretation, is 'isolation' from the critical ego" (p. 73). This is certainly a fundamental basis for work, but sounds beguilingly uncomplicated and does not deal with the manifold accessory problems. It is clear enough that incompletely analyzed transference attitudes are expressed subsequently in continued direct or reversed form toward the analyst, or produce excessive pressures in other life relationships onto which they may be displaced postanalytically. Sometimes indeed the unanalyzed transference residuals seem to have amalgamated rather than dispersed neurotic attitudes.

Usually, except in certain cases of severe disturbances, the transference neurotic manifestations do not form a fabric of consistent pattern and thickness. Since they are in part historically and genetically determined, there is a constant panoramic procession of transference pictures merging into each other or momentarily separating out with special clarity, in a way which is frequently less constant than the symptoms and other manifestations of the neurosis itself.[1] The degree to which the transference attitudes are played out in current relationships (other than the analytic relationship) also varies considerably. For this reason, I have myself been a little questioning of the blanket term "trans-

---

[1] There is also a considerable variability of the margin of the ego's therapeutic alliance, not only from case to case or in different forms of neurotic disturbances, but in the same patient at different times.

ference neurosis," which may be misleading. I would prefer to speak of *active transference neurotic manifestations.* The need for a distance or isolation of the neurotic transference manifestations from the critical ego (site of the therapeutic alliance) has already been noted. But it is also true that one of the conditions facilitating analytic work is the flexibility within the psychic structure permitting regression during the analytic hour and free movement back and forth between the various regressively oriented experiences on the couch and a return to the seeing eye of the critical ego. Where this is possible without producing a sense of inner violence to the ego organization, i.e., where the ego organization is fairly firm but has a quality of inner plasticity, the analytic work is much facilitated.[2] Where the critical ego is overburdened with especially strong superego attitudes, however, the isolation may be only apparent and the superego form too ironclad a bridge to the central neurosis, vitiating or immobilizing the work of the therapeutic alliance. On the other hand, there are many instances in which, in spite of a fairly good working ego outside of the analysis, there is an overfluidity in the transference; and especially at certain critical times, the therapeutic alliance is lost sight of or can be maintained only with the greatest difficulty at exactly those times when it is most needed.

I am purposely avoiding categorizing situations according to diagnosis at this time. Further, the effort of this presentation is to focus on the interplay between these two parts of the transference relationship and to suggest, at least to myself, additional avenues of investigation, rather than to make any suggestions regarding standard technical procedures or desirable variations from them. Within this general frame of reference, then, I shall attempt to examine certain problems under two general headings: (1) the transference complications in handling questions of reality with the patient—not only in those cases in which there is some special difficulty of reality testing or of perception, but in other cases as well, where there are potential complications in the inevitable contact outside the analytic relationship between analyst and analysand; (2) certain conditions, already referred to, of too great fluidity between regressive neurotic manifestations and the criti-

---

[2] I would especially refer here to Glover's (1955) description of the manifestations of different aspects of the transference in different types of neurosis.

cal ego, with a resultant tendency to temporary swamping or crowding out of the latter. I shall try to describe these situations and raise questions, answering them only incompletely if at all.

It would probably be generally agreed that in any psychoanalytic treatment, based as it is on the goal of producing change in the analysand through the agency of interpretation and the production of increasing insight, there must be a careful guarding of the autonomous attitude of the patient. Naturally, this also implies a prerequisite of at least such a degree of adequate functioning of the ego, even during the illness, that autonomy has not already been grossly sacrificed. For the furtherance of the preservation of autonomy, supportive measures, persuasion, direct encouragement, advice, and manipulation of the environment (such as interpretation and advice to the relatives) are consequently contraindicated. They are sometimes used as expedients under such exceptionally critical conditions as would be considered to endanger the life of the patient or the future of the analysis. Even in such situations there may be some risks of unsatisfactory sequelae, some of which may become immediately apparent and others remain hidden yet active for a considerable length of time or even impair the analytic result, and so approximate the very condition for which they have been invoked. The immediate result of such active support or intervention is to weaken the critical functioning of the patient's own ego. The practical impairment unfortunately sometimes spreads by rapid displacements to involve an increasing area, and undermines the therapeutic alliance rather than strengthening it—which is usually the result hoped for. The therapeutic alliance is thus insidiously diluted with ingredients of a narcissistic alliance. If the various elements of the recent crisis appear in the analysis quickly enough to be worked with fairly promptly, a favorable result may nonetheless ensue. But this does not always occur spontaneously and pressures from the analyst to bring them to the surface are not always satisfactory or productive. In most instances, it will be some time before they are brought out again, and the risk of the situation having a distorting effect on the analysis in the meantime has occurred.

Some of the sequelae which may be recognized are: the production of an attitude of special gratitude (or its opposite), which interferes with the freedom of subsequent transference expressions; an increase in the appetite of the patient for such interventions, with an accompanying increase in the provocations to the analyst.

One instance of this is the granting to the patient of the right to telephone at any time that he is panicky. Under such circumstances there may grow up a kind of indulgence in subacute panic, with the sweetness of continued placation which then interferes with its analysis. A similar and sometimes more difficult situation may occur with the patient who achieves an even greater sense of contact on demand by writing full and frequent letters by which he further avoids full verbalization and also deposits material which belongs in the analysis—in his stuffed letters which serve as unreachable pockets. It may be a condensed form of acting out which cannot be quickly analyzed and makes serious inroads on the progress of the immediate analytic work. While it cannot always be analyzed quickly and sometimes must be tolerated until it can be understood, it should at least not be positively encouraged.

Finally, it is worth mentioning that interventions or the use of active accessory therapeutic measures outside of the restrictions of the usual analytic relationship may constitute an inadvertent and unrecognized playing into the transference and risk a rearousal of some old unrevealed traumatic experience, originating in fantasy or in the actual life of the patient's childhood, toward which he draws the analyst with subtle unconscious provocation and seductiveness, even in the production of his crisis. One thinks here of Fenichel's warning (1941) that not joining in the game is the principal task of handling the transference. Yet it is infinitely easy to be drawn into the game in seemingly neutral measures during near crises or pseudocrises, and the worst of it is that one may not discover until much later, and sometimes not at all, the full meaning of what has been thought of as neutral intervention. Many times what appear to an unwary person as critical situations in the patient's external life are at least partly due to un-understood transference demands, which may be increased in repeated or converted forms if met with active assuagement devoid of understanding. In this connection it can be emphasized that transference acting out, whether in a massive, clearly patterned form or in less clearly distinguishable outlines extending into the behavior in external life—that such transference acting out is given a special force and tends to become more fixed in spite of the specious appearance of relief through the discharge. The fixation is the greater, the more the acting out is discharged clearly in the transference, unless it is not only defined but is traced back to its nuclear source and seen in its various current manifestations. This increase in fixation is inevitable since the person of the analyst may assume even greater significance than that of reality relationships of past or present, and the experience in the transference, if uninterpreted, has then an extraordinary confirmatory effect on the neurosis itself.

Other special problems having to do with the attitude of the analyst toward the external reality of the patient may be considered under two headings: those derived from the analyst's need to help the patient to see and to define the outlines of the actual external reality elements in certain life situations which the patient's neurosis tends to present in a distorted form; and especially those arising from complicated situations where the analyst and analysand share certain external reality experiences, e.g., where they know some people in common and have occasional unplanned contacts outside of the analytic office. Obviously, the conditions of this latter group are obligatory in the analysis of analytic students.

It is an analytic platitude to observe that the patient may hold to his neurotic distortions with great conviction and that this can be changed only by analysis which lessens the inner contributing pressures. Such distortions may appear in severely disturbed patients as transitory or quasi-permanent false perceptions (illusions or hallucinations). Again it is clear that correction by persuasion is either futile or is accomplished by the overwhelming of the neurotic pressures by the intensity of the patient's wish for approval or protection by the analyst, and again risks a narcissistic rather than a therapeutic alliance with a transference alleviation rather than an analytic one. Illusions of considerable tenacity may occur during the analysis of not even very grossly disturbed neurotic patients and are probably basically due to individual variations between the intensity of the different sensory responses and the degree to which these could be communicated by speech in the patient's early childhood. What is true about the susceptibility to form visual misperceptions of objects or mishearing of spoken words is naturally even more true of the susceptibility to neurotic distortions of interpretations of other people's attitudes. Here I think we have quite definite technical dilemmas. On the one hand, it may be possible, and conceivably advisable, to confront a patient with a misperceived object and show him in a neutral way that he has misperceived. This may be necessary where the patient has clung to his distorted impression with such tenacity that it has seemed to preclude dealing further with the nature or reason for his distortion.

I recall once actually getting a hat to demonstrate to a patient who insisted erroneously that that particular hat was of a certain shape and color, and she had happened to see me wear it just a day or two earlier. In this instance the confrontation did shake her conviction of the rightness of her perceptions, in a way beneficial in itself, and also sufficiently to permit her to examine the significance of her determined mistake. Parenthetically, the intensity of such an isolated illusion indicates that the distortion is referring in some way to an actual and important experience of the patient's childhood.

On the other hand, trying to help the patient to define reality as a frame of reference for examining exaggerations, false emphases, or additions of extraneous elements in situations involving interpretations of other peoples' attitudes presents many pitfalls. Freud (1912) emphasized that in questions involving a discrepancy between the patient's observation or memory and that of the analyst, the analyst's observation must be depended upon, since he is less likely to be emotionally involved than the patient. This seems as fundamentally sound a principle now as it was then, though it can never be regarded as *invariably* true, without implying an authoritative attitude in the analyst.

In situations outside the direct relationship between the analyst and analysand, the field becomes murkier and more difficult. While it is undoubtedly necessary under exceptional conditions to "nail down" the objective reality elements of a given specific situation of the patient's or to suggest certain probabilities for the patient's consideration, the analyst may have to resist a temptation to slip into a tendency to define external reality more and more, lest after a time he may find himself analyzing the patient's whole situation and the various people in it rather than focusing on the analysis of the patient and his attitudes toward various aspects of his situation. If the analyst continues to "define reality" to his patient, he gradually assumes a parental role in the transference reality rather than only in the patient's transference neurotic manifestation. Again this insidiously jeopardizes the patient's autonomy, compromises rather than develops the strengthening of the ego, and develops a reality situation in the transference more powerful than the original one. The patient will take up this game and, instead of focusing on himself and questioning his own attitudes, begin to deflect his concern and interpret the unconscious motivations of those around him. This is one of the easiest and most destructive bypaths away from a thorough analysis. Unless it is recognized by the analyst in time, it furnishes the patient with a set of tools, intended for his understanding of himself but misappropriated and used for resistance against such understanding. In any case, the analyst should know very clearly what he is about in any defining of reality with the patient; his assertion of the actual facts in a given situation should be securely founded and not represent simply a counteropinion or another person's interpretation. The analyst is obligated to be careful in any assertion of this kind, not only on the grounds of accuracy and aptness, but because the weight of his opinion in an active transference setting is such as to exaggerate the effect of these malapropos qualities of his statements.

Where analyst and analysand have mutual friends or acquaintances and certain experiences overlap outside the analytic relationship, there is especially likely to be a further complication in the transference relationship in deflections of certain attitudes from the analyst to others associated directly with him, and a concealed and rationalized acting out of them there. It may be that we pay too little attention to this phenomenon of the splitting of the transference relationship, even though it always occurs at some time in the course of the analysis, and may be one of the major defensive maneuverings in the analysis of analytic students.

I will attempt to bring out a further example of the possible implications of the reality contact between analyst and analysand, and question the significance of its handling. This is somewhat different from the other examples, since it is one of the conditions which is obligatorily present in every analysis, viz., the implications of the influence of the sex of the analyst in relation to the sex of the analysand. At present this subject is one of the most frequently spoken of topics in connection with finding an analyst or particularly a second analyst for a patient. It is my fortune to see a number of prospective analytic patients in initial consultative interviews. In quite a large number of instances these preanalytic patients ask, at the end of the interview if not during it, "Should I have a man or a woman analyst?" (There has been a distinct change in the increasing frequency of this query in the last decade.) Specific advice on the subject may have been offered by the first analyst, or by some analyst friend or sometimes by some recently analyzed friend; or an analytically interested social worker may have cautioned that this is an important question which should be settled by the interview; or the patient may himself have gotten it out of the air, as it were. When the inquiry is put to me I always pay attention to it with as much consideration as such a preliminary interview affords, to determine on what this anxious inquiry is based. In many instances the anxiety does not really seem to belong to this question itself but seems more to be part of the anxiety about beginning the analysis at all.

In 1936 Grete Bibring published a paper in which the significance of the sex of the analyst was dealt with in connection with certain aspects of what was then spoken of as transference resistance. The points which she made still seem valid, important, and worth reconsideration and restatement. She described the fact that sometimes when an analysis had become partly or almost completely stalemated and was interrupted because of this or for external reasons, it not infrequently went along better after its resumption with the original analyst or with a different analyst. This was to be attributed to the fact that the interruption served as a warning to the patient, convincing him of his need, which then increased his energetic cooperation. She emphasized very clearly that beyond this situation, there might exceptionally be certain others. She asserted that although the transference relationship is ordinarily not a reactive manifestation regulated by external reality, but is an active manifestation coming from the spontaneous neurotic instinctual (and I would now add defensive) pressures from within the patient, there are certain instances in which the analyst may (through the possession of certain marked idiosyncratic traits of appearance or character) represent some important, even crucial part of the patient's past reality to a degree which may block the patient, since it is a continual reminder of that which was impossibly difficult for him in the past. Under these circumstances, the analysand may either withdraw into himself or act out so violently in the transference as to impede progress drastically, unconsciously trying to provoke the analyst to do exactly that which he has most suffered from in his childhood. It was further apparent that the stimulus of this partial revival of reality through its actual repetition in current reality focused in the transference relationship itself might be enhanced if the sex of the analyst coincided with the sex of the crucial person—usually a parent—of the past. Under these circumstances, then, it is clear that transfer to another analyst may undo the blocking and that a change in the sex of the analyst may simply be a background part of this. This is most likely to happen at the first stages of the analysis or at some crucial point involving a situation for which the analyst has a blind spot in regard to himself. Otherwise the chances are he will have detected the difficulty even before the patient reacts so forcibly and this "similarity" will be exploited for the benefit of the work. Bibring further warns, however—and this seems to me of the utmost importance —that the analysand may then attempt to keep the negative transference allocated to the first analyst and enjoy only the positive with the second.

This whole discussion of the reality effect of the sex of the analyst on the patient is a very useful one, since we have often tended to overlook the fact that the important factor is not the reality of the sex per se but rather that it is the conveyer of the other less apparent partial reality. Unless these elements are disentangled in the handling of the transference of the subsequent analysis, the patient will continue to suffer the effects, one way or another, of the initial displacement. There is obviously another situation in which the reality sex of the analyst may exert a strong and sometimes a drastic effect on the patient, viz., the situation of strong unrecognized homosexual tendencies with latent possibilities of panic. This is usually announced by the patient in some emphatic statement—often with a deceptively assured surface—

that he or she "simply would not care to," or "could not possibly consider," or "has no confidence in" going to a man or to a woman, as the case may be. In such consultations, if a little discussion indicates that this is a definitely established attitude of the patient's, I myself always treat it with the utmost respect and compliance, since I recognize that such a patient really *would* find it difficult, if not impossible, to work with an analyst of the undesired sex. But I also know that in a number of these cases, a change in the analyst to one of the opposite sex may be desirable later.

It has seemed, however, that this question of the significance of the sex of the analyst has been clouded by the overly ready advice to a patient in a dragging or stalemated analysis that changing the sex of the analyst will have a beneficial effect on the analysis. Certainly, it may make the beginning of the next analysis easier. It has seemed, however, too often to be a terminal rationalization when the analysis has not gone well, and not sufficiently based on careful thought of where and how the stalemate has occurred. It is a recommendation which has sometimes delayed, I believe unnecessarily, the finding of a new analyst and has sometimes been ultimately disregarded, due to the pressure of an inadequate market supply of analysts of the desired sex. I must add that I have seen few catastrophes from this disregard if the replacement was with a thorough and careful therapist who handled the transference with discrimination and thoughtfulness. A timely consultation may help matters.

In recent years I have had the chance to know of a case in which an analysis never got off the ground, as it were, and dragged along for two years with some basic early work seemingly accomplished, and yet it could not really progress. It was discontinued then because the analyst, who was a very skillful and careful man, believed that the patient could not be analyzed. No recommendation was made by him to the patient to seek any further treatment. The patient did seek a consultation on his own initiative. During this it was revealed that not only did the analyst reproduce with striking fidelity certain of the qualities of the patient's older brother in an ever-stimulating way, much as in the case of Grete Bibring's patient, but furthermore, certain events had occurred in connection with the patient's first visits to the analyst's office, events about which the analyst did not and could not know, and which the patient in turn could not relate to the analyst, first, because their significance was such as to have a paralyzing effect on him, and second, because he was totally unaware of their significance. It happened to be a strange concatenation of several apparently incidental circumstances surrounding the first visits which thus stymied the analysis. The consultant sensed that these might be the source of the block and recommended a second analysis, which subsequently progressed satisfactorily.

Still another matter of concern about actual external reality components in the relationship between the analyst and the analysand consists in the everyday business of their relative postural positions. There is the assumption among many analysts that a neurotic patient must be analyzed prostrate and that a psychotic one must be treated sitting up. The firmness of this "rule" seems to me even greater among the younger than among the older analysts. It seems sometimes to be applied with a clichélike unquestioning attitude I have heard more than one analyst say quite confidently something like the following: "Well, when he [the patient] began to talk that way, I just sat him up and I've kept him that way since!" Usually this has occurred when the patient showed paranoid or other passive aggressive dissociative attitudes. Sometimes the analyst has felt that having the patient sitting up was the index of transforming the procedure from a psychoanalytic one to a psychotherapeutic one; and that once the patient sat up, he might figuratively never lie down again. Psychoanalytic restriction was then dissipated and the program was changed to an emphasis on day-by-day reality occurrences and relationships, supplemented by advice and generously supportive encouragement. Certainly, after a time then it becomes impossible to retrace the road back to an analytic relationship unless there is a change of therapists. It has seemed to me that the analyst who accepted this "rule" so uncritically was not generally much at home with psychotic patients and had a good deal of fear of them. He might prefer to keep his eyes directly on the patient and, although such a belief is not factually supportable, he believed himself safer with the patient sitting up.

The origin of the use of the couch is familiar to all psychoanalytic students. The usefulness of the procedure has been justified through the decades, even though it has been much criticized.

Certainly, the position of relaxation on the couch limits distraction, suggests sleep, and promotes thinking by free association. It has been asserted (Macalpine, 1950) that the recumbent position may create a feeling of dependence and helplessness in the patient. This must sometimes be true, though it is most likely to be so in some specially susceptible patients. In others it places the patient more definitely in the world of his own private life and fantasies and diminishes the social obligation for conversation. The analyst, being out of sight, can then more readily and naturally become the conveyor of an accessory function to the patient than if he loomed up straight in the line of the patient's vision, with his unique appearance and bearing obligatorily and continuously brought to the patient's notice. The analyst's position behind the patient favors the therapeutic alliance as well as the development of the transference neurotic manifestations.

Some analysts have the patient sit up when they wish to talk to him "outside of the analysis"—to settle some factual matter. It would then seem that sitting up means to the patient, "You are fully conscious. You should speak in a factual rational way. Do not confuse us with your fantasies now." While this change of position quite often does mark such a separation from the varyingly regressive movement of the usual analytic production, it by no means does so automatically or in a very consistent way. Everything that happens or is spoken between analyst and analysand is really a part of the analysis and may ultimately assert itself as such.

In my own experience with patients, the change from recumbent to sitting posture has seemed to have many different meanings, first of all dependent in some measure on whether the change is initiated by the analyst or by the analysand. If I think a patient is saying in one way or another that he would like to sit up, I may simply ask him if he would prefer to sit up, but I leave the decision up to him. I do note, however, the point at which he feels this need and what the significance of it seems to be. The sitting up, in this particular setting, is a limited acting out in the transference and a part of the analysis rather than an escape from it. I have found patients who wanted to sit up in order to watch me and check their fantasies about me; others who wanted to sit up because they felt a desire to fight, and also had a fear of a retaliative attack from me; still others where the sitting up was a wish to assure themselves that they were alive; and again others where the rise to a sitting position was part of a body-phallus expression of an erection. There were some—quite a few—who had some temporary problem of identity and wished to sit up in order to orient themselves better in their surroundings and in space. I do not often work with schizophrenic patients, but I have had a few ambulant schizophrenic patients who generally preferred the recumbent position but would sit up if they felt a danger of losing contact. This may, in any case, depend on how much the person relies on vision for contact.

Please do not think that my patients bob up and down continuously during treatment. I have never had one who did this capriciously. Only very rarely indeed have I suggested to a patient that he sit up. But I always accept the suggestion at least as a possibility if it comes from the patient in whatever way it is communicated. Actually, all in all, the question does not often arise. When it does, I treat it like any other symptomatic transference act.

In connection with this question of couch or chair, it should be noted that the superficial sophistication of the public concerning analysis now includes knowledge of the couch, which appears in magazines, cartoons, in movies, plays' and TV productions. To lie on the couch for analysis now is socially sanctioned and no longer considered queer, as it was twenty or thirty years ago. Rather if the analyst does not suggest the couch, the patient may readily become worried lest he is considered unanalyzable. This is a secondary development but nonetheless sometimes exerts a powerful influence on the patient if the analyst suggests sitting up.

To return to a discussion of the situation referred to earlier in this paper, in which there is too great a regressive fluidity during the hour so that the critical ego of the therapeutic alliance is crowded out—where the capacity to regress is not a sufficiently controlled one, to use Ernst Kris's term (1952), we know that if this is generally true throughout the analysis, little can be accomplished. It means that much will be brought to the analysis but in an acting-out way, with such pressures that they figuratively elbow the analysis out while the patient seemingly earnestly seeks it. The few patients whom I have had of this type are people whose whole lives seem to have been a series of repetitive living out of basic fantasies, so extensively as to engulf almost the total personality. If these patients can be analyzed at all, it is only after a long preliminary preparation and consistent patient work over a long period of time. I might say, however, that I have found that certain unusually creatively talented people, in whom any adequate use of their talents has been blocked, may also react in this way. Although some analysts would place members of this group in the categories of schizoid, latent schizophrenic, essentially psychotic, or borderline patients, it is not from the angle of diagnosis that I am at the present interested, but from the angle of the transference—the shifts in relationship between the different parts of the transference, the movement within it, etc. It also seems dangerous to base a diagnosis on the behavior in the transference.

I want, however, especially to present illustrations from two cases which are closely related to this group. These two patients are both women, whose lives have been dominated by the living out of massive neurotic patterns. It was not so much that they had obviously weak egos—both would have impressed people generally as being potentially very effective people, and it probably would have seemed puzzling why they had achieved little direction in their lives, although they were exceptionally bright and even talented. Both were crippled in their sexual interests, performance, and enjoyment. It was through a careful watching of the transference flux and movement within the different parts of the transference relationship that I came to understand certain important parts of the patients' development.

To speak more specifically of one of these patients: at certain times, often seemingly related to the menstrual period, she would behave in the most intensely provocative way toward me.[3] This consisted in a kind of frenzied demand for reassurance. Focusing on some relatively unimportant and sometimes patently absurd issue, she would return again and again to this with obsessionally hairsplitting ramifications of her central question. Sometimes it would be a question as to whether I thought she would ever be able to accomplish a certain thing—often trivial in itself—but somehow representing the question of whether or not she could ever get well. Sometimes the manifest pivot of her demands did

[3] For further details of this patient's developmental history, see ch. 10.

not even have this much clarity of significance. At other times she would focus on the question of whether, on the basis of some minutia of behavior, I thought the current man friend was really interested in her or looked down on her. I cannot now go into all of the variations of my mistakes in attempting to deal with these infantile and gluttonous tantrums. She was not one of those patients who, if she succeeded in provoking me to some counter-response, was immediately calm and triumphant, and sometimes her frenzy would continue for more than one hour. Usually in any hour after the onset of the tornado, she would return in a kind of sultry, quiet, brooding state, determined not to let herself go, but it would not be long before she would again be involved in her exceedingly intricate doubts and questions—the whole thing usually ending by attrition rather than by a final satisfying fulminating explosion. This was superficially at least in contrast to the other patient who behaved in a somewhat similar way, but with less hairsplitting, more triumph if she succeeded in provoking me and more fear that I would discontinue the analysis. In both instances, although there was a great deal of neurotic shame in regard to other parts of the analytic revelations, there was no manifest shame or embarrassment over these extraordinary upheavals, and for a long time no ability to discuss them afterward. It was as though, once they were over, she turned into a rather different person with no curiosity about and no contact with this storming child. It was obvious, too, that during the tantrum itself the critical ego was abolished.

It was true that in the first patient if the tantrum lasted more than an hour, sometimes at the beginning of the subsequent hour she would apparently be struggling to hold herself in check in a way that suggested that the self-critical faculty of the ego, probably largely invested in the superego, had been at work: but my presence was enough to restimulate the tantrum and any sense of a therapeutic alliance was completely lost from the picture. At other times her margin of therapeutic alliance varied but was sufficiently present to permit slow but consistent work. It had become apparent to me that while she had shown a marked sensitivity in regard to possible homosexual implications in her positive feelings toward other women and especially toward me—and I had thought for a time that this was the essential nuclear tension involved—I had gradually become convinced that in a direct form this was only a contributing factor and that the tantrums had much of an acting-out quality of directly repeating some infantile situation and relationship. While she showed slightly comparable episodes of aggrieved feelings toward other people, with tendencies to get into obsessional whirls involving pressure for some discharge, there was never the same insistent demand for reassurance which was so central a part of her transference upheavals. It was only through watching this for a considerable period of time and allowing myself to drift into almost reveries of her life as it had been revealed to me that I was able to see the nucleus of these fits of acting-out in the transference.

What had gradually emerged and could be reconstructed had to do with a period especially during her third and fourth years. She was a bright and apparently very beautiful little girl, the fourth child and very much her father's favorite. He was a compulsive man, a civic leader, always interested in the welfare of the community and especially of his own small domestic group. The family possessed considerable wealth, which permitted this father to retire early from the profession to which he had been trained, spending much time at home engaging in his own obsessional ruminations and ritualistic training of his young children. My patient entered into a disturbed state, with much masturbatory activity during the infancy of a younger sister, who was born toward the end of the patient's second year, and of whom she seems to have been intensely jealous, especially of the mother's nursing and care of the young baby. The masturbatory activity was so great that the troubled father determined to cure the little girl by staying with her when she was put to bed either to nap or at night. He talked to her, admonished her not to touch herself in order to please him, and constantly reassured her that everything would be all right so long as she would cease masturbating. There developed between the father and child an intense attachment, something akin to a focal symbiotic relationship based on their mutual need to suppress masturbation. The suppression had been successful, but had carried with it a loss of awareness of the clitoris; and it had been followed during latency by an aggressive acting out of combined oedipal and sibling jealousy with a brother six years older than herself, the oldest of the children.

This had been practically unchecked and had been accompanied by sleeping beauty fantasies of marrying a Prince or a Duke. It had finally terminated by the brother's desertion of her when she was still in early puberty and he was entering college. The overt obsessional and compulsive neurosis had broken through very soon with the definite onset of the menses.

What concerned me most here was the re-enactment of these focused symbiotically determined masturbatory tantrums in which there was an intense unconscious pressure to draw me into the game, during which it was demanded that I should become frenzied with her and promise her incessantly that everything would turn out all right. The successful understanding of these episodes helped very much not only in the understanding of this particular case, but in evaluating certain less acute transference states in other patients who had temporary abrogations of any capacity for critical self-scrutiny and were, one way or another, trying to re-establish states of anxious parental concern which had given considerable gratification. In the second patient who was mentioned along with this one, there was a somewhat comparable history in that it was the father rather than the mother who had been so intensely distressed by the little one's masturbatory activities, to an extent that he was unable to stand her presence at such times and would demand that she be taken to her room and out of his sight. In her provocative tantrums with me, there was then not the demand for reassurance, such as the first patient had, but a real need to gain the upper hand through her provocation, after which she could sometimes be calmer, even though she repeatedly feared that I would terminate the analysis. In both patients, my transference role during the tantrums was predominantly that of the father.

This paper had not aimed to present anything new—unless possibly this last matter of the intrusion of a symbiotically based infantile experience, acted out in the transference in a way to intrude and completely upset the therapeutic tenor of the work, is a small contribution. Essentially, however, the intent has been to restate principles which were stated emphatically some years ago, but which may need re-emphasis in relation to newer concepts in analysis and in the setting of its wider scope, in which there appear some untoward tendencies to use psychotherapeutic methods rather than the stricter and, I believe, more effective analytic ones.

Especially would it seem worthwhile to pay consistent attention to the special forms, variations, and movements within the transference relationship itself. I suppose fundamentally my paper attempts to suggest caution in regard to the introduction of active procedures, since these may undermine the patient's sense of autonomy, and risk establishing an actual relationship in the transference which may be more powerful than the corresponding one of the infantile neurosis, and have a confirmatory effect on the neurosis.

CHAPTER THIRTY-FOUR

A Critical Digest of the Literature on Selection of Candidates for Psychoanalytic Training (1961)

This review of the literature on the selection of candidates for psychoanalytic training will attempt to give as comprehensive a picture as possible of the ideas about selection which have evolved and prevailed in the past. This is a more complex task than the mere abstracting of a number of articles (a list of which is appended in footnote 5). It will be noted that the list contains few articles which are limited to problems of selection. However, an article by Eisendorfer (1959), and those of the Panel on Selection presented at the meeting of the American Psychoanalytic Association in May, 1960 (Eisendorfer, 1960; Fleming, 1960a, 1960b; Pollock, 1960a, 1960b; see also Greenson, 1961) are limited to this subject. Some are considered by their authors to be in a preliminary form and to deal with investigations still in their formative stages. However, they seem to me vital and important contributions, significant expressions of present-day concern about educational matters—a concern which gave rise to the Survey of Psychoanalytic Education and has subsequently been more or less influenced by it. The chapter on selection from the survey report by Lewin and Ross (1960) may also be cited here, but it too is a part of a study of much wider scope and is seen against this background. I have not included articles that deal with special testing methods. It seemed more appropriate to study these separately, after considering other conditions and issues influencing selection needs.

Selection of candidates for training is an omnipresent practical problem absorbing and harassing institute faculties rather widely. It is remarked as the weakest link in present-day planning of training (Lewin and Ross, 1960), and gives rise to the questions: Must this be so? Can there really be no methods that will serve efficiently? Or have we just not developed them? It is apparent that some special procedures have to be used since the growth of the knowledge of psychoanalysis and its acceptance have been such that more teachers, psychologists, and sociologists, as well as physicians, are seeking training (and getting it one way or another) than would have been dreamed possible fifty years ago. There are many more applicants for training than can be dealt with by the informal methods—almost self-selection—which prevailed in the early days of psychoanalysis when to be an analyst meant a struggle against attack and misunderstanding. This struggle was in itself a selecting process. It also meant greater ties to and within the small group of persons working together who inevitably became intimately known to each other.

The very acceptance of psychoanalysis—fundamentally by its own infiltration into the intellectual thought of the world arising from the force of its own truth—has produced curious and paradoxical problems and attitudes. One gets the impression that some of the older analysts, missing the special relations of the smaller group and the unique inspiration of association with Freud, resent the loss of the old struggle and in the need to carry on in this, perhaps too quickly developing, expansion of psychoanalytic interest, they would prefer to ignore it and attempt one way or another to reinstate bygone conditions which no longer fit.[1] We "later comers" naturally envy them; but because we did not experience that golden era we may not have so great and so moving a wish to turn time back to it.

Be that as it may, problems of selection and the attempts to cope with them have changed greatly during the last fifty years. It is obvious that selection, so important a link in the planning of

[1] This may be responsible for a great deal of the informal training outside of institutes which is more or less promoted by some analysts.

training, must be dealt with as part of the whole set of problems of organized training. As the sensitive spot between a training program and the outside world, it is also affected by changing times and conditions. To present an integrated digest of all the articles (listed in footnote 5) means the unfolding of a picture in which problems of selection present a central subpattern, rarely highlighted and not always clearly defined, in the development of psychoanalytic education in general. In this digest, I shall focus on: (1) what qualities are considered desirable in an analyst, and are therefore to be looked for in the applicant for training (and the insistent corollary, viz., what qualities are particularly defeating and should rule out the applicant if they are detected before training is begun); (2) methods of selection, often implied rather than explicitly stated; and (3) special conditions influencing or modifying points of view in regard to these subjects. Thus the need to change the conception of what qualities make a good analyst involves not only refinement and greater care in their definition, but a consideration of whether changes in the work of analysis itself demand different qualities in those undertaking it.

In these articles three major influences are impressive, confluent in the late 1930's and early 1940's, and even more conspicuous in the 1950's. These are: (1) the inevitable growth of the knowledge of psychoanalysis; (2) the impact of World War II; and (3) the development of ego psychology. The teaching of psychoanalysis was indubitably already expanding by the force of its own value. But the special needs of the war gave a forced growth, grafted onto the endogenous one, by demonstrating its value—not so much as a technique of individual therapy but as an essential aid in the understanding and better handling of the wide variety of human problems in both military and civilian life under the conditions of war. It has always been recognized that the greatest contributions of psychoanalysis are indirect ones—the stimulation of new vistas in related fields of endeavor rather than simply the therapeutic gains to the limited number of people who can be analyzed. This was spectacularly evident during World War II but gave rise to some difficulties, since those who were especially stimulated by the greater depth and usefulness of psychoanalytic understanding, and who saw it at work in the field rather than in the therapist's office, were young psychiatrists in military service. Many sought training immediately after the war, partly out of conviction and partly because they were at loose ends anyway and had government money to subsidize further training. It was inevitably a confusing situation.

In addition, migrations of European analysts, caused by the conditions preceding and during the war, involved a dislocation of the main centers of psychoanalytic training from the Continent to England and to the United States. The effect of all this on formally (as well as informally) organized training in the United States undoubtedly has been extremely great and complex. In some ways it also influenced problems of selection. Perhaps we are only beginning to get a sufficient distance from this period to be able to look at it with discerning objectivity. But whether or not the time is or soon will be ripe for studies of such influences, they seem to me basic in extending the work of evaluating and developing psychoanalytic training in this country.

Especially is there a need for a careful consideration of the role of the culture from which the applicant is drawn in furnishing characteristics which are favorable or unfavorable for the development of analysis and future analysts. One hears occasional but most emphatic statements regarding the improbability or even impossibility that the American culture can furnish worthwhile analysts. Certainly the role of the culture as part of the background of the analyst, so often alluded to in articles on training, and especially the influence of certain specific cultural attributes in their interplay with ego ideals, deserves special and thoughtful examination.

The influence of the development of ego psychology on questions of training, and specifically on the selection of candidates, is probably even more subtle and more direct. Anna Freud's book, *The Ego and the Mechanisms of Defense,* published in 1936, crystallized and gave further impetus to focusing on practical and theoretical considerations of ego development and their incorporation into analytic technique. This development was stimulating, yet it was also somewhat unsettling to many analysts, probably more in this country than in Europe where closer contact with Freud had meant a fuller development and greater assimilation of many concepts of ego psychology than had occurred here. At any rate, it seems that neither European nor American analysts really use this knowledge fully or effectively in the work of selection. This subject will be referred to later in connection with abstracts of specific articles. The material of articles referring in any way to problems of selection will be grouped roughly under decade headings, which relate not so much to the time of publication as to the period of analytic training referred to or described.

In the early days training was personal, informal, and tentative. Selection was based largely on the intensity of the individual's interest. We read of Freud conducting Eitingon's analysis by twice-a-week conversations during evening walks (1907-1909), and that Eitingon was then going to Berlin to further psychoanalytic work there. This sounds like a preceptor system.

When the Berlin Psychoanalytic Institute was founded in 1920, Sachs was the first training analyst. The demand that the analyst be analyzed was "theoretically acknowledged" but not yet tried. "Far from being based on precedents and strictly prescribed, it was still inchoate and receiving its definition by a coöperation in which the foremost analysts of the period coöperated." This was probably the beginning of an organized institute, in contrast to the group in Vienna which naturally congregated around Freud. Sachs's posthumously published article (1947), written in 1946, was still too close to the war period to have much perspective on incipient changes produced by the war. It dealt mostly with his impressions from 1920 to around 1940, thus including the two periods, in Berlin and in Boston. Throughout this article, as well as many others reviewed in this digest, the question is repeatedly raised as to whether or not the beginning student of analysis should be selected for his normality. In 1947 Sachs still believed that there was no essential difference between the analysis of training candidates and of neurotic patients, and clearly stated that it was to be expected that the candidates would have neurotic problems. "Psychoneurotic trends in our present state of civilization are so universal that a person who is practically free of them is a rare exception . . . still less likely to be found among those who want to be analysts because the vivid interest in psychoneuroses . . . is regularly motivated by one's own neurotic problems." He thus implied that neurosis in the applicant is not a handicap but to be expected and probably helpful. Regarding the selection of candidates, he mentions the general requirements (honesty, intelligence, reliability, and sufficient professional and cultural training) which he would consider necessary in any profession. He then adds a discussion of qualities necessary for the specific profession of the psychoanalyst, naming especially the faculty of access to and the *will to face* one's own unconscious, and absence of such a degree or magnitude of blind spots as would inhibit an intimate acquaintance with the mechanisms and contents of the unconscious or would substitute theoretical academic interest for it. He considers that the extent and nature of the blind spots cannot be determined in advance but only through a personal analysis. He therefore recommends a trial analysis. Among the qualities which may be determined without or before analysis, he mentions as favorable a lively interest in and understanding of the intuitive psychologists—the great poets, writers, and artists; and he further stresses that it is the degree of intactness and integration present in spite of the neurosis which is important. In discussing the question of the "normal" candidate, it is fairly clear that he is referring to *normal* in the sense of freedom from overt neurosis, for he remarks that normal candidates often have more distortions and anxieties than those presenting a downright neurosis. He warns against applicants who show a tendency to avoid emotions, who have shown chronic neurosis since childhood without remission during adolescence, who have psychotic and psychopathic trends, definite perversions and addictions, or rigidity based on firm defense of narcissistic traits. (It would appear that the last might require analysis for its detection as it cannot always be foretold.) He further warns against accepting those whose aim it is to make a career of psychoanalysis as a way of making a living, since he considers that psychoanalysis demands a total responsiveness (i.e., dedication) and that without this an analyst cannot attain or maintain a good balance between personal and private life. Thus he sees this "career for a living" problem as important in the long-term life situation rather than as an interference in the process of training, as we see it in highly organized institutes now.

In another posthumously published article (1947), Ella Sharpe deals largely with the qualities she considered favorable or necessary in an analyst. Her experience in England was rather different from that of Sachs and did not extend back to as early a time. The tone of her article—similar to that of his—does not imply a grappling as yet with postwar problems. In addition to those basic general qualifications to be considered for any profession, she stresses specifically that the prospective analyst should have an *insatiable curiosity* about man's mental and emotional life, and that the essential requirement of a personal analysis is to produce a conviction rather than merely an understanding of psychoanalysis. She implies rather than asserts that the insatiable curiosity with which the learning of psychoanalysis is approached must be capable of developing into a continual and *patient* search for psychological truth, and that the work of an analyst requires a combination of being an eternal student with capacity for creative work or at least for creative appreciation. She warns against the would-be student whose primary goal is to make a living, as she does against any situation in which financial or other gain from the patient outweighs the goal of search for truth. Among all the articles reviewed here, Sharpe's is the only one which emphasizes especially that the very young person is not the most desirable for analytic training, since his requirements for activity in life are generally too great, and he has, furthermore, not gained sufficient experience in actual living. Her use of the term *gravitation*, to describe the routes of access to psychoanalytic study, in its connotations is in significant contrast to the pressured clutching toward the career of psychoanalysis encountered in so many applicants since the war.

In "Analysis Terminable and Interminable" (1937), Freud discusses briefly some of the qualities desirable in an analyst. The question is raised largely in connection with considerations of what should be the achievements of a training analysis. In regard to the necessary character of the analyst, Freud states: "It is therefore reasonable to expect of an analyst, as a part of his qualifications, a considerable degree of mental normality and correctness. In addition, he must possess some kind of superiority, so that in certain analytic situations he can act as a model for his patient and in others as a teacher. And finally we must not forget that the analytic relationship is based on a love of truth—that is, on a recognition of reality—and that it precludes any kind of sham or deceit" (p. 248). He considers that the training analysis must be *"short and incomplete."* Freud then states the results desired from a training analysis as follows: "It [the training analysis] has accomplished its purpose if it gives the learner a firm conviction of the existence of the unconscious, if it enables him, when repressed material emerges, to perceive in himself things which would otherwise be incredible to him, and if it shows him a first sample of the technique" (p. 248). He formulates the ideal sequelae of the training period as a situation in which these stimuli will not cease to act upon the trainee, and when the training analysis ends the processes of ego transformaton will go on of their own accord, bringing new insight to bear upon all subsequent experience. But Freud further recognized that so favorable an outcome was not uniformly manifest, and adds, "Hostility . . . and partisanship . . . create an atmosphere which is not favourable to objective investigation. . . . a number of analysts learn to make use of defensive mechanisms which allow them to divert the implications and demands of analysis from themselves (probably by directing them on to other people), so that they themselves remain as they are and are able to withdraw from the critical and corrective influence of analysis. . . . It would not be surprising if the effect of a constant preoccupation with all the repressed material which struggles for freedom in the human mind were to stir up in the analyst as well all the instinctual demands which he is otherwise able to keep under suppression" (p. 249). This danger to the analyst then is the basis of Freud's suggestion of periodic reanalysis of the analyst.

Although this article was published as late as 1937 there is naturally much of it that reflects a period already passing. I am not sure that I understand fully the meaning of the demand for psychic normality. Freud speaks of the need for psychic normality and correct adjustment because the analyst must serve as a model to his patient in some situations and act as a teacher in others. Does he mean that this use of the analyst as model is desirable, or only that it is unavoidable in a training situation and must be coped with there? Although this statement of the need for psychic normality has been quoted in support of the idea that one should select normal individuals as candidates, this is not the necessary implication. It seems instead that psychic normality in the training analyst is the desired result of his personal analysis, and an achievement of his own training, rather than a condition required of the candidate.

It is interesting too that the further development of ego psychology and the careful analysis of defenses has tended to prolong the personal analysis. Few of us now would anticipate such favorable results from a short and incomplete analysis as were still somewhat hoped for in 1937. The question may still be raised whether or not our demands are too great and infiltrated with narcissistic expectations. Freud's statement regarding the incompletely analyzed analysts, who learn to apply defense mechanisms and to divert the conclusions of an analysis from themselves by applying them to others, gives rise to a further consideration which may be useful in the selection of candidates for training. We frequently hear expressed as a positive recommendation of an applicant that he has a "psychological gift" or "access to the unconscious" or "a high degree of intuitive understanding." Is it feasible and desirable to determine in preliminary admissions interviews or other procedures how this psychological gift has been used and has seemed to influence the applicant's life? That is to say, is it used largely for narcissistic gratifications and defensive purposes, or has the individual grown through its use in self-understanding and the development of such interests, as those in the arts?

The great migration of European analysts to the United States began in the 1930's, continued throughout the 1940's, and was probably at its peak in the period between 1935 and 1940. It immediately enriched all the resources of training throughout the United States, especially in the cities of the east and west coasts. In general, American analysts were touchy but basically grateful, and American students were especially responsive to a deepening and increased stimulation in the teaching. At first the stress of war conditions did much to mask and even partly to solve some of the problems arising from conflicts of culture, mores, and values—one might say simply "ways of going about things"—within both analytic practices and the general ways of life. Throughout, certainly the esteem and prestige of European training has been strong. Subsequently, certain problems began to emerge, and especially troublesome were the outcroppings of mutually ambivalent attitudes arising from those very individual problems which Freud warned about in "Analysis Terminable and Interminable." Again I must say, we may be too close to all this to be objective about it, but certainly it is an area meriting study as soon as it is at all feasible. These considerations would have no place in the present résumé, however, if the conditions involved did not affect our training programs, our ideas of what qualities are desirable in an analyst, and sometimes even our procedures of selection.

Naturally enough, there was a considerable stirring of interest in the problems of training in the 1940's, especially in discussions in the American Psychoanalytic Association. In the 1930's, requirements for acceptance for training had as their stated base, "maturity of personality, integrity of character, and aptitude for psychological work"—undoubtedly important general requirements, but not very specific. These had been formulated by a committee which presented a report at the 1932 Congress of the International Psycho-Analytical Association, and they were published in its *Journal* in 1933. This same report emphasized that selection should be a function of a committee of an organized institute and not of any one training analyst working privately. In 1939, David Levy called attention to the acceptance of too many neurotic individuals as candidates in training. He advised a stricter checking on credentials, the use of the Rorschach test, a rigorous course of training, and the dropping of undesirable students even after they had begun training. In this connection, it should be noted that only recently have there been plans to study this problem of the dropping of undesirable students. In earlier days this occurred very rarely. In a recent discussion (September 20, 1960) of training at a faculty meeting of the New York Psychoanalytic Institute, Anna Freud assumed that this was still true, and implied that no student would be dropped except for some extraordinary reason. Certainly, the policy in regard to dropping students must influence greatly the reciprocal policies and judgments concerning admissions of applicants. At present there are some training analysts who believe that there should be much greater freedom to discontinue training of candidates who seem unsuited for the profession. But in actual practice this is very difficult for many to do—especially where the burden of the decision lies almost wholly with the training analyst (G. Bibring, 1954; Console, n.d.).

George Pollock's "Historical Perspectives in the Selection of Candidates for Psychoanalytic Training" (1960a) gives some details concerning the discussions of 1939, in which Helene Deutsch, French, Kaufman, Rado, Blitzsten, and Alexander all participated, and also the later discussions in 1940, 1946, and 1948, all of which were initiated and carried on in the American Psychoanalytic

Association. In the 1940 Round Table Discussion, Levy defended the "healthy, but not stereotyped personality" as most suitable for training. Special attention was paid to questions of detecting disqualifying characteristics. In 1946, a conference on "Postwar Problems of Psychoanalytic Training" focused on the very large number of physicians applying for training and the distinct imbalance between this number and the number of available training analysts. The aim of the conference seemed to be to strengthen standards of training against the strong pressure to let down in order to admit as many as possible. In the 1948 panel on "Problems of Psychoanalytic Training," the selection discussion focused for the most part on detecting the promising student.

It should be noted here that in the 1940's there was a growing interest in the possible use of psychological tests either as main or adjunct facilities in admissions procedures. On the whole this tendency seemed to wane in the 1950's. At this earlier period there was also the definite concern in some places about linking psychoanalytic training with postgraduate medical organizations and incorporating it into academic settings. As part of this there was an interest in training young analysts who might become teachers of psychoanalysis in such academic settings and this may have influenced local selection criteria and procedures as well as the organization of training. There is an older history related to this in an early attempt to train analysts for special psychiatric posts in medical schools. I do not know of any published study regarding the relation between medical academic programs and psychoanalytic training, except the necessarily preliminary report in the Lewin and Ross study (1960) of psychoanalytic education. The further development of this would be extremely valuable.

We now reach the period of the 1950's. Ekstein (1950) presented a discussion of trial analysis as a period of exploration of analyzability and motivation. Trial analysis might, in many instances, explore analyzability in the sense of rigidity of defenses, especially in relation to marked narcissistic problems as well as problems of ego defect which might be masked in interview situations. Again it appears that the influence of ego psychology is felt here and that more careful consideration of this in admissions interviews would be helpful. It is doubtful, however, whether the problem of motivation could be adequately dealt with in a trial analysis. There might be a risk of directing and distorting the analysis itself by having this as too decided a goal.

In 1953 a panel on "Selection of Psychoanalytic Students" was presented at the Midwinter Meeting of the American Psychoanalytic Association, with the main focus on comparison of instruments of selection. The chief paper was that of Holt and Luborsky (1955). They emphasized criteria that a selector has for the position applied for, and the question of the conscious awareness during the interview with the applicant of whether or not these necessary essentials were present or could eventually be developed. As I have not myself made an adequate study of the Holt and Luborsky work, no summary of its implications for psychoanalytic admissions procedures can now be included. While their emphases seem to involve recommendations essentially similar to those made in various earlier terms, they demand greater precision of method and also introduce a vocabulary which would seem to consider analytic work as a "position applied for" and to connote a similarity between analytic training in institutes with job and skill development in industry.

In 1953, there was a panel on Problems of Training at the International Congress held in London. The papers given there were published in the *International Journal* in 1954. As this panel covered all problems of training, not all papers dealt with problems of selection. The question of the qualities desirable in an analyst, however, entered directly or indirectly into many of the discussions. Only those papers dealing with these aspects of training will be quoted in the present digest.

In a lively, stimulating, and provocative paper, "Analytic Training and Training Analysis" (1954), Michael Balint takes issue with that development in psychoanalytic training which he refers to as the "period of supertherapy," resulting from a demand for a fully completed analysis for the future analyst. He is apparently describing the situation in London, where the analysis is often carried out throughout the period of institute training and may be continued for a considerable time afterward. (This is certainly true in New York also.) He feels that it is even impossible to study the reasons for this or its effects since analysis which occurs after graduation is considered a private affair and is secret. He concludes that the need for so long an analysis reflects a suspicion of *inadequacy of original selection* and graduation criteria. (Whether or not this is true, such prolonged and repeated periods of analysis after graduation which are kept secret enormously complicate freedom of work relationships in psychoanalytic institutes.) My own suspicion is that the almost indefinitely long analyses may be partly due to the absence till now of good criteria concerning the degree of exploration of ego structure and functioning that is desirable in a training analysis. Balint says something related to this when he speaks of supertherapy as penetrating into the preoedipal and preverbal, and what he considers the overanalysis of transference phenomena "especially in their aggressive sadistic aspects." This is obviously aimed largely at the very long analyses of the Kleinian school.

It is interesting then to turn to the paper of Paula Heimann (1954), who at that time was a prominent follower of Melanie Klein but has since shifted her point of view. She states very specific qualities she thinks desirable before the applicant is definitely accepted for training: (1) deep conviction of the dynamic nature of the unconscious (which seems to imply for most people a period of analysis before decisive acceptance for training); (2) intuition and innate psychological flair, comparable to what we call talent in the artist; (3) curiosity (alert interest?) in human beings, combined with respect for the other's individuality (which is similar to the specific and implied requirements stated by Ella Sharpe in 1947); (4) capacity to make and maintain object relationships over a considerable period of time; (5) capacity to recognize limitations in the self and to tolerate frustrations involved in personal problems capable of long-term rather than immediate solution; (6) absence of denial techniques in regard to one's own problems. This is one of the most concisely stated and helpful summaries in the panel.

Lampl-de Groot (1954), in the same panel with Balint and Heimann, agrees substantially with Heimann's criteria for acceptance, but especially emphasizes integrity of character. She states quite definitely, however, that she feels a real inability to define objectively (and precisely?) the criteria of suitability of analysts for their profession due to the nature of the work itself, which is concerned with feelings, needs, impulses, and values—i.e., with human mental processes. In this respect she would probably feel unable to comply fully with the recommendations of Holt and Luborsky (1955). She recognizes the postwar pressure to finish analytic training rapidly and agrees with Grete Bibring that this might be especially true in America, although it was also the experience of the Dutch Institute. In discussing the increased scope, intensity, and duration of analysis, she states that these are necessary if it is to give the analysand a thorough knowledge of his own ego development and not merely those aspects involved in neurotic symptoms.

The rather brief article by Nielsen (1954) of Copenhagen is here quite interesting, especially since he is an older analyst working in a relatively isolated setting. He thinks there is too much emphasis on quantitative standards, such as the number of hours of analysis; he wishes to see more normal applicants for training, more active technique in training analysis, and shorter and more didactic training analyses. Thus he would more or less return to some of the older standards. He does not take into consideration either that the trainee is likely to follow the same shortcuts in therapeutic analyses that have been involved in his own training analysis, but he does mention that there is a change in the type of person wishing to become an analyst: the students of the 1920's were idealists who were ready to champion a cause, whereas the students of the 1950's are matter-of-fact seekers after a career.

Grete Bibring's paper, "Training Analysis and Its Place in Psycho-Analytic Training" (1954), was also a part of the International Congress Panel. It too emphasizes the preponderance of career seekers in applicants for training but adds that this often covers a secondary motivation for therapy, if the character symptoms are not ego-syntonic. She indicates that inevitably there is a preponderance of character problems rather than overt neuroses among career seekers. The rest of the paper, which is extremely interesting, is not reviewed here as it deals with other problems of training.

This takes us to the two excellent papers of Gitelson, one published in 1954 as part of the panel at the International Congress, the other six years earlier, in 1948. The 1948 paper shows definitely the influence of a greater closeness to the war than was evident in the 1954 discussion, when the hump of reaction to the war situation seemed passed or passing. In 1948, after reviewing a large number of opinions expressed in discussions concerning training and especially selection of candidates, held at the special conference and meetings between 1940 and 1946, Gitelson asked the question, "Do we have the obligation to continue to develop personnel capable of conducting definitive psychoanalyses of patients and ordering relevant psychoanalytic data from their work, or are we morally obligated to turn out psychotherapists—more or less trained—in as great numbers as possible in the interest of some mass therapeutic goal?" He concluded, "This is not simply a postwar issue. It is an issue for the entire future of analysis." He quotes from Waelder's "Present Trends in Psychoanalytic Theory and Practice" (1944), stressing that the knowledge of ego psychology shows the necessity and nature of the deepening of the psychoanalytic work as extending far beyond a glimpse of the unconscious—rather to a careful, precise reconstruction of the earlier stages of the neurosis and its precipitating conflicts, "to roll the process of neurosis back along the path of its development." Gitelson believed that it was this progressive but unsettling influence (the need for further knowledge of ego development) which made a consensus of opinion as to criteria for disqualifying candidates so difficult, as had been indicated by Knight's questionnaire and study (1953). Gitelson's discussion of the question of the so-called normal candidate, whose normality is based largely on rigid and deforming defenses, led him next to the opinion that positive criteria must consist rather in what the applicant has done in his life despite his neurosis: "What has survived of creativity, effective energy, of emotional flexibility and resonance, and of interpersonal interest, regardless of the formal diagnosis? One should look for these qualities in the initial interviews and let the analysis take care of the rest." He further took the rather extreme view that the student should not undertake a supervised analysis of a patient until his own analysis is in a stage of resolution or is satisfactorily ended.

Gitelson's paper of 1953 (published 1954) on "Therapeutic Problems in the Analysis of the 'Normal' Candidate" is a natural sequel to the earlier paper. He now deals first with Hartmann's conception of mental health as based on the structure of character, involving mobility or plasticity of the ego, especially with a good degree of plastic balance in the utilization of the defenses. He reviews the change in the character and interest in psychoanalytic candidates which had been occurring gradually and which became strikingly manifest during the war years and soon after. There then follow some interesting comments on the place of psychoanalysis in relation to the culture in which it is developing.

Finally, this digest arrives at the last grouping of pertinent articles—that of the last two years—especially influenced by the survey of psychoanalytic education and the activity of its directors. In Chapter IX of the Lewin and Ross (1960) *Psychoanalytic Education in the United States*, there is presented a summary of the varying procedures and emphases in regard to selection of candidates in various institutes. In a discussion of the suggestion that scrutiny of the applicant's work in supervised psychotherapy (where the supervision has been done by well-trained analysts) might aid in determining his potential psychoanalytic talent, one becomes aware of the fact that any such evaluation must depend upon a clearer conception of the nature of the given therapeutic practices than is usually possible at present.

General principles of decision about suitability of applicants may be summarized under four headings: (1) A certain amount of neurosis is inevitable and is not a deterrent. (2) If it is mastered through the personal analysis, it may be an asset. (3) The admissions committee may serve as a clinical conference in which prognosis of the patient (applicant) is the important issue. (4) Questions of special aptitude for psychoanalytic study and practice are considered. Research studies in selection have been undertaken at Columbia and Chicago, and a description of the Chicago undertaking is given. This chapter also includes some comments on preacceptance analysis which is often undertaken in the hope of influencing the admissions committee, and on the group of analyzed psychiatrists (not otherwise analytically trained and not connected with any institute) which has grown up around psychoanalytic centers. It seems that these men may later drift into the practice of psychoanalysis of some sort.

The Panel on Selection at the May, 1960 meeting of the American Psychoanalytic Association included papers by Eisendorfer (1960); Fleming (1960b), who also gave introductory comments as chairman (1960a); Pollock, whose paper on "The Selection Process and the Selector: The Individual Interview" deals especially with selection philosophy and practice in the Chicago

Institute; and Henriette Klein (1960), who reported briefly on the Columbia research on selection.[2]

In a paper amplified from a letter published in the Lewin and Ross study, Eisendorfer in 1959 summarized his experience from ten years of work in the service of admissions at the New York Institute. The method there has been through consideration of credentials and the development of special interviews which are pooled and discussed by a committee, much in the fashion of a clinical conference. Eisendorfer emphasizes that in interviewing skill grows with the actual experience augmented through the clinical conferences. The qualities considered here as revealing indications of capacity to become an analyst are defined as: (1) subtlety with which the applicant reveals himself; (2) selective specificity of his spontaneous productions (a sample illustration would help); (3) the degree of his spontaneity; (4) evidence of genuine curiosity about the unconscious; (5) appearance of self-examination in regard to his own feelings, problems, and ability; (6) his estimate of the nature of psychoanalysis; (7) capacity for articulate communication; (8) cultural background.

These points are again summarized in Eisendorfer's paper of 1960. He now adds an interesting picture of the interaction of the interviewer and the applicant during an admissions interview. According to his conception, the interviewer generally has a conscious or preconscious image of what he considers a good analyst to be—often narcissistically colored to be sure. During the interview this image constantly hovers over the impressions made by the applicant's self-revelations, which gradually coalesce more or less into some sort of character image. The interviewer is striving

[2] In 1956 Klein published an article on "The Columbia Psychoanalytic Clinic: A Development in Psychoanalytic Training," one section of which was devoted to selection of students. The procedure here, in addition to the usual scrutiny of credentials, included: (1) three psychiatric interviews with experienced psychoanalysts which were evaluated independently on a one-to-four scale; (2) psychological tests done over a two-day period; (3) a conference in which there was a joint evaluation of the pooled data. Earlier, Rorschach tests had been used routinely, but these were subsequently given up except for special situations. They were replaced by a series of psychodiagnostic tests, results of which were considered to indicate that almost all applicants "score high on a cultural or intellectual basis." Klein reports that the model of the desirable student was found to be largely fictitious and there was greater agreement about what was undesirable than about what was desirable in a student. Certain biases were noted in the interviewers in the following respects: (1) the examiner's exaggeration of the anxiety; (2) an avoidance of the aggressive applicant; and (3) overemphasis on cultural status.

throughout to determine in what ways the two images agree. Eisendorfer considers that the decision of the interviewer depends largely on the degree of confluence between the two images.

Of particular interest are the presentations of the philosophy and methods of admissions of the Chicago Institute as stated by Fleming (1960a, 1960b) and Pollock (1960b), chiefly at the recent panel of the American Psychoanalytic Association. The latter also has a paper on the historical perspectives of selection to which I am much indebted. The Chicago procedure for full admission to training apparently grew out of dissatisfaction with methods previously in use where there had been too much dependence on the recommendation of the personal analyst, or, in instances in which the applicant was not in analysis, on the recommendation of some analyst who knew him and was especially interested in him. Some students accepted before beginning their psychiatric residency proved to be unsatisfactory residents and the acceptance had to be reversed (Lewin and Ross, 1960). It was felt further that in general too many students were being accepted who did not develop well. These difficulties were common to many institutes especially in the postwar period.

The Chicago Institute has now set up a research study on selection, begun approximately three years ago. Full details are not yet available as it is still in a developmental stage. The following digest is based on the papers of Fleming and Pollock read at the May, 1960 meeting of the American Psychoanalytic Association, on the account given in the Lewin and Ross (1960) survey, and on the Greenson panel report (1961). From these joint sources it appears that the focus of the research is to establish scientific methodology which will be effective and applied with a sufficient approach to uniformity to be used in comparative studies.

There are now two stages in the admission: a preliminary tentative acceptance and a re-examination at the time of matriculation in courses before supervised work has even begun (Lewin and Ross, 1960). The original interviewing is done by two people, "if possible one man and one woman."[3] These interviews are followed

---

[3] This is of considerable interest. It has been repeatedly noted in the New York Institute that the content of the interviews often varies greatly according to the sex of the interviewer. This is rarely mentioned, however, in discussions of selection methods.

(after an unspecified time) by a group interview of about thirty minutes' duration. "Members of the interviewing panel study the record and make their rating, each group interviewer independently. Then a consensus is put in writing. Individual interviewers dictate reports and also rate. After the ratings are compiled and compared, an evaluation on the basis of both individual and group interviews is made, usually on the following day." The decision may tend to follow the group consensus rather than the results of individual interviews. While it is noted that these methods often reveal interesting material, there is some difference of opinion as to whether or not the tendency to depend on group consensus makes for any better approximation of an understanding of the applicant. Lewin and Ross (1960) point out that in the consensus, the findings of a specially astute individual interviewer may be lost. On the other hand, the effect of strong biases on the part of individuals on the interviewing panel may similarly be diminished. This group interview was instituted not for the time of matriculation but as part of the original tentative acceptance stage.

In her Introduction to the Panel on Selection (1960a), Fleming puts forward the questions: What are we selecting for? How do we recognize and evaluate the presence or absence of these special talents and skills? She deduces that it is desirable to have a test situation in which to observe the applicant in a position approximating as closely as possible the analytic situation. In her discussion she also elaborates on the question, What are we selecting for?, by likening the examination and definition of the work of an analyst roughly to job analysis, as scientifically determined in industry and business. She also believes that the interview serves the purpose of a test situation for the applicant, in that it approximates the conditions of the analytic situation in many ways. It is not quite clear to me whether she is considering the applicant as being in the place of analyst or analysand in this interview-analytic situation, but if these interviews for matriculation are after the applicant has already had a period of analysis, it may be felt that he has been able to view and understand the work of his analyst with what one might call counterempathy to an extent that makes this difference less marked. This seems to me implied in the further statement that the really ideal test situation would be an observation of the applicant's work with a patient. It is felt, however, that the interview "may be so focused that the information obtained about the applicant bears close relevance" to what would be observed in the ideal test situation.

All this must be looked at, however, with the realization that in this undertaking "the goal is not just the selection of good prospects for therapy, but rather of those relatively normal persons, often not motivated toward change in themselves, but wishing to learn how to change other people through the analytic process." One misses here a qualifying recognition that the wish to change other people so often springs from defenses in regard to the need for change in one's self, and that such defensive use of analytic understanding is clinically an unfavorable sign for the welfare of the individual. But setting this consideration aside, one can see more readily that such an analysand-applicant might be more focused on the maneuvers of the analyst and more in a situation of interchangeable identification with him than could be true of an analysand deeply involved in struggles with his own neurosis; i.e., in a "therapeutic" rather than a "didactic" analysis. His frame of mind in the interview-test situation might therefore also be different and he would be better able to straddle the analyst-analysand roles. The paper emphasizes, too, that the research investigation is focused on the question of predictability, but this aspect is not yet ready for presentation.

In Pollock's paper on "The Process of Selection and the Selector" (1960b), there is a more detailed likening of the admissions interviewing to the analytic session and a defining of the interaction between the interviewer and the applicant in these terms. Again the interview is described as a test situation which will show the degree of development of the skill and talent of analytical understanding in the applicant.

While there is here an attempt to understand and to record carefully the investigations of the ego functions in connection with analytic work, which seems to me the most forward-looking endeavor presented in this digest of studies of admissions methods, yet some serious questions arise. For example, the emphasis on prediction and the de-emphasis on therapeutic goals (for himself) in the candidate may contribute to a point of view which tends to present the work of analysis in a somewhat mechanistic way. It leaves out the element of growth and development and the consideration of the stability of their balance in the individual, or their vulnerability to external conditions, in the whole set of problems involved in predictability about human beings. I do not believe the comparison between the admissions interview and the analytic session can be a delicately precise one. It tends to minimize the passive receptive attitude in the analyst with the necessary reliance on permitting a *sequence of sessions* for the unfolding and developing of the subjective material of the analysand, and to substitute permission for a much more active questioning and subtly directing attitude on the part of the analyst. Neither do I think that the analytic session can be described as an analytic interview or as a one-to-one relationship. To emphasize such comparisons seems to risk insidious distortion of the analytic relationship, as it ordinarily exists in a therapeutic analysis.

In contrast to this inevitable degree of direction of the admissions interview, the theme is developed of the free empathic identification which must go on between the interviewer and the applicant. Pollock cites Freud's essay, "Project for a Scientific Psychology" (1895), and recent papers by Fliess and Grotjahn. The conception of this kind of empathic communication, which Pollock is requiring, seems to me more applicable to the period when an analysis is already well established, and to be of much less relevance in the admissions interview situation.

Fleming's paper on "What Analytic Work Requires of the Analyst" (1906b) was stimulated in part by the work of certain writers[4] who considered that job analysis is the important place to begin in undertaking a study of and improvement in methods of selection, and includes as an essential the need to understand explicitly what goes on in a so-called intuitive interview. Between these two points is the need to develop *measures* of success and failure, together with ways of identifying factors which indicate the potential for success or failure. Fleming's paper, closely interrelated with that of Pollock, states the aim to present an analysis of the job of analyzing in terms of the relation of its specific and unique aspects to the special abilities in the analyst. She sees this

---

[4] Paul Horst's monograph on *The Prediction of Personal Adjustment* (1941) and the study of Holt and Luborsky on *Personality Patterns of Psychiatrists* (1958) are especially referred to.

as especially involving an exploration of the ego functions and their operations in the work of analyzing. She sees the goal of therapy as the development of the patient's capacity for communication with himself and with others. (I am not sure that I understand this—whether it means his becoming aware of the previously unconscious elements and forces in himself, or whether it puts in a primary position the development of a new kind of relationship, drawing both on himself and others for cooperative empathy involving greater depths than otherwise would occur.) Fleming then attempts to describe the analyst's functions: "It is easy to see that the analyst must already possess a high level of capacity for this kind of communication if he is to use himself as an instrument in facilitating the communication processes of another person." The idea of a *work ego* is developed—i.e., ego functions which must be well developed in good analytic work, especially functions involving perceptual apparatus and systems of communication with himself and with others. The analyst's integrative and regulative systems must possess free energy for productive, creative activity not bound to serve defensive purposes but freely perceiving and translating the messages of his patient.

This work from the Chicago Institute is still in a preliminary stage and doubtless will be clarified and presented later. The project shows such genuine and energetic concern with problems of selection and is so stimulating that it needs much further consideration. It is the only presentation which attempts a definite account of the selector as well as of the selectee, and which gives so much attention to the ego functioning. To be sure this latter is dealt with in a way which focuses largely on suggested delineation of specific ego functioning of the analyst, rather than on the determination of the applicant's ego strengths or weaknesses. The ego work-model seems to me too isolatedly precise. This together with the vocabulary of hiring-for-a-job interviewing, with the use of such terms as "job analysis," "the job of analysis," "what tasks an analyst is called upon to perform," "what skills and tools an analyst must possess in order to perform these tasks"—the use of instruments and techniques for the skills—all this seems to me to overemphasize a mechanistic point of view in the effort to be precisely scientific. It diminishes the difference between the conception of a job and that of a profession, for me a fundamental and necessary difference.

SUMMARY

There seems to be general agreement that the selection of candidates for psychoanalytic training is one of the most important and vulnerable spots in the establishment of educational programs. The main issues rest on these considerations: (1) what qualities form an essential core in the character of the "good analyst"; (2) the extent to which they are present; (3) in what degree they can be discerned, or their maturing or development forecast, before the individual has been analyzed and had some experience with analyzing; and (4) what criteria and methods can be used for their evaluation either in developed or in larval form.

The digest of literature bearing in any way on the problems of selection of candidates revealed three main influences on training which converged in the 1940's.[5] These were the growth of the knowledge of psychoanalysis by the force of recognition of its value; the effects of the Second World War, especially in dislocating the centers of psychoanalytic training from the Continent to England and the United States; and the development of ego psychology.

All writers were in general accord with the basic requirements of intelligence, honesty, and sufficient educational and cultural background, such as would be necessary for the pursuit of any profession. The special qualities mentioned as important for an analyst were: sustained curiosity about the behavior and mental activities of human beings; respect for *the other* (i.e., capacity for object relationship); some facility of access to the unconscious: love and persistent pursuit of the truth—not implying conviction of knowledge of the truth; a modest degree of creativity or at least of creative appreciation; and a capacity for reflection and introspection in contrast to a habitual demand for action. Various opinions were expressed regarding the degree of neurosis admis-

[5] The following papers were surveyed in the preparation of this report: Balint (1954), G. Bibring (1954), Console (n.d.), Ekstein (1950), Eisendorfer (1959, 1960), Fleming (1960a, 1960b), A. Freud (1950), Freud (1937), Gitelson (1948, 1954), Greenson (1961), Grotjahn (1954), Heimann (1954), Holt and Luborsky (1955), H. Klein (1956, 1960), Knight (1953), Lampl-de Groot (1954), Lewin and Ross (1960), Nacht (1954), Nielson (1954), Pollock (1960a, 1960b), Sachs (1947), Sharpe (1947), Waelder (1944).

sible in a candidate or—stated in reversed form—the special emphasis on normality as a requirement. This of course leads to questions of what is meant by normality and the "normal neurosis." The most frequent opinion was that neurosis, provided it could be analyzed, was not a handicap in training but might furnish effective motivation and add to psychoanalytic sensitivity.

The dislocation of the centers of psychoanalytic training from continental Europe to England and the United States has brought an enormous enrichment and vitalization of our training but has also contributed special conditions and problems that arise from conflicts of cultural standards and values. This state of affairs cannot be quickly evaluated or resolved.

In general, a digest of the literature indicates a relatively slow degree of absorption of ego psychology into the thinking about general requirements of psychoanalytic work and of the needs of the psychoanalysts. For example, there is little emphasis on consideration of the types of defense which may be favorable or unfavorable in the character of the analyst, or in what kind of reciprocal or antithetical relationship these may be with the "ease of access to the unconscious," or how much can be determined regarding the probable analyzability of a prospective candidate by studying what his life story reveals of his systems of defense.

From the general background of this survey of literature, I would, in a preliminary way, suggest the following areas for consideration:

1. Re-evaluation of the qualities recommended as desirable in the "good analyst." Might it be possible to study the qualities, not just of candidates but of analysts who have proved themselves?

2. Special investigations of problems of normality and of mental health, about which much has already been written.

3. Study of the role of culture in the development of analysts, if the time is yet ripe for this. This would include contrasts between conditions of European and American culture; special problems (assets and difficulties) in American culture; the American-European situation especially in the larger institutes; and ecological problems of institutes in different parts of the country.

4. Investigation of special problems of the place of selection in the institute's organization and plan of training. This would include:

(a) *Special* goals of selection. Can we separate such goals—for research, for furthering teaching in academic or medical centers, or even for developing analytic practice in a given community —from the basic core of consideration of "what makes a good analyst"?

(b) Problems of size of institute—large or small—within the institute organization; and in relation to the community.

(c) The meaning of analysis prolonged after graduation, or a second analysis begun rather promptly, especially in regard to its effect on selection.

(d) The effect of "dropping" students and its antithetical counterpart, the effect of graduating students who are not really qualified to practice analysis.

This outline was submitted to the Committee on Psychoanalytic Education of The American Psychoanalytic Association at its meeting in November, 1960.

CHAPTER THIRTY-FIVE

Problems of Acting Out in the Transference Relationship (1963)

This paper will describe and discuss a form of massive acting out in the transference relationship. An attempt will be made to explore its genetic basis and to suggest its significance in some acute psychopathological states as well as in more prolonged conditions. Questions of its amenability to treatment will not be dealt with except to a very limited extent. These comprise especially complicated aspects of the overall subject, and require considerably more detailed and thorough study of the clinical situations and progress than is now available.

First of all, let us consider what we mean by *acting out*. It is a term used frequently in many different ways and sometimes with some degree of discouragement on the part of many young analysts. Unfortunately, it often carries an undertone of disparagement of the analysand who is not being a good and compliant patient bringing his dreams and his free associations to the daily hour. Instead he is misbehaving or even cutting up—in fact, causing trouble in the analysis by indulging in impulsive, unusual, and sometimes dramatic conduct elsewhere. He may tell in the hour some fragments of what has been going on, usually as though it were something which had just incidentally happened to him and not as though he had any initiative in producing it. Quite as frequently these events occur away from the analysis and remain unknown to the analyst for a long time (sometimes forever) unless he happens to hear of them from other patients or from some other incidental and unexpected source.

Every analyst knows that such acting out means that the patient is expressing in action old and as yet not thoroughly conscious conflictful memories instead of bringing them to the analyst in the tedious and fragmentary way in which such memories piece themselves together and are expressed in words in the analytic sessions. These old memories seem to have found their resting place in action tendencies in the patient, which are rearoused and claim precedence over—almost literally "get the jump on"—his capacity for reflection, introspection, and verbalization. We might define acting out, then, as memory expressed in active behavior without the usual sort of recall in verbal or visual imagery.

Because the patient is in one sense conscious of his actions, for generally he does not seem to be in a fugue or somnambulistic state, it is easy to slip into a feeling that he should know better than all this, that he is in fact being uncooperative; and to forget that he is not at all conscious of the significance of his behavior or of the underlying neurotic drives which bend outer reality to his needs in quite well-rationalized ways. Because the acting out gratifies and discharges the rationalized drives, no insight is ordinarily attained and the analysis is stymied or delayed. Consequently, the patient who frequently acts out is at least a very difficult patient. One hears the statement occasionally even from quite experienced analysts that the patient must be forbidden to act out, if the acting out seems in danger of becoming habitual; or at least that the acting out *must* be stopped somehow, otherwise the analysis cannot go on. In my experience, prohibition or direct intervention are generally useless, increasing rather than ameliorating the tendency.

But there are patients with a habitual repetition of specifically patterned acting out, who continue with such episodes even after they have gained some insight into the conflict and become aware of the peculiar excitement which often initiates such a burst of acting out. Such stubbornly held-to patterns seem then to be expressing hostility of a deeply ambivalent nature. It is necessary to indicate to the analysand that the analysis cannot possibly continue as long as this kind of indulgence is accepted by the patient. In this way the expression of hostility can be forced into the analysis. This is the situation sometimes in the patients I shall describe.

Fortunately, however, most acting out in neurotic patients is sporadic, and the contents of the special episodes gradually find their way back into the analysis and can be interpreted in the various new forms in which they then appear.

It is almost an analytic truism that acting out may appear in the neurotic patient because of inadequate expression and interpretation of the transference relationship. And this makes sense, for if neurotic tensions and patterned unconscious memories are mobilized and are blocked or impeded in their communication one way or another to the analyst, then their expression will seek other outlets, i.e., away from the analysis and the analyst. I think that acting out is also increased if the analyst becomes too active and oversteps the boundaries of neutrality, gratifying the patient in benevolent or moralistic interventions.

In general, it seems to follow that as long as the material is brought into the transference relationship, even as a combination of words and action, the analytic sailing is fairly clear and the storms will not be too frequent or insurmountable. But there are other conditions, already referred to, in which acting out in the transference occurs readily, is not easily open to interpretation, and furnishes a strong barrier against therapeutic progress. I shall direct this paper to a consideration of these cases.

GENERAL CONDITIONS

We may first take a look at those developmental factors which contribute to all acting out and then attempt to distinguish which are most powerful in our special group of patients. The predisposition to be active, which is certainly based in some measure on constitutional build, probably plays some part, though a minor one, in the promotion of acting out. As an indication of the influence of body structure, one has only to recall the developmental differences between boys and girls. Boys begin to walk earlier and are definitely more active in the nursery years than are girls. The girls in turn talk earlier than boys do. But here we come to the two meanings of the verb *to act,* both of which have some significance in acting out: *act* in the sense of movement and activity, and *act* in the sense of dramatic behavior and impersonation. For at the same time that little boys show a predilection to more vigorous motor activity, little girls are definitely more precocious in play acting. The score seems fairly even.

It has been generally recognized that disturbances in the oral phase increase tendencies to impulsive activity and may be important influences in the matrix in which acting-out pressures develop. Urgencies of the oral phase which are not mastered in accordance with the appropriate maturational stage may then be perpetuated in the trait of impatience. Such urgencies may of course be due to a variety of interferences, among which are excessive indulgence or deprivation, and especially erratic alternations of the two, impeding the stabilization of a natural rhythm. Disturbances of mastery of toilet control may contribute their part, especially if these too are a continuation of erratic and contradictory attitudes in the behavior of adults who are part of the infant's milieu and responsible with him for the direction of his developmental prowess. Sometimes too early toilet training is genuinely combined with the oral phase, and the uncertainties and urgencies of toilet functioning then leave their imprint in augmenting the inability to wait.

Multiplicity of authoritative figures in childhood may contribute to later acting-out tendencies, especially if there is tension among these "parents." Common situations of tension are due to conflicting attitudes between the actual parents, or between mother and nurse, but other individuals may be readily drawn in. This situation favors acting out during later analytic treatment since it is reproduced in the splitting of the transference and the more than ordinary utilization of others than the analyst for transference projections. This complication is generally not difficult to handle through interpretation so long as any substantial part of it is brought into the analysis, even though the major acting out may be away from the analysis. An exception to this is encountered in those cases in which one or another of the contending early parental figures has made a special ally of the child or had secrets with him, giving him thereby great gratification while at the same time arousing special anxiety about their betrayal. This situation may become almost inextricably bound up with guilt about the wish for oedipal betrayal. The old admonition of secrecy may then become a powerful reinforcement to keep the content away from the analyst. A complication may occur here through the use of the neurotic defense mechanism of denial which such patients have developed early in childhood and depended upon greatly throughout their lives.

It is also obvious that traumatic events in early childhood will tend to be repeated in acting-out episodes of which the traumatic neurosis is a paradigm. This occurs in the most clearly recognizable form, nonetheless often overlooked, in which the trauma has been an actual one with direct involvement of the child, though this naturally gains its significance largely from the degree to which the traumatic experience coincides with special fantasies of that period. It is my impression that the acting out is most forceful and persistent when the child has suffered humiliation in the traumatic episode, being forced from a desired active position to a seemingly devaluated passive one. When this situation is rearoused in the analysis, the acting out, representing an unconscious effort at regaining an active role, is usually carried out away from the analysis. The sense of humiliation which has originally promoted the repression now comes into play in the transference and therapy and is experienced temporarily but acutely as a degradation. Whenever this latter attitude crops out in the transference in a neurotic patient who does not generally suffer from a negative therapeutic attitude, the analyst may be alerted to the imminence of acting out outside of the analytic hour. It is in situations of this kind that patients may wish to discontinue the analysis.

A less well-focused type of acting out in connection with trauma occurs sometimes in a fuguelike re-enactment of some fairly well-organized fantasy of the past (Greenacre, 1950a). In such cases there has often been a minor sexual or aggressive incident in childhood which is based on and associated with elaborate fantasies derived from passive participation in (watching or hearing about) the behavior of adults. The original nucleus of this has generally occurred in the oedipal or immediately preoedipal period. But there may have been other, sometimes more extensive, re-enactments in prepuberty and early adolescence, and again in the course of analysis. These latter occur away from the analytic hour, are rationalized by the patient as things that have just unfortunately happened to him. Consequently they usually are reported in whole or in part in the analysis and can be worked with there.

There are other situations, too, in which a special premium has been put on the child's acting or acting up, rather than on his verbalization. This may amount to his being able to gain special indulgence by action in some way outwitting adult prohibition, when reasonable verbal communication would only have meant clearer frustration. The acting up may be the use of a stormy tantrum as blackmail, or it may be infantile delinquent behavior (e.g., taking surreptitiously that which is forbidden), or cute behavior which bypasses restrictions with charm. In any case, exhibitionism is greatly involved.

In an early paper on acting out (1950b) I described a small group of cases in which a tilted balance between action and speech had developed because speech itself had been deformed and devaluated for one reason or another. Infantilisms of speech were then paradoxically valued as part of the cute behavior but not as a means of communication. This was repeated subsequently during treatment and was usually associated with acting out in the analytic hour itself.[1]

ACTING OUT IN THE TRANSFERENCE RELATIONSHIP

General conditions which contribute in different degrees to the production of acting out have been reviewed because they appear in varying combinations and intensities in the type of *acting out in the transference* which is the special focus of this paper. But they have been referred to particularly in relation to acting out in the neuroses. The group of patients on whom I shall concentrate, however, does not belong to the anxiety hysterias or other anxiety and phobic states or the compulsive neuroses, which form the bulk of the conservative analyst's practice. Probably some clinicians would call them psychopathic or at least impulse-ridden characters. But in general they are not conspicuously impulse-ridden except under the pressure of analysis, and even there it is mainly within the transference relationship. Others would tend to put them in that general group of the "borderline" cases. But this seems too often not to define where the borderline approxi-

[1] The role of speech in psychoanalytic treatment is discussed further in chs. 18 and 39.

mately lies, or what is partially divided from what by it. I have thought that some were character neuroses with special deformations of the ego development. But I have also thought that some might be cases of major hysteria, a group which we have thought of as hardly existing any longer. It is possible that this is a clinical group that does exist but has been excluded from our vision by reclassification and the difficulty of their treatment. (This is referred to again later in this paper.)

Whether or not the acting out occurs mainly or exclusively outside of the immediate transference relationship and is excluded from the analytic hour, and whether or not it is reported to the analyst by the patient are considerations obviously of much importance in facilitating or hindering its understanding and its possible utilization through interpretation. This has been implicit in much of what has already been said regarding the place of acting out in the neurosis.

Massive acting out which is frequent, repetitive, and sometimes lasting over a considerable period of time is characteristic of the special group to be discussed. It mainly occurs in the analytic relationship and in the analytic hour. In some patients, it may on occasion extend into relationships outside of the immediate contact with the analyst. But it is then aimed directly at individuals known by the analysand to be associated with the analyst in either a positive or negative way. Such people are patently substitutes for the analyst. It is soon clear that whether the activity takes place inside or outside of the analytic hour, the analyst is the prime target and bears the force of the analysand's energetic efforts, whatever their content may be. During the period of acting out, the analysand generally loses all communication with the judging self-critical part of the ego and the therapeutic alliance is consequently diminished to the vanishing point. Interpretations therefore cannot be given at such times.

Once the period of acting out is over, the analysand has little inclination to examine it, and in some cases will neither spontaneously refer to it nor show any interest if the analyst tries to bring him to it. The analyst is then left almost empty-handed until the next attack occurs. To be sure, by a gradual process of erosion through recurrent periods of this kind and the occasional possibility of linking up the content with material arrived at from associations to dreams in the intervals between the attacks, it is sometimes possible to get a gradually increasing wedge of therapeutic interest, but it is very slow going.

It might be thought that these patients were psychotic from the way in which emotions entirely incongruous to the setting in which they are expressed are allowed to color the total picture and to dominate the behavior usually without any apparent even superficial insight into their inappropriateness. Certainly the psychotic patient distorts reality in the interest of his displaced emotional reactions. But if the distortion invades the sensitive transference relationship, it generally has colored and continues to color aspects of reality relationships elsewhere as well. In these patients, reality outside of the transference relationship is hardly at all involved or impaired.

I have already referred to the acting out in *attack* form. This is generally but not invariably true. One of my patients described the attacks as being something like an addiction, a description also used by Fenichel (1945b). But in what do the attacks of acting out consist; when do they occur? They are mainly provocative and seductive. The provocativeness takes many forms. But there is always the effort to seduce the analyst into some sort of reality involvement with him. The analysand may present himself as suffering and mistreated with a constant worrying over some current grievance which has a core or at least a kernel of realistic truth in it. But this is now brooded over in an obsessional way with a quiet drama aimed at getting the analyst to make an emotional response, form an alliance with the analysand, or intercede in his behalf. No other responses are acceptable. More frequently the other side of the coin is up and the analyst is represented as the misunderstander. There is then a persistent insidious nagging accusation with taunting ridicule. Anything the analyst says is taken out of context and distorted or shaded to fit the accusatory need. If the analyst says nothing, this is interpreted provocatively as indicating the justification of the complaints. There is a trying out of the analyst in a wearing-down effort to see where the limit of tolerance really is. This whole performance has a tantrum form, but of a special kind in which there is a relentless demand for reciprocation and discharge through or with the *other*, the analyst. One understands here a special significance of the term *projective identification.* Sometimes there is clearly a beating fantasy behind this provocativeness.

In the course of these episodes, certain details of behavior and verbal content may reveal quite clearly that a repetition of incidents of childhood is taking place. These may already be partly known to both the analyst and the analysand, but have not yet been adequately worked through. Attempts to point this out and to interpret the nature of the feelings toward the analyst are generally repudiated. The effort is to deny the past by making it come true in the present. It has been noticeable that quite often in patients with this kind of acting-out addiction, the tantrum occurred on the Monday following a "good" week or at least a few good days of analysis during which the analysand seemed to be gaining new ground of insight. This would be ruminated about over the weekend and followed by a violent effort at spewing out the gain and re-establishing the earlier state of affairs.

During the periods of acting out the analysand shows a heightening of alertness with a sensitivity to everything about the analyst (including his voice, expression, movement, etc.), all of which are pounced upon and felt as confirmatory to the analysand's emergent theme. There is also a mild kind of excitement which is sometimes detectable even before the attack has gotten well under way. In two patients, it was only possible to get some therapeutic leverage on the acting out when I was somehow able to get the patient interested in detecting this quiet excitement in himself preceding the attack which seemed to surprise him as well as me.

This is not a large group of patients. My material is drawn from five patients worked with during the last twelve to fifteen years. All five came into analysis with me in a state of anxious crisis, four coming from earlier analytic experiences which had not worked out. All five were unusually bright and able people, distinctly above the average in intellectual ability; and four had a special flair for understanding and working with other human beings. Three of the five were women, and were only children. The fourth, a man, was the youngest, most gifted member of a large family and was distinctly the family darling. The fifth also was the youngest child but in a smaller family. Bright and precocious, from infancy he had been abnormally adored by his father. His attacks of acting out differed from the others in that they consisted chiefly of glum angry silences. If there was any speech at such times, it was scanty and in so low a tone as to be scarcely audible. It was clear that this was a bid for me to come to him. Nonetheless, if I bent forward in my chair ever so little in order to hear better, he became more alarmed and bristled.

It will probably not be surprising to any analyst that these attacks, almost like states of being possessed, were especially precipitated by situations which stirred up the castration complex which was extraordinarily strong anyway. In the women, they were a good deal influenced by the menstrual rhythm. Separation, too, was a strong precipitant. Once accomplished, it was borne extraordinarily well. The first reaction to gaining of insight was exactly as though this had been a castrative attack, a phenomenon attributable to the fact that so much of the sense of ego strength and self-realization was narcissistically dependent on the feeling of ability to hold a negative attitude—to desert rather than be deserted.

Study of the genesis of these disturbances indicated that they had taproots in earliest infancy, i.e., in the oral phase and even into the preverbal part of it. In general, there was an overcloseness of the infant to both parents, not quite of the kind of focused tenacious interdependence described by Mahler (1952) as symbiosis, but with great physical contact and constant handling; being played with by the father as well as by the mother—understandable enough in immature parents with their first baby. This at least was the situation in infancy of the three women patients who were to grow up as only children.

But it is further conspicuous that in these three, the overzealous devotion of the father to the infant daughter was rather abruptly withdrawn when the child reached the oedipal period. It was the sort of break which more frequently comes later and dramatically when the little girl begins to mature at puberty. In one instance this withdrawal of the father was clearly precipitated by the child who, being used to the closest physical intimacy including daily showering with the father, developed an overt and intolerably aggressive attitude toward his phallus. One may surmise, however, that the unconscious, unresolved, and peculiarly infantile oedipal problem in the father found outlet toward his young daughter and cooperated with hers in producing his climactic disturbance. The children in all five instances were exposed to extremely inconsistent and even erratic handling. Without exception the parents were inharmonious, held together by bonds of jealousy, with frequent quarrels, in some instances possibly worsened by the birth of the child. In all cases, at least one parent was subject to marked rages. Yet in only two instances did divorce occur, and in one of these the parents remarried before the child reached puberty.

The early infancy of these patients was not generally characterized by feeding problems, although in two cases they played some part. In one, this was early and soon righted itself; in the other, there was a prolonged siege of colic during much of the first year. In spite of there being no history of delay or of marked distortion in the development of speech in any case, all showed symptoms later which indicated a susceptibility for speech to become secondarily involved in the neurotic manifestations of young adulthood. This leads us at once to the obvious participation of speech in problems of exhibitionism and scoptophilia which in direct or inhibited form were conspicuous in all members of this acting-out group.

It should be emphasized that, in the oral phase, the mouth is not the only source of gratifying contact with the mother and then with other animate and inanimate objects. Although at birth it is the most active and organized in its function of taking in, this function is soon shared with vision and with general body contacts. At first, relatively passive since the infant is not then capable of great initiative, these become increasingly more active and directed. Skin contact and kinesthetic reactions to the mother's body and its movements are partly superseded by more definite reaching and other outgoing movements to elicit and receive a response from the other, i.e., mother or her substitute. In this balanced triangular interplay of functioning, the mouth and the hand soon become partners, with the eye generally acting as supervisor—the whole setup fortified by the growing capacity for accessory body movements and changes in posture. The latter part of the oral phase is also characterized by the increasing strength and rhythmical quality of the activity of the body sphincters and merges into the early part of the period of gaining mastery of these, synchronously with the development of speech. Hoffer's paper (1950b) on the early stages of development of the body ego presents the reciprocity between hand and mouth, but does not much emphasize the role of vision. As much as thirty-five years ago, Hermann (1927) too pointed definitely to the question of dominance of hand or mouth in the oral phase, and was inclined to attribute the differences in balance between them in different individuals to inherited constitutional factors. These doubtless may play a part comparable to that played by the basic differences between the sexes, referred to at the beginning of this paper. Still, it seems that the emphasis on one or another part of this triangular interplay may be determined by the degree to which that part has become specially libidinized by an erotization of its aggressive activity.

Experience has led me to conclude that, in the group of patients now being described, the disturbances in the oral phase have been due largely to excessive and repeated visual and motor stimulation. The mouth and speech problems as such are, to a considerable degree, the result of secondary involvement, and may be accentuated by the confluence of the exigencies of early speech with those of sphincter control. This general state of affairs rests on two sets of conditions: *first,* the abnormal closeness to one or both parents, an intensity of relationship both enjoyed and suffered by the growing infant; and *second,* the infant's constant inclusion in both primal scenes and chronic marital quarreling. The combination of these two sets of factors interferes with the infant's sense of safety, reliability, and even reality of the parents. The image of one or both parents may then remain split into two components—the good and bad. The tension of the child may become so extreme that it breaks through from time to time and precipitates some change in the patterns of family life. Already mentioned is the patient who had such aggressive interests in her father's phallus, both to possess and to degrade it, as to cause a family crisis. The two forms of outbreak most frequent, however, were tantrums and early frenzied or insistent masturbatory activity.

The abnormal closeness to the parents depends in these cases not so much on a symbiotic type of relationship, nor yet on what has elsewhere been referred to as an appersonation of the infant by the parent (O. Sperling, 1944), as on an almost total exposure of the young child to the gamut of the activities of the parents. Such children are loved by their parents—narcissistically to be sure—and often with more expressive warmth than discriminatory judgment. This means that the child's own maturational needs, his individuality, are not sufficiently appreciated and often can be expressed only through aggressive outbursts, the patterns for which may be furnished by the parents themselves. Separation, whether through endogenous maturational pressure or enforced by outer circumstances, is felt as a hostile aggression or a counter-aggression. Too much of the budding sense of independent self is bound up then in an ambivalence, in which the appreciation of power is through outburst.

Exactly these situations of primal scenes and of parental quarreling create a temporary milieu in which the infant, if present, is both in and out of the affair. He is, as it were, "included out." At the same time, he is greatly stimulated both visually and motorically with an implicit, fearful, and excited participation through primary identification.[2] The fact that he frequently cannot get the attention of the parents at such times may produce a situation approximating abandonment. It would probably be inaccurate to consider this as evoking a feeling of definite humiliation in so young a child. Yet this early state of helplessness and loss, combined with jealousy (something similar to what one sees in pets who are in disfavor), is a forerunner of and may predispose to the production of special reactions to humiliation later in life.

The infantile—even larval—masturbation which is set up may occur partly from the direct erotic stimulation of the primal scene and partly from the general excitement which may invade all zones overflowing into premature genital excitation. When this is early, it is nonorgastic and frenzied, with the child's inability to find relief by himself. He rather seeks a discharge of relief through further involvement with the parents. Above all, a response is desired which might also be a token restitution. Certainly this is sometimes achieved and may result in a spanking. Other auto-

---

[2] The nature of primary identification and its continued activity later in life in states of hysterical and religious fervor or frenzy is beautifully illustrated in some of the fifteenth- and sixteenth-century paintings of saints, receiving the stigmata through the appearance of an angel representing Christ on the Cross. I refer especially to paintings of St. Francis in which rays of influence from Christ's body parts to corresponding points on Francis's body are represented by dotted lines of light.

erotic habits may develop alone or in combination with the genital rubbing. In any case, they generally do not resolve the tension. Although they may serve to focus and organize the diffuse stimulation into this activity until the child becomes tired out by himself, they have more often an oral rhythmic form than a true genital one.

What has already been described is the original nuclear form and background of the attacks of acting out in the transference relationship—the subject of our paper. It should be remembered, however, that attacks as they appear in and around the analyst's office carry with them a large burden of further accretions of later related experiences and developments. In configuration, they may vary from an almost endless, angry, brooding provocativeness (the oral form from the first year or so of life) to a more clearly orgastic type of behavior. There is then a brooding prodrome gradually working up to some generally self-destructive pitch of activity. It is sometimes openly and directly self-destructive, but it is always self-destructive if for no other reason than that it is clearly driven by a wish to delay or demolish the analysis and so achieve a negative therapeutic victory.

There is invariably a jealous identification with the analyst who then naturally forms the eye of the hurricane. But this jealousy is rarely consciously felt; and its component positive and negative parts may be acted out consecutively, or divided between the analyst and an accessory person in the general transference area. In one patient, such orgastic activity seemed to carry a total displacement of genital libido, for during these attacks of acting out the patient had a genital "deadness," with lack of interest in and inability to respond to genital stimulation.

One further element in the early genesis of the condition should be mentioned. This has to do with the amalgamation of the scoptophilia and the exhibitionism in a special fixation at the state of imitativeness. This is *acting* in the sense of taking on the behavior of another, in mimicry and simple forms of impersonation. It is not so developed a form of identification as to carry a really sustained wish to be like the person imitated. Yet it is distinctly more developed than the automatic mirroring reaction of the earliest months. It may be observed as early as sixteen to twenty months when it appears rather as a trying out of the own capacities in comparison with others—children, adults, or even pets—in the immediate environment. But in these overexposed children who have grown up to become my patients and be discussed in this paper, it may have become a highly developed skill. I have thought that it arose not only from the enormous importance of the scoptophilic drives and the need to reverse these in exhibitionism, but that it was prolonged and perfected through the early years out of the child's necessity to observe quickly the mood and state of responsiveness of those around him.

In this paper no single clinical case report has been included. An attempt has been made rather to present in summary the common factors in the genesis of this type of acting out in all the patients I have worked with. I have omitted more personal clinical illustrations since, at this period in my practice, many of my patients come from fields of work adjacent to our own. Neither am I at a professional stage in which I can feel any assurance that I can afford to wait a number of years as a seasoning time to insure the stability of any therapeutic gain. I submit these findings, then, subject to these restrictions which are unavoidable.

Before closing, however, I wish to make a few comments and raise questions concerning the possible relationship of the conditions in these patients with similar but more intense conditions contributing to the production of certain forms of delinquency. Here I am largely speculating, since I have no well-worked-out cases and only limited experience. It has seemed to me, however, that the conditions of strong stimulation of the very early aggressive and sexual drives of the young child did not permit a separation of the two, and that sexuality developed in the service of aggression and narcissism; further, that inconsistency of handling was such as to interfere with adequate object constancy to an extent which might strike at the roots of object relationship, promoting ambivalence expressed through action with a minimum of self-awareness. Is it possible that in certain cases of delinquency or criminality in which there is clearly a repetitive patterned form of the offending behavior, there might have been, in addition, a particularly strong fixation at the imitative stage, acting somewhat like an early imprint or engram on the developing child?

LITERATURE

In reviewing the literature on acting out as it bears on the findings presented in this paper, I have been impressed with how many of the factors just discussed have been described or mentioned in other clinical constellations. The relationship of neurotic acting out to delinquent activity especially in children is frequently stressed. These cases probably are rather different from those I have been studying. But even so, it is noteworthy that the cooperation through nonverbal communication between parent and child has been frequently observed as promoting impulsive acting out in which the child appears to gratify the poorly repressed aggressive drives of the parents, especially the mother. This was clearly emphasized in the work of Szurek et al. as early as 1942, and was further elaborated in later reports (Johnson, 1949; Johnson and Szurek, 1951; Giffin et al., 1954). Many of the papers dealing with acting out in adults in psychoanalytic treatment are expressed largely in dynamic and structural rather than predominantly in clinical genetic terms. It is not always easy then to extrapolate and interpret clearly the comparative findings.

Freud clearly indicated the reciprocal relation between memory and acting out when he stated that the patient reproduces instead of remembering (1941a); and in his paper on the two types of mental functioning (1911), he gave a formulation of the different stages in the development of communication which furnishes the fundamental background for understanding the acting out by the individual. It is apparent, too, that there can be no absolute line between the development of tendencies toward action as a general way of communication and that of the more specifically organized forms of acting out which may replace conflict-burdened memories, as indicated by Freud. Fenichel (1945b) pointed out that disturbances of the orality in the first months of life give an important etiological background for future acting out. This is emphasized again in a more recent paper by Altman (1957) in which there is the additional emphasis on the reciprocality of disturbance between mother and child in ways somewhat similar to those described by Szurek, Johnson, etc. In their cases, however, it would seem that the provocative stimulation of the child by the parent(s) was more severe and continuous, with greater impairment of superego development. Bird (1957) defined a somewhat comparable disturbance more specifically as resulting from a prolonged and accentuated symbiosis between mother and child causing a defective development with an incomplete differentiation between the child's ego and that of the mother. Ekstein and Friedman (1957), dealing especially with acting out of a delinquent type in adolescence, describe acting out not so much as merely a repetition of conflictual memory as an unconscious effort at solution of conflicts. They consider it to represent a more primitive stage of reality testing than is true in play action or play acting. The latter is seen as representing an effort to modify the past identification by new cue-taking. One suspects that such a condition might be more characteristic of acting out in adolescence than in other periods of life. Their conception seems related to that of Kanzer (1957b) on the relation of acting out to sublimation and reality testing.

The paper which gives a picture closest to the one I have presented is that of Spiegel (1954) who also stresses the massive nature of the acting out in his cases and the prominence of a sense of humiliation which is being warded off by the acting out. It is evident, however, that Spiegel's patients showed an extensive acting out both in and outside of the transference. He refers to their making acting out a way of life. The question has arisen in my mind how much some of my own cases, as well as the one reported by Spiegel, resemble the fate-neurosis type of hysteria described by Helene Deutsch in 1930. The precocious genital stimulation, with habitual masturbation generally without climactic discharge, would then form an important part of the "dispositional factor" mentioned by Deutsch, and would inevitably contribute to the peculiar malignancy of the oedipus complex.

Jan Frank emphasized both the tendency to imitativeness and the influence of multiple (split) authoritative figures in the childhood of acting-out patients (see Kanzer, 1957a). Zeligs's paper on "Acting In" (1957) is also pertinent to my material. He describes special types of body activity on the couch with postural attitudes which proved to be compromise representations of conflicts. These protect the ego from unconscious unacceptable impulses. He recognized them as masturbation equivalents which were also associated with troublesome amnesias. His observations have special significance for the one of my cases in which there were periods of rigidity with provocative silence, followed by the later development of repetitive expressive movements, not as deeply automatized as tics but a bit suggestive of them.

The literature on transference naturally contains many references to acting out. I would especially mention the 1951 paper of A. Reich on "Countertransference." This points clearly to the fact that, in a countertransference overidentification with the patient, there may be a kind of acting out on the part of the analyst which cooperates with and intensifies that of the patient. It probably is a clear reproduction of some of the early childhood situations described by Szurek et al., Johnson, Giffin, et al., Bird, Altman, and myself.[3]

---

[3] Acting out in the transference is discussed further in ch. 39.

CHAPTER THIRTY-SIX

Discussion of Bernard Brodsky's Paper on "Working Through" (1964)

It was a pleasure to read Dr. Brodsky's paper[1] which deals with a subject that has preoccupied and often baffled me (see chs. 12, 30, and 32). I found his discussion interesting and stimulating, and am grateful for it. He speaks of the *widening scope of working through*. I suspect that this widening is due not only to our increasing metapsychological knowledge, especially of ego development and of psychic structure, but also to the *widening scope of psychoanalytic therapy* itself, due to the growth of general knowledge of psychoanalysis on the part of the public, with increasing demands upon us to pay attention to a large group of patients who do not fit neatly into the earlier diagnostic categories, yet who may be able people, greatly in need of help.

Brodsky has taken as a starting point for discussion the definition of working through given by Ralph Greenson (1965b) as follows: "Working through is the analysis of those resistances and other factors which prevent insight from leading to significant and lasting changes" (p. 282). Brodsky quotes Greenson as enumerating the techniques of working through to be: repetition and elaboration of interpretation, and reconstruction of the past and its patterns, with the addition that the accurate reconstruction of the past seems the most capable of creating a sense of conviction

[1] Published as "Working Through: Its Widening Scope and Some Aspects of Its Metapsychology" (1967).

for the analysand. This conviction of the source of the neurotic patterns and of the rootedness of the interpretations in his own experience is achieved by the reconstructive work giving the analysand a sense of real familiarity with the walled-off, defended-against parts of himself. But Brodsky asks what the *modus operandi* of working through is, and focuses especially on the mastery of painful affects, in particular anxiety and humiliation, which must be accomplished in the interplay of transference neurosis and therapeutic alliance, with especial emphasis on the latter.

He thinks that it is this mastery which appreciably diminishes the adhesiveness of the neurotic patterns and so loosens or dislodges them. This can occur because the relative benignity and neutrality of the analyst provide an unparalleled situation for the anxiety to rise in relation to current situations and be interpreted by the analyst. Essentially the techniques are those mentioned by Greenson, but Brodsky considers that the essential area of operation is on the anxiety or other painful affect.

I would be inclined to agree with this, but wish to make certain additions to the discussion, considering the significance of the relation to reality and to reality testing, which is at least a concomitant and probably an essential part of working through, and should be scrutinized as part of the whole process. This is probably especially important in those cases in which anxiety or other painful affect are especially strong and stubborn in the course of treatment.

Brodsky quotes Valenstein's paper on "The Psycho-Analytic Situation" (1962) and Kris's paper on "The Recovery of Childhood Memories" (1956c), both of which have some bearing on this subject. In grappling with the problem of how working through leads to change in behavior and actions, Valenstein assigns the role of making insights more convincing to affect, the relevant emotions making the insights more subject to reality testing and rational cognitive evaluation, which lead to a dissolving of neutoric ego structuralization and thus make possible altered styles of ego functioning in the form of new action patterns. Kris also states the importance of transforming insight from intellectual into *total* experiences.

Now it seems to me that the actual move toward reality testing marks an important stage in the working through process. *First* of all, it implies that some insightful awareness of neurotic patterns has been achieved through the early analytic interpretative work. *Second,* the setting of the benign scrutiny of the therapeutic alliance has permitted a beginning loosening or softening of the rigidity of the neurotic patterns (whether affecting id, ego, or superego), not so much by abreaction as due to the analyst's attitude being already established as different from that of the people in the early situation in which the neurotic patterning had its inception so that the re-experience is in part a new experience. *Third,* reality testing implies getting a response from the "other" or "others" in the outer world, and not merely in that intermediate world of the analyst's office. As the internal loosening progresses, the response from the outside also changes and tends to solidify the modification going on in the analysand. The incipient change can generally hardly be thought of as a definite therapeutic gain until it does so begin to be reflected from the environment, and not merely subjectively felt by the analysand. This may be the total experience referred to by Kris. I think it may have been an emphasis on this, but with an impatience for quick results, that influenced Alexander in his ideas of the corrective experience.

This stage of working through always seems to me a very ticklish and repetitive therapeutic hazard, since the temptation of the analyst may be to seduce, encourage or in some way pressure the analysand in his wish to confirm such changes. But insofar as such attitudes on the part of the analyst may become positive or negative re-enactments of earlier parental attitudes, they risk weakening the analysand by establishing "corrective" behavior and auxiliary superegos. Moderation and careful timing of any such activity on the part of the analyst are essential. I feel confident that better results come when there is some conscious appreciation of the troublesome neurotic patterns, but the therapeutic correction is mostly silent and more automatized, taking on then some of the qualities of growth. Brodsky has touched on this certainly, and I am only restating and elaborating what he has said.

In regard to the relative importance, in working through, of the recovery of childhood memories compared to that of the realization of the patterning which has been established around the childhood memories, I would say with Kris that it is not the actual remembering of the events which is therapeutically so significant.

Certainly this is not valuable at all if it is divorced from working with the individual patterning which has been so set in motion by these experiences. But I do doubt whether the patterning can be adequately understood and in a sense claimed by the analysand without the recovery of critical events of childhood. I think that working with any group of memories interrelated in the process of screening does in fact inevitably uncover the progressive patterning. Stated in another way, the history of screen memories is an important part of the history of the establishment, shifts, substitutions, etc., of infantile defenses, and so may contribute much to the understanding of the developing neurotic patterns.

Screen affects seem to me much harder to deal with—especially that form of diffuse screening with anger which often takes the place of panic, shame, guilt, or jealousy. Here the anger is particularly difficult when it is frequent and of such proportions as to shut the patient off from any adequate communication with or receptivity toward the analyst. It permits a primitive projection to occur and temporarily destroys the therapeutic alliance. It seems then to be an erotized explosion with a temporary sense of exhilaration and power. It is closely related to the fabrication of crises as a way of neurotic progress in life; and I am not sure how much or in what ways mastery can be established.

I would return now to the topic of the influence of the special qualities of the analysand's sense of reality on the working through process. Perhaps one sees this set of problems most clearly when they appear in an exaggerated form in certain patients—in my experience, usually very able and sometimes definitely talented—who have an extraordinary ability to embellish reality with their own wishful fantasies or even to interchange reality and fantasy with unusually convincing agility. They are bright people, and I am convinced that in those cases that I have seen there is a special, probably constitutional, factor in the capacity for richness of fantasy and the ability to grasp the phenomenon of patterning as it occurs in the developments of childhood. But there have also usually been severely undermining influences in the early lives of these patients, so that their potential capacities for fantasy have developed overly luxuriantly and been used opportunistically for defense very early. A sense of drama is strong, and adds much to the secondary gain of the neurosis with every attempt to sustain this in the analytic setting. Such patients seem to progress well and convince themselves and often the analyst that they have made fundamental changes, which for short times seem to be reflected in constructive changes in relationships in the environment, but which may be—or seem to be—washed out again too readily. These patients may be in love with their own suffering, and have always a degree of voyeurism and a split in the ego development and functioning which permits an unusual degree of self-watching, and is much deeper than that required in the analytic situation. At times, however, this self-watching can genuinely be enlisted in the therapeutic alliance, but does not have the ordinary durability, and some residue of magic expectation is always a complication. Because of my interest in creativity, I have had several people come to me who showed these problems, which interfered with their work as well as with their analytic progress. Sometimes they were people of genuine creative ability, and sometimes this was a mirage, built on identifications and fantasies from one source or another beginning early in childhood. I mention these rather atypical cases, however, because they have given me a realization of how important an appraisal of the patient's working sense of reality is in the process of working through. There are certain aspects of Brodsky's case that suggest that the patient might have some of these problems.

I would add that in these patients, with an active and fluid interchange of reality and fantasy, there is sometimes an encapsulation of memories of very disturbing experiences which are guilt and anxiety provoking. These are valiantly defended through the very confusion of fantasy and reality, in a way to make the analysis almost interminable. I have discussed this somewhat in a paper dealing with "the secret" which is often withheld until the end of the analysis (see ch. 12).

CHAPTER THIRTY-SEVEN

Problems of Training Analysis (1966)

This paper is based on one prepared for a small meeting that took place before the Congress of the International Psycho-Analytical Association in Amsterdam, July 1965. It was circulated in advance to all analysts who were attending the special meeting. This version has very few revisions and includes a considerable portion of the introductory remarks made by the author.

When the discussion was planned, it was decided to limit the presentation to problems encountered in training analysis which have a direct impact on and may influence the outcome of the psychoanalytic process itself. Attempts might then be focused on understanding the extent and nature of the intrusions of training into the therapeutic process and the actual work of analyzing. These limits were imposed to exclude such other problems involved in the planning and administration of training as criteria for admission, selection of teachers, the curriculum, requirements for graduation, and others. There are also training problems which vary specifically according to the location of an institute; whether, for example, it is part of an academic, nonmedical, or a medical organization, or is a wholly independent institution. There are further problems too, much influenced by the structure of the community in which each institute has developed. Important as these are, and with due respect for the fact that they sometimes play an accessory part in the complication of the personal analysis of the student, still it seemed better not to attempt to include them in this paper lest the field under consideration be-

come so broad that the discussion might at this time become un-
manageable.

The literature is not comprehensively reviewed. Only a brief
summary of the main trends in training analysis published since
the Second World War is given. This survey of the literature,
made by the author in 1961 for the Committee on Psychoanalytic
Education of the American Psychoanalytic Association, served as
the basis of discussions in that committee (see ch. 34).[1]

As a practical expedient the review of the literature was limited
to the chief articles published in 1950 and after. This was a time
when the considerable growth in the size of institutes following
the Second World War had become somewhat stabilized. The development of analysis of the ego had furthermore progressed so far
that it was being more thoroughly assimilated, and it was influencing not only psychoanalytic instruction but the conduct of
analysis itself. There were thus two important changes: one intrinsic in the analysis of applicants for training, the other in the
organizational setting in which training analyses were conducted.

The articles reviewed were those of A. Freud (1950),[2] and
G. Bibring, M. Gitelson, Grotjahn, Nacht, Lampl-de Groot, Heimann, M. Balint, all of them presented at the International Congress in 1953 and published in the following year. There were also
some other articles not specifically reviewed (Nielson, 1954; Calef,
1954; Weigert, 1955a, 1955b; Windholz, 1955).[3] From then until
1960, there were a few articles but no comprehensive dealing with
the subject until the Survey of Psychoanalytic Education in the
United States (1960). It was the philosophy of the surveyors,
Lewin and Ross, to report on the conditions, standards, and official practices in the various institutes throughout the United
States, rather than to enter at once into any statement or intensive
study of the psychodynamics of the problems of the individual
student. The report stresses throughout the prevalent conflict be-

---

[1] It contributed to a paper later published by David Kairys (1964).

[2] This paper was originally written in 1938 as a report to the International
Educational Commission in Paris and first published in 1950. My translation was
obtained through the courtesy of Dr. Paul Kramer of Chicago.

[3] One also should mention a discussion by Bernfeld written in 1953 for the San
Francisco Psychoanalytic Society and published in 1962. He stated his strong conviction that organized institutes were so strongly "teacher-centered" as to interfere
with sound training of psychoanalytic students; but he did not take note of many
of the specific problems we are considering here.

tween the therapeutic and the administrative (sometimes including the pedagogic) roles of the training analyst, and that this conflict is acknowledged but cannot be wholly resolved by shifts from one aspect to another of the training analyst's functions. Lewin and Ross find it important that the environment in which different institutes operate influences their special problems. The basic troublesome conflict of roles among training analysts has been recognized to some degree time and time again since personal analysis of the prospective analyst was found to be essential in his training.

Another change which has occurred in the principles of training and has influenced its practice is the shift from the expectation that students regarded as normal would be adequately served by shorter terms of analysis than are usually required by analytic patients. The literature indicates, however, that this expectation was originally based on the absence of overt clinical symptoms or clear evidence of definite defects of character and of gross instabilities. At a time when psychoanalysis was struggling to establish itself against formidable opposition and prejudice, superior intellectual endowment and achievement were valued together with indications of great interest in making a life work of analysis.

It soon became apparent that the absence of overt symptoms was not infrequently associated with unusually rigidly organized ego-syntonic defenses which either defied analysis or required a much longer and more painstaking analysis than was necessary in applicants with clearly defined neuroses. Such candidates as appear normal by virtue of massive defenses do not readily empathize with the neurotic patient. They are inclined to rely on intellectual insight into the deeper aspects of neuroses, and require too great a systematic approach in dealing with neuroses. They are unaware of, or impatient with, many fundamental emotional nuances and implications in the irrational aspects of their patients' productions.

It should be remembered that the plan of training applicants was determined pragmatically and empirically, according to the needs both of the developing science of psychoanalysis and of the changing conditions of its practice. It developed even through the periods of two world wars in which the need for psychological understanding and therapy became imperative. Especially in the Second War it gained many adherents through the practical evidence that men trained in psychoanalysis were better able to understand and resolve problems of the troops (under conditions in which the technique of psychoanalysis was not in the least feasible), simply because they understood them better from the depth of their knowledge from psychoanalysis than was the case in the disciplinary and regimentational methods of the neurologists and of the behavioral psychiatrists and the psychologists.

We are now in the third generation of psychoanalysts. In the first, Freud was clearly the master and the great leader; the science was in its beginning, and the attitude of the medical profession and of the public was suspicious and hostile. In this setting those whose interest was so enlisted that they sought to become analysts did so out of conviction from a sturdy scientific curiosity and an imagination which responded to Freud's discoveries. Those who were psychiatrists were often influenced by their realization that other forms of treatment were inefficient.

All this of course meant that the original group of analysts was small. All or most of its members were individually chosen and were, in a sense, "special"; they were bound together by the ties of intense dedication and enthusiasm that emanate from a great leader. This was intensified by the then unpopularity of their interests. At the present time the degree of acceptance of psychoanalysis has enormously increased, though it varies greatly from place to place. In the United States there are localities where it may be looked upon with almost as much distrust and hostility as that which first greeted Freud's discoveries. But, by and large, it has become definitely established and has even gone through a period of overpopularity such that, as was so marked in the period immediately after the Second World War, more young professional people sought to become analysts than could possibly be trained.

While there is a nostalgic yearning among many older analysts (shared by younger ones as well) to return to the individualized and less formal training of the past, and to see this as the answer to many of our present dilemmas, this is not feasible. Furthermore, many of the problems to be discussed in this paper were apparently existent among the earlier groups, and some may even then have been more intense. Time cannot be turned back, and with the increased number of student analysts it is virtually impossible to divorce the personal analysis from its reference to the training organization and setting. Even in those few psychoanalytic institutes in which the student is not formally accepted until he has had a certain period of his personal analysis, or has "completed" it, insofar as he undertakes it with the intention of becoming a student and in most instances is being analyzed by a training analyst, the shadow of the institute still intrudes itself both on the aspiring student and on his analyst. The training situation leads inevitably to a conflict of aims in the student between that of being relieved of his neurosis and that of starting his career as an analyst as soon as possible. Career often exceeds therapy in importance. In his analyst a reciprocal conflict may supervene with a division of his interest between a concern about his analysand's welfare as a patient and his involvement in the student's success in undertaking his career.

It is evident that conditions of training vary greatly from place to place. The whole historical development of training is more or less represented in the spectrum of problems presented in different places, dependent on the cultural milieu influencing the nature of the community response to a psychoanalytic point of view. We cannot hope to cover all the diverse conditions of psychoanalytic training, and it should not be assumed that the content of this discussion is only influenced by the setting in which we work. We shall depend on others to diversify, correct, and elaborate these impressions according to the degree to which they apply to other communities.

STATEMENT OF PROBLEMS

The presentation of the ways in which the personal analysis of the student may be interfered with or complicated by the setting of the training situation has been divided into three sections based, perhaps arbitrarily, on the stages of his progress in the training program. These are first, the *opening phase* in which the student begins his personal analysis; second, the *middle period* in which he becomes involved in attendance at seminars and lectures, and is undertaking supervised analysis; third, the *closing phase* usually extending to some time after he has finished formal teaching. Problems are grouped under these headings according to the phase during which a given problem seemed to occur most frequently and most severely. It is evident that the timing and the severity of problems depend largely on individual situations.

THE OPENING PHASE

Practically, we may at present divide accepted applicants for psychoanalytic training into three groups. (1) Those who have had some kind of psychoanalytic treatment before applying for training. Such treatment has obviously been undertaken for therapeutic reasons, but has led to a further interest in psychoanalysis, perhaps as a career in the ordinary sense or perhaps with an even deeper sense of dedication to it as an art or a science, as the case may be. This is the group which includes some individuals who, in modern times, most nearly approximate the original group who responded through the avenue of their personal needs and interests to Freud's discoveries. (2) Those who may or may not have had such a period of analysis but whose psychiatric training has been in a psychoanalytically sophisticated hospital or training center in which analysis is thought to be the *sine qua non* of thorough psychiatric training.[4] (3) Those relatively naïve individuals, often from outlying districts, who have read little or much of psychoanalytic literature, and come with a zeal for training which often masks a (sometimes desperate) need for treatment. This need may be quite conscious, or more or less unconscious. Such students have no acquaintance with analysts, except those whose publications they have read. They may or may not have understood the psychoanalytic literature they read. They are generally earnest, and frequently have a quite severe neurosis.

In any case, becoming a student arouses or increases their narcissistic and competitive problems. The student's analysis is no longer an isolated relationship, for both he and his analyst are members of a competitive group. The student first becomes aware that he is one of the successful ones among a large group of applicants. He has suddenly attained the advantage of being one of the "in" group, often in contrast to friends or colleagues who have appeared to him to be as suitable as he, or even superior. This is especially true among those students who have had preliminary

---

4 Somewhat similar conditions obtained particularly in the years after World War II, when it was extremely difficult for veterans' hospitals to get adequate staff unless the hospital was close enough to a psychoanalytic institute that members might consider the possibility of beginning psychoanalytic training during their service.

psychiatric training in hospitals or organizations where psychoanalysts are on the staff and many psychoanalytically tinged lectures
have been given and psychoanalytically oriented psychotherapy
and research undertaken. Such programs may have had much of
value to offer him, but they may also contribute to his problems
during psychoanalytic training. The narcissistic aura of being an
analyst sometimes unfortunately gains a magic quality which may
be a handicap in the personal analysis. Verbalization of analytic
concepts has sometimes begun before there is the basic experience
for genuine assimilation. As with the child who talks precociously
and attracts attention by his cleverness, such early glibness may
become a defense against real recognition of therapeutic need, and
a resistance and rather superficial form of intellectualization.

The existence of psychoanalysis and some general idea of its
basic findings have been so long well known that most students
have in one way or another had some contact with analysts. They
have, therefore, various incipient transference attitudes already
established. In the further development of these it makes some
difference whether he has already been in a therapeutic analysis, or
is to begin his preparatory analysis as soon as possible after his
acceptance for training.

In the latter case, he is confronted by the need to select his own
analyst from a list of training analysts, or he is assigned to a training analyst, generally by a committee. One method or the other
may be used, and in some institutes both methods are available as
alternative possibilities, or in combined form. In the last instance
the student is given the choice between two or among three analysts. In some of the larger institutes the choice may be made by
direct assignment, and only if the student and the analyst seem
definitely incompatible is a second choice made. While it seems
desirable to permit some modicum of autonomy and allow some
selectivity to the student, this tends to be reduced by its cumber-
someness and the amount of time involved in multiple interviews
closely following the admissions interviews.

In some instances analysts, who are friends of the applicant, intercede unofficially with members of the placement committee and
in this way a student may indirectly have more of a choice than is
recorded in the minutes of the committee, even in an institute
where the placement is made ostensibly only by a committee.

Subtle complications of basic problems may later arise in these instances, even though there may be the advantage of an otherwise expeditious and in many respects an essentially suitable placement. Such intercession may have been made with or without the student's knowledge but, even when great discretion has been exercised, it generally becomes either known or suspected by the favored student and gradually by his colleagues as well. One such intercession tends to breed another.

To the candidate it means that he is a special student, even further "in," and that his analyst is a special analyst. This can, although it does not always, make for serious complications in an analysis depending on the attitude, skill, and freedom of the analyst in sensing and analyzing it. Insofar as such intercession has been unofficial and is contrary to the printed procedures, it may promote an insidious, fundamental distrust of analysis and analysts which cannot be frankly faced but is overcorrected by an intensified "positive" transference. It contributes then to unhealthy identifications in which the unresolved, equivocal transference later becomes acted out in the formation of cliques and in distorted political ambitions to attain power in society and institute matters. There is something very seductive about an atmosphere of conspiracy in good company. Occasionally, too, the neglected negative aspects of the transference emerge and contribute to later deviant theories and practices.

If the student is less favored, has no special friend at court, and has become aware that some others do, not only are his jealousy and resentment enormously aroused but his feelings of inferiority may be increased and projected onto his analyst. This is not only a confirmation to him of any similar jealousies and rivalries in his childhood, but it is now intensified to a particularly enlarged scale.

It has been my experience that the new student rather generally includes "His Institute" among his early transferences, reacting at first as though it were a person either identical with or at least consort to his analyst. The tendency is to want and to expect special understanding and tolerance and thus to feel betrayed by indications of differences in procedure in the case of other students. The analysis then starts with unwarrantedly negative feelings which delay its progress. But under any circumstances as soon as the student becomes the member of a group, his enhanced, competitive strivings are alerted and include his analyst (affirm-atively or negatively), as well as himself.

The syncretism of the dual role of the analyst, who must act both as personal therapist and as judge, comes into play when the decision must be made whether or not the student should proceed to take courses. This occurs generally a year or two after the be-ginning of the analysis, but varies in different institutes. The decision may be postponed in individual cases, but such a post-ponement is then generally an extra severe blow since it becomes known to the student's classmates. The student also becomes realistically aware of the analyst as judge, as the analyst is the only representative of the institute who has knowledge of him beyond what was revealed in connection with his acceptance as a student.

The situation is further complicated by the fact that if this decision must be made fairly early in the analysis, the student may not yet be aware of or ready to analyze the very conditions which may have made his analyst cautious. In cases where the clinical picture shows such severe and malignant features that the analyst feels that there is little chance that the student can ever qualify, the decision, however unfortunate, is simpler. There are, how-ever, other initial psychoanalytic complications from which the analyst expects an ultimately favorable outcome yet where a care-ful choice must be made between allowing the student to begin courses or insisting on delay, knowing that he is not only not yet ready for this type of study but that attendance at classes may seriously fortify his defenses and resistances. This seems to be one of the most ticklish areas in the process of analytic training.

Some of the clinical problems which are most difficult here are those that occur among very bright and fundamentally sensitive students, seemingly well organized, with a history of uninterrupted academic success, sometimes associated with qualities of lead-ership. In these instances it proves to have a background of strong compulsive character traits. Anxiety has so far been dispelled through successful intellectual competition, and there are few symptoms of which the student is aware. In my experience in these instances, there is usually a moderate to severe disturbance in the sexual life. The facts frequently do not even emerge until late in the analysis because the degree of narcissism is such that the deficiency in object relationship is not sensed and the sexual disturbance is not a matter of complaint unless there is an almost complete impotence. The susceptibility to reinforcement of the major defenses is especially high with respect to involvement in the academic aspect of analytic training, and the vulnerability to narcissistic collapse by delay in being admitted to participation in it is also equally great.

THE MIDDLE PERIOD

We shall consider the period of study in classroom and seminar, which is simultaneous with the personal analysis, as the middle period of the training analysis. There is now a solidification in the student of a sense of group participation, and there may be an enrichment through the sharing of common experiences. There is a definite advancement in his identification as an analyst; and the strengthening of his aim to be an effective analyst may in many instances reinforce his determination to see his personal analysis through, no matter how tough the going may be. The professional zeal, if it is fused with the real grasp of the necessity to uncover and lighten the neurotic areas in himself, may do much to compensate for any lessening of the therapeutic aims at the outset due to the division of interests with which he had entered training. It is inevitable that in a classroom there is the stimulus for an increase in competitiveness among students, with a flowering of exhibitionistic and other narcissistic elements. Insofar as these narcissistic wishes achieve satisfaction or are met with severely realistic affronts in a setting closely associated with his own analyst in the student's feelings, the experience may complicate the personal analysis especially if—as is common in acting out—it is not readily accessible in the analysis.

If the student at this time takes the further steps of participating in clinical seminars and of beginning supervised analysis, his identification of himself as an analyst generally becomes fixed. This seems inevitable. Training today is different from that of the early years of analysis when students from all over the world went to Vienna or Berlin where they spent one, two, or more years in training. When subsequently they re-established themselves in this country, they might or might not have gone into analytic practice. If they had, it often had the elements of an initial professional start. At present, the student more frequently takes his training in a city in or near the one in which he lives; or he goes first to a city where he intends to establish a practice. If he is not already established in the practice of psychotherapy, he commonly establishes an office when he undertakes supervised psychoanalytic treatment of patients. In the eyes of the community he is an analyst, and certainly the actual treatment of his patients confirms this ambition in his own eyes. This means that after this step is taken he is very much more vulnerable practically as well as subjectively if he suffers delays or disqualification in his training; yet the initial step of undertaking supervised work must often be taken before it is soundly possible to prognosticate his ability to function adequately as an analyst.

The rest of the presentation of the problems of this middle period of the training analysis is organized under three headings: first, the intrusion of reality into the analytic relationship between analyst and student; second, complication in the transference or the countertransference; third, increase in certain defenses in the training situation when classroom work is concurrent with personal analysis.

Under the first heading, most analysts would agree that in order to keep the field of analysis as clear as possible from extraneous contamination, it is well to limit association between the analyst and the analysand to the analysis itself. This is not only because the therapeutic analytic relationship becomes contaminated by artifacts which may conceal the true feelings, or are at least very distracting—much as artifacts confuse a microscopic field of examination—but if an active relationship (social or professional) is established between analyst and analysand outside of the consulting room, there is the risk that it may involve a repetition of elements of past conflicts as yet unresolved in the analysand. In other words, whether such outside contact is episodic or continuing, it often furnishes a medium for the development of an acting out which is prone to become mutual. The pressure of the neurotic pattern in the analysand unconsciously urges him to provoke or seduce the analyst into a response gratifying to his neurosis, rather than being strictly appropriate to the realistic work or situation. If this involves the repetition of an older situation which the analysand has not yet brought into the analysis, the analyst may be quite unaware of the nature and extent of his own cooperation in such an acting out, or in fact that it is an acting out at all.

For these reasons the solution frequently offered that problems arising from extra-analytic relationships will be analyzed at one time or another seems to me overly optimistic and tinged with rationalization. It has been my experience that this may certainly occur when the episode of acting out has involved analytic "material" which had already entered into the analytic process but has been incompletely worked through; but in instances where it represents the first eruption of the disturbing complex—which actually has been promoted by the stimulus and the anxiety of the contact in reality with the analyst—it not infrequently becomes further encapsulated. This means that it cannot be analyzed, that it makes for future trouble both in the personal and the professional life of the student. Sometimes it may later be identified and worked with in a subsequent analysis with another analyst. Such strangulated transference problems may be the source of a good many ambivalent attitudes toward analysis itself among analysts.

In my judgment the repetition of an infantile conflict—in which an analyst unwittingly provides the means for an acting out in the transference—may strengthen the effects of the infantile experience and render later working through more difficult. This untoward effect is probably due to the fact that in that part of the relationship to the analyst which lends itself to the development of the therapeutic alliance, the analyst is expected, both consciously and unconsciously, to conform to the ideal of the parent who will be both all understanding and completely neutral. This expectation is encouraged by the restrictions of the analytic situation, which seems to guarantee safe ground for the emergence of the elements of the transference neurosis. No analyst can completely justify these expectations; but if unfortunately he contributes to a failure corresponding exactly to one that the analysand had earlier experienced, the effect may be sharper and sometimes disastrous.

Such problems are more likely to occur in analysis in which the student is in a working cooperation of one kind or another outside of the analysis, as, for example, in hospitals or social organizations. The danger of complications which may jeopardize the neutrality of the transference is even greater when the student is directly or indirectly dependent on his analyst for approval and remuneration for his work.

Reality inevitably intrudes into the analytic relationship from contact between analyst and analysand in the classroom and other fortuitous contacts in an institute. This may be somewhat minimized and controlled by special arrangements and need not approach the extent that readily occurs in hospital and other organizational work.

There is furthermore at present an endeavor among some analysts to "change the public image" of psychoanalysis by increasing his activity in various social causes, through radio and television and journalistic reporting. This is a relinquishment of any serious attempt to preserve even the relative anonymity of the analyst. The value of the time-honored usage of the couch with the analyst's chair behind it would seem to be vitiated by the television screen out in front, even if the latter is seen only in the mind's eye of analyst and analysand. I believe these problems are worthy of examination, discussion, and the consideration of how and how much their results can be analyzed in an analysis itself.

Second, we come to the consideration of complications of the transference and countertransference during this middle period of training. It has already been emphasized that a latent or apparent transference to an institute and some of its representatives has been formed in some students at the time of their acceptance for training. While these transferences become focused in the relationship to the person of the analyst during the first period of studentship, they later become diffused and may be displaced especially to teachers or supervisors.

In other words, the transference relationship becomes split, and parts of it may tend to be removed from the personal analyst. The patterning of this is always influenced in part by the constellations of family relationships in the student's life. This kind of distribution of transference attitudes occurs of course in group situations in life, entirely independent of any analytic process and may be the basis of intense rivalries and tensions in almost any organization. But in analytic training, the very intensification of the transference by the personal analysis and the special activation in this way of previously dormant infantile attitudes makes studentship more significant and susceptible to disturbances. The possibility of splitting of the transference among the training personnel is pretty generally recognized by experienced analysts. It is nonetheless frequently ignored in the very instances in which it is most powerful. An unwary analyst may be too ready to accept such attitudes, however persistent, as though they were entirely the reality problems which naturally enough always play a part in them.

This raises the question: how much does countertransference play a reciprocal role? Certainly there are rivalries and jealousies among training analysts. Students may preconsciously sense and utilize these in provocative and rationalizing ways. But let us return to the problems of the training analyst. In any analysis it may be necessary under special circumstances for the analyst to make his analysand aware not only of the latter's disturbed attitudes, but even of the distortions and neurotic behavior of those associated with him. Interpretations to him of the behavior of those in the analysand's milieu seem to me to be something which should be used only rarely and with extreme caution. If such interpretation is given incautiously and involves colleagues who are active in his training, it can obscure not only essential elements in the student's neurosis, but create a disruption in the progress of his training and at the very least promote his ambivalence, encouraging a polarization in his transference. It has the greater force to the student since he is aware that his analyst knows the colleague well; hence the interpretation may at first be taken as a pronouncement of a fact rather than as an interpretative deduction from what the analysand has related.

There are of course problems arising from countertransference which occur in training analyses very much as they might in any analysis with an analyst in whom unresolved neurotic residues interfere with his adequate understanding of the analysand's neurosis. There are, however, three other interrelated main areas in which problems of the training analyst may promote countertransference interferences worth mentioning: first, overzealousness to have the student do well and show well academically; second, overt or covert active participation in effecting arrangements in regard to training matters which are, however, outside the sphere of the personal analysis; third, endeavors to keep the student's allegiance to him once the training analysis is finished. Finally, problems derived from or operating in conjunction with these have to do with the use and vicissitudes of the student's identification with his analyst.

Naturally an analyst has some interest in the welfare of his analysand. This is inherent in the empathy which is essential for carrying on the work. But unless this interest is combined with and largely devoted to a concern for tracking down and rooting out the analysand's neurosis, an analyst runs the risk of exploiting his analysand to gratify his own emotional and narcissistic needs— his wishes to be loved and admired; particularly to appear successful. From an unconscious fear of his own sadism, or that of his analysand, he may be overly kind and too reluctant to allow his patient the necessary suffering. Any of these defects leads to too strong a therapeutic zeal with a failure to analyze adequately many important areas of conflict in the analysand.

The training of analysts in an institute seems to favor increased competitiveness among analysts as well as among students. The training analyst's intense wish for his student to excel is sometimes all too apparent and not always helpful. It may lead him to advise the student whom to seek as supervising analysts or to arrange this for him, even if this is not the custom. He may furthermore inadvisedly give opinions regarding decisions about curriculum or the content of courses, or refer patients to his analysand.

In some larger institutes small cliques develop, and if a student is being analyzed by a member of one circle, he will almost surely have his supervision from others in the same circle. All of these exceptions to the regular way of conducting an analysis, in its relation to other aspects of training, give the student a feeling of being specially favored though he may be robbed of wider and more varied experiences, especially in his supervision. His narcissism is fed, and the analysis of negative transferences is impeded. When an analyst grants special favors to a student, makes him a gift in a sense, only rarely does the student analysand bring the matter up in his analysis later. The analyst is apt to have little inclination to respond to cues which indicate such a need, and to which he might ordinarily be sensitive. This at least is my impression from subsequent analyses required among analysands, and from discussing the subject with colleagues.

It is paradoxical that these problems of the induction into training by excessively benevolent and other exceptional procedures which tend to bind the student to his analyst seem to occur quite frequently among the older well-established analysts of some repute. It certainly cannot be attributed to their lack of analytic understanding. It seems rather to be connected with a spotty blindness to their own narcissism, protected by the defensive mechanism of isolation. Visibly it appears that there is a strong and only partly conscious drive to be a leader, rationalized as a need to keep a close relationship with promising younger colleagues, even perhaps "to save" them for the future of psychoanalysis. One influence may be the fact that a fair proportion of these older analysts were in their early training at a time when the principles of training and practice were in process of development and incompletely formulated. It was a time when there was an extraordinarily close bond among those who were struggling to establish a new science. The tendency of the young analyst to repeat what he experiences in his own analysis, even when he does not approve of it and "knows better," has been variously observed. It is conceivable that this tendency may persist or be revived among older analysts when centers of training are being established in new areas under conditions which somewhat suggest the pioneer days of psychoanalysis. The pioneer analyst in an authoritative position which permits him his individual variations and exceptions in the conduct of training is most conspicuously transparent to an outsider observing small training groups where two or three people are the core of the training activity. It is nevertheless also often present, but much less obviously, in the larger training centers.

Another problem of transference, and sometimes of countertransference, based largely on competition among training analysts (omitted from the original paper) was brought to our attention by Dr. Rudolph Loewenstein. He described the bewildering confusion in transferences when there are strong tensions of rivalry between a student's analyst and his supervisor. A divergence of point of view concerning technical handling or even of theoretical considerations may be puzzling but ultimately an enrichment to the student, if these attitudes are not combined with personal rivalries and resentments; but a dispute between a training analyst and a supervisor who consciously or unconsciously exchange messages through the student, catches the student in the middle and invites reinforcement of his familial conflicts. This then may not only impede the progress of the student's analysis but sometimes involves him in practical dilemmas as well.

In a personal communication Dr. Brian Bird suggested the additional consideration of a countertransference which tends to impede students by the analyst's giving unduly pessimistic reports about them, showing a seeming reluctance to have them graduate and become training analysts themselves. Superficially this is quite the opposite from the motivation of the training analyst who exploits his students, makes interventions on their behalf, and wants them not only to excel but to remain his satellites; nevertheless these opposite countertransferences may occur in one training analyst with regard to different students. In such instances the ambition of the training analyst to retain power seems central to his countertransference. Both attitudes can be rationalized by him as having necessary superego values. Both appear to have their roots in insufficiently resolved oedipal problems. In both instances there seems to be the desire to retain an influence over the student.

There are some misanthropic training analysts whose disturbance appears to be due to an unresolved negative transference which has been displaced onto an institute. In one instance at least, there was a deeply positive conviction regarding the fundamentals of psychoanalysis associated with a rigid, persistent doubt about certain specifics. It seemed that this analyst, as well as others less well known to me, was himself caught in quite a severe neurosis in which obsessional elements were superficially apparent. Such people may distrust themselves and fundamentally wish to hide; consequently, their participation in the activities of an institute is likely to be perfunctory, or to be exaggerated in a way to be self-defeating. Their work may deteriorate into an essentially educational or psychotherapeutic approach. They would probably be happier not to be training analysts, but the narcissistic wound in withdrawing from it is too great. These analysts may doubt their students because they doubt their own analyses of them. Generalizing from limited experience, it seems that they are not among those who try to hold their students in postanalytic allegiance or to form coteries of former students; nevertheless they may claim credit when a former student develops to take an important place in institute or society affairs, even though this may have occurred after a second analysis with someone else. The two orders of their ambivalence are thus reflected in their conflicting countertransferences toward their students. All this leads into questions involved in the nature of the identification between analyst and student. This is a complex and intricate relationship to which I cannot hope to do justice.

THE CLOSING PHASE

It seems better to speak of the closing phase of the training analysis than of its termination. It is evident that in many ways training impedes and interferes with the full development of the therapeutic aspects of a personal analysis. There are experienced analysts in whose judgment personal analysis during training is so complicated or even deformed as to make it therapeutically almost valueless. In the opinion of some, the training analysis had best be accepted largely as a teaching situation, a truly didactic performance in which therapeutic goals are secondary. A therapeutic analysis may then be sought at a later time according to the individual's awareness of unresolved problems as he discovers them in the course of his practice. Such a second analysis is then for one's self, in contrast to the first, which was for training.

There is much to be said for this. It nevertheless is apparent that few situations are this clear-cut, and that in the period of formal training there is an amalgam of training and therapy for personal demands that cannot be postponed. However, when the therapeutic needs are not urgent, the didactic elements in the training can be usefully promoted without so far reinforcing the defenses by intellectualization and its accompanying withdrawal from emotional problems that the idea of a later therapeutic analysis will not be abandoned as unnecessary. Stated in another way, it seems that the delicate part of such a training (didactic) analysis consists in dealing with the blend of gratification of the student's intellectual interests with sufficient stirring of his emotional problems to make him aware of the probability of increased anxiety as he later works with his patients. Unless he is alerted in some way to this possibility, there is great likelihood that he will drift into a repetition of his own didactic analysis with his patients. He will then tend to teach them how to think about themselves instead of analyzing them. He may himself become a theorist, bewildered or impatient with clinical complications which seem not to fit his theory. Such analysts frequently disqualify an unusually large number of their patients as being unanalyzable; or they may remain satisfied with conducting a predominantly intellectual form of analysis.

There were some instances of this kind in which the young analyst tended to develop a stereotyped theoretical approach to therapy which in the end became a caricature of psychoanalysis. This approach ignored clinical research, and because of the insistent demands of his intellectual narcissism (which bore the brunt of the analyst's own untouched emotional conflicts) he attempted more and more to make a closed and absolute theoretical system which gave him an illusion of safety.

I do not sufficiently understand the extensive and subtle ramifications of the identification between analyst and analysand to clarify their advantages and dangers. Some considerations which have impressed me are noted in the hope that discussion will add to the understanding of these and other problems.

It has been pointed out by some that the identification of the student analysand with his analyst may do much to repair the divided aims (therapy and career) with which the student generally approaches his training. The wish to be an analyst then fortifies him in the need to rid himself of his neurosis as part of the process of qualifying. While this may often be true, it sometimes miscarries. The student may make his identification on an infantile, imitative level in which interpretations are accepted compliantly rather than with a full experiencing of their meaning. The student characteristically then promptly discovers the need for making similar interpretations to his patients. Certain very narcissistic students inevitably react in this way; however, it depends not only on the character of the student but on the reaction of his training analyst as well.

It has seemed to me that this danger might be greater when the analyst was a person of some prestige in his analytic group. This is an added difficulty because the student feels that the analyst, so experienced or renowned, *must* be right. Unless the student is exceptionally tough minded, and in considerable neurotic distress as well, he may achieve a facsimile of self-understanding.

The analyst not infrequently becomes a "family-romance-father" through whom he may win at a professional level the success which he is seeking. This often not only leaves the fundamental oedipal conflict unresolved, but results in a hidden homosexually tinged relationship in which the tie to the professional relationship may appear to outweigh in importance even the personal emotional ties. The negative aspects of the relationship to the analyst are then readily projected onto anyone who criticizes him.

How does this identification come about? It is my belief that the matrix of the transference lies in the early period of the mother-child relationship, involving especially the period of the development of speech. Ingredients from this early state are regularly remobilized in the analytic situation with the analysand in a passive position while the analyst is near at hand in an atmosphere of quiet safety. This guarantees the basis of confidence, which will further the development both of the transference alliance and of the transference neurosis. This is an optimal climate then for the progress of the analysis so long as the analyst actually remains neutral. If, however, he grants special indulgences to the student, making him gifts in the form of advice, intercessions in his behalf, or by other benevolences, the student's reactions to these circumstances may combine with and vitiate the clarity of parts of the developing transference neurosis. Even more importantly, there is an increase in the infantile narcissism which infiltrates the therapeutic alliance and weakens the mature, self-critical functioning of the ego. The therapeutic alliance may be so jeopardized that it tends to be replaced by an infantile dependence on the analyst whose interpretations have become a voice of benevolent authority. In the most extreme cases, the student's copying of his analyst may progress to a startling degree, encompassing mannerisms, interests, and attitudes toward life as well as technical procedures in analyzing. The force of this undesirable analytic authority is apt to be greatest where the analyst is well known for his ability, and yet provides these indulgences. The influence of these combined factors is almost unshakable.

As has been mentioned, attendance at theoretical courses, with their extensive reading programs, sometimes reinforces defenses by intellectualization, especially in students in whom this is an already formed defense which has worked successfully for them in the past in promoting academic progress, generally with a warding off of the emotional conflicts. Their intellectual functioning and their ego ideals have an unusually high narcissistic value to them. Keen observation of patients takes the place of true empathy.

For many other students, exposure to the teaching of theoretical concepts is a real help in the progress of their own analyses. The understanding so gained, piecemeal and even blurred as it often appears to be, serves then to crystallize insights which they have been struggling to gain. The subjective feeling and the reaction is similar to the effect of a specially well-timed and succinct interpretation. This result seems to have come from the organization of various elements of their insight, under the influence of a degree of distance and impersonal objectivity which relieves their floundering. A paradoxical state of affairs sometimes appears in the classroom. Such students characteristically seem not to "show up well" in class; they often appear to be puzzled for they assimilate theory slowly and only after they have reapplied it to and tested it on themselves and on their patients.

Such a favorable reaction resembles what the analyst sometimes encounters in the analyses among certain of his patients. These, at certain stages, make great gains from the grasp of a simple formulation of some principle of dynamic organization which enables them to proceed to more detailed self-revelation and scrutiny in the processes of working through.

A still further area of complication for the student analysand lies in the invasion of his personal analysis by elements of his analytic work with patients. This is of varying degrees and types, and at the very least furnishes another dimension in his analysis. It might well have been discussed in the section having to do with the middle period of studentship, for it may begin as soon as the student begins to analyze. In my experience it most often flourishes after he has begun to analyze without supervision. There are probably few student analyses, or reanalyses of analysts, in which this does not occur to some extent. The effect is sometimes like looking at a lighted screen on which a picture is projected in which the main character and narrator holds up another extensive screen with his own picture, which is, however, only spottily illuminated.

This intrusive effect may be negligible or it may be quite confusing and represent a considerable resistance in the student who unconsciously wishes to distract his analyst from himself by exhibiting his own competence. This is conspicuous when the student recounts or refers to his special interests in, or to his successes with, his patients. As with defenses, it often combines a degree of resistance in the analysand who has an unconscious need to reach himself in an indirect way by describing, comparing, or implicitly contrasting his own problems with those of others. This may not be very different from the analysis of patients in which parents endlessly recount problems of their children, or of their siblings, as detours from themselves.

Among students, the latter defense is followed and evaluated with more difficulty, partly because the communications are more fragmentary and the analyst is less well informed of the basic emotional relationship between the student analyst and his patient. He is often ignorant too of the nature of the latter's neurosis. If he asks for further details he runs the risk of diverting the associative flow and so strengthening the resistance. Quite often the student's references to his patient contain a hidden plea for help or act as a seduction of the analyst to advise him or enter into clinical discussion with him. This may be because he is really in need of help or because unconsciously he wishes to turn the analysis into a relationship with a colleague rather than continue to be an analysand. The ability of the training analyst to see through the complex defenses may sometimes be impaired by his countertransference. How he can deal immediately with this situation determines the chances that there may or may not be ultimate benefits to the analysand. It depends on the extent of his awareness of the various complexities of which it is composed.

There is one more set of problems in the closing phase of a student's analysis which demands mention even though it cannot be satisfactorily answered, nor can the direction of a search for answers be clearly indicated. Stated in one way these problems have to do with timing the conclusion of a student's analysis. Should it be prolonged beyond graduation and brought to a natural conclusion when the realization is reached that the major areas of neurotic conflict have been worked through? From other angles it may involve other questions. (1) What will be the effect of graduation on the student's personal analysis? Graduation usually implies the official recognition of the student's acceptance as an independent analyst and removes him from the limitations of student status. (2) What are the criteria for a student's graduation? (3) What are the effects of continuing a student's analysis uninterruptedly into his postgraduate period? What also is the effect on him of keeping secret his continued analysis, or a second analysis entered into after he has become an active member of his institute or society? In a broader sense these questions belong to problems of the training period; technically they might be excluded.

The nature of the closing phase of the student's analysis in his formal training must, however, still be examined. This seems to me to depend in good measure on the strength and quality of his neurotic, narcissistic investment in being an analyst, and the degree to which this has been analyzed and modified during the analysis. Ideally, then, the closing phase will be marked by the assiduous and detailed working through of the major neurotic conflicts—as in any analysis.

In the analysis of those who are not students there is ordinarily a stage reached in which both analyst and analysand agree that the analysand is ready to depend on himself, having gained the means to do so; the association of patient and therapist then ceases. There is no further relationship, and any that might occur socially is avoided if possible. There are nevertheless those analysands who contrive occasions for social relationships with the analyst. There is at any rate a cooling-off period during which the analysand gets his own stance more securely and has the inner obligation to use or to discard whatever insights he had gained in his analysis. It would be naïve to assume that all transference reactions to the analyst cease with the closing of an analysis; but certainly they are in a process of diminution. After a thorough analysis the analysand is ready to reinvest himself, and may already have definitely begun to do so.

This cooling-off time is, then, of great value. It does not, however, exist in the training analysis. Under many circumstances the graduate comes into immediate contact with his former analyst in the affairs of his society or institute. He becomes aware that his analyst differs from other colleagues, and he begins to affiliate himself pro or con according to realistic considerations or to what he retains of his transference attitudes.

If the student is one of those in whom competition (usually

intellectual) has been the primary way of quieting anxieties in the past, and his training analysis has been a largely didactic one, there has probably not been the opportunity for a working through of the unresolved and sometimes almost untouched personal problems. The sound progress of the young analyst is then jeopardized. Such a degree of ego-syntonic competitiveness (which in my country is generally valued highly in the business world and highly promoted by advertising) furthers a one-sided vision of oedipal jealousy and sibling rivalry as well as an inadequate resolution of the rivalry between the sexes. There is then an intensified tendency to recreate infantile attitudes in an especially strong form in the relation to colleagues and an impairment of the full valuation of and respect for patients.

CONCLUDING REMARKS

The necessity of conducting personal analysis as part of a training program tends to produce conditions which appreciably interfere with this psychoanalytic process itself. The basic incompatibility in functions of the training analyst as therapist, judge, and teacher is probably the source of most of the important complications. The fact that the analyses must be carried on in the setting of a group organization affects both the training analyst and the student in many ways. It not only increases markedly the intrusion of current realities into the content of the analysis, but insofar as these not infrequently involve the training analyst as well as the student they tend to increase and complicate the transference and countertransference problems and often obscure the analysand's basic neurotic constellations; furthermore, and perhaps most important, the narcissism of both student and training analyst is actively excited, and competitiveness is promoted. Intellectualization unduly interferes with adequate working through.

SUMMARY

Problems of training analysis are described in detail, and these are discussed in their various ramifications. While these difficulties, implicit in the training situation, cannot be wholly eliminated, their consideration and discussion may be of value in resensitizing training analysts to their significances and so diminish their untoward effects.

It appears that inadequate attention to the subtle narcissistic pressures in the student's analysis, and in the reciprocal self-analysis of the training analyst, are the source of the most crucial problems described. Alertness to these hazards and strict adherence to the underlying principles, and to the basic rules of analysis, offer our best safeguards in the complicated relationships of analytic training.

CHAPTER THIRTY-EIGHT

Problems of Overidealization of the Analyst and of Analysis: Their Manifestations in the Transference and Countertransference Relationship (1966)

In this paper I shall limit myself to a relatively small but, I believe, important area in the vast field of transference and countertransference relationships. I shall deal only with overidealization of the analyst and of analysis. Before discussing this specific problem, however, I want to say a few words about the development of transference in general for it is a basic and most sensitive tool in the work of psychoanalysis, and its neglect or mishandling may interfere with the successful course of therapy by those who understand other aspects of psychoanalysis quite well.

The phenomenon of "transference" seems to be omnipresent in human relationships (see ch. 31). It is based on two essential psychological ingredients: first, the difficulty of the individual to exist long in emotional isolation; and second, the capacity to shift or transfer patterns of emotional relationship from one person or situation to another, provided there is a connecting link of some similarity between them.

The imperative nature of the demand for human contact was

brought home to us in a dramatic way some years ago by the pediatric observations of foundlings (Bakwin, 1942). The efforts to improve the lot of these infant waifs had been focused mostly on bettering their physical care in the early months of life, in order to give them as good a start as possible before placing them for adoption. It was obvious from this investigation, however, that babies abandoned at birth or in the first weeks of life did not thrive and rarely survived infancy under adequate or "good" physical conditions (warmth, care of nutrition and cleanliness) unless this included some mothering.[1] In other words, mechanical or impersonal substitutes for personal care simply do not work adequately. This demand for emotional contact, which is at first mediated through body contact, continues throughout life. Naturally in the first years after infancy, speech, memory, and imagination can offer substitutes for much of the physical contact which is so necessary in the early months. Still, solitary confinement in adult life is one of the severest punishments we know; an enforced abandonment by others, it rivals physical torture in the hierarchy of cruelty. Under conditions of confinement, too, those who enter imprisonment with some substantial emotional attachment to a person or a deeply felt cause have better chances for survival than the stranded ones (Jacobson, 1959).[2]

The second point, the ability to shift emotional patterns from one person to another on the basis of resemblances of varying im-

---

1 The experimental work of Harlow and Zimmerman (1958, 1959) on the rearing of infant monkeys seemed to indicate that the body warmth of a mother, even an artificial one constructed from a wire body covered with terry cloth and heated by electric light bulbs, was the most important element in contributing to the developmental welfare of the babies. They showed further that the young monkeys needed to have a mother to whom they could literally cling at the same time that they experienced the body warmth. These findings are important contributions to the understanding of the needs of human infants. It may be risky, however, to extrapolate from them completely and apply them too literally. It is obvious that the arboreal life of monkeys demands the development and persistence of clinging far beyond the requirements of humans. It is my impression, however, that in early psychoanalytic theory, anchored too strongly in the libido theory, there was too exclusive an emphasis on orality, in the first phase of life, and that the importance of clinging (Hermann, 1936), touch, smell, vision, and kinesthetic stimulation was insufficiently appreciated.

2 Also note the effect of imprisonment on fertile and active, but alienated minds: Adolf Hitler who wrote *Mein Kampf* while in prison; or the murderer Perry, whose waning warmth for humans turned to burning coldness touched with sentimentality as described by Truman Capote in *In Cold Blood* (1966); or the elaboration of a cult of hate during a period of confinement of Malcolm X—to be reversed later into a frank religious conversion to Moslemism (Malcolm X, *Autobiography*, 1965).

portance, is so much taken for granted in ordinary life that it may seem an unnecessary belaboring even to mention it. Yet because of the universality of this transference ability we may overlook its importance, on the one hand, in stimulating and promoting the sound incorporation of new experiences into the process of growth if the transference is based on valid and significant similarities; or, on the other hand, in contributing to the development of strongly prejudiced attitudes based on highly charged personal emotional elements which have a specious or at least not very significant similarity to other personal or more general situations.

A corollary to all this is that when a few people are gathered together, especially under conditions of relative isolation or secrecy, the lines of emotional relationship become intensified. This is more marked if the situation is protected against the influx of new stimulations bringing in new problems. There is then a tendency to a definite shift of emotional expectations into some kind of patterning representing the combination of repetition with compromises, as each individual seeks to adjust the attitudes generated by past experience to utilize the present situation for his own needs.

In the setting of analytic work, the group is reduced to two: the analyst and the analysand. Every care is taken to avoid intrusion of extraneous stimulations. The analyst then can give his attention entirely to the analysand who attempts through the various channels at his disposal to lay bare his innermost thoughts and feelings. The analyst's aim is to gain an understanding of the nature of the patient's disturbance. This understanding is then communicated to the latter at appropriate times and in appropriate terms. Naturally, such an undertaking cannot be begun unless the analysand has some basic confidence in the analyst or in the method of analysis or in both. He is further propelled by his wish to be relieved. The emotional attitudes of the analysand may then develop and be strengthened since they are not met by conflicting reactions from the analyst, who ideally makes no effort to argue, to persuade or to direct the analysand, but solely listens, clarifies, and interprets. The relative privacy usually serves as a protective isolation furthering feelings of safety rather than of loneliness. This part of the situation with its progressively developing confidence forms the primitive basis of the working alliance (or therapeutic alliance), which is essential as the medium of new understanding for the analysand. It is evident, I think, that it has many characteristics of the early infant-mother relationship in which the mother is the protection against unwelcome intrusions as well as against coldness and loneliness for the infant. I believe, indeed, the transference has its roots in this early and necessary relationship of infancy. However, in therapy, communication through bodily contact and direct gratification (other than that of privacy and watchful attentiveness) is replaced as much as possible by verbal communication. This situation makes possible the utilization of the adult's self-critical capacities, which probably could not operate well without anchorage to this primitive infantile trust.[3]

On this foundation the analysand finds himself developing attitudes, reactions, and illusions in regard to the analyst which are surprisingly inappropriate to and sometimes in marked contrast to his basic confidence. It becomes evident then that these are repetitions or revivals of earlier states arising from experiences with those with whom he has been in close relationship in years past. Although these attitudes may seem to carry hostility or suspicion, they have been able to develop because of the strength of the basic confidence reinforced by the absence of personal reactions from the analyst; and they may appear in remarkably clear outline in the analytic relationship. I am speaking here of course of the development of the transference neurosis or what I prefer to call transference neurotic attitudes.

It is probably obvious that the transference relationship in analysis contains by its very nature the seeds for idealization of the analyst in its rootedness in the early omnipotent stage of the mother-child relationship. It is my intention to examine certain other elements of early life which, if exaggerated, may favor an overidealization of analyst or analysis to a degree that is not helpful and may become rigidly binding and tenacious.

In years past, the basic importance of the mother-child relationship could be deduced from the very nature of its transference reproductions on the stage of the analytic relationship. But the growing concern with ego development pushed our interest back to the earliest months of life, and the utilization of direct observation of babies has enormously enriched our knowledge and

---

[3] This was first described by Sterba (1934).

made it more precise. It is noteworthy, however, that the role of the father in the first two years of the child's life has on the whole been rather neglected. This may be due in part to the fact that studies of well babies, and in some instances of severely disturbed ones, have necessarily been carried on mostly in clinics and day nurseries. Here the contact was largely with the mother through the use of techniques to gain information about the infant and to supply necessary aid and support to her. It is my belief, however, that the father is very important in these early months, not only as his influence is mediated through the mother but by his own contribution to special magic and omnipotent qualities of the child's life in ways which may be important in tendencies to overidealization, later appearing in the transference relationship to the analyst and to analysis itself.

Under most conditions, the mother is the infant's constant companion and very much the center of his universe, while the father is a more peripheral figure. This is especially marked during the first six to eight months. In caring for the baby's physical needs and alleviating his distresses, the mother's activity must contain a great variety of bodily contacts and handlings. There is a play of emotional responses—observable in her facial expression, her tone of voice, the briskness, smoothness or tension of her muscles, and in any number of details which may soon become significant to the infant. He probably senses her at first almost wholly insofar as she gratifies his needs and literally comforts him, or fails in these functions. But there is gradually increasing awareness of her separateness as he gains reciprocal awareness of his own parts and sensory functions.

The father, on the other hand, is never as close and constant in bodily relationship with the young infant as the mother (or her representative) must be. Nature has seen to that. At first he is probably most frequently sensed as a twilight figure, taking shape one way or another, actually associated with morning and evening; only appearing periodically in the full light of day as on weekends or holidays. Sometimes he is a nighttime marauder or ogre, but I shall say more of that later. How much he remains a distant figure or what part he plays in his own right or as an adjunct or an interference in the relationship to the mother depends on his own temperament, that of the mother, and especially on the nature of the relationship between them. The presence or absence of other siblings also plays a role.

If the father is a physically active person who really enjoys his children's infancy, he will play with the baby in a romping way, generally after the child has learned to sit up or shown an inclination to stand or walk. Playing with the child with wide tossing or sweeping movements or carrying the little one on his shoulders astride his head seem to be favorite paternal games. They are most exciting, especially in that period toward the end of the first year and during the second year when the child is beginning or has recently learned to walk. It seems then that the baby may feel a strong push for muscular activity and become demanding in seeking it. In this, there is not only a diffuse body erotism but, on the ego side, an increase in the sense of body self and degree of exploring of space. Some identification of his own movement with that of his father may occur with great exhilaration. The child may temporarily take on the illusion of being very big and active and the ensuing excitement may be enhanced by his for-real experience of being smaller, but on the way up.

Watching this as an onlooker I have thought that this illusion was a beneficial one, giving the child a sense of vigor and power through participation with the father, in contrast to some other father-child games in which the child continuously feels his own smallness and helplessness. Here again the effect may depend as much on the father's use of the game as on the child's. When the game results in overwhelming excitement, it may produce a premature genital stimulation associated with submission and leave some distorting influence on the later sexuality.

In either event I have been struck with the fact that children of both sexes seem to enjoy this sort of romping play much more with the father than with the mother, who may, it is true, be less well equipped muscularly to undertake it and consequently less smooth and assured in her movements. The child is more likely to initiate hide-and-seek games with the mother, dosing himself and her with his needs for separateness.

Thus, after the first weeks of life, the movement in the child is toward a gradual separation from the mother, which may ultimately allow the growth of a relationship on a different level. The father, however, must emerge from a murky figure "off there" to one with whom the child is familiar, after which at least an incipient object relationship is possible. This difference in relationship to the parents progressively diminishes but is not lost as long as the child remains at home. For usually the mother is concerned with the details of the immediate care of the children, the management of the household, food, clothing, and cleanliness, even though her care no longer requires much direct bodily handling. The father, on the other hand, is off at work during the day, because his provision and care for his children consist in his being the breadwinner. To the preschool and young school child the father's activity is generally more mysterious, powerful, and glamorous than the everyday familiar concerns of the mother. These earliest of all parental figures, the all-giving mother and the more than life-sized heroic father (dating actually from the first two years of life and representing the positive form of the murky figure at first sensed) tend to persist more or less until the oedipal period and the entrance into the school world, which usually occurs about the same time. But they are the parental figures which reappear later in a new embellished form in the family romance[4] if there has been an especially strong disillusionment regarding the parents in the oedipal and again in the pubertal periods.

What I have presented thus far deals only with the perception of the *good* parents. It is obvious that there are other aspects which the young child reacts to—the angry parent, the distant unresponsive parent, the punishing parent, etc. In general these different parents tend to line up into the two categories: good and bad. These parental images with their roots in the first year or two of life are formed not only from the perceptions of the actual parents (or substitute parental figures) but also from the good (comfortable) or bad (uncomfortable) feelings in the child himself; for they originate in a period when the differentiation of the self from the other is in process.

We can deduce then that the more troubled and painful the early preoedipal years are, whether through endogenous physical distress within the child or injurious influences from without (i.e., any situations in which distress is of such proportions that it cannot or at least is not alleviated readily by comforting ministra-

---

4 Frosch (1959) has described extensively the appearance of derivatives of the family romance in the transference.

tions), the greater will be the increase in the natural ambivalence of the child. While this develops most often in relation to the mother with whom early contact is the greater, it may spread readily to include others in the environment. Commonly the hostile distrust becomes covered with an anxious overattachment and overvaluation of the parent(s), which is, however, extremely susceptible to being upset.[5]

Some years ago as a consultant to a group of institutions caring for children from broken homes, I was much impressed with this state of affairs. In some instances these children had parents who really were *bad* parents in that they were neglectful, cruel, and not to be depended upon. However, rarely is any parent completely bad and the child generally had some kernel of pleasant memory to use as the basis of an expectation. The tendency of these children was to idealize, even glamorize, the absent parents. But if they went "home" to visit, there was likely to be trouble, as reality forced itself upon the child and outbursts of anger or other forms of aggression were frequent and severe. The social stratification of the children among themselves within the institution depended not so much on skill in competition of one sort or another but on how much the child was in contact with his parents: how often they visited, wrote, or sent him presents.

This is a rather long prelude to the consideration of the overidealization of the analyst and sometimes of analysis, a development which may present a subtly based transference problem with severe sequelae after the analysis is over, especially if it is not understood during treatment.

It is evident that the analytic situation, characterized by the analyst giving his total attention to the analysand in an atmosphere of privacy and protection with the aim of ultimately relieving the analysand, is one which meets many of the requirements of the good parent. And this is helpful for the formation of the basic transference, the site of the working or therapeutic alliance. But it also has some hazards in permitting a degree of idealization of the analyst or of analysis which is not beneficial.

<hr/>

[5] I discussed this somewhat in my paper on "The Predisposition to Anxiety" (1941). The emphasis there was on the earliest distresses of all, those occurring at birth and the very first months of life.

The general transference situation develops according to several different combinations of factors which impinge upon and may influence the intensity and configuration of the developing oedipal attachment. (1) If there has been a preponderance of discomfort in the earliest months but the care of a good parent has been available, then there is generally enough margin of positive response for the development of a sound basic transference and a workable transference neurosis. There may be a special tendency to idealization of the analyst which does not get out of bounds, however, unless it is augmented by a strongly seductive or protective analyst. When the idealization of the analyst is extreme, the patient may "analyze" to please the analyst and be fearful of admitting any hostile feelings. Characteristically, then, the analyst is nearly perfect, but the world remains insidiously hostile, and the analysand does not realize fully enough his own ability to deal directly with disturbing situations. Instead he is likely to resort to analyzing others before or in place of taking appropriate action himself. (2) There are some patients who have suffered *severe* physical distress in the preoedipal years (but not in the first months of life) and have been well cared for through the illness, who show in analysis an expectation of magic relief through simply coming to the analysis itself. They express few emotional reactions to the analyst, and in fact have generally a limited vocabulary for emotions, sometimes reacting as though an expression of any feeling is an indication of weakness. Their dreams may be vivid and show marked transference allusions of which they remain insistently unaware. One cannot say that the patient specifically idealizes the analyst or analysis, but rather that on a very primitive emotional level he expects magic relief from a procedure. (3) In a third group of patients, in whom there has been a prolonged severe degree of sensory and emotional deprivation soon after birth, no adequate clinging seems ever to have developed. In these cases, I believe, hostile attitudes will appear and persist from the beginning of the analysis. I am thinking here of a few patients who were institutionalized soon after birth or cared for under practically institutional conditions because of severe illness of the mother combined usually with unfavorable socioeconomic conditions. The care was not as sterile as in the case of the babies reported by Bakwin, but was grossly lacking in warmth

and responsiveness. Subsequent to these early conditions the patient finds the privacy of the analytic relationship disturbing as it
demands more than he is ready to give. His fear of passivity is so
great that it is met by a need to feel omnipotent. In rare instances
when a positive transference to the analyst does develop, it may
tend to become persistently clinging and to exclude the hostile
elements, which are deflected onto accessory transference figures
and subject to some analytic work. It is not a very satisfactory or
complete therapeutic procedure.

In type 3, however, if the patient shows a prolonged open hostile attitude toward the analyst or analysis, and his history indicates that he has not been able to sustain any good relationships in
his life, then I think it is generally useless to attempt to analyze. I
would emphasize the significance of the history of interference
with sustained personal relationships rather than with achievements. For there are many bright and even perceptive people who
have stacked up an impressive number of achievements which are
nonetheless built with a pervasive hostile attitude and a drive to
be on top at all costs. I have not been successful with such patients
myself, but have heard other analysts report some favorable results when the analysis was undertaken after a prolonged period
of psychotherapy. Such patients sometimes seem to idealize themselves as part of the narcissistic inflation necessary to counteract
their fear of passivity. They occasionally seek analysis because of
loneliness.

The group of patients who are chiefly to be considered here are
patients of the first type described. They do not show *open*
marked ambivalence. Hostility has early been controlled by reaction formation and superego development, but there are also
pockets of denial. They may be gentle and quiet people, or the
latent aggression may appear in a pressure of fervor and too consistent goodwill, associated with a general tendency to idealize.
Their compensation in life is fairly good, and they may seek treatment with fairly typical and not very severe neurotic symptoms.
As has already been implied, some idealization of the analyst is to
be expected from the very nature of the analytic situation. In
these patients there is at first little to mark any problems as more
severe than in most neurotic patients, unless it is that they seem
to be unusually "good" patients. They accept interpretations

overreadily, complying with free associations which will support or elaborate what the analyst has said. They tend to keep overt hostile reactions outside of the transference responses, and often deal with hostility by converting it into too great benevolence.

These patients do not want ever to relinquish the analyst. This wish to hold on expresses itself further in the wish to be an analyst or to do something at least related to analysis. It is easy to consider this idealization as part of a postoedipal identification and to accept it as the development of postoedipal values established as part of the resolution of the oedipus complex. But the fact that some of these patients never free themselves from the analyst or from the defensive use of analysis becomes apparent in later years and is rationalized as part of the analysis terminable-or-interminable question. As a matter of fact, this is not the case. It seems rather that the analyst and then analysis have been accepted as part of a special and magic world of omnipotence, which really belongs to early childhood. There is not as full an assimilation of the content of interpretations as one would have expected in the course of analytic work. Analytic concepts are understood in a quasi-intellectual way and, being used too much in the service of defense, they do not enrich life so much as replace it. The phase of analyzing others, which practically every analysand goes through in the course of his own analysis, persists, is indefinitely prolonged, and gratifies a narcissistic sense of in-ness and power. There are other patients who cannot sustain this clinging attitude toward the analyst or analysis; they again repeat the disappointments that they have experienced with their own parents, often in a peculiarly bitter way, and become aggressively hostile. In either case, whether the postanalytic attitude is one of persistent clinging or of hostility to the analyst or to analysis, it is likely to be one of fervor approaching fanaticism.

A complicating set of circumstances in a number of patients belonging generally to this group is found in the consistent and repetitive exposure to the primal scene beginning in the first weeks after birth and continuing without great interruption until puberty or even later. It has seemed to me that such a state of affairs, while usually occurring together with other untoward experiences, did nevertheless produce rather characteristic disturbances. It would take a more detailed careful study of a larger number of cases than I have yet had time to make to give a report on the variety of ways in which these experiences impress the child and combine with the fantasies endogenously generated in him, resulting then in rather severe distortion of later sexual interests and of passive and aggressive attitudes (Zetzel, 1965). The instances of prolonged sharing of the parental bedroom involving repeated primal scene exposures occurred in my patients almost exclusively in only children or in the youngest of several children. This situation may be contrasted with that in which there are sporadic chance participations in the primal scene, but then the experience is regarded as exceptional. In the latter instances, there is more likely to be a shock reaction and the impact on the child depends very much on the age of the child, the actual nature of the primal scene exposure itself, the circumstances surrounding it, and the reactions of the parents to the child's intrusion. In any event, the experience is likely to color the child's developing sexual theories and expectations. In the cases of repeated exposure over a number of years, it was necessary for the child to develop strong defensive reactions which shaped not only his sexual attitudes and expectations but invaded other parts of the character as well.[6]

In two cases (one an only child and the other the younger of two) the child shared the bedroom with the parents for several months of the year until well after puberty. The situation in both instances was furthered by the fact that the family lived in a Southern community in which the house, though sufficiently ample in size, was not heated throughout and during the winter months the family all slept in the one warmest room of the house. In other instances of only children of moderately poor but not really impoverished families, the child had been kept in the parents' room, while another room was rented out to a roomer. The arrangement was due to frugality rather than to real need. In still other families, well-to-do and with no special economic pressure, a variety of factors seemed to promote this sleeping arrangement: the parents might enjoy having the little one at hand and treat him more or less as a plaything; or a sexually inhibited mother might keep the child at hand as a barrier to frequent sex

---

[6] Some variations of the primal scene experience are indicated but not elaborated in my paper on screen memories (1949a).

relations. A neurotic anxious parent might need to reassure himself of the child's safety during the night. It is my impression, in fact, that the situation of such prolonged sleeping-together arrangements is rarely due as much to drastic impoverishment as to a kind of clinging, a continuation in one or both parents of old infantile wishes for closeness due to many different neurotic reasons. I shall describe some of the typical developments and then whatever visual memory associated with the sounds is aroused. This may be felt as though in the body or projected outward, with a reconstruction of the sense of being at the breast or close to the mother's body.[7] In some instances there is also a marked and circumscribed disturbance in the infant's motor and kinesthetic sense, due to special awareness of the rhythmic motions of intercourse and the shaking of the bed.

In one patient who showed this disturbance in a marked degree during the analysis, I finally made a tentative interpretation that it seemed she actually might have shared the bed with the parents for some time and participated unusually intimately in the movements of their sexual relationship. After a pause she confirmed this probability, saying it was true that during her second year the parents had taken her with them on a belated honeymoon in which she had shared their bed in the various hotels in which they stayed.

The specific direct stimulation of visual curiosity in this situation ordinarily comes, I think, at a later date—perhaps beginning in the latter half of the first year and continuing especially in the second and third year. There is then a clearer differentiation of self from the other, and the child is able to stand up in his crib and take in the situation more fully if there is even a dim light on. This situation is stressed by Zetzel (1965) who indicates that a later desire for visual mastery may be stimulated, although free fantasy is interfered with. I had come to the same conclusion in my cases, but would emphasize that the mastery is highly narcissistic with strong competitive and exhibitionistic content, while the inhibition of imagination robs it of richness. In some cases the process of learning is even more drastically involved. The in-

---

[7] Here then may be one source of the later experience described by Isakower (1938) and known rather generally as the "Isawoker phenomenon," which was elaborated in Lewin's studies (1946, 1953) of the "dream screen."

tensity and elaboration of curiosity also depend upon the specific nature of what the child sees and on the parents' reaction to his activity. In this later period, too, he is more likely to feel some beginning genital stimulation accompanying the pressure for excretory discharge. Furthermore, jealousy may now begin to be a strong ingredient in the feeling of exclusion and intensified loneliness.

My experience with patients in whom the sharing of the parental bedroom has extended practically uninterruptedly well into latency has impressed me with the degree to which selective denial and an amnesia of varying dimensions have developed. As a result, what the analyst hears about may be a few or many screen memories which are more than ordinarily inaccessible to elaboration, reconstruction, and interpretation. There may be an extremely strong resistance even on the part of very intelligent reasoning people to the idea that the parents indulged in sexual activity at this period and sometimes very improbable rationalizations are offered to account for such an asexual life.

It was very difficult to generalize about these cases. The clinical symptomatology varies according to the form of early stimulations and the ways in which they combine with later specific traumas and disillusionments affecting the oedipal struggle and its solution. There are many patients who overtly cling not to the analyst, but to the analysis in a paradoxical way. In spite of a continued rigid resistance and apparent discouragement they are quite unwilling to give up analysis. If induced by the analyst to discontinue treatment, they return later hoping this time it will be better. It is noteworthy that the maintenance of an extraordinarily enduring attachment to analysis may be their means of keeping an idealized version of the parents.

In general whether there was direct clinging to the analyst or to analysis, what the patient absorbed from interpretation was accepted pretty much on an intellectualized basis. Often this was hazy too. In some of the overt clingers there might be an attempt at cliché learning of analysis and a repetition of bits of analytic theory which the patient accepted as belonging to himself. Or there might be expressions of devotion to the analyst and of aggrandizement of him, but without the development of any clear transference neurosis. In some, such an attitude was punctuated by episodes of acting out which really expressed deep hostilities to the analyst and which were difficult to analyze (see ch. 35). Then again there might be a kind of Chinese wall shutting out of the analysis any frankly sexual thoughts, memories or feelings, even when their presence was startlingly clear in dreams or definitely implied in reactions to current situations.

One patient of this type had sought treatment because of impotence, beginning relatively soon after marriage and apparently in connection with his wife's desire to have a child. He could not accept the fact that the time relationship pointed the way to a possible connection worthy of exploration, but strongly insisted that it was a pure coincidence. He was more than reticent about the details of his sexual life, and did not mention spontaneously sexual successes or failures.

A prolific dreamer, this man brought clear, informative dreams, which appeared to tell the story of his difficulties in an almost forthright way. But he was singularly incurious about them. He would give a few associations and then tend to paraphrase the dreams. When there were "wet dreams" or specific sexual references, he would then admit that the dreams *might* have something to do with his sexual symptom, but he would not venture much beyond that. When I gave a tentative interpretation, I would get a cautious admission that what I said *might* have some significance, usually followed by a firm assertion, "But of course I don't remember anything about it!" With that he firmly shut the door which had momentarily been slightly ajar.

The patient was one who had shared the parental bedroom in winter into his adolescence because it was the warmest room in the house. (The details of childhood, though important, are not here enumerated.) He had graduated from the foremost professional school in his field with a magna cum laude. Now in his mid-thirties he was very inhibited in his social relationships, but in his work seemed efficient and self-assured (as I happened to hear from outside sources). It is true that he had somehow found a specialty within a specialty in which his sharp intellect could stake out problems with great skill and clarity. But he lacked encompassing vision and was restricted in professional areas requiring appreciation of human emotions.

He clearly used his concern with professional worries as a defense against his sexual problems. When he could not go to sleep readily or was awakened by an anxious dream, he shifted immediately to thoughts about unfinished work in his office and planned the work of the next day in detail.

He could not admit even the possibility that his parents had had intercourse or any other sexual activity at any time after his birth. Neither did he seem to feel that the absence of any sexual relationship between them would have indicated some severe personal problem. What did emerge fairly clearly and repetitively—to an extent that seemed convincing to me—was that the father had been involved with a young girl in some way which caused gossip. This would come up with associations to older men who had impregnated young girls. Just what the facts in regard to his father were, I could not tell, but his unadmitted fantasies were clear enough. The father was certainly a well-respected man in the community, and the patient emphasized this with such strength that one suspected a certain defensiveness in it. He seemed to have a need to keep an early idealized vision of the powerful all-good father. This he did in his symptoms, his character defenses, and his transference attitudes.

It has been the aim of this presentation thus far to indicate some of the general and specific situations in the early years of the later analysand which contribute to the development of over-idealization of the analyst or to passive magic expectations from the ritual analysis, and further to describe the relation of these to the origins of transference itself. I believe this is rooted most deeply in the physical dependence of the infant on the mother (partaking of the oceanic feeling described by some as religious); however, it also contains elements of the second year of life when the infant is accomplishing his own separateness but would still react to the parents, especially the father, as being all-powerful and godlike. The regression that occurs in the analytic transference relationship contains elements of both, but one or the other may be so accentuated as to focus the overly strong transference dependence on the analyst in a personal way or on the method of analysis, which then cannot really be utilized because it serves such a strong defensive need.

In the patient whose case has been scantily sketched, it appears that his normal postoedipal idealization of his father was interfered with both by the fantasies of violence repeatedly and annually reinforced by subjection to primal scenes, and further by hints and gossip concerning his father's behavior in the latter's young manhood. Both sets of experiences had obviously made indelible impressions on the boy, but had to be obliterated from consciousness by one of the strongest walls of denial I have ever encountered. It should be added, however, that in prepuberty the patient had a physical illness which focused attention on his genitals intensifying and fixating castration fears.

What interests me specially, however, is the way in which he built a strong reaction formation of almost religiously ritualized aims of perfection in his work. Although engaged in a profession dealing essentially with human relations, he had succeeded in finding a place for himself in which he could do a very specialized piece of work which did not demand that he look deeply into human motivations. In his own way he was courageous and efficient to an extreme degree. It was not that he sublimated conflicts but rather that he transferred them, in life as well as in analysis, to rather institutionalized social goals in which concepts of right and wrong played a considerable part. In this way he reinstated the glorious powerful father of his early childhood—the figure which might under some circumstances be the basis of a family romance fantasy. In the analysis itself, he clung to the feeling that if he followed the rules of analytic procedure conscientiously, he *must succeed*—thus giving the analysis too a rather firm disciplinary ritualistic quality resembling some religious practices.

But what are the countertransference attitudes of the analyst which permit or even promote his overidealization by the analysand? They appear as precisely those counterparts of the transference problems which occur in the analysand. Mainly they consist of the persistence in the analyst of strong narcissistic competitive drives with high demands for success. This appears under the guise of therapeutic enthusiasm. This may have been dislodged from its original appearance as personal ambition and give rise to an overvaluation of the power of analysis itself. Such analysts will see "more analysis" too readily as the answer to recurrent neurotic difficulties, without giving sufficient attention to why the previous analysis failed. They may be too ready to attribute a failure to the inadequate work of the first analyst, without assessing the real complexity of the neurosis. If they concur with the patient in blaming the previous analyst and sympathize with him, they are likely to find themselves enmeshed in too strong a positive transference in which it is difficult to decipher the negative elements. This is particularly likely to be true when the analyst has himself a need for emotional gratification—to be loved and admired by his analysands. In such instances, the analyst often appears disarmingly modest, but has a faith in the almost divine power of analysis.

The expectation of therapeutic omnipotence in the process of analysis was more frequent in years past. Freud's early discoveries were so profound and far-reaching and the realization of the power of unconscious forces to modify the course of life was so startling that the process of uncovering these forces and diminishing their effects was awe-inspiring. At the same time the analyst's position in the community set him apart in a way which tended to enhance or to wound his narcissistic image of himself. With the increase of the general public's knowledge about analysis, the analyst no longer occupies this special role, and this particular social increment to his narcissism is largely relieved. But the total problem is by no means eradicated.

It is not only the narcissistic needs of the analyst but his failure to recognize his own hostile aggressive drives which seem to make trouble by dovetailing with the problems of these analysands. He may then too readily identify with his patient and accept the latter's splitting of transference with projection of negative transference onto others, especially accessory members of the patient's family or of the analytic community. The therapeutic enthusiasm of the analyst is sometimes part of a latent rescue fantasy (Sterba, 1940), which is aroused by the analysand's suffering and pleas for help. An intense transference situation approaching a family romance may then develop. The patient's wish to find an ideal and all-powerful parent is met by the analyst's gratification in being the sympathetic parent through whom the patient will find a complete cure, approximating even a rebirth.

In such rescue operations the analyst's aggression may be allocated to those relatives or therapists who have previously been in contact with the patient and are, in fact or in fantasy, contributors to his disturbances. The analyst then becomes the savior through whom the analysand is to be launched. If this situation is further complicated by the analyst's succumbing to the patient's clinging seduction to the point of modifying the analytic treatment by interventions and active procedures, this naturally increases the attachment of the patient and tends to augment the secondary narcissism in giving him a sense of being specially favored. However, it further acts to keep him in a state of continued dependence or even transference bondage. This is sometimes gradually altered by time, but it is also prone to feed upon itself to the point of becoming irksome to either analyst or analysand, after which the latent negative transference may emerge in a troublesome or destructive way.

There is one situation which may interfere considerably and insidiously even in the treatment of patients whose problems are similar but less severe than those of the group described in this paper. This situation arises when the analyst is very well known and carries considerable prestige in the community from which the analysand comes. These circumstances, outside the control of the analyst and analysand, tend to enhance the image of the analyst and give the treatment a kind of magic power, with improvement deriving from association with the analyst rather than from the analysand's own development. It is impressive how many analysts, wrapped in the cloak of supposed anonymity in the consulting room, do not genuinely realize the complication of being well known and even in contact with the analysand in the outer world. In such situations transference cures may result without fundamental change or growth in the patient. This constitutes a special complication in the training of analytic students (see ch. 37), but it is also met in other patients. It approximates a reality gratification to the patient by the analyst, and tends to fixate special problems in the analysand. It is a situation which cannot be entirely eliminated; but awareness of its significance may modify therapeutic results considerably.

CHAPTER THIRTY-NINE

The Psychoanalytic Process, Transference, and Acting Out *(1968)*

Anna Freud opened the Symposium on Acting Out (1968) by stressing especially the use of the term itself. Considering it one of those technical terms which has lost meaning through the over-expansion of its application, she proposed to limit its usage along with that of other terms such as "transference" and "trauma" to phenomena within the psychoanalytic situation, in this way hoping to increase the precision of its definition. She gave a concise account of the birth, growth, and changing forms of certain analytic concepts according to what fits and is accurate for the needs of the expanding findings of clinical work itself. This forms an interesting and stimulating background for my topic, i.e., the impingement of acting out on the psychoanalytic process through the medium of the transference relationship.

In this paper, I am in fact less concerned with the definition of the term itself than I am with trying to understand the dynamics and effect of the substitution of action for verbal communication in its impact on the psychoanalytic process. I may have paid too little attention to the precision of definition because I find it difficult so completely to separate the dynamics of events within the confines of the analytic situation from their reciprocal relationship with both current and earlier events of the patient's life. This paper has become focused especially on the nature of the psychoanalytic process. Since the concept of the psychoanalytic process emerged gradually, its literature is not very compact, being scattered through papers on theory, technique, and clinical findings. This is probably due to the fact that the theory of analysis was based first of all on therapeutic aims and clinical discoveries, followed by a period of promoting the interdependent roles of technique and theory, while technique has also given the tools for clinical investigation (Hartmann, 1951).

In his paper on the vicissitudes of insight (more often referred to as the "good analytic hour" paper), Kris (1950a) describes psychoanalytic therapy as having the property of a process "with the motion of progressive development over time in a definite direction." He is chiefly concerned with the integrative forces at work in the patient and the change in alignment which begins to be felt when an interpretation—not necessarily in the setting of immediate evidence of positive transference—"hits home"; and both analyst and patient are aware of a beginning change in the analysand. Kris believed that libidinal and aggressive energy was now at the disposal of the patient for freer reinvestment. He made it clear that this "good hour," announcing a change, is part of a process, the result of other hours which have gradually led up to it, and that the liberation of energy does not ideally come so much from compliance to the analyst as to the meaning and structure of other elements as well, in the therapeutic process. It is this fabric of the ongoing analytic process including reaction to the analyst as well as the explicit content of the interpretation, with which this paper is largely concerned.

In considering the analytic process we think not only of the realignments of force which occur, but also of the elements which set these in motion. Here it is difficult to deal with process entirely separate from procedures. Kris described these stimuli as coming from interpretations given at "the right time" after a period of preparatory work in the preconscious of the patient. This generally consists of some moderately dim mulling over of what one might call "preliminary interpretations in a low key." These may include delineation of defense reactions and of patterns of overt behavior which have been discerned from the patient's accounts of himself. Such material builds up until it includes far-reaching interrelated references to current situations, events of the recent and remote past, representations in dreams, and sometimes references to the analyst. Kris saw the good analytic hour as comprising these elements which had at first appeared in a murky conglomeration but gradually took shape in a fairly consistent picture of which the central issues are illuminated by the analyst's final interpretation. These issues may not be immediately clear to the patient, but if important sensitive areas have been touched in this synthesizing way, he continues to work them over both in a silent preconscious process and in subsequent working through in analytic sessions. Often the "good analytic hour" really extends over several hours either in succession or with intervals between them. In any case it is led up to and followed by a preconscious pondering by the analysand.

Kris considered that the preliminary work of the analysis had loosened countercathectic energy and energy attached to repressed material; and that some of this was now available to participate in the integrative functions of the ego, promoting reorganization; and that this is the essence of the analytic process of which the good hour is a nodal point. But we have to recognize that the transference is the main medium through which this works. The term transference is used here to mean the total relationship between analyst and analysand during the course of treatment.

There are then two parts to the general transference relationship: first, the attitude of the analysand with which the analysis opens, usually, but not always, a sufficiently positive feeling to permit a fair degree of rapport; second, the transference neurosis. The initial tentative rapport is intensified by the restrictions of the analytic situation and furnishes the climatic background for the development of the transference neurosis.[1] This means that a

[1] To interpolate here some further remarks concerning Anna Freud's presentation: if I understood her correctly, she deplored a too-wide application of the term "transference" and suggested confining it strictly to what occurs in the analytic situation in relation to the analytic process, and so abandoning its use in favor of other terms designating various parts of what is now included under the general term transference. I can certainly see the value of this, especially in the effort to make classifications easier and perhaps more precise. But I think that the feeling with which the prospective analysand approaches his analysis and his analyst has an integral relationship and continuity with the basic feeling after he begins his analysis; that this initiates the analytic process and leads to the development of the transference neurosis. It might be useful to designate this "basic transference" as a condition of "special rapport." But I would want certainly to try this out before definitely suggesting it as a *term*. At any rate, in this paper I am concerned very much with the relationship of elements in the analytic therapy to the texture of the patient's life.

substantial healthy part of the ego, with its self-critical and integrative functions, forms a kind of working alliance with the analyst, strengthened by some degree of identification (Sterba, 1934; Strachey, 1934; E. Bibring, 1937). It is the transference neurosis, however, that furnishes most of the specific material for interpretation (Loewenstein, 1951). Concurrent with the growing interest in ego psychology and early ego development there has been an increasing interest in the character and variations of the working therapeutic alliance (Greenson, 1965a).

My own clinical observations led me to consider that this basic transference relationship had its roots in the earliest mother-infant bond and reproduced the helpless infant's primitive trust in the need-fulfilling mother (ch. 31). Spitz (1956) has also given a detailed statement, based on his studies, of the infantile prototype of the transference development. On first consideration, this basic element in the transference appeared to me as a regressive revival of infantile dependence. Subsequent reflection brought the further idea that the mere existence of such a need for relationship is not in itself necessarily regressive, since it is an essential ingredient for the maintenance of life itself in infancy and is a necessary component in all later productive activities in life. It certainly contains strong regressive pulls in situations of suffering which, together with the limitations of the analytic situation, act to extrude the transference neurosis. It may also catalyze the therapeutic alliance at the same time that its regressive elements act as contaminants. Perhaps one may say that it is the continuous viability of this first slight step of conversion of primary narcissism into the very beginning of object relationship which must be retained if object relationships are to develop and withstand untoward conditions later in life. This capacity for rapport seems also to be essential if learning, other than by conditioning, is to progress.

It is my conviction that the psychoanalytic process, at its best, involves essentially a progression of growth. This is not so much stimulated as liberated to take its own course. Here we may remind ourselves of the biological background of maturational change. What we are aiming at in psychoanalytic therapy is the reinstatement, insofar as is possible, of maturation which has been interfered with. Maturational shifts have a high degree of autonomy in their developmental patterning and proceed in accordance with an overall principle of individuation. Development always involves a response of the total organism, and growth of any of its component parts or systems does not readily get out of bounds separately from the rest of the organism.

Recent work of analytically trained observers in studies of infants has enlarged our understanding of the beginning of ego development and shown us the behavior patterning occurring in these early years. These patterns are at first much influenced by physiobiological factors in the body state and proceed according to biological maturation in cooperation with, or deterred by, the reciprocal response of the mother. There seems to be a natural landmark of individuation and attainment of separation in the second year of life with the achievement of walking and talking. There is a great leap forward in which mental and psychological functions attain increasing dominance, when communication can be carried on economically and independently of body contact or gross body activity.

While I arrived at certain observations regarding the significance of this period through my clinical findings and reconstructions with adult patients, it was gratifying to find that these were in harmony with the experiences of some of my colleagues working directly with young children. (I am especially indebted to Mahler for her discussions with me concerning this period of infancy.) It appears that in this second year of life with its high degree of maturational flux, sensitivity to sensation, and heightening of excitement, the attainment of walking and talking also gives an enormous expansion in the development of communication. It is further a time of special sensitivity to external stimulation and, especially in children whose even earlier development has been such that there is an impairment of incipient object relationship, there seems to be a susceptibility to traumas which are more readily induced and make a deeper impression. On the other hand, gifted people have often had experiences at this time which they later reported as involving special brilliance of sensation. These contribute the qualities of brightness, invigoration, and special responsiveness as they appear in later repetitions and screen memories.

On the basis of accumulated clinical observations it seemed

probable that the second year of life is rather generally a time of increased body animation accompanied by some focused genital awareness. Especially when the transition from primary to secondary process thinking is occurring with a gradual evolution of abstract thinking and of sense of self, the pattern of emotional development is greatly influenced by concomitant physical growth changes. Just before and during the establishment of speech, the biological maturation patterns exert a strong influence, sometimes with startling precision, on those of emotional development.[2]

I see the psychoanalytic process as a recreative growth process, similar in certain outlines to the creative process itself, which in my estimation is a special form of accelerated, intensified, and continued growth of which only the gifted ones, however, are capable (Beres, 1957). But whereas growth of the ordinary individual and the insistent growth of especially creative individuals are largely autonomous after the person has passed the first few years of life, the renewed or restored emotional growth occurring as the result of the psychoanalytic process requires another person to be regularly on hand, ever watchful, ever listening, and occasionally explaining (interpreting). The responsiveness of the analyst resembles very much that of the ideal mother or the ideal teacher of a young child. In our work, too, we must aim for the same respect for the autonomy of the patient that the ideal mother or teacher would have for the growing child and that the creative individual demands so compellingly for himself.

Growth proceeds in stages with fluctuations of activity which culminate in periods of stabilization or nodes representing the achieved organization of a new function. Such nodes are preceded by a fluttering, seemingly random, activity which gradually settles down as it is integrated into the new developmental stage. It is probably arrived at by cooperation between internal maturational forces and external stimulation (including the presence of a friendly audience and opportunity). The earlier experimental quality of this prenodal activity gives way then to a state when the total organism seems to click and the new function is in place. Gratification or even triumph in the exercise of the achieved function (e.g., finding a lost object and later walking and talking)

2 The role of speech and the development of secondary process functioning are discussed further in chs. 19 and 20.

appears with a period of playful practice. This overlaps then with the beginning experimentation with further activity, ultimately leading to the next developmental stage.[3]

With extraordinary intuition Freud gradually fashioned the methods for psychoanalytic therapy after the principles of growth. This was the more remarkable in that the new method of treatment involved the undoing of strictures of the past which impeded and distorted normal psychic development, so that the latter might emerge and proceed by itself. This was in contrast with the most advanced theories of the day which depended largely, but often unofficially, on support, suggestion, and direction in the current situation against a background of neurologizing hypotheses without much consideration for the individual's historical background.

Free association, one of the cornerstones of the psychoanalytic method, is somewhat comparable to the fluttering, seemingly random activity of the child before he reaches a new stage. It also resembles the pondering rumination which goes on in the preconscious dreamy states of a creative individual when he is in process of arriving at some new idea, formulation, or discovery (Freud, 1920b).[4] In the analysand it naturally finds its way back to the sources of his difficulties in the past as well as to his disappointments of the present and his hopes for the future. Since he is already caught in an inner nexus of binds, he might arrive at a state of unproductive brooding with obsessional repetition or rationalization if he were left entirely to himself. The analyst having traveled these or similar pathways in himself and with others recognizes the road signs and at appropriate times may point out the significances of the patient's being drawn to the familiar path even though in the past it has led to pain and frustration. He may even indicate the presence of paths which have been previously

---

[3] Described by Gesell (1946) in his article on ontogenesis of infant behavior.

[4] Free association as a method of promoting productivity had been described by Schiller in correspondence with Körner in 1788, and by Ludwig Börne in an article written in 1823 and reprinted in 1862. This latter may have been known to Freud who, at fourteen, read and enjoyed some of Börne's works. Freud rather objected, however, to Havelock Ellis's appreciation of his work as an artistic rather than a scientific production, especially as Ellis likened the free association to the method of "impression" used in a volume of doggerel published by J. J. Garth Wilkinson, who was known as a Swedenborgian mystic and poet rather than as a physician. E. Jones (1953) also gives some discussion of this in his biography of Freud.

bypassed. Gradually then courage for new development emerges.

The analyst thus supplements the patient's self-observing and self-criticizing functions and may operate almost as though he were a part of the patient. Insofar as the analyst's interpretations are clarifying, apt, and timely they may be accepted and gradually absorbed. Sometimes one may sense something almost like a click in the analysand when an interpretation which has been approached through its various aspects suddenly takes hold. This resembles a child who, fortified by the presence of an interested adult, regains courage and balance after a fall and takes more steps with renewed assurance.[5]

The importance of the basic transference must be considered not only in terms of the mother-infant relationship and the splitting of the ego. For the extent to which the interpretation can be made assimilable for the analysand depends not only on the analyst's sensitivity to the content of the patient's transference productions and his adequate knowledge of technique and principles but further on the construction—the stuff of which the patient's early attachments and identifications have been made in the period up to and including the acquisition of speech and the time immediately afterward. By this time, the role of the father, the relationship of the parents to each other, and the presence of other siblings are active influences. Identification at this time influences certain problems of affect, aspects of the sense of identity, and the early stages of object relationship. It contributes to the later oedipal development and influences its intensity, and possibly, the degree of firmness of postoedipal identifications.

The conduct of analysis is clearly dependent on communication through speech. While posture, mannerisms, facial expression and gestures are regularly seen during analysis, the analytic situation is set up in such a way as to minimize action as a major channel of communication and make it necessary for the patient to rely very largely on speech. The obvious value is that speech is the most economical, quickest, and clearest way of getting a message across. The analytic situation assures the delivery of the message

5 This auxiliary function of the transference relationship utilized in the therapeutic alliance raises questions of energy distribution and availability and of cathexis variability which are beyond my own reach, even for speculation. They are fascinating, but I must leave them for more theoretically minded clinicians than myself.

to a live listener. Further, speech entails both objectivation and social participation, albeit in a society of two.

Distortions of speech such as stammers, lisps, and disturbances of enunciation are common, and may interfere much or little with the analytic work, but are generally less disrupting than the disturbance of function in which the form of speech is well preserved but is not used very fully in the service of communication. Thus, speech may be used fundamentally as a discharge of tension, sometimes clearly comparable to a body excretory discharge; or for exhibitionistic purposes without real contact with the listener; or for ingratiation in which sympathy and self-justification rather than clarification is desired; or compulsively to fill a void of silence; or as a magical assertion to counterfeit fact. These narcissistic degradations of function occur at some time in any analysis, but are hardest to detect and work with when the misuse is consistent and largely ego-syntonic.

The misuse of speech in its function as communication may be reflected not only in the basic transference, but in that very part which is the gateway to and blends with the transference neurosis. Such deformations represent a fixation in early ego development, at which incipient defense reactions have begun to form at the very threshold of the oedipal period. This is after the acquisition of speech, when it is in the process of adaptive refinement to the new relation to reality, consistent with logical and abstract thinking. Such disturbances in the development of speech may contribute to an insecure transference as well as to a tendency to act out in the course of treatment. Acting out is in itself disruptive and disorganizing to treatment since it may remove highly charged memories from being worked with as they are expressed in action rather than being brought verbally into the analytic sessions. It always leads to interruption in the analytic process, sometimes to discontinuance, and may result in new complications in life.

Constitutional tendencies to action may certainly play some part in the propensity to act out in treatment. Inadequate interpretation of the transference and problems of countertransference are also important contributors. It has been the intention of this paper not so much to review all of the factors conducive to acting out as to focus on elements of disturbances in the use of speech and language which may interfere with the processes of growth as they are re-enacted in analytic treatment. Perhaps the most difficult misuse of the function of speech during analysis is its employment as a magical assertion, a substitute for reality-tested fact. This is a fraudulent objectivation. It is a question how much or how effectively such problems may be worked with. My hope is that this paper may stimulate further examination of the nature and effect of this special area in transference which represents the zone between action and speech, especially as I believe that this may have been overlooked or underplayed in its relation to other aspects of transference—more often being at least partially but inadequately dealt with in work with the defenses.

The other papers in this Symposium supplement my own in that they deal more explicitly with the consideration of acting out. The two papers of Grinberg and Vangaard touch rather closely and variantly on ideas I expressed in earlier papers on acting out (1950b and ch. 35). Using Freud's paper on "Remembering, Repeating and Working-Through" (1914a), Vangaard has developed his thesis on the basis that (i) the term acting out should be limited precisely to action arising during the analysis in the work of the analytic process—and not due to or affected appreciably by external happenings; (ii) acting out may serve to reduce tension created by unconscious conflict which has been activated in the analytic situation. This reduction of tension is not useful since resolution of the conflict has not been appreciably attained.

He then makes a sharp differentiation between actions due to unsolved unconscious conflict and behavior motivated by the need for reality testing when the unconscious conflict has been largely resolved. Thus acting out serves as a resistance and reality testing is a sign of therapeutic progress. The attitude of the therapist should then change accordingly, permitting more active benevolent intervention in the latter situation than would be permissible in the former. Now all this contrast is didactically very neat and in many instances helpful. But in my experience, in the actual treatment situation, it can rarely be as clear-cut as this.

Acting out certainly may become extreme when it is focused, channeled, and increased by the analytic process under the stress of an intense transference relationship. If we limit the term acting out to describe only this, and very precisely, we must recognize the intrinsic connection of such behavior to the tendency to repeat organized memories of old events or fantasies in action, instead of and sometimes as a step toward bringing them into conscious and verbally communicable form, and that this occurs outside of analysis and may be stimulated by external events of large or small proportions. Such stimulation from external sources may occur even in the course of an ongoing analysis and may combine with rather than predominantly arise from the work of the analytic process itself. Thus I cannot make as definite a differentiation as Vangaard seems to do. Similarly I think elements of attempts at reality testing may be discerned in many instances of acting out. If the unconscious conflict has been but little touched, then the reality testing is unsuccessful and may even be disastrous. In any case, the analytic patient is a living person and the analytic process constantly uses material from current situations in its relation to the drive and defensive tendencies from the past.

I would certainly concur with Vangaard's caution about the need to evaluate the significance of disproportionate or inappropriate action in terms of its relation to the degree of resolution of the underlying conflict. It is a temptation to speak of other points of Vangaard's paper, especially his distrust of the value of interpretation in dealing with ego problems and his apparent belief that analysis must be limited entirely to work with the transference neurosis. But this leads to more discussion than time will permit.

Grinberg's paper impinges on one of my own on (massive) acting out in the transference (see ch. 35). While I would say that all acting out must be viewed as having at least an implicit relation to the transference, this particular paper dealt with acting out which was manifestly and repetitively directed at the analyst within the actual analytic hour. Grinberg believes that acting out is *generally* based on a central nucleus of disturbance characterized by a "projective identification." He sees this as a repetition of mourning resulting from an early object loss, either real or fancied, before the sense of the wholeness of the self has been reasonably attained. The child then suffers from a splitting apart of the introjective-projective elements; and by a projective identification onto the substitute object, attempts to regain the lost part of the self-image. He states that "the child, who when experiencing the loss of the primal object (mother) and before finding a substitute object (father) feels acute anxiety because he is 'halfway,' reacts as though suddenly confronted with a void and gets into a tantrum of acting out so as not to lose himself into the void."

The behavior of the patients whom I was describing in my 1966 paper (ch. 35) resembled Grinberg's patients in that they showed a determined and repeated need to draw the analyst into the orbit of their disturbances, in a way which might be described under the heading of projective identification. But there are two main areas of striking differences: Grinberg sees this as a nuclear condition of mourning which forms the general core of acting out in its various manifestations. In contrast, my paper was based on five cases, which I regarded as unusual and even exceptional, occurring as they did as the only ones in thirty years of experience. I considered that their behavior might be classed as acting out since it appeared to be a rather direct repetition of early experiences which were not and could not be available for direct recall and verbal communication, because their strongest roots were in the first two years of life when there is no firm establishment of secondary process thinking. I wonder whether Grinberg's experience is based on a group of patients rather different from the general run of my own, and may include a much higher proportion of patients with severe distortions or deficits in early ego development.

The second important area of difference is in the genetic content of the situation giving rise to the projective identification. It is hard for me to conceive of a *general* developmental picture such as Grinberg describes. It would seem to me rather an exceptional situation. While the mother is the primal object during the first months of the infant's life, this relationship is supplemented gradually by that to the father, which may develop especially during the second year, and is substantially different from that with the mother. In any case, there would commonly be an overlap and mutual reinforcement rather than a chasm and void into which the child would feel a danger of being lost. My own cases were either only children or youngest children who, from birth on, had been in many ways in an abnormally close relationship with both parents, sharing the bedroom and sometimes even the bed throughout early childhood and well into latency. This complicated the progress of good separation from the parents as it generally develops through the introjective-projective stage. Further, the intensity of experiences both of closeness and of separation was increased by subjection to repeated primal scene experiences. Then the parents, though at hand, could not be reached except by crying, increasing to tantrums.

Grinberg notes the problem of identity in his patients and seems to attribute this to the projective identification in the early months. There were problems of bisexual identification in my patients too—which I thought were due to multiple determinants but might have been especially influenced by the constant bodily contact by touch and vision over a very considerable period of time with both parents. This then acted in a way to confuse the primitive body image.

As with Grinberg's patients, the tantrum behavior occurred frequently in relation to separations from the analyst even for weekends. It was also strikingly in evidence following "good analytic hours" in the Kris sense. It appeared that there was a fear of being incorporated and of submission as great as the fear of loss by separation. All my five patients were bright and even somewhat talented people whose mature development had been impaired by disturbances reaching a height in tantrum behavior. I had a modest success with three of the five patients. This was not the result of indoctrination or teaching, as Vangaard thinks may be necessary, but of constant interpretation of the various ways in which the narcissistic sensitivity had led to aggressive outbreaks, and of the gradual awakening of the patients to the need to master the temptation to gain a semblance of power through tantrum, grievances, and pseudoemergencies.

This leads me to Rangell's patient who had made a way of life from a similar form of acting out. It seems, however, that the disturbance arose from an exceptional series of actual traumas in the postoedipal period, such as to increase extremely the castration fears. I am also impressed by Rangell's statement of acting out as "a specific type of neurotic action directed towards interrupting the process of achieving effective insight—thereby seen mostly in the course of psychoanalysis but also elsewhere." This seems to me a concise summary and to represent pretty much what Freud was indicating in the 1914 paper referred to above.

I regret that I am unable to make any valid contribution to the discussion of Lebovici's paper, since I have no experience in the field of child analysis.

To return to further comments concerning Anna Freud's presentation—I was glad that she emphasized that there are differences in the origin and texture of acting out in the neuroses, impulsive characters, and psychoses, as there has been a recent tendency to oversimplify the application of our theories in a way to exaggerate common factors in these disorders and sometimes to overlook fundamental differences. I would also think that acting out in the neuroses occurs predominantly under the stimulus of the analytic process but may occur outside the analytic hour; further, that it resembles and is related to certain repetitive actions—no matter what we call them—which may occur even where there is no analysis. To me it seems a mistake to ignore these in our efforts to understand behavior. We may have to find terms or phrases which will adequately describe these and other differences. It is possible we are at a stage where the term acting out, now being used too loosely, may be on its way out. But I do not think this change can be demanded or hurried very much, since it depends on increasing precise knowledge and reciprocal theory to show its inadequacy and give rise, usually almost spontaneously, to new definition through which a new term will be assimilated. This may be implied in Anna Freud's succinct statements. When we use the term acting out now, we might well question and designate what constitutes the behavior we are describing and how we understand it.

My own paper has been so involved in considering the analytic process, that it may have skimped attention to the specific manifestations of the acting out and especially to the different types and origins of disturbances of the function of verbal communication in analysis. I see the development of speech as a significant stage, in which verbalization is combined with other motor expressions in varying ways. The scrutiny of these, within the analytic situation during treatment, may contain avenues for understanding early ego disturbances which have not been adequately explored.[6]

---

6 The role of speech in psychoanalytic treatment is taken further in ch. 18.

Notes on the Influence and Contribution of Ego Psychology to the Practice of Psychoanalysis (1970)

I

It is the purpose of this presentation to discuss certain aspects of the contribution of ego psychology during the last thirty-five years, especially with regard to its influence in psychoanalytic practice. A precise historical survey of the work that has been done would certainly extend beyond the scope of this paper. I shall try rather a brief sketch of this period in which external conditions, especially in this country, have brought an increased general knowledge of psychoanalysis and consequently a greater demand for its use. This situation has interacted with the developments within the science itself to produce a certain deepening of our knowledge, the expansion and consolidation of theory, and a gradual impact upon the technique of practice.

As an illustration I shall use a clinical case the course of which can be traced through twenty years of treatment, with a number of therapists, all one way or another under the aegis of psychoanalysis. This case is, first, an example of the group of patients who now form a considerable proportion of those seeking treatment. Then I have attempted to indicate the genetic background of its development which could not have been as well understood without the recent investigations and formulations of ego psychology. Finally, I have exploited this material to indicate how its detailed study may throw additional light on problems of therapy.

The period of thirty-five years dates from the years just before the Second World War. Then the coming of so many European colleagues meant an enrichment of our teaching and a general quickening stimulation to psychoanalytic thought and work. This was soon followed by an increased demand for training young psychiatrists who had been in war service. They were generally impressed by the greater understanding and effectiveness of the men who had been trained in psychoanalysis, even though there was naturally no opportunity for the practice of psychoanalysis itself under conditions of war. This meant that in the immediate postwar period there were many more applications for training than could possibly be met. Similarly there was—at least along the Eastern coast—a much greater demand for treatment on the part of the public than the number of well-trained analysts could supply. As a consequence, there grew up a number of enthusiastic but sometimes deviant schools of psychoanalytic thought, sometimes referred to as "neo-Freudian." This was undoubtedly more true in the New York area than in other parts of the country.

The length of time both for training and for the conduct of any individual analysis has always been one of the obstacles in the way of an easy assimilation of the practice of psychoanalysis. Among these accessory "psychoanalytic" groups there was often an emphasis on a shortening of both training and therapy and in some instances a de-emphasis on the importance of infantile sexuality and the role of the sexual development in the formation of neurosis. In some there further tended to be a greater attention to environmental factors and "interpersonal relations." All this tended to dilute psychoanalytic theory and sometimes seriously to degrade psychoanalytic practice when not only rules of technique but principles suffered. It was a sign, nonetheless, of the growing infiltration of psychoanalytic thought into the general understanding and interest in allied fields as well as in the general public.

In addition, patients seeking treatment presented clinical pictures of very great variety, and analysts found themselves confronted with requests for help from many whose disturbances did not fit neatly into the group of psychoneuroses for which analysis had been considered especially suitable.

The years just before the outbreak of World War II had been a period in which interest in ego psychology was germinating and would soon lead to further formulations based on clinical observations. The publication of Anna Freud's (1936) *The Ego and the Mechanisms of Defense* was probably the most important single stimulus to definite changes in the practice of analysis, and in retrospect can be seen as a landmark in the further development of ego psychology. Theoretically minded analysts who, like Freud, had been interested in the relation of analysis to other psychological systems continued to concern themselves with problems of the functioning of the ego, in relation to both libido and aggression, their interaction forming the basis of the autonomous core of the individual. Here we must be especially grateful to the intellectual leadership of Hartmann, whose work and publication beginning in the prewar era were continued in association with other colleagues, both psychoanalysts and psychologists, in the postwar years and the decade of the 50's.

It seems to me that in the last twenty to twenty-five years, there have been three general trends of investigation in psychoanalysis: (1) new formulations of theory; (2) observations of infant development and of mother-child relationships; and (3) clinical research reports of special problems in well-studied cases. Actually the first two areas of interest have seemed to complement each other very much; the furtherance of analytic theory has gone hand in hand with a burgeoning growth of studies of infants by analytically trained observers, and both have contributed largely to the background understanding of our clinical findings in the neuroses of both children and adults. But the practical application of this new knowledge to the work with neurotic disorders of childhood has naturally been more quickly envisioned than its utilization in the actual practice of psychoanalysis of adults. This may be inevitable because of the time necessary to test our findings as they are aligned with theoretical principles and finally observed in their later forms in adulthood.

The assimilation of the results of research in such ways as to make changes in analytic techniques, whether of principles or procedures, is a slow and may be a staggering process. The fundamental influence on technique can often be seen only after the lapse of a considerable time. New formulations may be accepted enthusiastically and overapplied by some analysts with an idea that these may shorten analysis. This sometimes occurs with an optimistic feeling that the new theoretical formulations have settled things once and for all, and that everything will now fall into line to make a satisfactorily closed system on which one can thoroughly depend. Or innovations in theory or practice may be greatly resisted by conservative analysts, especially those who with a kind of law of talion wish to continue analyzing in the way in which they have themselves been analyzed and taught. But this may be true in some measure in any science where there are always oscillations between periods of theoretical reformulations so satisfactory that they become accepted as basic facts, only to be followed by new surges of expansion of discovery for which the older theories are no longer adequate.

It has seemed that the increased interest in psychophysical development of the early years has not yet been sufficiently exploited and substantially used in the actual clinical practice of psychoanalysis. The reasons for this are not altogether clear. It may be the result in part of pressures of the times which tend to look forward rather than into the past and to shift from interest in individual therapy to more socialized forms of treatment. This interest seems perhaps to be more prevalent among analysts than among the patient population. But it may also be part of a natural lag in the assimilation of new knowledge requiring a change of emphasis with new and flexible technical procedures.

A seemingly paradoxical situation arises, however, from the fact that with the greater, often inaccurate knowledge of psychoanalysis by the general public, a more varied group of patients seeks treatment than the group of psychoneurotic patients for whose treatment we have in the past considered psychoanalysis to be especially indicated. Many of these have already had a "go" at one or another form of what they supposed to be analysis. This has sometimes included rather unusual forms of group therapy, "wild" analysis, combinations of drug therapy with other forms of psychotherapy, and sometimes treatment in one of the "neo-Freudian" schools. (Only three times in recent years have I had patients seeking treatment who had not already had some treatment, usually of the kind such as has already been mentioned.) Thus the public demand has forced or at least encouraged the widening scope of analytic practice.

A sign of the clinical way station at which we find ourselves seems indicated by the growing attention to the "borderline" patient. This term "borderline state," however, is essentially a temporary and noncommittal diagnostic compromise as it is too indefinite and in addition has the connotation of a near or potential psychosis. But many of the so-called borderline patients are not on the edge of psychosis, but are competent people with histories of disturbances in early infancy which contributed to faults in the ego and superego development, making for certain lacunae and distortions there, and also for irregularities in sexual functioning. Some of these cases are closer in structure to the perversions than to psychoses, having polymorphous perverse tendencies but without any leading perversion.

II

The rest of this paper will be devoted to a description of a small subgroup of the larger group of patients showing defects in early development. I have selected this smaller group for presentation as these patients show types of massive behavioral defenses with which I have sometimes found it possible to work successfully in such a way as to be able to carry through to satisfactory results. These special behavioral defenses are not uniformly characteristic of the total larger group. They are often overlooked as some of them may seem at first sight to be adequate character traits serving a sound defensive function and rather adding to the social acceptability of the patient. This social shell was one, however, which made use of language and certain pleasant behavior in ways to ward off deeper understanding at the same time accruing the vocabulary and interest in analysis which had a deceptive similitude to a real understanding. I found that if I detected this early and began to work gradually with these special defensive maneuvers and bits of behavior, there was some chance of getting through to a more genuine rapport permitting a real analytic process to occur.

In contrast to the earlier idea that the work of analysis proper was to be concentrated almost entirely on the content brought out by free association, Anna Freud indicated, in 1936, the important revision of this fundamental rule in emphasizing that attention must be paid to the (defensive) nature of any difficulties in maintaining free association. This is particularly pertinent in the group of patients presented here, as complex behavior may obstruct free association, or more frequently free association may be enjoyed rather than used. In many respects these patients resemble some of Freud's early cases in the vividness with which pathogenic relationships and dynamic patterns stand out, and the immediacy of the apparent response to therapy is impressive. But this rapid improvement is often followed by a relapse.

The group of patients with whom I am dealing does not comprise those neglected cases in which the patient came late to seek psychiatric help or psychoanalytic treatment and already had such strongly established appetites for secondary gain that the earlier inappropriate medical and surgical measures might in themselves have assumed the nature of addiction. They were on the whole more sophisticated and had sought some sort of psychological help early and repetitively, sometimes with well-trained and careful analysts, but perhaps more often with enthusiastic, variously trained therapists who might hope for an early cure with less intensive treatment.

Their defensive behavioral patterns express attitudes and maneuvers rather than mechanisms of defense, although specific mechanisms make up their component parts. Such patterned behavior, being usually, though not always, ego-syntonic, is rarely felt as symptomatic by the patient, who tends to ignore or justify it. Although ego-syntonic, it is not usually well organized and rigid, as in rather firmly, integrated character disorders. The patient appears rather flexible and at first these massive behavior reactions may seem to be only episodic and largely reactive, but after a time one realizes how persistent, extensive, and repetitive they are.

Treatment is begun often because of acute anxiety attacks, masked and experienced as peculiarly alien and sometimes appearing rather as anxiety-driven tantrums, which have gotten out of hand and are embarrassing or constricting in the life situation. Or it may be begun because of vague dissatisfactions with the way that life is going and the conscious wish for help in straightening things out. Many of these patients are bright, alert, and attractive people, appreciative of their own appearance and readily responsive to others with whom they make ready contact. They may be moody, but rarely appear really solitary. They are, on the other hand, often ingenious and practical, as well as being perceptive and verbal. They usually have a keen sense of humor and some wit. Keenly sensitive to the attitudes and behavior of others, they may show an astute perceptive understanding which is strikingly in contrast to the lack of genuine introspective interest in their own attitudes. I have thought that this was due in part to the fact that these patients seem to have a habitual undercurrent of anger which is mostly denied and unconscious, and appears rather in a pseudoexhilaration, lending a sheen to contacts and a pressure to activities which is attractive and charming. They may describe their own behavior with vividness which at first glance may be mistaken for insight. But it is from the stance of an onlooker at themselves and with less depth than is shown in their observations of others.

The treatment seems to begin auspiciously, especially if the patient has come to it largely on his own initiative, rather than by persuasion or pressure from others. Characteristically, he appears to have a good feeling for psychological understanding, learns free association rather readily,[1] is relieved and even enthusiastic to be in treatment. It is, however, rather difficult to gauge what he has gained from earlier treatment. The first hours seem in other respects unusually productive and informative. The special defensive behavior usually becomes obvious after a few weeks or months. Soon it may be noted that the knowledge which the patient seems to be gaining about himself is quickly seized upon and exploited in explaining the situations and attitudes of others, including the analyst, as well as (but more often instead of) leading to a deeper self-examination. Coupled with this is a compelling inclination toward diffuse competitive comparison with others, which gives the impression not only of general ambivalence but of such uncertainty in the self-image as to border on disturbance in the sense of identity. Even when these patients seem to grasp in-

---

[1] This is in contrast to the smaller group who find free association difficult largely because of open anger or fear of passivity.

terpretations of their own neurotic behavior, there is often a pleased gratification and a kind of relish in the discovery, which is then converted into a clever descriptive form which gives an armor against further understanding. The interpretation may subsequently be discarded or kept as of intellectual or even exhibitionistic interest but often fails to lead to appropriate working through.

As the analysis progresses, the stubbornly recurrent defensive behavior patterns become clearer. Very conspicuous in the *reaction to separation*. The capacity for rationalization is great and each untoward reaction is well explained in terms of immediate conditions. The idea that there is a difficulty in accepting separation is not tolerated. In general separations can only be accepted when they have been initiated by the patient. Even weekends, especially those elongated by a holiday, are too much if the situation is of the analyst's asking. The patient then often seeks to make an extra contact with the analyst under one pretext or another, or more extremely, has an outburst of anger in anticipation or in memory of the separation, or goes into a state of angry withdrawal. If there has already been a marked symptomatic improvement, this may collapse. Related to, but operating in the opposite direction from the poor tolerance of separation is the patient's difficulty in maintaining prolonged continuous relationships *outside of the analysis*. This is not always flagrantly apparent but can be detected in the life story. There may be a continual hunt for close relationships which are readily elicited and poorly borne. One gets the impression that the closeness becomes frightening because of a fear of submission or of engulfment, and the relationship breaks off in anger, which is justified on one or another pretext. As the analytic relationship which does not permit the full play of intimacy is safer for such patients, they generally sustain it reasonably well. Yet after the early stage is past, they may be less constant in attendance, show less rather than more interest in analytic work, and be unfaithful to it in their overreadiness to talk outside the analytic hour about what has gone on during the analysis. Such talk is likely to be complaining or picturesque. In this respect, they differ from the patients who split the deeper transference relationship and confide in and discuss their personal problems with friends as well as with the analyst.

Provocativeness, crisis and scene making are defensive patterns which appear both in and outside of the analysis. In my experience, however, once they appear in the analytic hour they may become grounded there, so that the behavior outside may be improved for considerable periods of time, especially in official positions in the world. The provocativeness often starts with a diffuse irritability which is like the overcast prelude to a storm; and, with the use of some trivial specific exchange with the analyst, leads to a circular form of increasing anger in which reason is lost sight of. There is an effort to draw the analyst into the storm by eliciting an angry or forbidding response from him, or by utilizing any change in the analyst's voice or attitude which can be so interpreted. Then the provocative tantrum may, but does not always, subside. It is then generally forgotten. Such provocativeness is closely related to *scene and crisis making* which are common in the history of the patient and may be more frequent in life situations than in the analytic setting itself. The difference may be due to the fact that the embellishment of a scene often utilizes the effect on an audience, which is greater in the outer world than in the privacy of an office. As is to be expected, however, such people may be efficient and well controlled for considerable periods of time in situations in which they have achieved some esteem. But even so, it is difficult for them to maintain a balance of equanimity long enough for the best development in work and personal relationships, both of which may be vulnerable to sudden breakdown.

Dramatization with its essential ingredient of exhibitionism is sometimes so strong as to offer a substantial substitute for reality. It often appears as an adjunct to humor and wit, may be combined with activity and sometimes with considerable organizing and executive ability in a way which would appear to offer the opportunity and need for reality testing. But the tolerance for frustration is low and just when the benefits of reality testing might be helpful, collapse may occur with the aid or sequel of a scene. This may then be associated with marked volatility of mood, which may quickly deteriorate into dramatic impulsiveness and helplessness. I have thought from work with my own patients that, in a paradoxical way, their sometimes excellent attainments in actual life had been reached under the goading influence of exaggerated fantasy-driven ambition which could never be satisfied. This situation was part of a lifelong tendency to grandiose fantasying, as a defense against early fears of destruction.

This leads to a consideration of the degree of *invasion of the sense of reality* by fantasying as well as a distortion of its functioning in peculiar and characteristic ways. What is so striking is that the patient has unusual perceptive alertness to the environment and often registers both details and gestalt formations with unusual vividness and accuracy. His perceptiveness is largely on the basis of observation, and his relationship to what is observed seems more visual than object-related. In certain limited respects he has an especially keen sense of reality. This capacity resembles that of the writer and in another way of the actor. But in writer and actor, it is supported by other character attributes which permit its consistent utilization. But in these patients, the graphic picture is subject to rapid distortion in the interest of defense, in meeting the exaggerated and temporary needs to bolster the self-esteem, to amuse and entertain, or to impress others with the uniqueness of any distress.

A rather severe distortion of reality observation is found in the temporary isolation and extreme exaggeration of some part of what has been observed or heard. Out of context this is then used as the focus of rationalization which also involves projection of a very simple sort. It has the earmarks of the early infantile state before individuation is securely established and the "I" is incompletely differentiated from the "other." Under stress then a self-induced hurt is quickly attributed to the "other" as is common in states of anger in early childhood. But in these patients, the focus is frequently on some insignificant point which may then become converted into a more extensive grievance which usually does not last long and is used as a weapon in temporary attack and then discarded. The content is often of only passing significance and the matter is soon dropped. While this symptom has a paranoid coloring, the content of the projection is not elaborated, organized or permanently established, although the tendency itself may be persistently repetitive. It arises against the background of a more fluid and volatile character structure containing hysterical elements and lacks the greater rigidity which is part of a more malignant paranoid tendency.

What appears to be the opposite of the grievance but is really only a negative form of it appears in states of prolonged silence in which the patient may fix his attention on one spot in the room or on one thought in his own mind and continue to look at or to think the same thing over and over, excluding everything else, until he has constructed a formidable crust between himself and the analyst. There is obviously a strong flavor here of ambivalent seduction. There is thus a vulnerability of the sense of reality to specially focused magnifying distortions which are usually transitory. They occur in the service of defensive rationalization and are accomplished by massive constriction of attention with denial and a peculiar capacity for self-suggestion, sometimes resulting in a definite though temporary illusion formation.

Related to these disturbances of perception of outer reality are the distorted perceptions of the own body, which are sometimes quite extreme and may be multiform and vary from time to time. This swing from concentration on the "other" to focused concern with the body self may have specific nuclear residues of unresolved disturbances in the early separation-individuation phases of infancy. In the cases I am considering, it occurred mostly in the setting of an unstable body image and went hand in hand with an insecure realization of the own identity, especially of sexual identity. But other body features might be involved as well. These are usually external body parts, especially those which may be examined visually and are open to direct comparison with others—facial features, hair, hands and feet.

The central focus of distortions in perception of the own body is announced in the not infrequent fantasy of the little girl that she possesses male genitals. While one sees this acted out very clearly in little girls of nursery school years, and sees its influence in later attitudes of women, occasionally it is encountered in the form of a definite illusion in an adult woman. I am not referring here to psychotic patients in whom the fantasy may appear as a full-fledged delusion, but rather to patients who have an established sensory illusion accompanied by a full realization of its absurdity. There are similar disturbances in men, certainly, some of which may be very persistent, e.g., misperception about the size of the penis or about the size of the nipples or of other body parts.

That such an illusion is a manifestation of the castration complex is evident. The question rather is: Why is this defensive illusion maintained (repetitively) with so much force when it is so clearly at odds with other aspects of reality appreciation and testing? The definite emergence of such an illusion in the girl by denial of the absence of external male genitals (or put another way, the denial that she is genitally different from the boy) or the denial of the possession of external genitals by the boy may be relatively frequent however, in dreams, in individuals who have severe castration complexes but never give any evidence of this disturbance of perception reaching the stage of an actual illusion.

This kind of an attempt at solution of the castration problem may be displaced onto other parts of the body relatively frequently both in these patients and in others. Such displacements appear in subjective distortion of form or function of other body parts or in hypochondriacal fears in regard to internal organs. Further, the dominant defensive mechanisms and patterning may involve thought processes and speech as well as shaping defensive behavior and body complaints. As is to be expected from what has already been said, these patients sometimes show rather rapid and massive shifts in subjective sexual identification, with an unusual degree of polarization of masculine-feminine with aggressive (active) submissive (passive) attitudes. The genetic relation of these symptoms to severe disturbances in the separation-individuation period of the infant's life will be discussed briefly later within this paper but really deserves more extensive and precise study than is available at present.

III

The presentation of a clinical case may be helpful to draw the picture together.

The patient was in her early forties when she sought a consultation presenting the questions whether or not she should resume analytic treatment; i.e., could she expect to gain more from treatment or must she settle for such gains as she had already achieved; if she returned for further psychoanalysis, should she change analysts?

Although it obviously had its roots much earlier, she dated her neurotic disturbance from about the age of twenty when she married soon after graduating from college. In her teens she had behaved in a passive and demure way, attracted few boys, felt left out, and was envious of other girls. She attributed her meek behavior to the influence of her grandfather with whom she had lived much of the time. Leaving college in a state of desperation over her lack of popularity, she determined to change herself and became an animated flirtatious girl. She felt this change of posture took a great deal of energy, but she was successful, and soon met and married a young professional man a few years her senior.

But this success turned at once into failure for she was afraid of intercourse and felt the penis was like a cannon. She developed severe rages at her husband and suffered from globus hystericus so relentless that it subsided only when she slept. She felt guilty and a failure as a woman, and anger at her husband for being a man. The whole marital episode lasted only three and a half months. She returned to her family home, having drifted into taking alcohol and drugs. She could not tolerate being married but was in terror of being alone. When her mother went out, leaving her alone, on the first day after she came home, she took an overdose of sedative sufficient to cause her to be taken to a general hospital after which she made her first venture into psychotherapy.

It should be mentioned that this young woman had for a long time been playing with the thought of suicide and promising or threatening herself with it from time to time if she did not live up to the demands she made of herself. It was probably under this self-imposed threat that she had pushed herself to play the role of the animated and flirtatious young woman. This preoccupation with suicide was evidently based on her identification with her parents for she was the only child of a gay and flirtatious young woman who had been drawn into marriage by the threat of the young man, who was to become her father, that otherwise he would commit suicide. It is interesting here to note that the patient's parents were also only children.

The patient's account of herself made clear that since early childhood she had her own secret world of fantasy in which the theme of romantic marriage more or less alternated with thoughts of poverty, degradation, and prostitution. She was never a withdrawn child, however, and her fantasy was continually combining with her forays into the world, so that she really was a dramatic role player. The thought of suicide was used much as it had been by her father—as a prod to herself and others, but also as a recourse in case of failure. Now when her mother deserted her for an evening at a time when she felt in great need, she did what her father had threatened twenty-one years earlier if the mother deserted him then. It is interesting that the patient's attempt, however, was of a passive nature—that of taking an overdose of sedative.

In the hospital she refused to see her family and on her discharge she refused to go home, but instead took a long trip with a woman friend, and then settled in a nearby city where she undertook to work and at the same time began some sort of psychotherapeutic treatment. This seems to have been what has recently been called psychoanalytically oriented psychotherapy. It was sustained for two years but was not intensive and a good deal of interpretation was—perhaps necessarily—given. Certainly she learned the term *penis envy* then even though she could not accept the concept. She also learned something of her hostility to her father for having neglected her. She soon gravitated back to her childhood home where her mother and stepfather were. Under the support of the therapy she began to work and did rather well. She felt that in other respects, she had not improved.

At twenty-six she returned to New York and perhaps catalyzed by her earlier initial success there, she again emerged into a kind of aggressive popularity. She had many lovers and many proposals; but never again committed herself to marriage. Each time she was interested in someone she developed the choking and was worse. Again she sought psychiatric help and eventually reached a woman analyst trained in one of the less conservative schools with whom she remained in treatment for about seven years. During this time she had not only the choking sensations when she was with men but a new symptom of acute pulling sensations in the eyes which felt as though they were being pulled from their sockets and she was attempting to get them back again. This occurred more often with women. Symptoms were predominantly but not strictly determined in this sex-differentiated fashion. Either might occur with either sex. If someone was warm and loving, then she developed the intolerable choking, while the eye symptoms came when she felt insecure because someone with whom she had felt closeness was retreating. The first choking episode occurred immediately after marriage, was associated with rage, and relieved only by screaming and yelling. This was in a situation, nonetheless, in which she felt loved by her husband but unable to love him in return. The eye symptoms emerged acutely when she was in treatment with the friendly woman therapist who allowed her many indulgences but had from time to time to enforce restrictions.

In general, she improved in this period of treatment in which negative transference was tolerated or ignored and the positive was exploited. But she had great trouble giving up the treatment. She fairly quickly fell into a morose depressed state, connected seemingly with the threatened loss of her therapist and influenced certainly by the death of her maternal grandmother, a rather harsh uncomfortable woman who had had a considerable hand in the patient's upbringing, and in childhood had openly complained of the mother's unacceptable behavior. This death had precipitated an ugly depression in the patient's mother, which the patient observed as so strong a postmortem identification with the grandmother that even her expression and appearance began to resemble that of the deceased woman. She herself felt doomed and enmeshed by this, as she felt she would also be compelled to resemble her mother and thus her grandmother. She was better, however, after a dream of two sisters in a suicide pact. In the dream the older one (the mother) must die while the younger one (herself) would survive.

On emerging from this depressed period and also having terminated her treatment, she was now again in one of her times of determined decision to seek relationships with men. At first seeking safety with older men, she soon was determined to be practical and seek a marriage with a man her own age with whom she thought she might anticipate a longer period of companionship. Energetically she established a more permanent home for herself and also threw herself into her work. Then about eighteen months after relinquishing therapy and again feeling the danger of an inner collapse, she was overtaken by a compelling fantasy of having a phallus—or one might better say, of having male genitals. This was so strong that she seemed actually to feel the organs as though they were attached to her own body. The way in which this occurred, spontaneously as she was walking down Fifth Avenue on a pleasant day, suggests that it was not just phallic envy, but that there was a very strong wish to be a man, or perhaps to be both sexes. Amused and appalled by this phenomenon in a way which suggests triumph, she was still sufficiently concerned to seek consultation and again entered a period of treatment which lasted for more than five years.

In this last treatment period there was a much more thorough exploration of both positive and negative elements of the transference neurosis without indulgent interventions or the use of supporting psychotherapeutic measures. The patient showed a predominantly appreciative though stormy response to this with outbursts of extreme provocativeness and tantrums, expecting that she would force termination of the analysis in this way and expressing contempt for the man who could tolerate her behavior. She improved a good deal during the analysis, becoming more self-sufficient, but remaining highly ambivalent, narcissistic, and impulsive.

At one time rather late in the analysis she began a period of delayed mourning for her maternal grandfather who had died rather suddenly some years earlier. After this she began to have more direct sexual transference feelings toward the analyst rather than his being used in scattered transference representations. Probably the urgency of these was too much for her to tolerate and she began to plan for and demand the end of the analysis. When she consulted me some eight or nine months later, it was clear that there was much unfinished business concerning the death of the grandfather. She still gave quite conflicting and confused statements about when this had occurred, but she associated it with her first or second coming to New York.

The period of delayed mourning had been initiated when she was away on a vacation some months before she terminated the analysis, but after termination had begun to be talked of. She then awoke one morning with a half-dream-fantasy of being locked in a sexual embrace with her grandfather, but without any rhythmic movement. She was very distressed and later that day drove alone through the country overwhelmed with tears, first thinking of the death of the paternal grandmother of whom she had been fond, and then soon of the death of the maternal grand-

father who had been closest to her in her childhood. It was on her
return to treatment after this vacation that she had begun to experience urgent sexual feelings toward the analyst, at the same
time feeling that she would die or be killed on the couch. She
recalled nightmares of childhood with a fear of being marked for
death by her pediatrician (who happened to have a last name
resembling that of the consultant who had sent her to her last
analyst). After this she refused to lie on the couch and really
forced the termination of the analysis.

She then had two operations, one a removal of a metatarsal
neuroma and the other a hysterectomy. Both operations were indicated, but not urgent. They did seem, however, to have the
significance to the patient of a life and death struggle and probably had the meaning of a necessity to be castrated. A few months
later she began a love affair with an older man, a widower, and at
first felt happy and lucky, but soon the relationship began to
deteriorate. The bed seemed a place of death, even as the analyst's
couch had been at the end of the analysis when she refused to
lie on it. It seemed probable that this man represented her maternal grandfather who was the truest oedipal figure in her life.
She felt that she was in love with him, but was both drawn to
him and felt she must escape. It was also clear in their sexual
relationship that for him to be potent she had to be extraordinarily passive. She at one time had the experience of a total emotional surrender, with a vaginal orgasm. But usually when this
occurred, it was followed the next day by a fear of disintegration
similar to the condition in which she had seen her mother and
grandmother when depressed. On occasion when she masturbated
with a fantasy of being very passive, she became panicky and felt
as though she were losing her mind.

It is essential to look back into the early years of this patient's
life to decipher the sources of her extraordinary ambivalence,
coupled as it is with gross disturbances of body, especially genital,
identity and involving further special capacities to produce and
exploit distortions of reality perceptions.

Some kind of sexual stimulation and need for genital discharge
apparently occurred early and involved a peculiar amalgamation
of oral, visual, and genital awareness. The patient's spontaneous
memory goes back to the age of three, with spotty memories even

earlier. According to her feeling, she masturbated all her life and almost daily. Her early memory is of some kind of genital excitement from the age of three, without remembered fantasy. This occurred in the presence of her mother especially when both napped together in the afternoon, and at times it was associated with sucking at the mother's breast. Both institutions continued until the age of four and a half when the mother deserted her in favor of a lover, disapproved of by the maternal grandparents. The genital activity of this early time was later checked with the patient's mother who recalled that the child had used a wadded-up sheet between her legs to help stimulate herself genitally. It is apparent that the whole set of nap activities almost surely was mutually gratifying (symbiotic) to mother and child. One surmises, but cannot know conclusively, that the genital excitement was a combination of oral and beginning genital rhythm without true orgasm, and that there was already some primitive conception of the need for an external organ (breast and/or penis) for satisfaction.

There is more amnesia for the period from four and a half to seven, when the mother returned, than for any other time in her life. While she felt collapsed by the mother's departure, she quickly bridged it and alleviated her fear of desertion by the grandparents by a constant flow of letters to her mother. At this time, she lived with the grandparents, and was accepted by her grandfather in a close bodily intimacy which was reminiscent of her earlier attachment to the mother. Further, he adored her as long as she did exactly what he wanted, and he made daydream plans for her to follow in his business as he had previously wanted her mother to do. She learned to manage situations with tears. There seemed also to be the beginning of masturbation fantasies about her mother's life with the lover, which seemed both glamorous and degraded.

At seven when the mother returned home to marry the lover, the child was definitely a "member of the wedding." As she had been her mother's confidante and witness to the mother's erotism and constant flirtations, she seemed to deposit this knowledge in proliferated and wildly embellished oedipal and prostitution masturbation fantasies, while in her official life she was innocent of any sexual knowledge and was a sedate and demure child.

In prepuberty her masturbatory interest changed from a concern with the vagina, which she also treated as a mouth,[2] to using manual pressure on the vulva in such a way as to elicit some clitoral sensation. All this was supplemented with fantasies of being watched by a man with an enormous erection about which he was helplessly frustrated. Obviously this was both a seduction and a revenge fantasy in which the genital elements were stronger than previously, and the whole performance contained efforts at establishing a sense of body separateness, but still supplemented by the sight of the large male organ. At other times there were frank oedipal fantasies.

Puberty and early adolescence brought a shift of body awareness. There was further strengthening of her focused genital feelings and masturbation seemed to have a new importance to her. She felt as though she had invented it herself and was both self-depreciating and important.[3] When a bit later she heard a name for her discovery and also that another girl had made the same discovery, her guilt was relieved and her importance may have been diminished.

Three other developments in the role of her genital feelings should be mentioned. *First,* in her young adulthood, when she was successful in work and was given a promotion, she would have a feeling of being "totally possessed" and get the choking feeling. *Second,* vaginal orgasm in young adulthood was satisfying only when in intercourse she could almost eliminate the man from her awareness, i.e., she had it "just for herself." (The use of the man as the impersonal complementary agent is reminiscent of her use of the wadded-up sheet in infancy.) The converse was also true: when she was relatively passive in intercourse and her partner could be fully potent, she would either withdraw into unresponsiveness or, if aroused to orgasm, would have panicky

---

[2] After pressing her finger into her vagina she would next put it into her mouth to taste the secretion. This seems probably a new version of the early sucking at the mother's breast while pressing a wadded sheet against her genitals. It seems also that the clitoral sensation may now have been stronger and more in the child's possession (i.e., part of herself) than it had been when she seemed to be dominated by the obligatory image of the external genital—the phallus-breast—represented by the wadded-up sheet.

[3] The chapter in Carroll's *Through the Looking Glass* which is entitled "It's My Own Invention" gives an account of the disguised terms in which a similar discovery is made by the White Knight. I have described this in *Swift and Carroll* (1955).

fears of disintegration. *Third,* related to this state was a phase in which the idea of intercourse as a killing or being killed came vividly to the fore. The shadowy appearance of this in the transference in the last period of analysis probably influenced her to precipitate termination of treatment. The nucleus of this death-dealing fantasy appeared to be in old symbiotic genital fantasies about her grandfather, about whose death some years earlier a delayed mourning had begun to appear. This grandfather's relation was, as already indicated, an almost total displacement from a similar state with her mother. The panic now, however, also influenced and was influenced by her need to have her foot operated on and to have a hysterectomy, both operations having been undertaken in the few months past.

Although there was no clear memory before the age of two and a half, it is justified to suppose that this period was one of considerable stimulation causing tension in the infant. Both parents were young, immature and unhappy. The indication is of a considerable amount of dissension between them. The mother was not one to shield her infant but rather to use the baby as a shield and comfort for herself. Whether there was frequent primal scene stimulation or whether it was more the excitement of constant quarreling may not, in this case, have made a great deal of difference in the reactive patterns stamped on the young child. That the separation of the parents removed the father just as a period when, under better circumstances, he might have begun to emerge as a separate and desirable influence in the child's life, seems to me very significant. That she later associated surrender with death may have been rooted in this period. In her later life it was not only the possession of the penis, both directly and as a symbol of power, but the feeling of being able to be aggressive which meant so much in her sense of her own value and even her existence.

IV

Although this patient was not one with whom I worked analytically, I have selected her case for presentation because of the accessibility of her rather long and vivid history of the development and variability of her symptoms. I saw her for five consultation visits. Further, the account of her various therapies is in itself something of a record of the influence of psychoanalysis on psychotherapy and the changing state of psychoanalytic practice in this country.

In spite of her extraordinarily disturbed family life in childhood and adolescence, she was evidently a person of fundamentally good physique and intellectual endowment, which allowed the semblance of good development and excellent progress in school, so that she graduated from college at twenty. When during her college years, she sought consultation with a psychoanalyst because of her social unease, no treatment was considered for her. It was only when soon afterward she was confronted with marriage and the permanent separation from her grandfather that the acute anxiety, emotionalism, and hysterical symptoms became manifest. In the next twenty-two years she turned from one therapy to another and was rarely able to go for any length of time without some kind of analytic help. This may in part have been due to the incompleteness of some of her early treatment. But the early confusion, stimulation, and inconstancy to which she was subjected in infancy as well as the pervasiveness of disturbances and distortions of practically all the family relationships would account in good measure for the adhesiveness of her symptoms. Nonetheless she was able to function quite well in the world where she was relatively successful except for her susceptibility to anger.

Looked at from a little distance one sees that the patterns of this patient's individual life were formed against the background of models and by interaction between family members, in whom aggression seemed generally to be the dominant drive, and was accepted as such. Love was not lacking, but was of a narcissistic type characterized by strong identification and possessiveness, which led in turn to retaliations and anger. It was an intrafamily situation in which sentimentality may have been accepted and tenderness seen as weakness. The exception in this was the patient's father, an interloper in the family, considered weak and ineffective with his inverted aggression appearing in threats of suicide. (He later turned out to be a fairly steady but mediocre man whom the patient scarcely knew until she was adult.) The head of the group was the maternal grandfather who had been successful in business and could see nothing better for his young granddaughter than that she follow in his footsteps in business. He did, however, wish her to look particularly girlish, innocent, prim, and pretty. He had apparently behaved very similarly with his daughter, the patient's mother.

The texture of this household is significant. Economically stable, and rather consistent in its own emotional turmoil, it furnished the stuff on which the child's important identifications and general sense of identity were to be based even though the individual, and specifically the sexual, identity were profoundly confused. Thus this disturbed but durably balanced family milieu must have contributed to the deepening of the character traits which later were used by the patient in exaggerated defensive maneuvers both in life and in her treatment; especially the readiness to let go in anger, the sardonic humor, and the relish for the drama of life.

The effect of the family attitudes (which one might call the family culture) was similar in its reinforcement of the early pathological but individual sexual patterns, strengthening and perpetuating them through repeated gratifications; that is, not only was the child an onlooker of the relationships of the adults of the family, but she was herself a participant in overerotized and aggressivized behavior with them. These infantile patterns were changed somewhat by her physical development with increasing genital demands asserting themselves. While there was clearly a struggle for a heterosexual development, the sexual behavior was repeatedly pulled into the service of attempts to complete the unstable body image and thereby to promote a sounder individuation than that of the false maturity of too early and strained self-reliance driven by aggression. Such progress was hindered by the frequent oscillation between masculine and feminine identifications, either one of which seemed dangerous by itself and might end in flight to the opposite. This state of affairs was fundamentally grounded in the specific experience of the first years of life. From the glimpses I had of this patient through consultations and the biographical material supplied to me, I believe that the body-image problems extended in rather specific patterns from body ego to psychic ego. The patient certainly offers a wide range of developmental constellations for a research-minded therapist.

Mahler's (1967, 1968) work has been of invaluable aid to me in understanding such cases as the one I have just attempted to describe in summary form. While we do not have memories from the first year of life or even material directly from the patient which might be the basis of psychoanalytic reconstruction, yet I believe we are warranted in considering that certain pathological patterns and problems had their origin in disturbances at that early time.[4] The patient's later behavior and symptoms carry the imprint of a marked and ever-*recurrent struggle to separate herself from "the other"* (whether mother, grandfather, lover or various therapists), resulting in a variety of problems of sexual identification and identity; *constantly recurring states of anger* in her efforts to establish object relationships which do not "come off" but end in flight out of *fear of killing or being killed; fluidity of body image* both in form and function, due to the constant contamination of the self-image by parts of the "other," in which there can nearly always be deciphered some version of the early relationship with the mother.

The intensification of looking and of attracting attention through crying was almost surely a necessary and inevitable development in this first year of life, and sowed the seeds for the scoptophilia and exhibitionism dramatically represented by the eye symptoms of her adulthood.

Throughout it all there developed a remarkable alertness, an outreaching and a watchful hold on external reality, which was, however, subject to quick shifts of denial and distortion. In addition to the clinical continuity of the patient's state with conditions such as are outlined by Mahler, the actual biographical data are also congruous with this picture. The patient was the only child of parents both of whom were only children. The marriage began with a burden, since the mother, who was gay, frivolous, and quixotic, married the father without love. He, apparently a rather passive-appearing man, showed his stubborn aggression with threats of suicide by which he achieved but could not sustain the

---

[4] In a recently translated article, D. Burlingham (1935) has stressed the exquisite early sensitivity of the infant to the mother so that the child reacts not only to the open mood of the mother but senses the mother's suppression or denial of disturbed emotional states. This is based on direct observations which are close to my own postulations expressed in early papers on the predisposition to anxiety (1941). I believe that the infant also reacts very definitely to changes in the body tension of the mother.

marriage. When the patient was two and a half (at a time when the father might have begun to be important to the young child), the divorce occurred and with it the father disappeared.

We can only assume that those first two years were troubled ones for the child as well as for the immature parents, and that relationships generally were inconstant and intense. In the years when the child was two and a half to four and a half, the mother, feeling degraded and dependent on her parents for support, seems to have turned to the child in an extraordinarily pathological symbiotic relationship, which may have been a recrudescence of an earlier one, and left deep marks on the girl's development. The desertion of the mother at four and a half brought the use of the grandfather as a substitute for both mother and father, but always with a fear of loss, and an actual denial of feeling when loss really was experienced.

One must ask further, how much do disturbances in these first months produce specific patterns against the background of obligatorily increased narcissism, accompanied by extreme ambivalence? How much is there a persistence of an unusual amount of primary narcissism especially in those who seem to be well endowed constitutionally but have a rough time in the first year of life. Is the later patterning influenced by any events of that early patterning, other than as in this patient in whom the same continuing influences which were distorting early led directly to later troubles as well? Mahler speaks of a normal symbiotic phase[5]

[5] Mahler uses the term *symbiosis* to express a mutuality between mother and infant which begins soon after or almost simultaneously with the beginning of the separation-individuation stage of development (i.e., sometime in the second or third month) and succeeds the initial period of dual unity within a common boundary. She bases the idea of symbiosis on the hypothesized picture from the infant's point of view; that while beginning to separate he still can get his needs fulfilled from "the other," the mother. Out of this the mutuality develops. Mahler supports her idea further by the work of T. Benedek (1938, 1959) who emphasized that this stage of mutual gratification represents a beneficial developmental stage in the mother as well. Mahler grants that the normal symbiosis of early infancy is an extremely uneven affair, being an absolute dependence for the child and a very relative (but never absolute) one for the mother. It seems to me that neither Benedek nor Mahler sufficiently takes into account that this early and apparently satisfactory mutuality occurs quite often in mother-infant relationships in which the infant represents a phallus to the mother, and that the mother feels fulfilled at this time, but that the degree of actual development in her may be a complex and not easily determined matter, the seamy side of which may not show up very promptly. Mahler does state that the term *symbiosis* is a metaphor and does not describe, as the biological concept does, what actually happens between two individuals. Per-

which is beneficial. But if the symbosis is of a pathological type, does this mean that the mother has already such pathological needs as to overdraw on her relationship to the child? Or may a sick child or one unevenly developed at birth, by his very needs, draw the mother into an abnormal symbiotic relationship, and through the activation of this and its polarization by guilt feelings and other complex sensitivities continue a disturbance of individuation into the later infant years?

The intensification of the ambivalence and its subsequent penetration into most of the departments of the life of the special patient I have been describing are impressive. It seemed to result in a constant tendency for oscillation between two poles, so that flight from one to the other could always be used as a defensive maneuver whenever either closeness or distance of whatever nature became threatening. This ambivalence and the readiness for anger seemed the most important character traits probably going directly back to these fundamental disturbances of the first two years of life. The anger, with its constant accompanying fantasy of killing or being killed, seemed to be a paradoxical, and often insidiously destructive, way of the patient's assuring herself that she was alive and active.

Of further importance is the distortion of the sex life by the impact on it of the aggressive drive and the accompanying fears and by its being drawn into the service of attempts to repair a faulty and too plastic body image. It was especially striking that the patient only experienced a full orgasm, first, when in masturbating she dispensed with her romantic fantasies and said, "I will do this just for myself"; or second, when she felt a complete surrender to a partner who could only be vigorously potent if she was completely passive. (This actually seemed to approximate her dream of sexual embrace with her grandfather; but the experience, in its greater violence, may have been more of a sadomas-

---

haps I am being too precious, but it still seems to me that Mahler's own term separation-individuation stage (which can be qualified with the adjectives "early" and "later") is so far superior in its accuracy that I prefer to use it. An appreciable symbiosis (in the biological sense) between mother and infant seems to me to imply such an underlying disturbed state in the mother as might intensify the tendency to polarization and partial reversal of roles in the separation-individuation phase and have untoward effects on the infant. By keeping the term *separation-individuation* for the normal stage in the infant, a confusion between symbiosis as normal and symbiosis as pathological is avoided.

ochistic affair than the dream represented.) But while a sexual experience could in these ways produce a full orgastic gratification, in each instance it was followed after some hours by a feeling and fear of disintegration.

V

The question arises whether the prognosis in such a case as this one is so limited as to make therapy contraindicated or at least wasteful from the patient's point of view. This cannot be decisively answered at present. In this particular case the disturbance in ego development has involved a relatively severe defect in object relationship. Our first question might be whether the necessarily long treatment permits any degree of filling in of such a defect through growth nurtured by sustained transference rapport —provided the analyst does not attempt to do this through interventions and indulgences which would convert the transference into an *actual* relationship in life. If this occurs, as it did with this patient and the benevolent female analyst, the situation tends to reproduce the nagging pull toward the early "symbiotic" relationship and risks simply repeating in a new form the old problems, so that neither object relationship nor self-reliance (without anger) is much improved.

One aspect of this might be formulated as follows: does the unique relationship in the analysis permit an experience of object constancy, which together with the work within the realm of the transference neurosis permits some degree of repair that may be carried over into nonanalytic relationships and improve these and the sense of autonomy as well.

The second question is concerned with the role of interpretation and reconstruction if such a well-contained transference development is established. I believe that there has been a gradual shift in the attitude of analysts toward the place of reconstruction in analytic therapy. In the eyes of many its importance is discredited or diminished. The aim is to work with attitudes involved in conflicts and defenses rather than to uncover the specific events which have been the turning points or crystallizing points about which these have developed. I would certainly agree that the uncovering of memories, either directly or by reconstruction, does not give the magic relief by abreaction originally ascribed to it. On the other hand, these memories are the carriers and currency of the developing attitudes and usually give the specific terms in which the patient has felt and has pictured himself. He is more in contact with himself when the disturbing attitudes of the present are seen and felt in relation to his own unique history than if no such reconstruction is attempted. For instance, there is no clearer record of the vicissitudes of conflicts with their defensive mechanisms and forward movement at the expense of certain restriction than can be seen in a screen memory if it is possible really to work with it sporadically over a period of time. Thus it is not just *per se* to fill in the amnesia of the past, but to put the patient in living touch with, and in this way help him to understand, the emotional trends developing out of significant events and crucial periods in his own life. This may lead him then, even imperceptibly, to attempts to master those action tendencies which have been interfering with his progress. Sometimes he is quite aware of this work of mastery. Even in the neuroses, especially in the phobic and compulsive states, we know that there are times when it is necessary for the patient to make conscious exertions to correct tendencies which have become embedded as habits, but that he does so in better spirit and with better effect if he has understood what these originally sprang from.

We may now raise a third question even more difficult to answer. Assuming that the patient has suffered a considerable impairment of the progress of individuation in the first two years of life, is it possible for him to recover some feeling conception and appreciation of this from the way in which evidences of the conditions giving rise to it filter through into the analysis in a great variety of ways: the earliest memories, pseudomemories, screen memories, family stories which he has picked up because he has a special affinity for them and uses them as screens, early symptoms, certain dream states, episodic physical peculiarities demonstrated on the couch, etc., all may play a part. Further, if he does recover some such ideas and so reaches a feeling of understanding something of his own early babyhood, is this of any use at all to him, or is it only to be an interesting encumbrance? It is impossible for any single analyst to accumulate enough firsthand experience with a large enough group of patients to justify a confident reply now.

In the few cases I have had, I have thought that the therapeutic results were influenced not only by the probable severity of the impairing conditions of the first years but by the degree to which in the therapy itself it was possible to achieve a fairly consistent and flexible communication with the patient. If I could reach that, then there was a better chance of getting the patient into a real contact with himself, a situation which is necessary if any desire for change involving mastery or reduction of sadomasochistic and exhibitionistic gratification is to be awakened.

This brings us back to the consideration of the massive behavioral defenses which were outlined earlier in this paper. These are difficult to modify. Since they originally had real narcissistic sustaining value for the patient and sometimes led to considerable social acceptance as well, they are implicitly felt to be the bulwarks of his personality. Pointing out that they are valuable but that their overuse has made a coat of plastic armor producing isolation from and noncommunication with both himself and "the other" is unwelcome and is met with anger, disbelief, and derision. Once the inoculation has been made, it depends a good deal on the tactful ingenuity and the persistent durability of the analyst whether any progress can be made. In my experience, such patients rarely can appreciate any gain or feel any liberation in response to such interpretations until a considerable time has passed, and even then the gain is seen in retrospect and sometimes without awareness of what it has been due to. One may say that there is a kind of re-education in this process, but it is a re-education in which direction and intellectualization—often craved by the patient—must be avoided. I would also want to make clear that it is the modification of these defenses which may make possible the greater use (absorption) of the content of the rest of the analytic work.

CONCLUDING REMARKS

The work which has been done on ego development has, in my estimation, allowed a much deeper understanding of all of our patients, especially as to the influence of the events of the preverbal months of life on later development. But of equal or greater importance is the insight into the role of aggression in its interplay with the libidinal phase development. I would see ag-

gression as having its origin in the enormous pressure of growth—
in the expansion and differentiation of the organism during the
parasitic period of foetal life. At this stage the foetus is totally
dependent on the mother for its existence and its development
may be grossly influenced by untoward conditions in the mother.
Yet its development proceeds largely according to autonomous,
biologically determined patterns. The force of growth would appear of necessity a nonhostile form of physical aggression and will
later contribute to the core of the autonomous ego, as the body
ego develops into the psychic ego. The aggression can then only
become hostile aggression when there is at least a beginning object relationship. Until this stage of development has been
reached, frustration leads only to an undifferentiated form of
suffering in which potential sadism and masochism are the same.
It is regarding this stage (or zone) of transition from body ego to
psychic ego that I would foresee the possibility of greater and
more precise knowledge regarding the somatopsychic as well as
sadomasochistic disturbances of balance and their sequelae. Such
information might be gained from psychophysiological research,
combined with carefully done and reported clinical observations
of infants and supplemented by psychoanalytical studies of adults.

Some analysts may raise the objection that such enterprises go
beyond the sphere of psychoanalysis. Certainly they do go beyond
the borders of the metapsychology of the psychoneuroses, for
which psychoanalysis as a therapy has been best suited. But at
least as I see it, if we are to understand early ego development we
must be ready to seek and to try to assimilate such knowledge. I
am not suggesting that the analyst become a physiologist who will
introduce adjunctive methods into the psychoanalytic therapy. I
am convinced that the analyst as therapist must keep his field as
free as possible from accessory modes of treatment which act as
interventions which are rarely justified and may be complicating.
But I am strongly endorsing the cooperation of and the pooling
of information from a well-done psychoanalytic therapy (which is
in itself a research) with the research in physiological psychology
and in the studies of the development of infants.

There are two other special areas which occur to me as ones in
which further knowledge of early ego development may be enriching to psychoanalysis. The *first* is the investigation of constitu-

tional variations; and the *second* is a more specific appraisal of the basic relationship between the analyst and his analysand in therapy. As to the *first*—with my belief that the core of the autonomous ego has its origin in the biological growth of the young organism, and that the patterns of physical growth and learning leave their stamp on later patterns of mental functioning, then it may be well worth examining the individual differences in infant responses even during the first year of life. We would wish to determine, for example, the variations in degree of sensory responsiveness in different infants; or the evidences and timing of an early organizing capacity as seen perhaps in the baby's ability to observe gestalt formations and similarities in patterns and rhythms. I have thought—on the basis of limited clinical work and from biographical and autobiographical studies of artists— that in the creative individual, special capacities of responsiveness along these lines are inborn. It may be that investigations of this kind have already been done by academic psychologists whose work may not yet have been sufficiently exploited in relation to the analytic approach. Some work of this kind may also be in process in infant studies by psychoanalytically trained observers. I think that the work of Mrs. Burlingham has some bearing on these problems, although she is dealing with handicapped (blind) children rather than normal or gifted ones.

The *second* area mentioned was the fundamental relationship between the analyst and analysand which must exist if therapy is to develop at all. More specific investigation of this may have a direct bearing on treatment procedures, as the nature of the relationship itself is in any case somewhat determined by the earlier one between mother and infant. I have spoken of this in earlier articles as the "basic transference" to distinguish it from the reactions of the transference neurosis. Since some analysts consider that the term transference should be limited to the phenomena of the transference neurosis, I have recently substituted simply the word "rapport". At any rate there must be the capacity for sufficient emotional engagement between therapist and patient to give some margin of real communication. Especially in patients who have had grave disturbances in the first two years of life, this basic relationship is usually a complex ambivalent one. The hostile aggression may be concealed by the patient, especially if he is in need and anxious. With a wish to get relief by compliance, he may tend to build up an artificially strong semblance of positive feeling, which may appear rather convincing but is not durable.

With most patients who come to me I do not begin treatment until I have made a diagnostic study in a few interviews. In this way I am forewarned about such patients who from their immediate symptomatology might appear to be less complicated psychoneuroses. Their life story will usually give some indication of whether there has been trouble in the first two years. If the patient is one who sinks at once into an overly strong positive transference relationship (as was true in the patient whose case has been given here) I watch for indications of the defensive armor, evident in behavior and character traits, and begin work gradually but persistently to uncover the hostility. If, on the other hand, the patient shows open ambivalence and direct hostility in relationship to the analyst, I work with it immediately. This is contrary of course to the usually recommended procedure of waiting for a strong positive transference to be established. I have found that some patients find relief in the fact that the analyst is aware of their hostility, can tolerate it, and that it will not threaten the treatment. My own question here is whether this early beginning of work with the hostile aggressive attitudes of the patient does not actually consolidate the rapport and by its maintenance throughout the analysis do something to give the patient a better hold on life through somewhat repairing the damage done in the earliest years.

One further comment—while communication through speech is our main channel of contact in analysis, it is especially important to scrutinize carefully how speech is being used. What are the individual's accessory needs for contact, and is speech genuinely subserving them, no matter how difficult that may be? Or are these being defended against and held further in check by an incomplete or specious verbal communication?

Bibliography

Abraham, K. (1907), The Experiencing of Sexual Traumas as a Form of Sexual Activity. *Selected Papers on Psycho-Analysis*. London: Hogarth Press, 1949, pp. 47-63.

—— (1910) Remarks on the Psycho-Analysis of a Case of Foot and Corset Fetishism. *Selected Papers on Psycho-Analysis*. London: Hogarth Press, 1949, pp. 125-136.

—— (1917), Ejaculatio Praecox. *Selected Papers on Psycho-Analysis*. London: Hogarth Press, 1949, pp. 280-298.

—— (1925), The History of an Impostor in the Light of Psycho-Analytical Knowledge. *Clinical Papers and Essays on Psychoanalysis*. New York: Basic Books, 1955, pp. 291-305.

Acworth, Bernard (1947), *Swift*. London: Eyre & Spottiswoode.

Alexander, F. (1925), A Metapsychological Description of the Process of Cure. *Int. J. Psycho-Anal.*, 6:13-34.

—— (1958), A Contribution to the Theory of Play. *Psychoanal. Quart.*, 27:175-193.

Altman, J. L. (1957), On the Oral Nature of Acting Out. *J. Amer. Psychoanal. Assn.*, 5:648-667.

Anonymous (1685), *The Life of Titus Oates from the Cradle to His First Pilloring for Infamous Perjuring* (A Broadside). Printed in London by Mallet in White Horse Alley near Fleet Bridge.

—— (1881), *The Life and Death of Captain William Bedloe, One of the Chief Discoverers of the Horrid Popish Plot*. London: Printed by George Larkin for John Hancock and Enoch Prosser.

Anstruther, I. (1957), *Dr. Livingstone, I Presume*. New York: Dutton.

Author of 'Digby' (1902), *Rochester and Other Literary Rakes of the Court of Charles II*. London: Longmans Green.

Baesjon, Jan (1956), *The Vermeer Forgeries*. London: Geoffrey Bles.

807

Bak, R. C. (1953), Fetishism. *J. Amer. Psychoanal. Assn.,* 1:285-298.

—— (1968), The Phallic Woman: The Ubiquitous Fantasy in Perversions. *The Psychoanalytic Study of the Child,* 23:15-36.[a]

Bakwin, H. (1942), Loneliness in Infants. *Amer. J. Dis. Child.,* 63:30-40.

Balint, M. (1935), A Contribution to Fetishism. *Int. J. Psycho-Anal.,* 16:481-483.

—— (1954), Analytic Training and Training Analysis. *Int. J. Psycho-Anal.,* 35:157-162.

Ball, F. Elrington, ed. (1914), *The Correspondence of Jonathan Swift.* London: G. Bell.

Bally, G. (1945), *Vom Ursprung und von den Grenzen der Freiheit.* Basel: Schwabe.

Baring-Gould, S. (1880), *Curious Myths of the Middle Ages.* Boston: Roberts, pp. 160-172.

Bell, A. I. (1961), Some Observations on the Role of the Scrotal Sac and Testicles. *J. Amer. Psychoanal. Assn.,* 9:261-286.

Benedek, T. (1938), Adaptation to Reality in Early Infancy. *Psychoanal. Quart.,* 7:200-214.

—— (1959), Parenthood as a Developmental Phase. *J. Amer. Psychoanal. Assn.,* 7:389-417.

Beres, D. (1957), Communication in Psychoanalysis and in the Creative Process: A Parallel. *J. Amer. Psychoanal. Assn.,* 5:408-423.

Bergman, P. (1947), Analysis of an Unusual Case of Fetishism. *Bull. Menninger Clin.,* 11:67-75.

Bernfeld, S. (1952), On Psychoanalytic Training. *Psychoanal. Quart.* 31:453-482, 1962.

Biancolli, L. (1951), The Great Fritz Kreisler Hoax (Copyright 1951 by Theodore Presser Co. Reprinted by permission of the author and *Étude, the Music Magazine*). In: *Grand Deception,* ed. A. Klein. London: Faber & Faber, 1955, pp. 147-153.

Bibring, Edward (1937), Therapeutic Results of Psycho-Analysis. *Int. J. Psycho-Anal.,* 18:170-189.

Bibring [Lehner], Grete (1936), A Contribution to the Subject of Transference Resistance. *Int. J. Psycho-Anal.,* 17:181-189.

—— (1954), Training Analysis and Its Place in Psycho-Analytic Training. *Int. J. Psycho-Anal.,* 35:169-173.

Bird, B. (1957), A Specific Peculiarity of Acting Out. *J. Amer. Psychoanal. Assn.,* 5:630-647.

---

[a] *The Psychoanalytic Study of the Child,* ed. R. S. Eissler, A. Freud, H. Hartman, M. Kris & S. L. Lustman; currently 24 Vols. New York: International Universities Press, 1945-1969.

Black, G. F. (1926), *Macpherson's Ossian and the Ossianic Controversy: A Contribution towards a Bibliography.* New York: The Public Library.

Bonnett, S. (1952), Personal communication.

Boveri, M. (1961), *Treason in the Twentieth Century.* London: Mac-Donald.

Bowman, Isa (1900), *Lewis Carroll.* New York: Dutton.

Brandeis, G. (1925), *Wolfgang Goethe,* tr. A. W. Porterfield. New York: Franc-Maurice, Vol. II, p. 32.

Breuer, J. & Freud, S. (1893-1895), Studies on Hysteria. *Standard Edition,* 2.[b]

Brewer, E. C. (n.d.), *A Dictionary of Phrase and Fable.* New York: Lippincott.

Brinnin, J. M. (1959), *The Third Rose.* Boston: Little Brown.

Brodie, F. (1945), *No Man Knows My History.* New York: Knopf.

Brodsky, B. (1959), The Self-Representation, Anality, and the Fear of Dying. *J. Amer. Psychoanal. Assn.,* 7:95-108.

—— (1967), Working Through: Its Widening Scope and Some Aspects of Its Metapsychology. *Psychoanal. Quart.,* 36:485-496.

Brody, S. (1956), *Patterns of Mothering.* New York: International Universities Press.

Brown, Thomas (August 18, 1693), *The Salamanca Wedding.* London.

Bryant, Sir Arthur (1964), *The Age of Chivalry.* New York: Doubleday.

Bulfinch, T. (1898), *Age of Fable.* Philadelphia: David McKay.

Bullitt, J. M. (1953), *Jonathan Swift and the Anatomy of Satire.* Cambridge: Harvard University Press.

Burlingham, D. (1935), Empathy between Infant and Mother. *J. Amer. Psychoanal. Assn.,* 15:764-781, 1967.

—— (1961), Some Notes on the Development of the Blind. *The Psychoanalytic Study of the Child,* 16:121-145.

Burnet, Bishop Gilbert (1838), *History of His Own Time.* London: William Smith, pp. 282-298, 308-311, 323-324, 337, 359, 383.

Cammaerts, E. (1925), *The Poetry of Nonsense.* London: Routledge.

Calef, V. (1954), Panel Report: Training and Therapeutic Analysis. *J. Amer. Psychoanal. Assn.,* 2:175-178.

Cannon, D. F. (1949), *Explorer of the Human Brain: the Life of Santiago Ramón y Cajal. With a Memoir of Dr. Cajal, by Sir Charles Sherrington.* New York: Henry Schuman.

Carroll, L. (1865), *Alice in Wonderland* [published as *Alice's Adventures Underground*]. London: Macmillan, 1876.

[b] See footnote c below.

—— (1871), *Through the Looking Glass.* London: Macmillan, 1876.

—— (1876), *The Hunting of the Snark.* London: Macmillan.

—— (1889), *Sylvie and Bruno.* London: Macmillan, 1893.

—— (1933), *Complete Works of Lewis Carroll.* New York: Random House.

Chauvire, R. (1952), *History of Ireland.* Dublin: Clonmore & Reynolds.

Chauvois, L. (1957), *William Harvey.* London: Hutchinson Medical Publications.

Chesterton, G. K. (1923), *St. Francis of Assisi; the Most Lovable of All Saints.* London: Hodder & Stroughton.

Church, Richard (1956), *Over the Bridge: An Autobiography.* New York: Dutton.

Cocteau, J. (1956), *The Journals of Jean Cocteau.* New York: Criterion.

Cole, J. A. (1965), *Lord Haw-Haw and William Joyce.* New York: Farrar Straus & Giroux.

Console, W. A. (n.d.), Training Failures. Unpublished manuscript.

Coremans, P. (1957), *Van Meegeren's Faked Vermeers and de Hooghs: A Scientific Examination.* Amsterdam: J. M. Meulenhoff.

Corner, G. W. (1944), *Ourselves Unborn: Natural History of the Human Embryo.* New Haven: Yale University Press.

Costain, Thomas B. (1958), *The Three Edwards.* New York: Doubleday.

Craik, Henry (1882), *The Life of Jonathan Swift.* London: John Murray.

Davis, Herbert (1942), *Stella: A Gentlewoman of the 18th Century.* New York: Macmillan.

—— (1947), *The Satire of Jonathan Swift.* New York: Macmillan.

Deakin, F. W. & Storry, G. R. (1966), *The Case of Richard Sorge.* New York: Harper & Row.

Despert, J. L. (1938). Schizophrenia in Children. *Psychiat. Quart.,* 12: 366-371.

Deutsch, H. (1930), Hysterical Fate-Neurosis. *Neurosis and Character Types.* New York: International Universities Press, 1965, pp. 14-28.

—— (1942), Some Forms of Emotional Disturbance and Their Relationship to Schizophrenia. *Psychoanal. Quart.,* 11:301-321.

—— (1945), *The Psychology of Women,* Vol. II: *Motherhood.* New York: Grune & Stratton.

—— (1955), The Impostor. *Psychoanal. Quart.,* 24:483-505.

Dillan, David J. (1964), *Soviet Espionage.* New Haven: Yale University Press.

Drame, A. T. (n.d.), *Saint Catherine of Siena and Her Time*. Quoted by A. Richardson, p. 23.

Eastman, M. (1936), *Enjoyment of Laughter*. New York: Simon & Schuster.

Eddy, William A., ed. (1951), *Satires and Personal Writings of Jonathan Swift* [reprinted]. London: Oxford University Press.

Ekstein, R. (1950), Trial Analysis in the Therapeutic Process. *Psychoanal. Quart.*, 19:52-63.

—— & Friedman, S. W. (1957), Acting Out, Play Action and Acting. *J. Amer. Psychoanal. Assn.*, 5:581-629.

Eiseley, L. (1962), *The Mind As Nature*. New York, Evanston, London: Harper & Row.

Eisendorfer, A. (1959), The Selection of Candidates Applying for Psychoanalytic Training. *Psychoanal. Quart.*, 28:374-378.

—— (1960), Notes on the Psychoanalytic Interview. In: Panel on the Selection of Candidates for Psychoanalytic Training. Abstr. in: *J. Amer. Psychoanal. Assn.*, 9:135-145, 1961.

Eissler, K. R. (1959), The Function of Details in the Interpretation of Works of Literature. *Psychoanal. Quart.*, 28:1-20.

—— (1963), *Goethe*, 2 Vols. Detroit: Wayne University Press.

Engelbert, O. (1950), *St. Francis of Assisi: A Biography*, tr. & ed. Edward Hutton. London: Burns Oates.

Erikson, E. H. (1937), Configurations in Play. *Psychoanal. Quart.*, 6: 139-214.

—— (1940), Studies in the Interpretation of Play. *Genet. Psychol. Monogr.*, 22:557-671.

—— (1951), Sex Differences in the Play Configurations of a Representative Group of Pre-Adolescents. *Amer. J. Orthopsychiat.*, 21:667-692.

—— (1956), The Problem of Ego Identity. *J. Amer. Psychoanal. Assn.* 4:56-121.

Ermakov, I. D. (1924), [*Essay in the Analysis of Gogol's Creative Forces*]. Moscow: Gos.

Fenichel, O. (1927), The Economic Function of Screen Memories. *Collected Papers*, 1:113-116. New York: Norton, 1953.

—— (1930), The Psychology of Transvestitism. *Int. J. Psycho-Anal.*, 11:211-227.

—— (1931), Respiratory Introjection. *Collected Papers*, 1:221-240. New York: Norton, 1953.

—— (1934), Concerning the Theory of Psychoanalytic Technique. *Collected Papers*, 1:332-348. New York: Norton, 1953.

—— (1935), Psychoanalytic Method. *Collected Papers*, 1:318-330. New York: Norton, 1953.

——— (1937), The Theory of the Therapeutic Results of Psychoanalysis. *Collected Papers,* 2:19-24. New York: Norton, 1954.

——— (1941), *Problems of Psychoanalytic Technique.* New York: Psychoanalytic Quarterly.

——— (1945a), *The Psychoanalytic Theory of Neurosis.* New York: Norton.

——— (1945b), Neurotic Acting Out. *Collected Papers,* 2:296-304. New York: Norton, 1954.

Fleming, Joan (1960a), Introduction to Panel on the Selection of Candidates for Psychoanalytic Training. Abstr. in: *J. Amer. Psychoanal. Assn.,* 9:135-145, 1961.

——— (1960b), What Analytic Work Requires of an Analyst. In: Panel on the Selection of Candidates for Psychoanalytic Training. Abstr. in: *J. Amer. Psychoanal. Assn.,* 9:135-145, 1961.

Flexner. James Thomas (1962), *The Benedict Arnold Case.* New York: Collier Books.

Forster, John (1876), *The Life of Jonathan Swift.* New York: Harper & Brothers.

Fraiberg, S. (1954), Tales of the Discovery of the Secret Treasure. *The Psychoanalytic Study of the Child,* 9:218-241.

——— & Freedman, D. A. (1964), Studies in the Ego Development of the Congenitally Blind Child. *The Psychoanalytic Study of the Child,* 19:113-170.

Frazer, J. G. (1890), *The Golden Bough.* New York: Macmillan, 3rd. ed. 1935, Vol. I:376-386.

Freeman, Martin, ed. (1921), *Vanessa and Her Correspondence with Jonathan Swift.* London: Selwyn & Bount, 1921.

Freud, A. (1936), The Ego and the Mechanisms of Defense. *The Writings of Anna Freud,* Vol. 2. New York: International Universities Press, 1966.

——— (1950 [1938]), The Problem of Training Analysis. *The Writings of Anna Freud,* 4:407-421. New York: International Universities Press, 1968.

——— (1951), Observations on Child Development. *The Psychoanalytic Study of the Child,* 6:18-30.

——— (1954), Psychoanalysis and Education. *The Psychoanalytic Study of the Child,* 9:9-15.

——— (1968), Acting Out. *Int. J. Psycho-Anal.,* 49:165-170.

——— & Burlingham, D. (1942), *War and Children.* New York: International Universities Press, pp. 49, 98.

——— & ——— (1943), *Infants Without Families.* New York: International Universities Press.

Freud, S. (1896a), Heredity and the Aetiology of the Neuroses. *Standard Edition*, 3:141-156.[c]

—— (1896b), The Aetiology of Hysteria. *Standard Edition*, 3:189-222.

—— (1898), Sexuality in the Aetiology of the Neuroses. *Standard Edition*, 3:261-285.

—— (1899), Screen Memories. *Standard Edition*, 3:301-322.

—— (1900), The Interpretation of Dreams. *Standard Edition*, 4 & 5.

—— (1901), On Dreams. *Standard Edition*, 5:629-686.

—— (1905a), Fragment of an Analysis of a Case of Hysteria. *Standard Edition*, 7:3-122.

—— (1905b), Three Essays on the Theory of Sexuality. *Standard Edition*, 7:125-243.

—— (1906), My Views on the Part Played by Sexuality in the Aetiology of the Neuroses. *Standard Edition*, 7:271-279.

—— (1908), Creative Writers and Day-Dreaming. *Standard Edition*, 9:141-153.

—— (1909), Analysis of a Phobia in a Five-Year-Old Boy. *Standard Edition*, 10:3-149.

—— (1910a), Five Lectures on Psycho-Analysis. *Standard Edition*, 11:3-56.

—— (1910b), Leonardo da Vinci and a Memory of His Childhood. *Standard Edition*, 11:59-137.

—— (1911), Formulations Regarding the Two Principles of Mental Functioning. *Standard Edition*, 12:213-226.

—— (1912), Recommendations to Physicians Practising Psycho-Analysis. *Standard Edition*, 12:109-120.

—— (1913), The Theme of the Three Caskets. *Standard Edition*, 12:289-301.

—— (1914a) Remembering, Repeating and Working-Through. *Standard Edition*, 12:145-156.

—— (1914b), On Narcissism. *Standard Edition*, 14:67-102.

—— (1914c) On the History of the Psycho-Analytic Movement. *Standard Edition*, 14:3-66.

—— (1916-1917), Introductory Lectures on Psycho-Analysis. *Standard Edition*, 15 & 16.

—— (1918), The Taboo of Virginity. *Standard Edition*, 11:191-208.

—— (1920a), Beyond the Pleasure Principle. *Standard Edition*, 18:3-64.

—— (1920b), A Note on the Prehistory of Analytic Technique. *Standard Edition*, 18:263-265.

[c] *The Standard Edition of the Complete Psychological Works of Sigmund Freud*, 24 Vols., translated and edited by James Strachey. London: Hogarth Press and the Institute of Psycho-Analysis, 1953-

—— (1923a), The Ego and the Id. *Standard Edition*, 19:3-66.

—— (1923b), The Infantile Genital Organization. *Standard Edition*, 19:141-145.

—— (1924), The Economic Problem of Masochism. *Standard Edition*. 19:159-170.

—— (1925), An Autobiographical Study. *Standard Edition*, 20:3-74.

—— (1926a), Inhibitions, Symptoms and Anxiety. *Standard Edition*, 20:77-175.

—— (1926b), The Question of Lay Analysis. *Standard Edition*, 20: 179-258.

—— (1927), Fetishism. *Standard Edition*, 21:149-157.

—— (1928), Dostoevsky and Parricide. *Standard Edition*, 21:175-196.

—— (1931a), Female Sexuality. *Standard Edition*, 21:223-243.

—— (1931b), The Expert Opinion in the Halsmann Case. *Standard Edition*, 21:251-253.

—— (1933a), New Introductory Lectures on Psycho-Analysis. *Standard Edition*, 22:3-182.

—— (1933b), Sándor Ferenczi. *Standard Edition*, 22:227-229.

—— (1937), Analysis Terminable and Interminable. *Standard Edition*, 23:209-253.

—— (1939), Moses and Monotheism. *Standard Edition*, 23:3-137.

—— (1940a [1922]), Medusa's Head. *Standard Edition*, 18:273-274.

—— (1940b [1938]), Splitting of the Ego in the Process of Defence. *Standard Edition*, 23:271-278.

—— (1950), *The Origins of Psychoanalysis*. New York: Basic Books, 1954.

Friedjung, J. K. (1927-1928), Wäsche-Fetischismus bei einem Einjährigen. *Z. psychoanal. Päd.*, 2:25-26, 235-236.

Fries, M. E. (1946), The Child's Ego Development and the Training of Adults in His Environment. *The Psychoanalytic Study of the Child*, 2:85-112.

Frinck-Brentano, F. (1902), *Cagliostro and Company*, tr. George Maidment. New York: James Pott.

Frosch, J. (1959), Transference Derivatives of the Family Romance. *J. Amer. Psychoanal. Assn.*, 7:503-522.

Galton, F. (1869), *Hereditary Genius: An Inquiry into Its Laws and Consequences*. London: Macmillan, rev. 1892, reprinted 1925.

Galenson, Eleanor (1969), The Nature of Thought in Childhood Play. In: *Separation-Individuation: Essays in Honor of Margaret S. Mahler*, ed. J. B. McDevitt & C. F. Settlage. New York: International Universities Press (in press).

Gerard, R. W. (1946), The Biological Basis of Imagination. *Sci. Monthly*, 62:477-499.

Gernsheim, H. (1949), *Lewis Carroll: Photographer*. New York: Chanticleer Press.

Gesell, A. (1940), *The First Five Years of Life*. New York: Harper & Row, pp. 29-50.

—— (1946), The Ontogenesis of Infant Behavior. In: *Manual of Child Psychology*, ed. L. Carmichael. New York: Wiley, 2nd ed., 1954.

Ghiselin, B., ed. (1955), *The Creative Process*. Berkeley: University of California Press.

Giffin, M. E., Johnson, A. M., & Litin, E. M. (1954), Specific Factors Determining Antisocial Acting Out. *Amer. J. Orthopsychiat.*, 24: 668-684.

Gilbert, M. S. (1938), *Biography of the Unborn*. Baltimore: Williams & Wilkins.

Gilbert, Michael (1957), *The Claimant*. London: Constable.

Gillespie, W. H. (1940), A Contribution to the Study of Fetishism. *Int. J. Psycho-Anal.*, 21:401-415.

—— (1952), Sexual Perversions. *Int. J. Psycho-Anal.*, 33:397-402.

Gitelson, M. (1948), Problems of Psychoanalytic Training. *Psychoanal. Quart.*, 17:198-211.

—— (1954), Therapeutic Problems in the Analysis of the 'Normal' Candidate. *Int. J. Psycho-Anal.*, 35:174-183.

Glasgow, Ellen (1954), *The Woman Within*. New York: Harcourt, Brace.

Glover, Edward (1933), The Relation of Perversion-Formation to the Development of Reality-Sense. *On the Early Development of Mind*. New York: International Universities Press, 1956, pp. 216-234.

—— (1939), *Psycho-Analysis*. London: Staples Press, 2nd ed.

—— (1955), *The Technique of Psychoanalysis*. New York: International Universities Press. pp. 119-120.

Glover, James (1927), Notes on an Unusual Form of Perversion. *Int. J. Psycho-Anal.*, 8:10-24.

Goodenough, F. L. (1931), *Anger in Young Children* [Inst. Child Welfare Monograph Series, 9.]. Minneapolis: University of Minnesota Press.

Gosse, E. (1934), *Father and Son*. New York: Oxford University Press, pp. 15-16, 27-42.

Graff, W. L. (1956), *Rainer Maria Rilke: Creative Anguish of a Modern Poet*. Princeton: Princeton University Press.

Grant, James (1814), *Thoughts on the Origin and Descent of the Gael:*

and Observations Relative to the Authenticity of the Poems of Ossian. Edinburgh: Walker & Grieg for Archibald Constable; London: Longman, Hurst, Reese, Arme and Brown; Inverness: John Young.

Grant, V. W. (1949), A Fetishistic Theory of Amorous Fixation. *J. Soc. Psychol.,* 30:17-37.

Green, R. L. (1949), *The Story of Lewis Carroll.* London: Methuen.

—— ed. (1953), *The Diaries of Lewis Carroll.* London: Cassell.

Greenacre, P. (1941), The Predisposition to Anxiety. *Psychoanal. Quart.,* 10:66-95, 610-638. Also in: *Trauma, Growth and Personality.* New York: International Universities Press, 1969, pp. 27-82.

—— (1945a), The Biological Economy of Birth. *The Psychoanalytic Study of the Child,* 1:31-53. Also in: *Trauma, Growth and Personality.* New York: International Universities Press, 1969, pp. 3-26.

—— (1945b), Urination and Weeping. *Amer. J. Orthopsychiat.,* 15:81-88. Also in: *Trauma, Growth and Personality,* New York: International Universities Press, 1969, pp. 106-119.

—— (1945c), Pathological Weeping. *Psychoanal. Quart.,* 14:62-75. Also in: *Trauma, Growth and Personality.* New York: International Universities Press, 1969, pp. 120-131.

—— (1947), Vision, Headache, and the Halo. *Psychoanal. Quart.,* 16:177-194. Also in: *Trauma, Growth and Personality.* New York: International Universities Press, 1969, pp. 132-148.

—— (1949a), A Contribution to the Study of Screen Memories. *The Psychoanalytic Study of the Child,* 3/4:73-84. Also in: *Trauma, Growth and Personality.* New York: International Universities Press, 1969, pp. 188-203.

—— (1949b), A Genetic Approach to the Problem of Inconsistency in Social Attitudes. *J. Soc. Issues,* 5:19-26.

—— (1950a), The Prepuberty Trauma in Girls. *Psychoanal. Quart.,* 19:298-317. Also in: *Trauma, Growth and Personality.* New York: International Universities Press, 1969, pp. 204-223.

—— (1950b), General Problems of Acting Out. *Psychoanal. Quart.,* 19:455-467. Also in: *Trauma, Growth and Personality.* New York: International Universities Press, 1969, pp. 224-236.

—— (1951), Respiratory Incorporation and the Phallic Phase. *The Psychoanalytic Study of the Child,* 6:118-205. Also in: *Trauma, Growth and Personality.* New York: International Universities Press, 1969, pp. 259-292.

—— (1952a), Pregenital Patterning. *Int. J. Psycho-Anal.,* 33:410-415.

—— (1952b), *Trauma, Growth and Personality.* New York: Norton;

second edition, New York: International Universities Press, 1969.

—— (1955), *Swift and Carroll: A Psychoanalytic Study of Two Lives.* New York: International Universities Press.

—— (1962a), The Early Years of the Gifted Child: A Psychoanalytic Interpretation. *Year Book of Education.* London: Evans, pp. 71-90.

—— (1962b), Discussion and Comments on the Psychology of Creativity. *J. Amer. Acad. Child Psychiat.,* 1:129-137.

Greenson, R. R. (1961), Panel Report: The Selection of Candidates for Psychoanalytic Training. *J. Amer. Psychoanal. Assn.,* 9:135-145.

—— (1965a), The Working Alliance and the Transference Neurosis. Psychoanal. Quart., 34:155-181.

—— (1965b), The Problem of Working Through. In: *Drives, Affects, Behavior,* Vol. 2, ed. M. Schur. New York: International Universities Press, pp. 277-314.

Groos, Karl (1898), *Play of Animals.* New York: Appleton; London: Chapman & Hall.

Gross, A. (1936), The Secret. *The Yearbook of Psychoanalysis,* 8:204-212. New York: International Universities Press, 1952.

Grotjahn, M. (1954), Psychoanalytic Training and Psychoanalytic Therapy. *Int. J. Psycho-Anal.,* 35:254-262.

Halverson, H. M. (1933), The Acquisition of Skill in Infancy. *J. Genet. Psychol.,* 43:3-48.

Hardy, Evelyn (1949), *The Conjured Spirit.* London: Hogarth Press.

Harlow, H. (1958), The Nature of Love. *Amer. Psychologist,* 13:673-685.

—— & Zimmerman, R. R. (1959), Development of Affectual Responses in Infant Monkeys. *Science,* 146:421-432.

Harnik, J. (1932), Pleasure in Disguise. *Psychoanal. Quart.,* 1:216-264.

Hartmann, H. (1939), *Ego Psychology and the Problem of Adaptation.* New York: International Universities Press, 1958.

—— (1950), Comments on the Psychoanalytic Theory of the Ego. *The Psychoanalytic Study of the Child,* 5:74-95.

—— (1951), Technical Implications of Ego Psychology. *Psychoanal. Quart.,* 20:31-43.

—— (1955), Notes on the Theory of Sublimation. *The Psychoanalytic Study of the Child,* 10:9-29.

—— Kris, E., & Loewenstein, R. M. (1946), Comments on the Formation of Psychic Structure. *The Psychoanalytic Study of the Child,* 2:11-39.

—— —— —— (1949), Notes on the Theory of Aggression. *The Psychoanalytic Study of the Child,* 3/4:9-36.

—— —— —— (1964), *Papers on Psychoanalytic Psychology [Psycho-*

logical Issues, Monogr. 14]. New York: International Universities Press.

Hatch, E., ed. (1933), *Letters of Lewis Carroll to His Child Friends.* London: Macmillan, pp. 64-68; 101-106.

Heilman, Robert B. (1950), Introduction to the Modern Library Edition of *Gulliver's Travels.* New York: Random House.

Heimann, Paula (1954), Problems of Training Analysis. *Int. J. Psycho-Anal.,* 35:163-168.

Hendrick, I. (1942), Instinct and Ego During Infancy. *Psychoanal. Quart.,* 11:33-58.

—— (1943a), The Discussion of the "Instinct to Master." *Psychoanal. Quart.,* 12:561-565.

—— (1943b), Work and the Pleasure Principle. *Psychoanal. Quart.,* 12:311-329.

Hermann, I. (1927), Charles Darwin. *Imago,* 13:57-82.

—— (1936), Sich-Anklammern, Auf-Suche-Gehen. *Int. Z. Psychoanal.,* 22:349-370.

—— (1949), The Giant Mother, the Phallic Mother, Obscenity. *Psychoanal. Rev.,* 36:302-307.

Hewins, Ralph (1966), *Quisling: Prophet Without Honor.* New York: John Day.

Hoffer, W. (1949), Mouth, Hand and Ego-Integration. *The Psychoanalytic Study of the Child,* 3/4:49-56.

—— (1950a), Oral Aggressiveness and Ego Development. *Int. J. Psycho-Anal.,* 31:156-160.

—— (1950b), The Development of the Body Ego. *The Psychoanalytic Study of the Child,* 5:18-24.

Holt, R. R. & Luborsky, L. (1955), The Selection of Candidates for Psychoanalytic Training: On the Use of Interviews and Psychological Tests. *J. Amer. Psychoanal. Assn.,* 3:666-681.

—— & —— (1958), *Personality Patterns of Psychiatrists.* New York: Basic Books.

Horst, Paul (1941), *The Prediction of Personal Adjustment.* New York: Social Science Research Council.

Howard, Mary W. (1855), *Hastings, Past and Present.* London: John Russell Smith.

Hudson, D. (1954), *Lewis Carroll.* London: Constable.

Hug-Hellmuth, H. (1915), Ein Fall von weiblichem Fuss-, richtiger Stiefelfetischismus. *Int. Z. f. ärzt. Psychoanal.,* 3:111-114.

Ingram, J. H. (1910). *The True Chatterton.* London: Unwin.

Isaacs, S. (1948), The Nature and Function of Phantasy. *Int. J. Psycho-Anal.,* 29:73-97.

Isakower, O. (1938), A Contribution to the Pathopsychology of Phenomena Associated with Falling Asleep. *Int. J. Psycho-Anal.,* 19:331-345.

Isherwood, Christopher (1947), *Lions and Shadows: An Education in the Twenties.* Norfolk, Conn.: New Directions.

Jackson, H. (1950), Introduction. *The Complete Nonsense of Edward Lear.* London: Faber & Faber.

Jacobson, E. (1946), The Child's Laughter. *The Psychoanalytic Study of the Child,* 2:39-60.

—— (1959), Depersonalization. *J. Amer. Psychoanal. Assn.,* 7:581-610.

Johnson, A. M. (1949), Sanctions for Superego Lacunae of Adolescents. In: *Searchlights on Delinquency,* ed. K. R. Eissler. New York: International Universities Press, pp. 225-245.

—— & Szurek, S. A. (1952), The Genesis of Antisocial Acting Out in Children and Adults. *Psychoanal. Quart.,* 21:323-342.

Johnson, Samuel (1778), *The Poetical Works of Dr. Jonathan Swift, With the Life of the Author* [Lives of the English Poets]. Edinburgh: Apollo Press.

Johnston, Denis. Personal communications.

Jones, E. (1953), *The Life and Work of Sigmund Freud,* Vol. 1. New York: Basic Books.

—— (1956), The Nature of Genius. *Sigmund Freud: Four Centenary Addresses.* New York: Basic Books, pp. 3-36.

Jörgensen, J. (1912), *St. Francis of Assisi,* tr. T. O'Conor-Sloane. New York: Longmans, Green.

Kafka, F. (1916), *Metamorphosis.* London: Vanguard, 1947.

Kairys. D. (1964), The Training Analysis: A Critical Review of the Literature and a Controversial Proposal. *Psychoanal. Quart.,* 33:485-512.

Kanner, L. (1943), Autistic Disturbances of Affective Contact. *Nerv. Child,* 2:217-250.

—— (1944), Early Infantile Autism. *J. Pediat.,* 25:211-217.

—— (1949), Problems of Nosology and Psychodynamics of Early Infantile Autism. *Amer. J. Orthopsychiat.,* 19:416-426.

Kanzer, M. (1955), Gogol: A Study on Wit and Paranoia. *J. Amer. Psychoanal. Assn.,* 3:110-125.

—— (1957a), Panel Report: Acting Out and Its Relation to Impulse Control. *J. Amer. Psychoanal. Assn.,* 5:136-145.

—— (1957b), Acting Out, Sublimation and Reality Testing. *J. Amer. Psychoanal. Assn.,* 5:663-684.

Kaplan, S. & Rank, B. (1962), Communication and Transitory Creativity in Response to a Trauma. *J. Amer. Acad. Child Psychiat.,* 1:108-128.

Kardos, E. & Peto, A. (1956), Contributions to the Theory of Play. *Brit. J. Med. Psychol.,* 29:100-112.

Kaye-Smith, S. (1937), *Three Ways Home.* New York & London: Harper & Row.

Kestenberg, J. S. (1956), On the Development of Maternal Feelings in Early Childhood. *The Psychoanalytic Study of the Child,* 11:257-291.

—— (1965, 1967), The Role of Movement Patterns in Development: Parts I, II, and III. *Psychoanal. Quart.,* 34:1-36; 34:517-563; 36:356-409.

Klein, H. (1956), The Columbia Psychoanalytic Clinic: A Development in Psychoanalytic Training. In: *Changing Concepts of Psychoanalytic Medicine,* ed. S. Rado & G. E. Daniels. New York: Grune & Stratton, pp. 4-14.

—— (1960), A Comparative Study of Trainees and Their Development During the Training Period. In: Panel on the Selection of Candidates for Psychoanalytic Training. Abstr. in: *J. Amer. Psychoanal. Assn.,* 9:135-145, 1961.

Klein, M. (1921-1945), *Contributions to Psycho-Analysis.* London: Hogarth Press, 1948.

Knight, R. P. (1953), The Present Status of Organized Psychoanalysis in the United States. *J. Amer. Psychoanal. Assn.,* 1:197-221.

Koestler, A. (1959), *The Sleepwalkers.* New York: Macmillan.

—— (1964), *The Act of Creation.* London: Hutchinson.

Kris, E. (1935), The Image of the Artist. *Psychoanalytic Explorations in Art.* New York: International Universities Press, 1952, pp. 64-84.

—— (1952), *Psychoanalytic Explorations in Art.* New York: International Universities Press.

—— (1955), Neutralization and Sublimation: Observations on Young Children. *The Psychoanalytic Study of the Child,* 10:30-46.

—— (1956a), On Some Vicissitudes of Insight in Psycho-Analysis. *Int. J. Psycho-Anal.,* 37:445-455.

—— (1956b), The Personal Myth: A Problem in Psychoanalytic Technique. *J. Amer. Psychoanal. Assn.,* 4:653-681.

—— (1956c), The Recovery of Childhood Memories in Psychoanalysis. *The Psychoanalytic Study of the Child,* 11:54-88.

Kronold, E. & Sterba, R. (1936), Two Cases of Fetishism. *Psychoanal. Quart.,* 5:63-70.

Kubie, L. S. (1939), A Critical Analysis of the Concept of a Repetition Compulsion. *Int. J. Psycho-Anal.* 20:390-402.

—— (1941), The Repetitive Core of Neurosis. *Psychoanal. Quart.*, 10:23-43.

—— (1958), *Neurotic Distortions of the Creative Process.* Lawrence, Kansas: University of Kansas Press.

LaForgue, R. (1930), The Eroticization of Anxiety. *Int. J. Psycho-Anal.*, 11:312-322.

Lampl-de Groot, J. (1954), Problems of Psycho-Analytic Training. *Int. J. Psycho-Anal.*, 35:184-187.

Lane, J. (1949), *Titus Oates.* London: Andrew Dakers.

Lane-Poole, Stanley, ed. (1885), *Swift's Letters and Journals.* London: Kegan Paul, Trench.

Langer, Susanne K. (1942), *Philosophy in a New Key.* Cambridge: Harvard University Press. New York: Mentor Books, 1951.

Lauder, William (1939), In: *Oxford Dictionary of English Literature.* Oxford: Clarendon Press.

Laurendeau, M. & Pinard, A. (1962), *Causal Thinking in the Child.* New York: International Universities Press.

Lavin, I. (1951), *Nikolai Gogol.* London: Sylvan Press.

Lear, Edward (1846), *Book of Nonsense.* London & New York: Frederick Warne, 1905.

—— (1872), *More Nonsense.* London & New York: Frederick Warne.

—— (1907), *Letters of Edward Lear, Author of "The Book of Nonsense," to Chichester Fortescue, Lord Carlingford and Frances, Countess Waldegrave,* ed. Lady Constance Strachey. London: T. Fisher Unwin.

Lewin, B. D. (1946), Sleep, the Mouth and the Dream Screen. *Psychoanal. Quart.*, 15:419-443.

—— (1948), The Nature of Reality, the Meaning of Nothing, with an Addendum on Concentration. *Psychoanal. Quart.*, 17:524-526.

—— (1950), *The Psychoanalysis of Elation.* New York: Norton, pp. 69-70, 75-78.

—— (1953), Reconsideration of the Dream Screen. *Psychoanal. Quart.*, 22:174-199.

—— & Ross, H. (1960), *Psychoanalytic Education in the United States.* New York: Norton, pp. 133-167.

Lewis, C. S. (1955), *Surprised by Joy: The Shape of My Early Life.* London: Geoffrey Bles.

Lewis, Flora (1965), *The Red Pawn: The Story of Noel Field.* New York: Doubleday.

Lewis, M. M. (1951), Infant Speech. *A Study of the Beginnings of Language.* New York: Humanities Press; London: Routledge & Kegan Paul.

Lipin, T. (1963), The Repetition Compulsion and 'Maturational' Drive-Representatives. *Int. J. Psycho-Anal.,* 44:389-405.

Loewenstein, R. M. (1950), Conflict and Autonomous Ego Development During the Phallic Phase. *The Psychoanalytic Study of the Child,* 5:47-52.

—— (1951), The Problem of Interpretation. *Psychoanal. Quart.,* 20: 1-14.

Löfgren, L. B. (1966), On Weeping. *Int. J. Psycho-Anal.,* 47:375-381.

Lorand, S. (1930), Fetishism in Statu Nascendi. *Clinical Studies of Psychoanalysis.* New York: International Universities Press, 1950, pp. 11-24.

Loti, P. (1890), *Le roman d'un enfant.* Paris: Calmann-Lévy.

McCaleb, Walter F. (1963), *New Light on Aaron Burr.* Austin, Texas: Texas Quarterly Studies.

Macalpine, I. (1950), The Development of Transference. *Psychoanal. Quart.,* 19:501-539.

Macaulay, Thomas Babington (1858), *History of England,* Vol. I. London: Longman, Brown, Green, Longmans & Roberts. pp. 234, 483.

MacDonald, G. (1871), *At the Back of the North Wind.* London: Nonesuch Press, 1963.

MacFall, Haldane (1911), *A History of Art.* London: T. C. & E. D. Jack.

Mack-Brunswick, R. (1940), The Preoedipal Phase of the Libido Development. *Psychoanal. Quart.,* 9:293-319.

Macpherson, Alexander (1893), *Church and Social Life in the Highlands.* Edinburgh: William Blackwood.

Magarschak, D. (1957), *Gogol: A Life.* London: Faber & Faber.

Mahler, M. S. (1952), On Child Psychosis and Schizophrenia: Autistic and Infantile Psychoses. *The Psychoanalytic Study of the Child,* 7:286-306.

—— (1963), Thoughts about Development and Individuation. *The Psychoanalytic Study of the Child,* 18:307-324.

—— (1967), On Human Symbiosis and the Vicissitudes of Individuation. *J. Amer. Psychoanal. Assn.,* 15:740-764.

—— (1968), *On Human Symbiosis and the Vicissitudes of Individuation.* New York: International Universities Press.

—— & Gosliner, B. J. (1955), On Symbiotic Child Psychosis. *The Psychoanalytic Study of the Child,* 10:195-215.

—— & McDevitt, J. B. (1968), Observations on Adaptation and Defense in Statu Nascendi. *Psychoanal. Quart.,* 37:1-22.

Mann, Thomas (1909), *Royal Highness,* tr. Cecil Curtis. New York: Knopf, 1916.

—— (1930), *A Sketch of My Life*. Harrison of Paris: Printed and made in Germany.

—— (1936), *Stories of Three Decades,* tr. H. T. Lowe-Porter. New York: Knopf.

—— (1948), *Doctor Faustus,* tr. H. T. Lowe-Porter. New York: Knopf.

—— (1951), *The Holy Sinner,* tr. H. T. Lowe-Porter. New York: Knopf.

—— (1954), *Confessions of Felix Krull, Confidence Man,* tr. Denver Lindly. New York: Knopf, 1955.

Masson, D. (1856), *Chatterton: A Biography*. New York: Dodd, Mead, 1899.

Maurois, André (1968), *Illusions*. New York & London: Columbia University Press.

Maxwell, Gavin (1960), *Ring of Bright Water*. New York: Dutton, 1965.

Medawar, P. B. (1957), The Uniqueness of the Individual. In: *The Pattern of Organic Growth and Transformation*. Edinburgh: Constable, pp. 110-114.

Meiss, M. L. (1952), The Oedipal Problem of a Fatherless Child. *The Psychoanalytic Study of the Child,* 7:216-229.

Menninger, J. L. (1942), Theories of Work and Play. M.A. Thesis. Lawrence, Kansas: University of Kansas.

Menninger, K. A. (1938), *Man Against Himself*. New York: Harcourt Brace.

—— (1942a), *Love Against Hate*. New York: Harcourt Brace.

—— (1942b), Play. *Virginia Quart. Rev.,* 18:591-599.

—— & J. L. (1942), Recreation for Morale. *Bull. Menninger Clin.,* 6:96-102.

Meredith, H. V. (1945), Toward a Working Concept of Growth. *Amer. J. Orthod. & Oral Surg.,* 31:440-458.

Milne, A. A. (1929), *The Secret and Other Stories*. London: Methuen.

Misch, G. (1951), *History of Autobiography in Antiquity,* 2 Vols. Cambridge, Mass.: Harvard University Press.

Modell, A. (1968), *Object Love and Reality*. New York: International Universities Press.

Moorehead, Alan (1963), *The Traitors*. New York: Harper & Row, 2nd ed.

Morris, D. (1962), *The Biology of Art*. New York: Knopf.

Muller, (Friedrich) Max(imilian) (1888), Identity of Language and Thought. *Three Introductory Lectures: Signs of Thought*. Chicago: Chicago Open Court Publications.

Murray, Linda & Peter (1959), *Dictionary of Art and Artists*. Baltimore: Penguin Books.

Mutch, J. R. (1944), The Lacrimation Reflex. *Brit. J. Ophthalmol.*, 28:317-336.

Nabokov, V. (1947), *Nikolai Gogol*. London: Nicholson & Watson.

Nacht, S. (1954), The Difficulties of Didactic Psychoanalysis. *Int. J. Psycho-Anal.*, 35:250-253.

Namnum, A. (1960), On Secrets. Paper read at the Western New England Psychoanalytic Society.

Nansen, F. (1931), *Through the Caucasus to the Volga*, tr. G. C. Wheeler. New York: Norton.

Nelson, W. E. (1933), *Textbook of Pediatrics*. New York: Saunders, 6th ed., 1954.

Nicolson, Harold George (1927), *The Development of English Biography*. London: L. & V. Wolff.

Nielsen, N. (1954), The Dynamics of Training Analysis. *Int. J. Psycho-Anal.*, 35:247-249.

Norman, Charles (1955), *Rake Rochester*. London: W. H. Allen.

Nunberg, H. (1930), The Synthetic Function of the Ego. *Int. J. Psycho-Anal.*, 12:123-140, 1931.

—— (1937), Theory of the Therapeutic Results of Psychoanalysis. *Practice and Theory of Psychoanalysis*. New York: International Universities Press, 1961, pp. 165-170.

—— (1955), Theoretical Principles of Psychoanalytic Therapy. *Principles of Psychoanalysis*. New York: International Universities Press, pp. 330-360.

O'Casey, Sean (1956), *I Knock at the Door: Swift Glances Back at Things That Made Me*. New York: Macmillan.

Oliphant, Mrs. (1907), *Francis of Assisi*. London: Macmillan.

Omwake, E. & Solnit, A. J. (1961), "It Isn't Fair": The Treatment of a Blind Child. *The Psychoanalytic Study of the Child*, 16:352-404.

Orrery, John, Earl of Orrery (1752), *Remarks on the Life and Writings of Dr. Jonathan Swift*. Dublin: George Faulkner.

Pater, Walter (1895), The Child in the House. *Miscellaneous Studies*. London: Macmillan.

Payne, S. (1939), Some Observations of the Ego Development of the Fetishist. *Int. J. Psycho-Anal.*, 20:161-170.

Peller, L. E. (1954), Libidinal Phases, Ego Development, and Play. *The Psychoanalytic Study of the Child*, 9:178-198.

Penkovsky, Oleg (1965), *The Penkovsky Papers: The Russian Who Spied for the West*. London: Collins.

Piaget, J. (1927), *The Child's Conception of the World*. New York: Humanities Press, 1951.

Pollock, G. H. (1960a), Historical Perspectives in the Selection of Candidates for Psychoanalytic Training. In: Panel on the Selection of Candidates for Psychoanalytic Training. Abstr. in: *J. Amer. Psychoanal. Assn.*, 9:135-145, 1961.

—— (1960b), The Selection Process and the Selector: The Individual Interview. In: Panel on the Selection of Candidates for Psychoanalytic Training. Abstr. in: *J. Amer. Psychoanal. Assn.*, 9:135-145, 1961.

Provence, Sally & Lipton, Rose (1962), *Infants in Institutions*. New York: International Universities Press.

Psalmanazar, George (1704), *Historical and Geographical Description of Formosa, an Island Subject to the Emperor of Japan*. London: Dan Brown, G. Strahan & W. Davis, & Coggan.

—— (1765), *Memoirs of   , Commonly Known by the Name of George Psalmanazar, a Reputed Native of Formosa*. London: R. Davis.

Quintana, Ricardo (1953), *The Mind and Art of Jonathan Swift*. Reprinted. London: Methuen.

Rado, S. (1928), An Anxious Mother. *Int. J. Psycho-Anal.*, 9:219-226.

Rank, O. (1924), *The Trauma of Birth*. London: Paul, Trench, Trubner.

Rapaport, D. (1960), *The Structure of Psychoanalytic Theory [Psychological Issues, Monogr. 6]*. New York: International Universities Press.

Read, Herbert (1940), *Annals of Innocence and Experience*. London: Faber & Faber.

Reich, A. (1951), On Countertransference. *Int. J. Psycho-Anal.*, 32:25-31.

—— (1957), Contribution to the Panel on Ego Distortion. Read at the Twentieth Congress of the International Psycho-Analytical Association, Paris.

Rexford, E. N., ed. (1966), *A Developmental Approach to Problems of Acting Out: A Symposium*. New York: International Universities Press.

Ribble, Margaret (1943), *The Rights of Infants*. New York: Columbia University Press.

Richardson, Aubrey (n.d.), *The Mystic Bride*. London: T. Werner Laurie, pp. 18-19.

Ritvo, S. & Provence, S. (1958), Form Perception and Imitation in

Some Autistic Children. *The Psychoanalytic Study of the Child,*
    13:155-161.
Rolland, R. (1910-1913), *Jean Christophe,* 3 Vols. New York: Henry
    Holt.
Romm, M. (1949), Some Dynamics of Fetishism. *Psychoanal. Quart.,*
    18:137-153.
Ronblom, H. K. (1966), *Wennerstrom, the Spy.* New York: Coward-
    McCann.
Root, Jonathan (1963), *The Betrayers.* New York: Coward-McCann.
Roper, Abel (1692), *The Life of William Fuller.* London: (printer not
    given).
Royidis, Emanuel (1896), *Pope Joan,* tr. Lawrence Durrell. London:
    Verschoyle, 1954.
Russell, C. E. (1908), *Chatterton.* New York: Moffat.
Sabatier, P. (1908), *Life of St. Francis of Assisi.* London: Hodder &
    Stoughton.
Sachs, H. (1947), Observations of a Training Analyst. *Psychoanal.
    Quart.,* 16:157-168.
Saunders, Bailey (1895), *The Life and Letters of James Macpherson.*
    London: Swan Sonnenschein.
Scammon, R. E. (1922), On the Weight Increments of Premature In-
    fants as Compared with Those of Fetuses of the Same Gestation
    Age and Those of Full-Term Children. *Proc. Soc. Exp. Biol. &
    Med.,* 19:133-136.
Schachner, Nathan (1961), *Aaron Burr.* New York: A. S. Barnes.
Schilder, P. (1935), *The Image and Appearance of the Human Body.*
    New York: International Universities Press, 1950.
Schweitzer, Albert (1955), *Memories of Childhood and Youth.* New
    York: Macmillan.
Scott, Sir Walter (1841), *Memoirs of Jonathan Swift, D.D.* Edinburgh:
    Robert Cadell.
Scott, Temple, ed. (1913), *Prose Works of Jonathan Swift,* ·12 Vols.
    London: G. Bell.
Seccombe, Thomas (1894), *Lives of Twelve Bad Men.* London: T.
    Fisher Unwin, pp. 95-154.
Segal, A. & Stone, F. H. (1961), The Six-Year-Old Who Began to See.
    The Psychoanalytic Study of the Child, 16:481-509.
Session of the International Training Commission. Reported at Weis-
    baden, September, 1932. *Int. J. Psycho-Anal.,* 16:155-159.
Sewall, E. (1952), *Field of Nonsense.* London: Chatto & Windus.
Sharpe, Ella F. (1947), The Psycho-Analyst. *Int. J. Psycho-Anal.,* 28:
    1-6.

Sheridan, Thomas (1785), *The Life of the Reverend Dr. Jonathan Swift*. Dublin: Luke White.

Sitwell, Osbert (1952), *Left Hand, Right Hand: The Autobiography of Sir Osbert Sitwell*, Vol. I. London: Macmillan.

Slenczynska, R. (& Biancolli, L.) (1957), *Forbidden Childhood*. New York: Doubleday.

Smart, J. S. (1905), *James Macpherson: An Episode in Literature*. London: David Nutt, Longacre.

Smith, David Nichol, ed. (1935), *The Letters of Jonathan Swift to Charles Ford*. Oxford: Clarendon Press.

Smyth, Ethel (1946), *Impressions That Remained*. New York: Alfred A. Knopf.

Spender, Stephen (1951), *World Within Worlds: An Autobiography*. New York: Harcourt Brace.

Sperling, M. (1959), A Study of Deviate Sexual Behavior in Children by the Method of Simultaneous Analysis of Mother and Child. In: *Dynamic Psychopathology in Childhood*, ed. L. Jessner & E. Pavenstedt. New York: Grune & Stratton, pp. 221-242.

—— (1963), Fetishism in Children. *Psychoanal. Quart.*, 32:374-392.

Sperling, O. (1944), On Appersonation, *Int. J. Psycho-Anal.*, 25:128-132.

Spiegel, Leo A. (1954), Acting Out and Instinctual Gratification. *J. Amer. Psychoanal. Assn.*, 2:107-119.

Spiegel, Nancy T. (1967), An Infantile Fetish and Its Persistence into Young Womanhood. *The Psychoanalytic Study of the Child.*, 22:402-425.

Spitz, R. A. (1933), Ein Beitrag zum Problem der Wandlung der Neurosenform: Die Infantile Frau und ihre Gegenspieler. *Imago*, 19:454-467.

—— (1945), Hospitalism. *The Psychoanaytic . Study of the Child*, 1: 53-73.

—— (1951), The Psychogenic Diseases in Infancy: An Attempt at Their Classification. *The Psychoanalytic Study of the Child*, 6: 255-279.

—— (1956), Transference, the Analytic Setting and Its Prototype. *Int. J. Psycho-Anal.*, 37:380-385.

—— (1957), *No and Yes*. New York: International Universities Press.

—— (1965), *The First Year of Life*. New York: International Universities Press.

Sprigge, Elizabeth (1957), *Gertrude Stein, Her Life and Work*. London: Hamish Hamilton.

Stanley, D., ed. (1909), *The Autobiography of Sir Henry Morton Stanley*. Boston: Houghton Mifflin.

Stanley, Henry M. (1874), *My Kalulu, Prince, King, and Slave*. New York: Scribner.

Stein, Gertrude (1933), *The Autobiography of Alice B. Toklas*. New York: Harcourt Brace.

—— (1934), *The Making of Americans*. New York: Harcourt Brace.

—— (1937), *Everybody's Autobiography*. New York: Random House.

—— (1951), *Two—Gertrude Stein and Her Brother*. New Haven: Yale University Press.

Stephen, Sir Leslie (1889), *Swift* [English Men of Letters Series]. London: Macmillan.

Sterba, Editha (1935), An Important Factor in Eating Disturbances of Childhood. *Psychoanal. Quart.*, 10:365-372, 1941.

Sterba, Richard F. (1929), The Dynamics of the Dissolution of the Transference-Resistance. *Psychoanal. Quart.*, 9:363-379, 1940.

—— (1934), The Fate of the Ego in Analytic Therapy. *Int. J. Psycho-Anal.*, 15:117-126.

—— (1940), Aggression in the Rescue Fantasy. *Psychoanal. Quart.*, 9:505-508.

Stevenson, O. (1954), The First Treasured Possession. *The Psychoanalytic Study of the Child*, 9:199-217.

Strachey, J. (1934), The Nature of the Therapeutic Action of Psycho-Analysis. *Int. J. Psycho-Anal.*, 15:127-159.

Swift, Deane (1755), *An Essay upon the Life, Writings, and Character of Dr. Jonathan Swift*. London: Charles Bathurst.

Swift, Jonathan (1735), *The Works of Jonathan Swift, D.D., D.S.P.D.* Dublin: George Faulkner.

Symposium (1968), Acting Out and Its Role in the Psychoanalytic Process. *Int. J. Psycho-Anal.*, 49:165-245.

Szurek, S. A., Johnson, A. M., & Falstein, E. (1942), Collaborative Psychiatric Therapy of Parent-Child Problems. *Amer. J. Orthopsychiat.*, 12:511-516.

Tamassia, N. (1905), *Saint Francis of Assisi and His Legend*, tr. Lonsdale Rag. Venice: Istituto Veneto di Arti Grafiche.

Tausk, V. (1919), On the Origin of the "Influencing Machine" in Schizophrenia. In: *The Psychoanalytic Reader*, ed. R. Fliess. New York: International Universities Press, 1948, Vol. 1, pp. 52-85.

Taylor, A. L. (1952), *The White Knight: A Study of C. L. Dodgson*. London: Oliver & Boyd.

Taylor, J. H. (1934), Innate Emotional Responses in Infants. *Ohio Univ. Stud. Cont. Psychol.*, 12:69-81.

Terman, L. M. (1917), The Intelligence Quotient of Francis Galton in Childhood. *Amer. J. Psychol.*, 28:209-215.

Thomson, J. Arthur (1927), *The Minds of Animals*. London: Newnes.

Tovey, Rev. Duncan C. (1899), In: *Reviews and Essays in English Literature*. London: George Bell, pp. 138-155.

Townsend, C. W. (1896), Thigh Friction in Infants under One Year of Age. *Arch. Ped.*, 13:833-835.

Undset, S. (1935), *The Longest Years*. New York: Alfred Knopf.

Valenstein, A. F. (1962), The Psycho-Analytic Situation. *Int. J. Psycho-Anal.*, 43:315-324.

Van Doren, Carl (1930), *Swift*. New York: Viking Press.

—— (1941), *Secret History of the American Revolution*. New York: Viking Press.

Van Doren, Mark (1958), *The Autobiography of Mark Van Doren*. New York: Harcourt Brace.

Van Ophuijsen, J. H. W. (1920), On the Origin of the Feeling of Persecution. *Int. J. Psycho-Anal.*, 1:235-239.

Vencovsky, E. (1938) Psychosexual Infantilism: Fetishism with Masochistic Features, Colostrophilia and Lactophilia. *Casopis Lekaru Ceskych (J. of the Czech Doctors)*, Vol. 77.

Vian, Alsager (1889), William Fuller. In: *Dictionary of National Biography*. London: Smith, Elder.

Waelder, R. (1932), The Psychoanalytic Theory of Play. *Psychoanal. Quart.*, 2:208-224, 1933.

—— (1944), Present Trends in Psychoanalytic Theory and Practice. *The Yearbook of Psychoanalysis*, 1:79-94. New York: International Universities Press, 1945.

Wallace, William M. (1954), *Traitorous Hero: The Life and Fortunes of Benedict Arnold*. New York: Harper.

Walls, G. L. (1942), *The Vertebrate Eye*. Bloomfield Hills, Mich.: Cranbrook Institute of Science.

Weigert, E. (1955a), Panel Report: Special Problems in Connection with Termination of Training Analyses. *J. Amer. Psychoanal. Assn.*, 3:314-322.

—— (1955b), Special Problems in Connection with Termination of Training Analyses. *J. Amer. Psychoanal. Assn.*, 3:630-640.

West, Rebecca (1964), *The New Meaning of Treason*. New York: Viking Press.

Wheatley, V. (1957), *The Life and Work of Harriet Martineau*. London: Becker & Warburg.

Whiteside, Thomas (1960), *An Agent in Place: The Wennerstrom Affair*. New York: Viking Press.

Wiener, N. (1953), *Ex-Prodigy: My Childhood and Youth*. New York: Simon & Schuster.

Wilde, W. R. (1849), *The Closing Years of Dean Swift's Life*. Dublin: Hodges & Smith, 2nd ed.

Williams, Harold, ed. (1937), *The Poems of Jonathan Swift*, 3 Vols. Oxford: Clarendon Press.

—— (1948), *Jonathan Swift: Journal to Stella*, 2 Vols. Oxford: Clarendon Press.

Wilson, C. H. (1804), *Swiftiana*, 2 Vols. London: Richard Phillips.

Wilson, Daniel (1869), *Chatterton: A Biographical Study*. London: Macmillan.

Wilson, G. W. (1948), A Further Contribution to the Study of Olfactory Representation with Particular Reference to Transvestitism. *Psychoanal. Quart.*, 17:322-329.

Wilson, M. (1927), *The Life of William Blake*. London: Nonesuch Press.

Windholz, E. (1955), Problems of Termination of the Training Analysis. *J. Amer. Psychoanal. Assn.*, 3:641-650.

Winnicott, D. W. (1953), Transitional Objects and Transitional Phenomena. *Int. J. Psycho-Anal.*, 34:89-97.

—— (1957), *Mother and Child*. New York: Basic Books.

—— (1959), *Collected Papers*. New York: Basic Books.

—— (1960), The Theory of the Parent-Infant Relationship. *Int. J. Psycho-Anal.*, 41:585-595.

—— (1965a), *The Maturational Processes and the Facilitating Environment*. New York: International Universities Press.

—— (1965b), *The Family and Individual Development*. New York: Basic Books, pp. 143-144.

Wittels, F. (1929), The Child Woman. *Critique of Love*. New York: Macaulay, pp. 282-313.

Woodruff, D. (1957), *The Tichborne Claimant*. London: Hollis & Carter.

Woollcott, A. (1936), Introduction. *The Complete Works of Carroll*. New York: Modern Library.

Wrighton, Charles (1962), *The World's Greatest Spies*. New York: Taplinger.

Wulff, M. (1946), Fetishism and Object Choice in Early Childhood. *Psychoanal. Quart.*, 15:450-471.

Zetzel, E. R. (1965), Repression of Traumatic Experience and the Learning Process. In Panel: Memory and Repression, rep. W. G. Niederland. *J. Amer. Psychoanal. Assn.*, 13:619-633.

Zeligs, M. A. (1957), Acting In. *J. Amer. Psychoanal. Assn.*, 5:685-706.

Bibliographical Notes

Part I

CHAPTER 1   CHILD WIFE AS IDEAL

was presented at the Annual Meeting of the American Or-
thopsychiatric Association, 1946. It was first published in
the *American Journal of Orthopsychiatry*, 17:167-171, 1947.

CHAPTER 2   CERTAIN RELATIONSHIPS BETWEEN FETISHISM AND THE FAULTY
DEVELOPMENT OF THE BODY IMAGE

was first published in *The Psychoanalytic Study of the Child*,
8:79-98, 1953.

CHAPTER 3   PENIS AWE AND ITS RELATION TO PENIS ENVY

was first published in *Drives, Affects, Behavior*, ed. R. M.
Loewenstein. New York: International Universities Press,
1:176-190, 1953.

CHAPTER 4   PROBLEMS OF INFANTILE NEUROSIS

was a contribution to a special all-day meeting of the New
York Psychoanalytic Society and Institute at Arden House,
N.Y. It was first published in *The Psychoanalytic Study of
the Child*, 9:18-24, 37-40, 1954.

CHAPTER 5   FURTHER CONSIDERATIONS REGARDING FETISHISM

was read at the 19th Congress of the International Psycho-
Analytical Association in Geneva, Switzerland, July, 1955. It
was first published in *The Psychoanalytic Study of the Child*,
10:187-194, 1955.

CHAPTER 6   EXPERIENCES OF AWE IN CHILDHOOD

was read as the Brill Memorial Lecture at the New York
Academy of Medicine, March 20, 1956. It was first published
in *The Psychoanalytic Study of the Child*, 11:9-30, 1956.

CHAPTER 7   THE IMPOSTOR

was first published in *The Psychoanalytic Quarterly*, 27:359-382, 1958.

CHAPTER 8   EARLY PHYSICAL DETERMINANTS IN THE DEVELOPMENT OF THE SENSE OF IDENTITY

was read in a panel discussion on "Problems of Identity" at the Annual Meeting of the American Psychoanalytic Association in Chicago, May 11, 1957. It was first published in the *Journal of the American Psychoanalytic Association*, 6:612-627, 1958.

CHAPTER 9   TOWARD AN UNDERSTANDING OF THE PHYSICAL NUCLEUS OF SOME DEFENSE REACTIONS

was read at the 20th Congress of the International Psycho-Analytical Association in Paris, July-August, 1957. It was first published in *The International Journal of Psycho-Analysis*, 39:69-76, 1958.

CHAPTER 10   ON FOCAL SYMBIOSIS

was first published in *Dynamic Psychopathology in Childhood*, ed. L. Jessner & E. Pavenstedt. New York: Grune & Stratton, 1959, pp. 243-256.

CHAPTER 11   REGRESSION AND FIXATION

was read at the Midwinter Meeting of the American Psychoanalytic Association in New York, December 4, 1959. It was first published in the *Journal of the American Psychoanalytic Association*, 8:703-723, 1960.

CHAPTER 12   FURTHER NOTES ON FETISHISM

was first published in *The Psychoanalytic Study of the Child*, 15:191-207, 1960.

CHAPTER 13   CONSIDERATIONS REGARDING THE PARENT-INFANT RELATIONSHIP

This paper, together with one by Winnicott (1960), formed the basis of a discussion at the 22nd Congress of the International Psycho-Analytical Association in Edinburgh, July-August, 1961. It was first published in *The International Journal of Psycho-Analysis*, 41:571-584, 1960.

CHAPTER 14   A STUDY ON THE NATURE OF INSPIRATION

was read at the plenary session of the Midwinter Meeting of the American Psychoanalytic Association, New York, on December 8, 1963. It was first published in the *Journal of the American Psychoanalytic Association*, 12:6-31, 1964.

CHAPTER 15   ON THE DEVELOPMENT AND FUNCTION OF TEARS

is based on and expanded from a discussion of L. Börje Löfgren's paper, "On Weeping," read at the 24th Congress of the International Psycho-Analytical Association in Amsterdam, July, 1965. It was first published in *The Psychoanalytic Study of the Child,* 20:209-219, 1965.

CHAPTER 16   THE INFLUENCE OF INFANTILE TRAUMA ON GENETIC PATTERNS

was first published in *Psychic Trauma,* ed. S. S. Furst. New York: Basic Books, 1967, pp. 108-153.

CHAPTER 17   PERVERSIONS

is an expanded version of a discussion of Robert Bak's paper, "The Phallic Woman: The Ubiquitous Fantasy in Perversions," read at the meeting of the New York Psychoanalytic Society on February 27, 1968. It was first published in *The Psychoanalytic Study of the Child,* 23:47-62, 1968.

CHAPTER 18   THE FETISH AND THE TRANSITIONAL OBJECT

was first published in *The Psychoanalytic Study of the Child,* 24:144-164, 1969.

CHAPTER 19   THE TRANSITIONAL OBJECT AND THE FETISH: WITH SPECIAL REFERENCE TO THE ROLE OF ILLUSION

is the second part of the above paper. It was originally planned as a contribution to a Festschrift in honor of Dr. Winnicott. It is to be published in *The International Journal of Psycho-Analysis,* Vol. 51, 1970.

CHAPTER 20   DISCUSSION OF DR. GALENSON'S PAPER ON "THE NATURE OF THOUGHT IN CHILDHOOD PLAY"

was presented at a meeting of the New York Psychoanalytic Society, in the spring of 1969. It is to be published in *Separation-Individuation: Essays in Honor of Margaret S. Mahler,* ed. J. B. McDevitt & C. F. Settlage. New York: International Universities Press.

CHAPTER 21   THE NATURE OF TREASON AND THE CHARACTER OF TRAITORS

was first published (under the title "Treason and the Traitor") in *American Imago,* 26:199-232, 1969.

Part II

CHAPTER 22   THE MUTUAL ADVENTURES OF JONATHAN SWIFT AND LEMUEL GULLIVER

was first published in *The Psychoanalytic Quarterly,* 24:20-62, 1955.

CHAPTER 23   "IT'S MY OWN INVENTION"

was first published in *The Psychoanalytic Quarterly*, 24:200-244, 1955.

CHAPTER 24   THE CHILDHOOD OF THE ARTIST

was adapted from a paper read as part of a panel discussion on "The Scope of the Contribution of Psychoanalysis to the Biography of the Artist," held at the Midwinter Meeting of the American Psychoanalytic Association in New York, December, 1956. It was first published in *The Psychoanalytic Study of the Child*, 12:47-72, 1957.

CHAPTER 25   THE FAMILY ROMANCE OF THE ARTIST

was adapted from a paper read at the Kris Memorial Meeting in New York, September, 1957. It was first published in *The Psychoanalytic Study of the Child*, 13:9-43, 1958.

CHAPTER 26   THE RELATION OF THE IMPOSTOR TO THE ARTIST

was first published in *The Psychoanalytic Study of the Child*, 13:521-540, 1958.

CHAPTER 27   PLAY IN RELATION TO CREATIVE IMAGINATION

was adapted from a paper read as the Sophia Mirviss Memorial Lecture in San Francisco, March 2, 1959; and in a revised form as part of a panel discussion on "Imagination," held at the Annual Meeting of the American Psychoanalytic Association in Philadelphia, April 25, 1959. It was first published in *The Psychoanalytic Study of the Child*, 14:61-80, 1959.

CHAPTER 28   WOMAN AS ARTIST

was read as the Second Alexander Lecture in Chicago, November 21, 1959. It was first published in *The Psychoanalytic Quarterly*, 29:208-227, 1960.

CHAPTER 29   ON NONSENSE

was first published in *Psychoanalysis—A General Psychology: Essays in Honor of Heinz Hartmann*, ed. R. M. Loewenstein, L. M. Newman, M. Schur, & A. J. Solnit. New York: International Universities Press, 1966, pp. 655-677.

Part III

CHAPTER 30   EVALUATION OF THERAPEUTIC RESULTS

was a contribution to a symposium held at the Boston Psychoanalytic Society and Institute, on January 17 and 18, 1948. It was first published in *The International Journal of Psycho-Analysis*, 29:11-14, 32, 1948.

CHAPTER 31   THE ROLE OF TRANSFERENCE

was read as part of a panel discussion on "The Traditional Psychoanalytic Technique and Its Variations," held at the Midwinter Meeting of the American Psychoanalytic Association in New York, December, 1952. It was first published in the *Journal of the American Psychoanalytic Association*, 2:671-684, 1954.

CHAPTER 32   RE-EVALUATION OF THE PROCESS OF WORKING THROUGH

was adapted from a paper read at the Symposium, "The Theory of Technique," held at the Centenary Scientific Meetings of the British Psycho-Analytical Society, May 5, 1956. It was first published in *The International Journal of Psycho-Analysis*, 37:439-444, 1956.

CHAPTER 33   CERTAIN TECHNICAL PROBLEMS IN THE TRANSFERENCE RELATIONSHIP

was read at the Midwinter Meeting of the American Psychoanalytic Association in New York, December 6, 1957. It was first published in the *Journal of the American Psychoanalytic Association*, 7:484-502, 1959.

CHAPTER 34   A CRITICAL DIGEST OF THE LITERATURE ON SELECTION OF CANDIDATES FOR PSYCHOANALYTIC TRAINING

was prepared as part of studies made by the Committee on Psychoanalytic Education of the American Psychoanalytic Association. It was first published in *The Psychoanalytic Quarterly*, 30:28-55, 1961.

CHAPTER 35   PROBLEMS OF ACTING OUT IN THE TRANSFERENCE RELATIONSHIP

was a contribution to the Symposium on "A Developmental Approach to Problems of Acting Out," held in Boston on June 15 & 16, 1962. It was first published in the *Journal of the American Academy of Child Psychiatry*, 2:144-175, 1963. Also in: *A Developmental Approach to Problems of Acting Out* [*Journal of the American Academy of Child Psychiatry*, Monograph No. 1], ed. E. N. Rexford. New York: International Universities Press, 1966, pp. 144-159.

CHAPTER 36   DISCUSSION OF BERNARD BRODSKY'S PAPER ON "WORKING THROUGH"

was read at the meeting of the New York Psychoanalytic Society on October 13, 1964. It is published here for the first time.

CHAPTER 37   PROBLEMS OF TRAINING ANALYSIS

was first published in *The Psychoanalytic Quarterly*, 35:540-567, 1966.

CHAPTER 38 PROBLEMS OF OVERIDEALIZATION OF THE ANALYST AND OF ANALYSIS

was presented at the Pan-American Psychoanalytic Congress in Buenos Aires, August 2, 1966. It was first published in *The Psychoanalytic Study of the Child,* 21:193-212, 1966.

CHAPTER 39 THE PSYCHOANALYTIC PROCESS, TRANSFERENCE, AND ACTING OUT

was a contribution to the Symposium on "Acting Out," held at the 25th Congress of the International Psycho-Analytical Association in Copenhagen, July, 1967. Among the other participants were Anna Freud, León Grinberg, Leo Rangell, Thorkil Vangaard. The individual papers were all published in 1968 (see Symposium, 1968). It was first published in *The International Journal of Psycho-Analysis,* 49:211-218, 1968.

CHAPTER 40 NOTES ON THE INFLUENCE AND CONTRIBUTION OF EGO PSYCHOL-OGY TO THE PRACTICE OF PSYCHOANALYSIS

is to be published in *Separation-Individuation: Essays in Honor of Margaret S. Mahler,* ed. J. B. McDevitt & C. F. Settlage. New York: International Universities Press.

Index